THE LEGENDS OF
THE JEWS

THE LEGENDS OF THE JEWS

BY
LOUIS GINZBERG

VOLUME I

FROM THE CREATION TO JACOB

TRANSLATED BY HENRIETTA SZOLD

WITH A NEW FOREWORD BY

JAMES L. KUGEL

THE JOHNS HOPKINS UNIVERSITY PRESS
BALTIMORE AND LONDON

Johns Hopkins Paperbacks edition, 1998
9 8 7 6 5 4 3 2

The Johns Hopkins University Press
2715 North Charles Street
Baltimore, Maryland 21218-4363
www.press.jhu.edu

Library of Congress Cataloging-in-Publication Data

Ginzberg, Louis, 1873–1953.
    The legends of the Jews / by Louis Ginzberg : with a new foreword by
James L. Kugel.
        p.   cm.
    Translated by Henrietta Szold and Paul Radin.
    Originally published: Philadelphia : Jewish Publication Society of America,
1909–1938.
    Includes bibliographical references and index.
    ISBN 0-8018-5890-9 (pbk. : vol. 1 alk. paper)
    1. Legends, Jewish. 2. Bible. O.T.—Legends. 3. Midrash—Translations
into English. 4. Aggada—Translations into English. I. Szold, Henrietta,
1860–1945. II. Radin, Paul, 1883–1959. III. Title.
BM530.G513   1998
296.1'9—dc21   97-46024
                                                                   CIP

ISBN 0-8018-5891-7 (pbk. : vol. 2); ISBN 0-8018-5892-5 (pbk. : vol. 3);
ISBN 0-8018-5893-3 (pbk. : vol. 4); ISBN 0-8018-5894-1 (pbk. : vol. 5);
ISBN 0-8018-5895-X (pbk. : vol. 6); ISBN 0-8018-5896-8 (pbk. : vol. 7)

A catalog record for this book is available from the British Library.

To
MY BROTHER ASHER

CONTENTS

Contents

FOREWORD

James L. Kugel

Louis Ginzberg was never entirely satisfied with his title *The Legends of the Jews*; he always said he would have done better to choose a name like *The Legends of the Bible.* The reason is clear. Ginzberg's magnificent, mammoth compilation is not of Jewish legends in general, but of legends connected specifically with the Hebrew Bible. What he sought to do was to assemble the many fanciful elaborations and embellishments of biblical stories that had arisen among the Jews in the centuries following the Bible's own creation and retell them as one continuous narrative. These elaborations, which belong to a body of writing known in Hebrew as *midrash* ("scriptural interpretation"), lay scattered here and there in a dauntingly varied body of works. They abound in the multivolume Jerusalem and Babylonian Talmuds as well as in a number of smaller books like *Genesis Rabba, Leviticus Rabba, Midrash Tanhuma,* and so forth. In bringing them together as he did, Ginzberg ended up producing a kind of parallel text to much of the Bible itself—a retelling of its stories embellished with all the imaginative material that Jews had developed piecemeal in the centuries following the Bible's completion. So in this sense his book is, truly, *The Legends of the Bible.* (This name was eventually given to

a posthumous—and not very successful—one-volume conden-
sation of his work, published by the Jewish Publication Society
[Philadelphia, 1956].)

At the same time, however, Ginzberg was well aware that the
material he had assembled was, at least in its broad outline, well
known to many Jews. Moreover, the corpus of books on which
he principally drew included, along with the Bible itself, most
of the classical library of Judaism; Jews had studied this material, or at least heard sermons preached about it and discussed
it among themselves, throughout their long history. In a sense,
then, despite its apparently too general wording, *The Legends of
the Jews* was, and is, an altogether apt name. The tales and
imaginative flights found herein are indeed the Jewish legends
par excellence, a literature that, more than any other, shaped
the Jewish consciousness for all time.

In undertaking the task of compiling and retelling these
biblical elaborations, Ginzberg was hardly on unfamiliar ground.
He himself was an extraordinarily gifted and free-ranging
intellect, and he had hesitated for quite a time before choosing
his field of specialization. He might well have pursued any
number of different fields and had, in fact, begun his university
studies as a mathematician, where his youthful genius would no
doubt have made for a brilliant career had he not soon come to
the sad realization that his religion posed an impassable ob-
stacle to any university appointment in that field. (Another,
somewhat different, indication of Ginzberg's great breadth of
mind is the fact that his earliest published book is not a work of
scholarship at all, but a collection of poems, *Gedichte*, written in
1894 in a language he had only begun to study five years
earlier.) But having eventually taken on "Orientalia" as his

specialty, Ginzberg swiftly made a name for himself. His doctoral dissertation was devoted to the same overall subject as the future *Legends*, specifically, to the survival of various Jewish elaborations of the Bible in the writings of the Church Fathers. He also studied the development of these same elaborations in another body of writings, the biblical apocrypha and pseudepigrapha, a field just then experiencing a rebirth of interest. And beyond his work in these specific areas, Ginzberg was known in general for his contributions to the study of rabbinic literature; indeed, by the end of his scholarly career he had left his mark on a half dozen major fields of research related to rabbinics, from the Dead Sea Scrolls to the Jerusalem Talmud to the study of post-Talmudic (Geonic) writings. He was thus, as much as any one person might be, the ideal candidate for the job.

In 1901 Ginzberg formally proposed the idea of the *Legends* to the Jewish Publication Society of America. He had arrived in the United States scarcely two years earlier (after wandering from his native Lithuania to various points in Russia, Germany, and France), and his English was still weak. He therefore suggested writing his work on "Jewish Legends Relating to Biblical Matters" in German and leaving to others the matter of translating it into English for publication. As for the work itself, Ginzberg decided to adopt a two-tiered approach to his material. He would begin by retelling these embellished stories in his own words, reconciling as best he could the various, sometimes jangling or contradictory versions of the same story found in different sources. Then, in a series of learned footnotes, he would make mention of his different sources and discuss any technical matters relating to parallel versions and philological or other difficulties, as well as occasional references to scholarly works by others. He promised to submit the manuscript two years later.

Neither in the timing nor the overall length of his work was Ginzberg able to keep his word. The first volume of the *Legends* did not actually appear until 1909, and the writing of the subsequent volumes stretched out until 1928, when the sixth (and last) volume of notes was printed. (It was still later that the seventh, index volume was compiled; yet another volume, to consist of six lengthy excurses on central biblical figures, is alluded to here and there in Ginzberg's notes, but it was apparently never completed.) In all other respects, however, the *Legends* not only met the publishers' expectations but mightily surpassed them. Long before the last volume was completed, Ginzberg's work had already become a classic. Its success is perhaps best indicated not by its overall sales— though more than half a million books have been printed in English alone—but by the simple fact that, for several decades now, *The Legends of the Jews* has been cited in scholarly works as if it were a primary source ("Ginzberg, *Legends*, 2:235," or the like), rubbing shoulders with the other, considerably older members of the "classical" Jewish library alluded to earlier. Read for pleasure by millions of Jews and Christians, consulted by students, scholars, and ordinary folk, *The Legends of the Jews* has itself become legendary, the master work of one of the twentieth century's greatest and most original Jewish scholars.

In seeking to introduce *The Legends of the Jews* to yet a new generation of readers, I thought it might be helpful to say something about the book from the perspective of the very late twentieth century, that is, something about how the book looks nowadays within its larger historical and intellectual milieu; and I should like to add a word about some recent developments in the various fields in which Ginzberg worked since the time he composed his—the phrase is appropriate here as rarely elsewhere—magnum opus.

As mentioned, Ginzberg himself had second thoughts about the *of the Jews* part of his title, but it is the word *legends* that, I daresay, probably most troubles scholars today, and this in turn says something about the intellectual climate in which Ginzberg worked. His predecessors and contemporaries did indeed like to speak of the biblical elaborations in question as "legends," as if somehow the popular imagination had just spontaneously created them out of thin air. Ginzberg's older contemporary M. Berdiczewski, compiler of *Mimmekor Yisrael*, had rigorously followed a folkloristic definition of the material, as had a number of slightly later scholars in the field. Other students of these biblical elaborations went further and spoke of them as the true "literature" of the Jews, a kind of submerged, postbiblical epic composed by different Jewish bards from various lands and periods. (This approach was followed most prominently by H. N. Bialik and H. Ravnitsky in their compilation, *Sefer ha-Aggadah*, undertaken at almost exactly the same time as Ginzberg's.)

Part of the reason for both views had to do, curiously, with ideas of Jewish self-definition at the time, and, more specifically, with the spread of Jewish national feelings, and, eventually, Zionism. If being a Jew were not, or not merely, a religious identity, if the Jews were in a fact a people like any other, then the existence of a great body of popular Jewish *legends* could certainly be enlisted to support this view: other peoples had their legends and—behold!—so did the Jews—their own legends and nobody else's. In addition, the nineteenth-century conception of nationhood held it as axiomatic that any self-respecting people was characterized by three things: its national homeland, its national language, and its national literature. The first two were easy enough to identify in the case of the Jews: Palestine was the ancient Jewish homeland, and Hebrew had been the Jews' language from time immemorial. But what about the third?

The Bible alone would not do well as an answer. First, if the Bible were the only literature that the Jews had produced, this was tantamount to saying that they had ceased to exist as a people shortly after the last chapter of the Bible had been written and the Jews cast out of their homeland—whereas many Jews were just then seeking to argue the opposite, that the continued use of Hebrew as, at least, a written language and the Jews' own ongoing literary creativity both supported the contention that they had, despite the loss of their homeland, remained a true people all those years. Moreover, the simple truth was that the Bible was not the only text that the Jews had been reading or studying during the centuries of their exile. The Babylonian Talmud also occupied a central position, as did other works associated with the study-house and the synagogue. True, much of this material could hardly be deemed worthy of the title "national literature"; dry discussions of rabbinic legal practice were hardly the stuff of the literary imagination. But alongside such things were those highly imaginative elaborations of the biblical stories, which existed in great abundance. Were *they* not the true literature of the Jewish people during their centuries of exile, these "legends" of the Jews? So it was that a body of writing that was, at least formally, biblical exegesis, a way of *interpreting* the Bible, came to be transformed by Ginzberg and others into works of the imagination, basically oblivious to the scriptural verses that were their original focus and raison d'être.

This is not the place for a detailed account of the nature of Ginzberg's raw material, traditional Jewish biblical interpretation. Suffice it to say that midrash is not "interpretation" in the modern sense. The (mostly anonymous) creators of midrash, who began to flourish as early as the third or fourth centuries B.C.E., did not seek to explain the Bible in an objective, dispassionate way. They were, on the contrary, engagé interpreters who sought everywhere to bring out what they believed to be the eternal, relevant, and fundamentally religious significance of the biblical text. In trying to understand the Bible in keeping with their own views, these ancient interpreters usually focused their attention on specific details in the biblical text—an unusual word or turn of phrase, for example, or anything that might seem out of place or contradictory. A modern interpreter might see such things as problems to be explained by philological inquiry. The ancient midrashist, on the contrary, saw them as opportunities, an invitation by the text itself to "fill in the blanks" and so account for the perceived anomaly, often using the same opportunity to bring out the story's religious or moral significance.

For example, the book of Genesis relates that Joseph was sold as a slave by his brothers and taken down to Egypt, where his master's wife attempted to seduce him. The Bible notes laconically: "Joseph was fair of form and appearance. And it came to pass after these things that his master's wife cast her eyes upon Joseph and said, 'Lie with me'" (Gen. 39:6–7). Now, the phrase "after these things" is somewhat troubling in this last verse: after all, Joseph's being handsome was not a "thing" that happened, but presumably a condition that had existed for some time. Why, then, did the Bible say "after these things"? No doubt a modern commentator, if he or she even bothered to notice this slight irregularity, would explain it as a broad reference to the preceding events and not specifically to the words that appear just before it ("Joseph was fair of form and appearance"). Moreover, the phrase "and it came to pass after these things" is a fairly common transitional phrase in the Bible: first X happened (here, Joseph was sold as a slave and caused his master's house to prosper), then, *after these things*, Y.

But such is not the way of midrash, where every slight detail in the Bible's form of expression is deemed significant. And so, one ancient interpretation held that the "things" referred to in this verse were actually things that Joseph did in order to make himself handsome: he primped and straightened and combed and *became* "fair of form and appearance. And it came to pass after these things that his master's wife cast her eyes upon Joseph and said, 'Lie with me.'" Accompanied by such an explanation, the text's "after these things" suddenly makes sense: she had barely noticed him before, but after Joseph primped and straightened, his master's wife made her indecent proposal. (This reading also pins the blame for Joseph's subsequent misfortune on Joseph himself: had he not been so vain, nothing would have happened.) Another line of interpretation held that the things referred to were things that Joseph's master's wife did: she snagged Joseph in the hall to chat seductively with him and even changed her clothes three times a day in order to invite his attention, hoping for some indiscre-

tion on his part. It was only *after these things* had taken place—
and failed!—that she looked him square in the eye and said,
"Lie with me." In both cases the midrashist has invented
something that is not in the Bible itself, and yet, to the
midrashic way of thinking, the invented material is *practically*
there, the phrase "after these things" inviting the interpreter to
supply the missing information.

The Legends of the Jews recounts both these traditions (2:44,
47–48; 5:339, nn. 108, 112). Characteristically, however, in
neither place does Ginzberg actually mention the biblical
problem (or even the biblical verse) out of which they originated. His focus was relentlessly on the content of these little
elaborations themselves, rather than on their exegetical dimension, and so he rarely addressed their precise relationship to
the biblical text. Lest this observation be misunderstood, I
should add that Ginzberg is not to be thought the worse for
having adopted his particular approach. If he submerged the
exegetical side of midrash, this was, as I have suggested, very
much in keeping with the then-dominant view of things: he
simply did not see explaining such things (which must have
seemed obvious to him most of the time) as part of his mission.
On the other hand, he was an extremely zealous collector of
different versions, mining the most obscure sources for yet
another variant; moreover, he showed, apart from his myriad
minute observations about the meaning of this or that obscure
word in a text (and myriad hypothetical restorations of the
pristine form of a text—many of which restorations have been
subsequently verified by the discovery of new manuscripts),
great zeal in tracing different forms of the same story, sometimes tracking down a resemblance between two items that

would otherwise have been altogether lost. The *Legends,* in other words, is a truly monumental work of scholarship, and its lack of interest in midrash as exegesis cannot detract from the rest of its achievement. Indeed, part of Ginzberg's genius was to have discovered a way of presenting what he knew in such a way as to satisfy two rather different clienteles, the general educated reader and the specialist working in the field.

Ginzberg's magnificent notes, the product of a truly prodigious memory and decades of hard work, thus remain for today's scholar an indispensable tool, nay, the heart of his great undertaking. It is safe to say that they will never be duplicated and probably not even revised in some future edition. It would take a team of experts in different fields many years to go back over all that Ginzberg covered in the *Legends,* and many more years for these same scholars to explore all the sources that were not available to Ginzberg but are now within reach. Even if such a grand revision of the *Legends* is thus highly unlikely, it might nonetheless be worthwhile to sketch in brief what the *Legends* might look like if Louis Ginzberg were beginning his work today, nearly a century after he actually did.

In some ways his undertaking would appear a good bit easier: this is an age in which new scholarly editions, manuscript facsimiles, microfilms, and the like are available as never before. Ginzberg loved manuscript work and would no doubt delight in today's abundance; indeed, computer technology promises not only greater resources for the future but also methods of textual search and storage of material, as well as other devices yet undiscovered, which all would have vastly simplified the work of compilation and comparison that he kept, principally, in his own head. This very abundance, however, would also have complicated his task. The "sea of learning" (*yam shel talmud*) has revealed itself to be of far greater dimension than previously imagined, so much so that the very standards by which scholarship is conducted have dramatically shifted.

Add to this the existence of whole bodies of texts unused by Ginzberg—most dramatically, the Dead Sea Scrolls. Ginzberg had studied (brilliantly) one text, the *Damascus Document*, whose origins are traceable back to the same community that assembled the Dead Sea Scrolls, but the rest of that great corpus of manuscripts only began to be discovered and published long after Ginzberg had finished the *Legends*, indeed, the publication process is only now coming to a close. Ginzberg would no doubt have mined the scrolls for their wealth of information about ancient biblical interpretation; indeed, the first stages of many of his *Legends* are attested within this corpus. Another source of new texts, the Cairo Geniza, was of course known to Ginzberg—he had used it brilliantly for his own research—but as far as the *Legends* are concerned, newly published Geniza texts, especially in the realms of *piyyut* (medieval liturgical poetry), targum, and basic rabbinic texts, would no doubt have further enriched his work. To these might be added yet other new manuscript troves—the Jewish libraries of Petersberg and Moscow, the gnostic texts from Nag Hammadi in Egypt, recently published works in Slavonic, Syriac, Coptic, and similarly obscure languages, all would have been put to good use by Ginzberg today. The first four volumes of the *Legends* might remain basically the same, but the two volumes of notes might have to be doubled to account for all the new material.

In saying this, however, I mean to assert that the basic shape of the *Legends'* overview and the depth and detail of much of its survey remain unchallenged despite the availability of new material. What Ginzberg succeeded in doing was sift through the mass of classical Jewish texts and much other material to restore the great body of what he called, modestly, "Jewish Legends Relating to Biblical Matters." He did not lose the forest for the trees; nor, remarkably, did he lose the trees. Nearly a century after he began, his work stands as both a fundamental tool of contemporary research and a Jewish classic, something no English-language collection of Judaica, or the ordinary Jewish home, should be without. No scholar dare aim higher.

PREFACE

*Was sich nie und nirgends hat
begeben, das allein veraltet nie.*

The term Rabbinic was applied to the Jewish Literature of post-Biblical times by those who conceived the Judaism of the later epoch to be something different from the Judaism of the Bible, something actually opposed to it. Such observers held that the Jewish nation ceased to exist with the moment when its political independence was destroyed. For them the Judaism of the later epoch has been a Judaism of the Synagogue, the spokesmen of which have been the scholars, the Rabbis. And what this phase of Judaism brought forth has been considered by them to be the product of the schools rather than the product of practical, pulsating life. Poetic phantasmagoria, frequently the vaporings of morbid visionaries, is the material out of which these scholars construct the theologic system of the Rabbis, and fairy tales, the spontaneous creations of the people, which take the form of sacred legend in Jewish literature, are denominated the Scriptural exegesis of the Rabbis, and condemned incontinently as *nugæ rabbinorum*.

As the name of a man clings to him, so men cling to names. For the primitive savage the name is part of the essence of a person or thing, and even in the more advanced stages of culture, judgments are not always formed in agreement with facts as they are, but rather according to the names by which they are called. The current estimate of Rabbinic Literature is a case in point. With the label Rabbinic later ages inherited from former ages a certain distorted view of the literature so designated. To this day, and even among scholars that approach its investigation with unprejudiced minds, the opinion prevails that it is purely a learned product. And yet the truth is that the most prominent feature of Rabbinic Literature is its popular character.

The school and the home are not mutually opposed to each other in the conception of the Jews. They study in their homes, and they live in their schools. Likewise there is no distinct class of scholars among them, a class that withdraws itself from participation in the affairs of practical life. Even in the domain of the Halakah, the Rabbis were not so much occupied with theoretic principles of law as with the concrete phenomena of daily existence. These they sought to grasp and shape. And what is true of the Halakah is true with greater emphasis of the Haggadah, which is popular in the double sense of appealing to the people and being produced in the main by the people. To speak of the Haggadah of the Tannaim and Amoraim is as far from fact as to speak of the legends of Shakespeare and Scott. The ancient authors and their modern brethren of the guild alike elaborate legendary material which they found at hand.

It has been held by some that the Haggadah contains no popular legends, that it is wholly a factitious, academic product. A cursory glance at the pseudepigraphic literature of the Jews, which is older than the Haggadah literature by several centuries, shows how untenable this view is. That the one literature should have drawn from the other is precluded by historical facts. At a very early time the Synagogue disavowed the pseudepigraphic literature, which was the favorite reading matter of the sectaries and the Christians. Nevertheless the inner relation between them is of the closest kind. The only essential difference is that the Midrashic form prevails in the Haggadah, and the parenetic or apocalyptic form in the pseudepigrapha. The common element must therefore depart from the Midrash on the one hand and from parenesis on the other.

Folklore, fairy tales, legends, and all forms of story telling akin to these are comprehended, in the terminology of the post-Biblical literature of the Jews, under the inclusive description Haggadah, a name that can be explained by a circumlocution, but cannot be translated. Whatever it is applied to is thereby characterized first as being derived from the Holy Scriptures, and then as being of the nature of a story. And, in point of fact, this dualism sums up the distinguishing features of Jewish Legend. More than eighteen centuries ago the Jewish historian Josephus observed that "though we be deprived of our wealth, of our cities, or of the other advantages we have, our law continues immortal." The word he meant to use was not law, but Torah, only he could not find an equivalent for it in Greek. A singer of the Synagogue a thousand years after Josephus, who expressed his sentiments in Hebrew, uttered the same thought: " The Holy City and all her daughter cities are violated, they lie in ruins, despoiled of their ornaments, their splendor darkened from sight. Naught is left to us save one eternal treasure alone—the Holy Torah." The sadder the life of

the Jewish people, the more it felt the need of taking refuge
in its past. The Scripture, or, to use the Jewish term, the
Torah, was the only remnant of its former national independence, and the Torah was the magic means of making a
sordid actuality recede before a glorious memory. To the
Scripture was assigned the task of supplying nourishment
to the mind as well as the soul, to the intellect as well as the
imagination, and the result is the Halakah and the Haggadah.

The fancy of the people did not die out in the post-Biblical
time, but the bent of its activity was determined by the past.
Men craved entertainment in later times as well as in the
earlier, only instead of resorting for its subject-matter to
what happened under their eyes, they drew from the foun-
tain-head of the past. The events in the ancient history of
Israel, which was not only studied, but lived over again
daily, stimulated the desire to criticise it. The religious re-
flections upon nature laid down in the myths of the people,
the fairy tales, which have the sole object of pleasing, and
the legends, which are the people's verdict upon history—all
these were welded into one product. The fancy of the Jewish people was engaged by the past reflected in the Bible,
and all its creations wear a Biblical hue for this reason.
This explains the peculiar form of the Haggadah.

But what is spontaneously brought forth by the people is
often preserved only in the form impressed upon it by the
feeling and the thought of the poet, or by the speculations of
the learned. Also Jewish legends have rarely been trans-
mitted in their original shape. They have been perpetuated
in the form of Midrash, that is, Scriptural exegesis. The
teachers of the Haggadah, called *Rabbanan d'Aggadta* in

the Talmud, were no folklorists, from whom a faithful re-
production of legendary material may be expected. Pri-
marily they were homilists, who used legends for didactic
purposes, and their main object was to establish a close connection between the Scripture and the creations of the popular fancy, to give the latter a firm basis and secure a long
term of life for them.

One of the most important tasks of the modern investigation of the Haggadah is to make a clean separation between the original elements and the later learned additions.
Hardly a beginning has been made in this direction. But as
long as the task of distinguishing them has not been accomplished, it is impossible to write out the Biblical legends of
the Jews without including the supplemental work of scholars in the products of the popular fancy.

In the present work, "The Legends of the Jews," I have
made the first attempt to gather from the original sources
all Jewish legends, in so far as they refer to Biblical person-
ages and events, and reproduce them with the greatest at-
tainable completeness and accuracy. I use the expression
Jewish, rather than Rabbinic, because the sources from
which I have levied contributions are not limited to the Rabbinic literature. As I expect to take occasion elsewhere to
enter into a description of the sources in detail, the following
data must suffice for the present.

The works of the Talmudic-Midrashic literature are of
the first importance. Covering the period from the second
to the fourteenth century, they contain the major part of the
Jewish legendary material. Akin to this in content if not
always in form is that derived from the Targumim, of which

the oldest versions were produced not earlier than the fourth century, and the most recent not later than the tenth. The Midrashic literature has been preserved only in fragmentary form. Many Haggadot not found in our existing collections are quoted by the authors of the Middle Ages. Accordingly, a not inconsiderable number of the legends here printed are taken from mediæval Bible commentators and homilists. I was fortunate in being able to avail myself also of fragments of Midrashim of which only manuscript copies are extant. The works of the older Kabbalah are likewise treasuries of quotations from lost Midrashim, and it was among the Kabbalists, and later among the Ḥasidim, that new legends arose. The literatures produced in these two circles are therefore of great importance for the present purpose.

Furthermore, Jewish legends can be culled not from the writings of the Synagogue alone; they appear also in those of the Church. Certain Jewish works repudiated by the Synagogue were accepted and mothered by the Church. This is the literature usually denominated apocryphal-pseudepigraphic. From the point of view of legends, the apocryphal books are of subordinate importance, while the pseudepigrapha are of fundamental value. Even quantitatively the latter are an imposing mass. Besides the Greek writings of the Hellenist Jews, they contain Latin, Syrian, Ethiopic, Aramean, Arabic, Persian, and Old Slavic products translated directly or indirectly from Jewish works of Palestinian or Hellenistic origin. The use of these pseudepigrapha requires great caution. Nearly all of them are embellished with Christian interpolations, and in some cases the inserted portions have choked the original form so completely that it is impossible to determine at first sight whether a Jewish or a Christian legend is under examination. I believe, however, that the pseudepigraphic material made use of by me is Jewish beyond the cavil of a doubt, and therefore it could not have been left out of account in a work like the present.

However, in the appreciation of Jewish Legends, it is the Rabbinic writers that should form the point of departure, and not the pseudepigrapha. The former represent the main stream of Jewish thought and feeling, the latter only an undercurrent. If the Synagogue cast out the pseudepigrapha, and the Church adopted them with a great show of favor, these respective attitudes were not determined arbitrarily or by chance. The pseudepigrapha originated in circles that harbored the germs from which Christianity developed later on. The Church could thus appropriate them as her own with just reason.

In the use of some of the apocryphal and pseudepigraphic writings, I found it expedient to quote the English translations of them made by others, in so far as they could be brought into accord with the general style of the book, for which purpose I permitted myself the liberty of slight verbal changes. In particulars, I was guided, naturally, by my own conception of the subject, which the Notes justify in detail.

Besides the pseudepigrapha there are other Jewish sources in Christian garb. In the rich literature of the Church Fathers many a Jewish legend lies embalmed which one would seek in vain in Jewish books. It was therefore my special concern to use the writings of the Fathers to the utmost.

The luxuriant abundance of the material to be presented made it impossible to give a verbal rendition of each legend. This would have required more than three times the space at my disposal. I can therefore claim completeness for my work only as to content. In form it had to suffer curtailment. When several conflicting versions of the same legend existed, I gave only one in the text, reserving the other one, or the several others, for the Notes, or, when practicable, they were fused into one typical legend, the component parts of which are analyzed in the Notes. In other instances I resorted to the expedient of citing one version in one place and the others in other appropriate places, in furtherance of my aim, to give a smooth presentation of the matter, with as few interruptions to the course of the narrative as possible. For this reason I avoided such transitional phrases as " Some say," " It has been maintained," etc. That my method sometimes separates things that belong together cannot be considered a grave disadvantage, as the Index at the end of the work will present a logical rearrangement of the material for the benefit of the interested student. I also did not hesitate to treat of the same personage in different chapters, as, for instance, many of the legends bearing upon Jacob, those connected with the latter years of the Patriarch, do not appear in the chapter bearing his name, but will be found in the sections devoted to Joseph, for the reason that once the son steps upon the scene, he becomes the central figure, to which the life and deeds of the father are subordinated.

Again, in consideration of lack of space the Biblical narratives underlying the legends had to be omitted—surely not a serious omission in a subject with which widespread acquaintance may be presupposed as a matter of course.

As a third consequence of the amplitude of the material, it was thought advisable to divide it into several volumes. The references, the explanations of the sources used, and the interpretations given, and, especially, numerous emendations of the text of the Midrashim and the pseudepigrapha, which determined my conception of the passages so emended, will be found in the last volume, the fourth, which will contain also an Introduction to the History of Jewish Legends, a number of Excursuses, and the Index.

As the first three volumes are in the hands of the printer almost in their entirety, I venture to express the hope that the whole work will appear within measurable time, the parts following each other at short intervals.

LOUIS GINZBERG.

NEW YORK, *March 24, 1909*

I

THE CREATION OF THE WORLD

I

THE CREATION OF THE WORLD

The First Things Created

In the beginning, two thousand years before the heaven and the earth, seven things were created: the Torah written with black fire on white fire, and lying in the lap of God; the Divine Throne, erected in the heaven which later was over the heads of the Ḥayyot; Paradise on the right side of God, Hell on the left side; the Celestial Sanctuary directly in front of God, having a jewel on its altar graven with the Name of the Messiah, and a Voice that cries aloud, " Return, ye children of men." [1]

When God resolved upon the creation of the world, He took counsel with the Torah. [2] Her advice was this: " O Lord, a king without an army and without courtiers and attendants hardly deserves the name of king, for none is nigh to express the homage due to him." The answer pleased God exceedingly. Thus did He teach all earthly kings, by His Divine example, to undertake naught without first consulting advisers. [3]

The advice of the Torah was given with some reservations. She was skeptical about the value of an earthly world, on account of the sinfulness of men, who would be sure to disregard her precepts. But God dispelled her doubts. He told her, that repentance had been created long before, and sinners would have the opportunity of mending

their ways. Besides, the Temple service would be invested
with atoning power, and Paradise and hell were intended
to do duty as reward and punishment. Finally, the Messiah
was appointed to bring salvation, which would put an end to
all sinfulness.[4]

Nor is this world inhabited by man the first of things
earthly created by God. He made several worlds before
ours, but He destroyed them all, because He was pleased
with none until He created ours.[5] But even this last world
would have had no permanence, if God had executed His
original plan of ruling it according to the principle of strict
justice. It was only when He saw that justice by itself
would undermine the world that He associated mercy with
justice, and made them to rule jointly.[6] Thus, from the
beginning of all things prevailed Divine goodness, without which nothing could have continued to exist. If not for
it, the myriads of evil spirits had soon put an end to the
generations of men. But the goodness of God has ordained,
that in every Nisan, at the time of the spring equinox, the
seraphim shall approach the world of spirits, and intimidate
them so that they fear to do harm to men. Again, if God
in His goodness had not given protection to the weak, the
tame animals would have been extirpated long ago by the
wild animals. In Tammuz, at the time of the summer solstice, when the strength of behemot is at its height, he roars
so loud that all the animals hear it, and for a whole year
they are affrighted and timid, and their acts become less
ferocious than their nature is. Again, in Tishri, at the
time of the autumnal equinox, the great bird ziz[7] flaps his
wings and utters his cry, so that the birds of prey, the eagles

and the vultures, blench, and they fear to swoop down upon
the others and annihilate them in their greed. And, again,
were it not for the goodness of God, the vast number of big
fish had quickly put an end to the little ones. But at the
time of the winter solstice, in the month of Ṭebet, the sea
grows restless, for then leviathan spouts up water, and the
big fish become uneasy. They restrain their appetite, and
the little ones escape their rapacity.

Finally, the goodness of God manifests itself in the preservation of His people Israel. It could not have survived
the enmity of the Gentiles, if God had not appointed pro-
tectors for it, the archangels Michael and Gabriel.[*] Whenever Israel disobeys God, and is accused of misdemeanors
by the angels of the other nations, he is defended by his
designated guardians, with such good result that the other
angels conceive fear of them. Once the angels of the other
nations are terrified, the nations themselves venture not to
carry out their wicked designs against Israel.

That the goodness of God may rule on earth as in heaven,
the Angels of Destruction are assigned a place at the far
end of the heavens, from which they may never stir, while
the Angels of Mercy encircle the Throne of God, at His
behest.[*]

THE ALPHABET

When God was about to create the world by His word,
the twenty-two letters of the alphabet[10] descended from the
terrible and august crown of God whereon they were engraved with a pen of flaming fire. They stood round about
God, and one after the other spake and entreated, " Create

the world through me!" The first to step forward was the
letter Taw. It said: "O Lord of the world! May it be
Thy will to create Thy world through me, seeing that it is
through me that Thou wilt give the Torah to Israel by the
hand of Moses, as it is written, ' Moses commanded us the
Torah.' " The Holy One, blessed be He, made reply, and
said, " No!" Taw asked, " Why not?" and God answered:
" Because in days to come I shall place thee as a sign of
death upon the foreheads of men." As soon as Taw heard
these words issue from the mouth of the Holy One, blessed
be He, it retired from His presence disappointed.

The Shin then stepped forward, and pleaded: "O Lord
of the world, create Thy world through me, seeing that
Thine own name Shaddai begins with me." Unfortunately,
it is also the first letter of Shaw, lie, and of Sheker, falsehood, and that incapacitated it. Resh had no better luck. It
was pointed out that it was the initial letter of Ra', wicked,
and Rasha', evil, and after that the distinction it enjoys of
being the first letter in the Name of God, Rahum, the
Merciful, counted for naught. The Kof was rejected, because Kelalah, curse, outweighs the advantage of being the
first in Kadosh, the Holy One. In vain did Zadde call attention to Zaddik, the Righteous One; there was Zarot, the
misfortunes of Israel, to testify against it. Pe had Podeh,
redeemer, to its credit, but Pesha', transgression, reflected
dishonor upon it. 'Ain was declared unfit, because, though
it begins 'Anawah, humility, it performs the same service
for 'Erwah, immorality. Samek said: "O Lord, may it be
Thy will to begin the creation with me, for Thou art called
Samek, after me, the Upholder of all that fall." But God

said: "Thou art needed in the place in which thou art;" thou must continue to uphold all that fall." Nun introduces Ner, "the lamp of the Lord," which is "the spirit of men," but it also introduces Ner, "the lamp of the wicked," which will be put out by God. Mem starts Melek, king, one of the titles of God. As it is the first letter of Mehumah, confusion, as well, it had no chance of accomplishing its desire. The claim of Lamed bore its refutation within itself. It advanced the argument that it was the first letter of Luhot, the celestial tables for the Ten Commandments; it forgot that the tables were shivered in pieces by Moses. Kaf was sure of victory. Kisseh, the throne of God, Kabod, His honor, and Keter, His crown, all begin with it. God had to remind it that He would smite together His hands, Kaf, in despair over the misfortunes of Israel. Yod at first sight seemed the appropriate letter for the beginning of creation, on account of its association with Yah, God, if only Yezer ha-Ra', the evil inclination, had not happened to begin with it, too. Tet is identified with Tob, the good. However, the truly good is not in this world; it belongs to the world to come. Het is the first letter of Hanun, the Gracious One; but this advantage is offset by its place in the word for sin, Hattat. Zain suggests Zakor, remembrance, but it is itself the word for weapon, the doer of mischief. Waw and He compose the Ineffable Name of God; they are therefore too exalted to be pressed into the service of the mundane world. If Dalet had stood only for Dabar, the Divine Word, it would have been used, but it stands also for Din, justice, and under the rule of law without love the world would have fallen to ruin. Finally, in spite of reminding one of Gadol, great,

Gimel would not do, because Gemul, retribution, starts
with it.

After the claims of all these letters had been disposed of,
Bet stepped before the Holy One, blessed be He, and pleaded
before Him: " O Lord of the world! May it be Thy will to
create Thy world through me, seeing that all the dwellers
in the world give praise daily unto Thee through me, as it is
said, ' *B*lessed be the Lord forever. Amen, and Amen.' "
The Holy One, blessed be He, at once granted the petition
of Bet. He said, " *B*lessed be he that cometh in the name of
the Lord." And He created His world through Bet, as it is
said, " *B*ereshit God created the heaven and the earth."

The only letter that had refrained from urging its claims
was the modest Alef, and God rewarded it later for its humility by giving it the first place in the Decalogue.[12]

THE FIRST DAY

On the first day of creation God produced ten things:[13]
the heavens and the earth, Tohu and Bohu, light and darkness, wind and water, the duration of the day[14] and the duration of the night.[15]

Though the heavens and the earth consist of entirely different elements,[16] they were yet created as a unit, " like the
pot and its cover."[17] The heavens were fashioned from the
light of God's garment, and the earth from the snow under
the Divine Throne.[18] Tohu is a green band which encompasses the whole world, and dispenses darkness, and Bohu
consists of stones in the abyss, the producers of the waters.
The light created at the very beginning is not the same as the
light emitted by the sun, the moon, and the stars, which

appeared only on the fourth day. The light of the first day was of a sort that would have enabled man to see the world at a glance from one end to the other. Anticipating the wickedness of the sinful generations of the deluge and the Tower of Babel, who were unworthy to enjoy the blessing of such light, God concealed it, but in the world to come it will appear to the pious in all its pristine glory.[19]

Several heavens were created,[20] seven in fact,[21] each to serve a purpose of its own. The first, the one visible to man, has no function except that of covering up the light during the night time; therefore it disappears every morning. The planets are fastened to the second of the heavens; in the third the manna is made for the pious in the hereafter; the fourth contains the celestial Jerusalem together with the Temple, in which Michael ministers as high priest, and offers the souls of the pious as sacrifices. In the fifth heaven, the angel hosts reside, and sing the praise of God, though only during the night, for by day it is the task of Israel on earth to give glory to God on high. The sixth heaven is an uncanny spot; there originate most of the trials and visitations ordained for the earth and its inhabitants. Snow lies heaped up there and hail; there are lofts full of noxious dew, magazines stocked with storms, and cellars holding reserves of smoke. Doors of fire separate these celestial chambers, which are under the supervision of the archangel Metatron. Their pernicious contents defiled the heavens until David's time. The pious king prayed God to purge His exalted dwelling of whatever was pregnant with evil; it was not becoming that such things should exist near the Merciful One. Only then they were removed to the earth.

The seventh heaven, on the other hand, contains naught but what is good and beautiful : right, justice, and mercy, the storehouses of life, peace, and blessing, the souls of the pious, the souls and spirits of unborn generations, the dew with which God will revive the dead on the resurrection day, and, above all, the Divine Throne, surrounded by the seraphim. the ofanim, the holy Ḥayyot, and the ministering angels.[22]

Corresponding to the seven heavens, God created seven earths, each separated from the next by five layers. Over the lowest earth, the seventh, called Ereẓ, lie in succession the abyss, the Tohu, the Bohu, a sea, and waters.[23] Then the sixth[24] earth is reached, the Adamah, the scene of the magnificence of God. In the same way the Adamah is separated from the fifth earth, the Arḳa, which contains Gehenna, and Sha'are Mawet, and Sha'are Ẓalmawet, and Beër Shaḥat, and Ṭiṭ ha-Yawen, and Abaddon, and Sheol,[25] and there the souls of the wicked are guarded by the Angels of Destruction. In the same way Arḳa is followed by Ḥarabah, the dry, the place of brooks and streams in spite of its name, as the next, called Yabbashah, the mainland, contains the rivers and the springs. Tebel, the second earth, is the first mainland inhabited by living creatures, three hundred and sixty-five species,[26] all essentially different from those of our own earth. Some have human heads set on the body of a lion, or a serpent, or an ox ; others have human bodies topped by the head of one of these animals. Besides, Tebel is inhabited by human beings with two heads and four hands and feet, in fact with all their organs doubled excepting only the trunk.[27] It happens sometimes that the parts of these double persons quarrel with each other, especially while eating and drink-

ing, when each claims the best and largest portions for himself. This species of mankind is distinguished for great
piety, another difference between it and the inhabitants of
our earth.

Our own earth is called Heled, and, like the others, it is
separated from the Tebel by an abyss, the Tohu, the Bohu,
a sea, and waters.

Thus one earth rises above the other, from the first to the
seventh, and over the seventh earth the heavens are vaulted,
from the first to the seventh, the last of them attached to the
arm of God. The seven heavens form a unity, the seven
kinds of earth form a unity, and the heavens and the earth
together also form a unity.[28]

When God made our present heavens and our present
earth, "the new heavens and the new earth"[29] were also
brought forth, yea, and the hundred and ninety-six thousand
worlds which God created unto His own glory.[30]

It takes five hundred years to walk from the earth to the
heavens, and from one end of a heaven to the other, and
also from one heaven to the next,[31] and it takes the same
length of time to travel from the east to the west, or from
the south to the north.[32] Of all this vast world only one-
third is inhabited, the other two-thirds being equally divided
between water and waste desert land.

Beyond the inhabited parts to the east is Paradise[33] with
its seven divisions, each assigned to the pious of a certain
degree. The ocean is situated to the west, and it is dotted
with islands upon islands, inhabited by many different peoples. Beyond it, in turn, are the boundless steppes full of
serpents and scorpions, and destitute of every sort of vege-

tation, whether herbs or trees. To the north are the supplies of hell-fire, of snow, hail, smoke, ice, darkness, and wind-storms, and in that vicinity sojourn all sorts of devils, demons, and malign spirits. Their dwelling-place is a great stretch of land, it would take five hundred years to traverse it. Beyond lies hell. To the south is the chamber containing reserves of fire, the cave of smoke, and the forge of blasts and hurricanes.[34] Thus it comes that the wind blowing from the south brings heat and sultriness to the earth. Were it not for the angel Ben Nez, the Winged, who keeps the south wind back with his pinions, the world would be consumed.[35] Besides, the fury of its blast is tempered by the north wind, which always appears as moderator, whatever other wind may be blowing.[36]

In the east, the west, and the south, heaven and earth touch each other, but the north God left unfinished, that any man who announced himself as a god might be set the task of supplying the deficiency, and stand convicted as a pretender.[37]

The construction of the earth was begun at the centre, with the foundation stone of the Temple, the Eben Sheti-yah,[38] for the Holy Land is at the central point of the surface of the earth, Jerusalem is at the central point of Palestine, and the Temple is situated at the centre of the Holy City. In the sanctuary itself the Hekal is the centre, and the holy Ark occupies the centre of the Hekal, built on the foundation stone, which thus is at the centre of the earth.[39] Thence issued the first ray of light, piercing to the Holy Land, and from there illuminating the whole earth.[40] The creation of the world, however, could not take place until

God had banished the ruler of the dark." "Retire," God said to him, "for I desire to create the world by means of light." Only after the light had been fashioned, darkness arose, the light ruling in the sky, the darkness on the earth."

The power of God displayed itself not only in the creation of the world of things, but equally in the limitations which He imposed upon each. The heavens and the earth stretched themselves out in length and breadth as though they aspired to infinitude, and it required the word of God to call a halt to their encroachments."

THE SECOND DAY

On the second day God brought forth four creations, the firmament, hell, fire, and the angels."

The firmament is not the same as the heavens of the first day. It is the crystal stretched forth over the heads of the Hayyot, from which the heavens derive their light, as the earth derives its light from the sun. This firmament saves the earth from being engulfed by the waters of the heavens; it forms the partition between the waters above and the waters below." It was made to crystallize into the solid it is by the heavenly fire, which broke its bounds, and condensed the surface of the firmament. Thus fire made a division between the celestial and the terrestrial at the time of creation, as it did at the revelation on Mount Sinai." The firmament is not more than three fingers thick," nevertheless it divides two such heavy bodies as the waters below, which are the foundations for the nether world, and the waters above, which are the foundations for the seven heavens, the Divine Throne, and the abode of the angels."

The separation of the waters into upper and lower waters was the only act of the sort done by God in connection with the work of creation.⁴⁸ All other acts were unifying. It therefore caused some difficulties. When God commanded, " Let the waters be gathered together, unto one place, and let the dry land appear," certain parts refused to obey. They embraced each other all the more closely. In His wrath at the waters, God determined to let the whole of creation resolve itself into chaos again. He summoned the Angel of the Face, and ordered him to destroy the world. The angel opened his eyes wide, and scorching fires and thick clouds rolled forth from them, while he cried out, " He who divides the Red Sea in sunder ! "—and the rebellious waters stood. The all, however, was still in danger of destruction. Then began the singer of God's praises: " O Lord of the world, in days to come Thy creatures will sing praises without end to Thee, they will bless Thee boundlessly, and they will glorify Thee without measure. Thou wilt set Abraham apart from all mankind as Thine own ; one of his sons Thou wilt call ' My first-born '; and his descendants will take the yoke of Thy kingdom upon themselves. In holiness and purity Thou wilt bestow Thy Torah upon them, with the words, ' I am the Lord your God,' whereunto they will make answer, ' All that God hath spoken we will do.' And now I beseech Thee, have pity upon Thy world, destroy it not, for if Thou destroyest it, who will fulfil Thy will ? " God was pacified; He withdrew the command ordaining the destruction of the world, but the waters He put under the mountains, to remain there forever.⁴⁹

The objection of the lower waters to division and separation" was not their only reason for rebelling. The waters had been the first to give praise to God, and when their separation into upper and lower was decreed, the waters above rejoiced, saying, " Blessed are we who are privileged to abide near our Creator and near His Holy Throne." Jubilating thus, they flew upward, and uttered song and praise to the Creator of the world. Sadness fell upon the waters below. They lamented: "Woe unto us, we have not been found worthy to dwell in the presence of God, and praise Him together with our companions." Therefore they attempted to rise upward, until God repulsed them, and pressed them under the earth." Yet they were not left unrewarded for their loyalty. Whenever the waters above desire to give praise to God, they must first seek permission from the waters below."

The second day of creation was an untoward day in more than the one respect that it introduced a breach where before there had been nothing but unity; for it was the day that saw also the creation of hell. Therefore God could not say of this day as of the others, that He " saw that it was good." A division may be necessary, but it cannot be called good, and hell surely does not deserve the attribute of good."

Hell " has seven divisions," one beneath the other. They are called Sheol, Abaddon, Beër Shaḥat, Ṭiṭ ha-Yawen, Sha'are Mawet, Sha'are Ẓalmawet, and Gehenna. It requires three hundred years to traverse the height, or the width, or the depth of each division, and it would take six thousand three hundred " years to go over a tract of land equal in extent to the seven divisions."

Each of the seven divisions in turn has seven subdivisions,

and in each compartment there are seven rivers of fire and seven of hail. The width of each is one thousand ells, its depth one thousand, and its length three hundred, and they flow one from the other, and are supervised by ninety thousand Angels of Destruction. There are, besides, in every compartment seven thousand caves, in every cave there are seven thousand crevices, and in every crevice seven thousand scorpions. Every scorpion has three hundred rings, and in every ring seven thousand pouches of venom, from which flow seven rivers of deadly poison. If a man handles it, he immediately bursts, every limb is torn from his body, his bowels are cleft asunder, and he falls upon his face.⁹ There are also five different kinds of fire in hell. One devours and absorbs, another devours and does not absorb, while the third absorbs and does not devour, and there is still another fire, which neither devours nor absorbs, and furthermore a fire which devours fire. There are coals big as mountains, and coals big as hills, and coals as large as the Dead Sea, and coals like huge stones, and there are rivers of pitch and sulphur flowing and seething like live coals.⁹

The third creation of the second day was the angel hosts, both the ministering angels and the angels of praise. The reason they had not been called into being on the first day was, lest men believe that the angels assisted God in the creation of the heavens and the earth.⁸¹

The angels that are fashioned from fire have forms of fire,⁸² but only so long as they remain in heaven. When they descend to earth, to do the bidding of God here below, either they are changed into wind, or they assume the guise of men.⁸³ There are ten ranks or degrees among the angels.⁸⁴

The most exalted in rank are those surrounding the Divine
Throne on all sides, to the right, to the left, in front, and
behind, under the leadership of the archangels Michael, Gabriel, Uriel, and Raphael.[65]

All the celestial beings praise God with the words,
" Holy, holy, holy, is the Lord of hosts," but men take prece-
dence of the angels herein. They may not begin their
song of praise until the earthly beings have brought their
homage to God.[66] Especially Israel is preferred to the angels.
When they encircle the Divine Throne in the form of fiery
mountains and flaming hills, and attempt to raise their voices
in adoration of the Creator, God silences them with the
words, " Keep quiet until I have heard the songs, praises,
prayers, and sweet melodies of Israel." Accordingly, the
ministering angels and all the other celestial hosts wait until
the last tones of Israel's doxologies rising aloft from earth
have died away, and then they proclaim in a loud voice,
" Holy, holy, holy, is the Lord of hosts."

When the hour for the glorification of God by the angels
draws nigh, the august Divine herald, the angel Sham'iel,
steps to the windows[67] of the lowest heaven to hearken to
the songs, prayers, and praises that ascend from the syna
gogues and the houses of learning, and when they are finished, he announces the end to the angels in all the heavens.
The ministering angels, those who come in contact with the
sublunary world,[68] now repair to their chambers to take their
purification bath. They dive into a stream of fire and flame
seven times, and three hundred and sixty-five times they
examine themselves carefully, to make sure that no taint
clings to their bodies.[69] Only then they feel privileged to

mount the fiery ladder and join the angels of the seventh
heaven, and surround the throne of God with Hashmal and
all the holy Hayyot. Adorned with millions of fiery crowns,
arrayed in fiery garments, all the angels in unison, in the
same words, and with the same melody, intone songs of
praise to God.["]

The Third Day

Up to this time the earth was a plain, and wholly covered
with water. Scarcely had the words of God, "Let the
waters be gathered together," made themselves heard, when
mountains appeared all over and hills,["] and the water collected in the deep-lying basins. But the water was recalci-
trant, it resisted the order to occupy the lowly spots, and
threatened to overflow the earth, until God forced it back
into the sea, and encircled the sea with sand. Now, whenever the water is tempted to transgress its bounds, it beholds
the sand, and recoils.["]

The waters did but imitate their chief Rahab, the Angel of
the Sea, who rebelled at the creation of the world. God had
commanded Rahab to take in the water. But he refused,
saying, " I have enough." The punishment for his disobedience was death. His body rests in the depths of the sea,
the water dispelling the foul odor that emanates from it.["]

The main creation of the third day was the realm of
plants, the terrestrial plants as well as the plants of Paradise. First of all the cedars of Lebanon and the other great
trees were made. In their pride at having been put first,
they shot up high in the air. They considered themselves
the favored among plants. Then God spake, " I hate arro-

gance and pride, for I alone am exalted, and none beside,"
and He created the iron on the same day, the substance with
which trees are felled down. The trees began to weep, and
when God asked the reason of their tears, they said: "We
cry because Thou hast created the iron to uproot us therewith. All the while we had thought ourselves the highest of
the earth, and now the iron, our destroyer, has been called
into existence." God replied: "You yourselves will furnish
the axe with a handle. Without your assistance the iron
will not be able to do aught against you." [14]

The command to bear seed after their kind was given to
the trees alone. But the various sorts of grass reasoned,
that if God had not desired divisions according to classes,
He would not have instructed the trees to bear fruit after
their kind with the seed thereof in it, especially as trees are
inclined of their own accord to divide themselves into species. The grasses therefore reproduced themselves also after
their kinds. This prompted the exclamation of the Prince
of the World, "Let the glory of the Lord endure forever;
let the Lord rejoice in His works." [15]

The most important work done on the third day was the
creation of Paradise. Two gates of carbuncle form the entrance to Paradise, [16] and sixty myriads of ministering angels
keep watch over them. Each of these angels shines with the
lustre of the heavens. When the just man appears before
the gates, the clothes in which he was buried are taken off
him, and the angels array him in seven garments of clouds of
glory, and place upon his head two crowns, one of precious
stones and pearls, the other of gold of Parvaim, [17] and they
put eight myrtles in his hand, and they utter praises be-

fore him and say to him, " Go thy way, and eat thy bread
with joy." And they lead him to a place full of rivers, surrounded by eight hundred kinds of roses and myrtles. Each
one has a canopy according to his merits,[18] and under it
flow four rivers, one of milk, the other of balsam, the third
of wine, and the fourth of honey. Every canopy is overgrown by a vine of gold, and thirty pearls hang from it, each
of them shining like Venus. Under each canopy there is a
table of precious stones and pearls, and sixty angels stand at
the head of every just man, saying unto him: " Go and eat
with joy of the honey, for thou hast busied thyself with the
Torah, and she is sweeter than honey, and drink of the
wine preserved in the grape since the six days of creation,[19]
for thou hast busied thyself with the Torah, and she is compared to wine." The least fair of the just is beautiful as
Joseph and Rabbi Johanan, and as the grains of a silver
pomegranate upon which fall the rays of the sun.[20] There is
no light, " for the light of the righteous is the shining light."

And they undergo four transformations every day, passing
through four states. In the first the righteous is changed
into a child. He enters the division for children, and tastes
the joys of childhood. Then he is changed into a youth, and
enters the division for the youths, with whom he enjoys the
delights of youth. Next he becomes an adult, in the prime of
life, and he enters the division of men, and enjoys the
pleasures of manhood. Finally, he is changed into an old
man. He enters the division for the old, and enjoys the
pleasures of age.

There are eighty myriads of trees in every corner of Paradise, the meanest among them choicer than all the spice

trees. In every corner there are sixty myriads of angels singing with sweet voices, and the tree of life stands in the middle and shades the whole of Paradise." It has fifteen thousand tastes, each different from the other, and the perfumes thereof vary likewise. Over it hang seven clouds of glory, and winds blow upon it from all four sides," so that its odor is wafted from one end of the world to the other. Underneath sit the scholars and explain the Torah. Over each of them two canopies are spread, one of stars, the other of sun and moon, and a curtain of clouds of glory separates the one canopy from the other." Beyond Paradise begins Eden, containing three hundred and ten worlds " and seven compartments for seven different classes of the pious. In the first are " the martyr victims of the government," like Rabbi Akiba and his colleagues; " in the second those who were drowned; " in the third " Rabbi Johanan ben Zakkai and his disciples; in the fourth those who were carried off in the cloud of glory; " in the fifth the penitents, who occupy a place which even a perfectly pious man cannot obtain; in the sixth are the youths " who have not tasted of sin in their lives; in the seventh are those poor who studied Bible and Mishnah, and led a life of self-respecting decency. And God sits in the midst of them and expounds the Torah to them."

As for the seven divisions of Paradise, each of them is twelve myriads of miles in width and twelve myriads of miles in length. In the first division dwell the proselytes who embraced Judaism of their own free will, not from compulsion. The walls are of glass and the wainscoting of cedar. The prophet Obadiah." himself a proselyte, is the

overseer of this first division. The second division is built
of silver, and the wainscoting thereof is of cedar. Here
dwell those who have repented, and Manasseh, the penitent
son of Hezekiah, presides over them. The third division is
built of silver and gold. Here dwell Abraham, Isaac, and
Jacob, and all the Israelites who came out of Egypt, and the
whole generation that lived in the desert." Also David is
there, together with all his sons " except Absalom, one of
them, Chileab, still alive. And all the kings of Judah are
there, with the exception of Manasseh, the son of Hezekiah,
who presides in the second division, over the penitents.
Moses and Aaron preside over the third division. Here are
precious vessels of silver and gold and jewels and canopies
and beds and thrones and lamps, of gold, of precious stones,
and of pearls, the best of everything there is in heaven." The
fourth division is built of beautiful rubies," and its wainscoting is of olive wood. Here dwell the perfect and the steadfast in faith, and their wainscoting is of olive wood, because
their lives were bitter as olives to them. The fifth division is
built of silver and gold and refined gold," and the finest of
gold and glass and bdellium, and through the midst of it
flows the river Gihon. The wainscoting is of silver and gold,
and a perfume breathes through it more exquisite than the
perfume of Lebanon. The coverings of the silver and gold
beds are made of purple and blue, woven by Eve, and of
scarlet and the hair of goats, woven by angels. Here dwells
the Messiah on a palanquin made of the wood of Lebanon,
" the pillars thereof of silver, the bottom of gold, the seat of
it purple." With him is Elijah. He takes the head of Messiah, and places it in his bosom, and says to him, " Be quiet,

for the end draweth nigh." On every Monday and Thursday and on Sabbaths and holidays, the Patriarchs come to him, and the twelve sons of Jacob, and Moses, Aaron, David, Solomon, and all the kings of Israel and of Judah, and they weep with him and comfort him, and say unto him, " Be quiet and put trust in thy Creator, for the end draweth nigh." Also Korah and his company, and Dathan, Abiram, and Absalom come to him on every Wednesday, and ask him: " How long before the end comes full of wonders? When wilt thou bring us life again, and from the abysses of the earth lift us?" The Messiah answers them, "Go to your fathers and ask them"; and when they hear this, they are ashamed, and do not ask their fathers.

In the sixth division dwell those who died in performing a pious act, and in the seventh division those who died from illness inflicted as an expiation for the sins of Israel."

THE FOURTH DAY

The fourth day of creation produced the sun, the moon, and the stars. These heavenly spheres were not actually fashioned on this day; they were created on the first day, and merely were assigned their places in the heavens on the fourth." At first the sun and the moon enjoyed equal powers and prerogatives." The moon spoke to God, and said: " O Lord, why didst Thou create the world with the letter Bet?" God replied: " That it might be made known unto My creatures that there are two worlds." The moon: " O Lord, which of the two worlds is the larger, this world or the world to come?" God: " The world to come is the larger." The moon: "O Lord, Thou didst create two

worlds, a greater and a lesser world; Thou didst create the
heaven and the earth, the heaven exceeding the earth; Thou
didst create fire and water, the water stronger than the fire,
because it can quench the fire; and now Thou hast created
the sun and the moon, and it is becoming that one of them
should be greater than the other." Then spake God to the
moon: " I know well, thou wouldst have me make Thee
greater than the sun. As a punishment I decree that thou
mayest keep but one-sixtieth of thy light." The moon made
supplication: " Shall I be punished so severely for having
spoken a single word?" God relented: " In the future world
I will restore thy light, so that thy light may again be as
the light of the sun." The moon was not yet satisfied. " O
Lord," she said, " and the light of the sun, how great will it
be in that day?" Then the wrath of God was once more
enkindled: " What, thou still plottest against the sun? As
thou livest, in the world to come his light shall be sevenfold
the light he now sheds." [100]

The sun runs his course like a bridegroom. He sits upon
a throne with a garland on his head.[101] Ninety-six angels
accompany him on his daily journey, in relays of eight every
hour, two to the left of him, and two to the right, two before
him, and two behind. Strong as he is, he could complete his
course from south to north in a single instant, but three
hundred and sixty-five angels restrain him by means of as
many grappling-irons. Every day one looses his hold, and
the sun must thus spend three hundred and sixty-five days
on his course. The progress of the sun in his circuit is an
uninterrupted song of praise to God. And this song alone
makes his motion possible. Therefore, when Joshua wanted

to bid the sun stand still, he had to command him to be silent. His song of praise hushed, the sun stood still.[102]

The sun is double-faced; one face, of fire, is directed toward the earth, and one, of hail, toward heaven, to cool off the prodigious heat that streams from the other face, else the earth would catch afire. In winter the sun turns his fiery face upward, and thus the cold is produced.[103] When the sun descends in the west in the evening, he dips down into the ocean and takes a bath, his fire is extinguished, and therefore he dispenses neither light nor warmth during the night. But as soon as he reaches the east in the morning, he laves himself in a stream of flame, which imparts warmth and light to him, and these he sheds over the earth. In the same way the moon and the stars take a bath in a stream of hail before they enter upon their service for the night.[104]

When the sun and the moon are ready to start upon their round of duties, they appear before God, and beseech him to relieve them of their task, so that they may be spared the sight of sinning mankind. Only upon compulsion they proceed with their daily course. Coming from the presence of God, they are blinded by the radiance in the heavens, and they cannot find their way. God, therefore, shoots off arrows, by the glittering light of which they are guided. It is on account of the sinfulness of man, which the sun is forced to contemplate on his rounds, that he grows weaker as the time of his going down approaches, for sins have a defiling and enfeebling effect, and he drops from the horizon as a sphere of blood, for blood is the sign of corruption.[105]

As the sun sets forth on his course in the morning, his wings touch the leaves on the trees of Paradise, and their vibration is communicated to the angels and the holy Ḥayyot, to the other plants, and also to the trees and plants on earth, and to all the beings on earth and in heaven. It is the signal for them all to cast their eyes upward. As soon as they see the Ineffable Name, which is engraved in the sun, they raise their voices in songs of praise to God. At the same moment a heavenly voice is heard to say, " Woe to the sons of men that consider not the honor of God like unto these creatures whose voices now rise aloft in adoration." [106] These words, naturally, are not heard by men, as little as they perceive the grating of the sun against the wheel to which all the celestial bodies are attached, although the noise it makes is extraordinarily loud.[107] This friction of the sun and the wheel produces the motes dancing about in the sunbeams. They are the carriers of healing to the sick,[108] the only health-giving creations of the fourth day, on the whole an unfortunate day, especially for children, afflicting them with disease.[109]

When God punished the envious moon by diminishing her light and splendor, so that she ceased to be the equal of the sun as she had been originally,[110] she fell,[111] and tiny threads were loosed from her body. These are the stars.[112]

The Fifth Day

On the fifth day of creation God took fire [113] and water, and out of these two elements He made the fishes of the sea.[114] The animals in the water are much more numerous than those on land. For every species on land, excepting only the weasel, there is a corresponding species in the water, and, besides, there are many found only in the water.[115]

The ruler over the sea-animals is leviathan.[116] With all
the other fishes he was made on the fifth day.[117] Originally
he was created male and female like all the other animals.
But when it appeared that a pair of these monsters might
annihilate the whole earth with their united strength, God
killed the female.[118] So enormous is leviathan that to quench
his thirst he needs all the water that flows from the Jordan
into the sea.[119] His food consists of the fish which go between his jaws of their own accord.[120] When he is hungry,
a hot breath blows from his nostrils, and it makes the waters
of the great sea seething hot. Formidable though behemot,
the other monster, is, he feels insecure until he is certain that
leviathan has satisfied his thirst.[121] The only thing that can
keep him in check is the stickleback, a little fish which was
created for the purpose, and of which he stands in great
awe.[122] But leviathan is more than merely large and strong;
he is wonderfully made besides. His fins radiate brilliant
light, the very sun is obscured by it,[123] and also his eyes shed
such splendor that frequently the sea is illuminated suddenly by it.[124] No wonder that this marvellous beast is the
plaything of God, in whom He takes His pastime.[124]

There is but one thing that makes leviathan repulsive, his
foul smell, which is so strong that if it penetrated thither,
it would render Paradise itself an impossible abode.[125]

The real purpose of leviathan is to be served up as a
dainty to the pious in the world to come. The female was
put into brine as soon as she was killed, to be preserved
against the time when her flesh will be needed.[126] The male
is destined to offer a delectable sight to all beholders before
he is consumed. When his last hour arrives, God will sum-

mon the angels to enter into combat with the monster. But
no sooner will leviathan cast his glance at them than they
will flee in fear and dismay from the field of battle. They
will return to the charge with swords, but in vain, for his
scales can turn back steel like straw. They will be equally
unsuccessful when they attempt to kill him by throwing
darts and slinging stones; such missiles will rebound without leaving the least impression on his body. Disheartened,
the angels will give up the combat, and God will command
leviathan and behemot to enter into a duel with each other.
The issue will be that both will drop dead, behemot slaughtered by a blow of leviathan's fins, and leviathan killed by a
lash of behemot's tail. From the skin of leviathan God will
construct tents to shelter companies of the pious while they
enjoy the dishes made of his flesh. The amount assigned to
each of the pious will be in proportion to his deserts, and
none will envy or begrudge the other his better share. What
is left of leviathan's skin will be stretched out over Jerusalem as a canopy, and the light streaming from it will illu-
mine the whole world, and what is left of his flesh after the
pious have appeased their appetite, will be distributed among
the rest of men, to carry on traffic therewith.[127]

On the same day with the fishes, the birds were created,
for these two kinds of animals are closely related to each
other. Fish are fashioned out of water, and birds out of
marshy ground saturated with water.[128]

As leviathan is the king of fishes, so the ziz is appointed to
rule over the birds.[129] His name comes from the variety of
tastes his flesh has; it tastes like this, *zeh,* and like that,
zeh.[130] The ziz is as monstrous of size as leviathan himself.

His ankles rest on the earth, and his head reaches to the very sky.[131]

It once happened that travellers on a vessel noticed a bird. As he stood in the water, it merely covered his feet, and his head knocked against the sky. The onlookers thought the water could not have any depth at that point, and they prepared to take a bath there. A heavenly voice warned them: "Alight not here! Once a carpenter's axe slipped from his hand at this spot, and it took it seven years to touch bottom." The bird the travellers saw was none other than the ziz.[132] His wings are so huge that unfurled they darken the sun.[133] They protect the earth against the storms of the south; without their aid the earth would not be able to resist the winds blowing thence.[134] Once an egg of the ziz fell to the ground and broke. The fluid from it flooded sixty cities, and the shock crushed three hundred cedars. Fortunately such accidents do not occur frequently. As a rule the bird lets her eggs slide gently into her nest. This one mishap was due to the fact that the egg was rotten, and the bird cast it away carelessly. The ziz has another name, Renanim,[135] because he is the celestial singer.[136] On account of his relation to the heavenly regions he is also called Sekwi, the seer, and, besides, he is called "son of the nest,"[137] because his fledgling birds break away from the shell without being hatched by the mother bird; they spring directly from the nest, as it were.[138] Like leviathan, so ziz is a delicacy to be served to the pious at the end of time, to compensate them for the privations which abstaining from the unclean fowls imposed upon them.[139]

THE SIXTH DAY

As the fish were formed out of water, and the birds out of boggy earth well mixed with water, so the mammals were formed out of solid earth,[140] and as leviathan is the most notable representative of the fish kind, and ziz of the bird kind, so behemot is the most notable representative of the mammal kind. Behemot matches leviathan in strength, and he had to be prevented, like leviathan, from multiplying and increasing, else the world could not have continued to exist; after God had created him male and female, He at once deprived him of the desire to propagate his kind.[141] He is so monstrous that he requires the produce of a thousand mountains for his daily food. All the water that flows through the bed of the Jordan in a year suffices him exactly for one gulp. It therefore was necessary to give him one stream entirely for his own use, a stream flowing forth from Paradise, called Yubal.[142] Behemot, too, is destined to be served to the pious as an appetizing dainty, but before they enjoy his flesh, they will be permitted to view the mortal combat between leviathan and behemot, as a reward for having denied themselves the pleasures of the circus and its gladiatorial contests.[143]

Leviathan, ziz, and behemot are not the only monsters; there are many others, and marvellous ones, like the reëm, a giant animal, of which only one couple, male and female, is in existence. Had there been more, the world could hardly have maintained itself against them. The act of copulation occurs but once in seventy years between them, for God has so ordered it that the male and female reëm are at opposite ends of the earth, the one in the east, the other in the west.

The act of copulation results in the death of the male. He is bitten by the female and dies of the bite. The female becomes pregnant and remains in this state for no less than twelve years. At the end of this long period she gives birth to twins, a male and a female. The year preceding her delivery she is not able to move. She would die of hunger, were it not that her own spittle flowing copiously from her mouth waters and fructifies the earth near her, and causes it to bring forth enough for her maintenance. For a whole year the animal can but roll from side to side, until finally her belly bursts, and the twins issue forth. Their appearance is thus the signal for the death of the mother reëm. She makes room for the new generation, which in turn is destined to suffer the same fate as the generation that went before. Immediately after birth, the one goes eastward and the other westward, to meet only after the lapse of seventy years, propagate themselves, and perish.[144] A traveller who once saw a reëm one day old described its height to be four parasangs, and the length of its head one parasang and a half.[145] Its horns measure one hundred ells, and their height is a great deal more.[146]

One of the most remarkable creatures is the "man of the mountain," Adne Sadeh, or, briefly, Adam.[147] His form is exactly that of a human being, but he is fastened to the ground by means of a navel-string, upon which his life depends. The cord once snapped, he dies. This animal keeps himself alive with what is produced by the soil around about him as far as his tether permits him to crawl. No creature may venture to approach within the radius of his cord, for he seizes and demolishes whatever comes in his reach. To kill

him, one may not go near to him, the navel-string must be
severed from a distance by means of a dart, and then he dies
amid groans and moans.[148]

Once upon a time a traveller happened in the region
where this animal is found. He overheard his host consult
his wife as to what to do to honor their guest, and resolve
to serve "our man," as he said. Thinking he had fallen
among cannibals, the stranger ran as fast as his feet could
carry him from his entertainer, who sought vainly to restrain
him. Afterward, he found out that there had been no intention of regaling him with human flesh, but only with the
flesh of the strange animal called "man."[149]

As the "man of the mountain" is fixed to the ground by
his navel-string, so the barnacle-goose is grown to a tree by
its bill. It is hard to say whether it is an animal and must
be slaughtered to be fit for food, or whether it is a plant and
no ritual ceremony is necessary before eating it.[150]

Among the birds the phœnix is the most wonderful.
When Eve gave all the animals some of the fruit of the tree
of knowledge, the phœnix was the only bird that refused to
eat thereof, and he was rewarded with eternal life. When
he has lived a thousand years, his body shrinks, and the
feathers drop from it, until he is as small as an egg. This
is the nucleus of the new bird.[151]

The phœnix is also called "the guardian of the terrestrial
sphere." He runs with the sun on his circuit, and he
spreads out his wings and catches up the fiery rays of the
sun.[152] If he were not there to intercept them, neither man
nor any other animate being would keep alive. On his right
wing the following words are inscribed in huge letters,[153]

about four thousand stadia high: "Neither the earth produces me, nor the heavens, but only the wings of fire." His
food consists of the manna of heaven and the dew of the
earth. His excrement is a worm, whose excrement in turn
is the cinnamon used by kings and princes.[152] Enoch, who
saw the phœnix birds when he was translated, describes
them as flying creatures, wonderful and strange in appearance, with the feet and tails of lions, and the heads of croco-
diles; their appearance is of a purple color like the rainbow;
their size nine hundred measures. Their wings are like
those of angels, each having twelve, and they attend the
chariot of the sun and go with him, bringing heat and dew
as they are ordered by God. In the morning when the sun
starts on his daily course, the phœnixes and the chalkidri[154]
sing, and every bird flaps its wings, rejoicing the Giver of
light, and they sing a song at the command of the Lord.[155]

Among reptiles the salamander and the shamir are the
most marvellous. The salamander originates from a fire of
myrtle wood[156] which has been kept burning for seven years
steadily by means of magic arts. Not bigger than a mouse,
it yet is invested with peculiar properties. One who smears
himself with its blood is invulnerable,[157] and the web woven
by it is a talisman against fire.[158] The people who lived at
the deluge boasted that, were a fire flood to come, they would
protect themselves with the blood of the salamander.[159]

King Hezekiah owes his life to the salamander. His
wicked father, King Ahaz, had delivered him to the fires of
Moloch, and he would have been burnt, had his mother not
painted him with the blood of the salamander, so that the
fire could do him no harm.[160]

The shamir was made at twilight on the sixth day of creation together with other extraordinary things.[161] It is about
as large as a barley corn, and it possesses the remarkable
property of cutting the hardest of diamonds. For this
reason it was used for the stones in the breastplate worn by
the high priest. First the names of the twelve tribes were
traced with ink on the stones to be set into the breastplate,
then the shamir was passed over the lines, and thus they
were graven. The wonderful circumstance was that the
friction wore no particles from the stones. The shamir was
also used for hewing into shape the stones from which the
Temple was built, because the law prohibited iron tools to
be used for the work in the Temple.[162] The shamir may not
be put in an iron vessel for safe-keeping, nor in any metal
vessel, it would burst such a receptacle asunder. It is kept
wrapped up in a woollen cloth, and this in turn is placed in a
lead basket filled with barley bran.[163] The shamir was
guarded in Paradise until Solomon needed it. He sent the
eagle thither to fetch the worm.[164] With the destruction of
the Temple the shamir vanished.[165]

A similar fate overtook the taḥash, which had been created
only that its skin might be used for the Tabernacle. Once
the Tabernacle was completed, the taḥash disappeared. It
had a horn on its forehead, was gaily colored like the turkey-
cock, and belonged to the class of clean animals.[166]

Among the fishes there are also wonderful creatures, the
sea-goats and the dolphins, not to mention leviathan. A sea-
faring man once saw a sea-goat on whose horns the words
were inscribed: "I am a little sea-animal, yet I traversed
three hundred parasangs to offer myself as food to the levia-

than." [167] The dolphins are half man and half fish; they even have sexual intercourse with human beings; therefore they are called also " sons of the sea," for in a sense they represent the human kind in the waters. [168]

Though every species in the animal world was created during the last two days of the six of creation, [169] yet many characteristics of certain animals appeared later. Cats and mice, foes now, were friends originally. Their later enmity had a distinct cause. On one occasion the mouse appeared before God and spoke: " I and the cat are partners, but now we have nothing to eat." The Lord answered: " Thou art intriguing against thy companion, only that thou mayest devour her. As a punishment, she shall devour thee." Thereupon the mouse: " O Lord of the world, wherein have I done wrong?" God replied: " O thou unclean reptile, thou shouldst have been warned by the example of the moon, who lost a part of her light, because she spake ill of the sun, and what she lost was given to her opponent. [170] The evil intentions thou didst harbor against thy companion shall be punished in the same way. Instead of thy devouring her, she shall devour thee." The mouse: " O Lord of the world! Shall my whole kind be destroyed?" God: " I will take care that a remnant of thee is spared." In her rage the mouse bit the cat, and the cat in turn threw herself upon the mouse, and hacked into her with her teeth until she lay dead. Since that moment the mouse stands in such awe of the cat that she does not even attempt to defend herself against her enemy's attacks, and always keeps herself in hiding. [171]

Similarly dogs and cats maintained a friendly relation to each other, and only later on became enemies. A dog and a

cat were partners, and they shared with each other whatever they had. It once happened that neither could find
anything to eat for three days. Thereupon the dog proposed that they dissolve their partnership. The cat should
go to Adam, in whose house there would surely be enough
for her to eat, while the dog should seek his fortune elsewhere. Before they separated, they took an oath never to
go to the same master. The cat took up her abode with
Adam, and she found sufficient mice in his house to satisfy
her appetite. Seeing how useful she was in driving away
and extirpating mice, Adam treated her most kindly. The
dog, on the other hand, saw bad times. The first night after
their separation he spent in the cave of the wolf, who had
granted him a night's lodging. At night the dog caught
the sound of steps, and he reported it to his host, who bade
him repulse the intruders. They were wild animals. Little
lacked and the dog would have lost his life. Dismayed, the
dog fled from the house of the wolf, and took refuge with
the monkey. But he would not grant him even a single
night's lodging; and the fugitive was forced to appeal to
the hospitality of the sheep. Again the dog heard steps in
the middle of the night. Obeying the bidding of his host,
he arose to chase away the marauders, who turned out to be
wolves. The barking of the dog apprised the wolves of
the presence of sheep, so that the dog innocently caused the
sheep's death. Now he had lost his last friend. Night after
night he begged for shelter, without ever finding a home.
Finally, he decided to repair to the house of Adam, who also
granted him refuge for one night. When wild animals approached the house under cover of darkness, the dog began

to bark, Adam awoke, and with his bow and arrow he drove
them away. Recognizing the dog's usefulness, he bade him
remain with him always. But as soon as the cat espied the
dog in Adam's house, she began to quarrel with him, and
reproach him with having broken his oath to her. Adam
did his best to pacify the cat. He told her he had himself
invited the dog to make his home there, and he assured her
she would in no wise be the loser by the dog's presence; he
wanted both to stay with him. But it was impossible to appease the cat. The dog promised her not to touch anything
intended for her. She insisted that she could not live in one
and the same house with a thief like the dog. Bickerings
between the dog and the cat became the order of the day.
Finally the dog could stand it no longer, and he left Adam's
house, and betook himself to Seth's. By Seth he was wel-
comed kindly, and from Seth's house, he continued to make
efforts at reconciliation with the cat. In vain. Yes, the enmity between the first dog and the first cat was transmitted
to all their descendants until this very day.[17]

Even the physical peculiarities of certain animals were
not original features with them, but owed their existence to
something that occurred subsequent to the days of creation.
The mouse at first had quite a different mouth from its
present mouth. In Noah's ark, in which all animals, to
ensure the preservation of every kind, lived together peaceably, the pair of mice were once sitting next to the cat.
Suddenly the latter remembered that her father was in
the habit of devouring mice, and thinking there was no
harm in following his example, she jumped at the mouse,
who vainly looked for a hole into which to slip out of sight.

Then a miracle happened; a hole appeared where none had
been before, and the mouse sought refuge in it. The cat
pursued the mouse, and though she could not follow her
into the hole, she could insert her paw and try to pull the
mouse out of her covert. Quickly the mouse opened her
mouth in the hope that the paw would go into it, and the
cat would be prevented from fastening her claws in her
flesh. But as the cavity of the mouth was not big enough,
the cat succeeded in clawing the cheeks of the mouse. Not
that this helped her much, it merely widened the mouth of
the mouse, and her prey after all escaped the cat.[113] After
her happy escape, the mouse betook herself to Noah and said
to him, " O pious man, be good enough to sew up my cheek
where my enemy, the cat, has torn a rent in it." Noah bade
her fetch a hair out of the tail of the swine, and with this
he repaired the damage. Thence the little seam-like line
next to the mouth of every mouse to this very day.[114]

The raven is another animal that changed its appearance
during its sojourn in the ark. When Noah desired to send
him forth to find out about the state of the waters, he hid
under the wings of the eagle. Noah found him, however,
and said to him, " Go and see whether the waters have diminished." The raven pleaded: " Hast thou none other
among all the birds to send on this errand? " Noah: " My
power extends no further than over thee and the dove." [115]
But the raven was not satisfied. He said to Noah with great
insolence: " Thou sendest me forth only that I may meet my
death, and thou wishest my death that my wife may be at
thy service." [116]   Thereupon Noah cursed the raven thus:
" May thy mouth, which has spoken evil against me, be ac-

cursed, and thy intercourse with thy wife be only through it." [177] All the animals in the ark said Amen. And this is the reason why a mass of spittle runs from the mouth of the male raven into the mouth of the female during the act of copulation, and only thus the female is impregnated. [178]

Altogether the raven is an unattractive animal. He is unkind toward his own young so long as their bodies are not covered with black feathers, [179] though as a rule ravens love one another. [180] God therefore takes the young ravens under His special protection. From their own excrement maggots come forth, [181] which serve as their food during the three days that elapse after their birth, until their white feathers turn black and their parents recognize them as their offspring and care for them. [182]

The raven has himself to blame also for the awkward hop in his gait. He observed the graceful step of the dove, and envious of her tried to emulate it. The outcome was that he almost broke his bones without in the least succeeding in making himself resemble the dove, not to mention that he brought the scorn of the other animals down upon himself. His failure excited their ridicule. Then he decided to return to his own original gait, but in the interval he had unlearnt it, and he could walk neither the one way nor the other properly. His step had become a hop betwixt and between. Thus we see how true it is, that he who is dissatisfied with his small portion loses the little he has in striving for more and better things. [183]

The steer is also one of the animals that have suffered a change in the course of time. Originally his face was entirely overgrown with hair, but now there is none on his nose, and that is because Joshua kissed him on his nose during the siege of Jericho. Joshua was an exceedingly heavy man. Horses, donkeys, and mules, none could bear him, they all broke down under his weight. What they could not do, the steer accomplished. On his back Joshua rode to the siege of Jericho, and in gratitude he bestowed a kiss upon his nose.[184]

The serpent, too, is other than it was at first. Before the fall of man it was the cleverest of all animals created, and in form it resembled man closely. It stood upright, and was of extraordinary size.[185] Afterward, it lost the mental advantages it had possessed as compared with other animals, and it degenerated physically, too; it was deprived of its feet, so that it could not pursue other animals and kill them. The mole and the frog had to be made harmless in similar ways; the former has no eyes, else it were irresistible, and the frog has no teeth, else no animal in the water were sure of its life.[186]

While the cunning of the serpent wrought its own undoing, the cunning of the fox stood him in good stead in many an embarrassing situation. After Adam had committed the sin of disobedience, God delivered the whole of the animal world into the power of the Angel of Death, and He ordered him to cast one pair of each kind into the water. He and leviathan together thus have dominion over all that has life. When the Angel of Death was in the act of executing the Divine command upon the fox, he began to weep bitterly. The Angel of Death asked him the reason of his tears, and the fox replied that he was mourning the sad fate of his friend. At the same time he pointed to the figure of a fox in the sea, which was nothing but his own reflection. The Angel of Death, persuaded that a representative of the fox family had been cast into the water, let him go free. The fox told his trick to the cat, and she in turn played it on the Angel of Death.[187] So it happened that neither cats nor foxes are represented in the water, while all other animals are.[188]

When leviathan passed the animals in review, and missing the fox was informed of the sly way in which he had eluded his authority, he dispatched great and powerful fish on the errand of enticing the truant into the water. The fox walking along the shore espied the large number of fish, and he exclaimed, "How happy he who may always satisfy his hunger with the flesh of such as these." The fish told him, if he would but follow them, his appetite could easily be appeased. At the same time they informed him that a great honor awaited him. Leviathan, they said, was at death's door, and he had commissioned them to install the fox as his successor. They were ready to carry him on their backs, so that he had no need to fear the water, and thus they would convey him to the throne, which stood upon a huge rock. The fox yielded to these persuasions, and descended into the water. Presently an uncomfortable feeling took possession of him. He began to suspect that the tables were turned; he was being made game of instead of making game of others as usual. He urged the fish to tell him the truth, and they admitted that they had been sent out to secure his person for leviathan, who wanted his heart,[189] that he might become as knowing as the fox, whose wisdom he had heard many extol. The fox said reproachfully: "Why did you not tell me the truth at once? Then I could have brought my heart along with me for King Leviathan, who would have showered honors upon me. As it is, you will surely suffer punishment for bringing me without my heart. The foxes, you see," he continued, " do not carry their hearts around with them. They keep them in a safe place, and when they have need of them, they fetch them thence." The fish quickly swam to shore, and landed the fox, so that he might go for his heart. No sooner did he feel dry land under his feet than he began to jump and shout, and when they urged him to go in search of his heart, and follow them, he said: " O ye fools, could I have followed you into the water, if I had not had my heart with me? Or exists there a creature able to go abroad without his heart? " The fish replied: " Come, come, thou art fooling us." Whereupon the fox: " O ye fools, if I could play a trick on the Angel of Death, how much easier was it to make game of you? " So they had to return, their errand undone, and leviathan could not but confirm the taunting judgment of the fox: " In very truth, the fox is wise of heart, and ye are fools." [110]

ALL THINGS PRAISE THE LORD

" Whatever God created has value." Even the animals and the insects that seem useless and noxious at first sight have a vocation to fulfil. The snail trailing a moist streak after it as it crawls, and so using up its vitality, serves as a remedy for boils. The sting of a hornet is healed by the house-fly crushed and applied to the wound. The gnat, feeble creature, taking in food but never secreting it, is a specific against the poison of a viper, and this venomous reptile itself cures eruptions, while the lizard is the antidote to the scorpion.[171]

Not only do all creatures serve man, and contribute to his comfort, but also God " teacheth us through the beasts of the earth, and maketh us wise through the fowls of heaven." He endowed many animals with admirable moral qualities as a pattern for man. If the Torah had not been revealed to us, we might have learnt regard for the decencies of life from the cat, who covers her excrement with earth; regard for the property of others from the ants, who never encroach upon one another's stores; and regard for decorous conduct from the cock, who, when he desires to unite with the hen, promises to buy her a cloak long enough to reach to the ground, and when the hen reminds him of his promise, he shakes his comb and says, " May I be deprived of my comb, if I do not buy it when I have the means." The grasshopper also has a lesson to teach to man. All the summer through it sings, until its belly bursts, and death claims it. Though it knows the fate that awaits it, yet it sings on. So man should do his duty toward God, no matter what the consequences. The stork should be taken as a model in two respects. He guards the purity of his family life zealously, and toward his fellows he is compassionate and merciful. Even the frog can be the teacher of man. By the side of the water there lives a species of animals which subsist off aquatic creatures alone. When the frog notices that one of them is hungry, he goes to it of his own accord, and offers himself as food, thus fulfilling the injunction, " If thine enemy be hungry, give him bread to eat; and if he be thirsty, give him water to drink." [172]

The whole of creation was called into existence by God unto His glory,[1a] and each creature has its own hymn of praise wherewith to extol the Creator. Heaven and earth, Paradise and hell, desert and field, rivers and seas—all have their own way of paying homage to God. The hymn of the earth is, "From the uttermost part of the earth have we heard songs, glory to the Righteous." The sea cxclaims, "Above the voices of many waters, the mighty breakers of the sea, the Lord on high is mighty."

Also the celestial bodies and the elements proclaim the praise of their Creator—the sun, moon, and stars, the clouds and the winds, lightning and dew. The sun says, "The sun and moon stood still in their habitation, at the light of Thine arrows as they went, at the shining of Thy glittering spear"; and the stars sing, "Thou art the Lord, even Thou alone; Thou hast made heaven, the heaven of heavens, with all their host, the earth and all things that are thereon, the seas and all that is in them, and Thou preservest them all; and the host of heaven worshippeth Thee."

Every plant, furthermore, has a song of praise. The fruitful tree sings, "Then shall all the trees of the wood sing for joy, before the Lord, for He cometh; for He cometh to judge the earth"; and the ears of grain on the field sing, "The pastures are covered with flocks; the valleys also are covered over with corn; they shout for joy, they also sing."

Great among singers of praise are the birds, and greatest among them is the cock. When God at midnight goes to the pious in Paradise, all the trees therein break out into adoration, and their songs awaken the cock, who begins in turn to praise God. Seven times he crows, each time reciting a

verse. The first verse is: " Lift up your heads, O ye gates ;
and be ye lift up, ye everlasting doors, and the King of
glory shall come in. Who is the King of glory? The Lord
strong and mighty, the Lord mighty in battle." The second
verse: " Lift up your heads, O ye gates ; yea, lift them up, ye
everlasting doors, and the King of glory shall come in. Who
is this King of glory? The Lord of hosts, He is the King of
glory." The third: " Arise, ye righteous, and occupy yourselves with the Torah, that your reward may be abundant in
the world hereafter." The fourth: " I have waited for Thy
salvation, O Lord!" The fifth: " How long wilt thou sleep,
O sluggard? When wilt thou arise out of thy sleep?" The
sixth: " Love not sleep, lest thou come to poverty ; open thine
eyes, and thou shalt be satisfied with bread." And the
seventh verse sung by the cock runs: " It is time to work for
the Lord, for they have made void Thy law."

The song of the vulture is: " I will hiss for them, and
gather them ; for I have redeemed them, and they shall increase as they have increased "—the same verse with which
the bird will in time to come announce the advent of the
Messiah, the only difference being, that when he heralds the
Messiah he will sit upon the ground and sing his verse,
while at all other times he is seated elsewhere when he sings
it.

Nor do the other animals praise God less than the birds.
Even the beasts of prey give forth adoration. The lion says:
" The Lord shall go forth as a mighty man ; He shall stir up
jealousy like a man of war ; He shall cry, yea, He shall shout
aloud ; He shall do mightily against his enemies." And the
fox exhorts unto justice with the words: " Woe unto him

that buildeth his house by unrighteousness, and his chambers
by injustice; that useth his neighbor's service without wages,
and giveth him not his hire."

Yea, the dumb fishes know how to proclaim the praise of
their Lord. " The voice of the Lord is upon the waters,"
they say, " the God of glory thundereth, even the Lord upon
many waters "; while the frog exclaims, " Blessed be the
name of the glory of His kingdom forever and ever!"

Contemptible though they are, even the reptiles give praise
unto their Creator. The mouse extols God with the words:
" Howbeit Thou art just in all that is come upon me; for
Thou hast dealt truly, but I have done wickedly." And the
cat sings: " Let everything that hath breath praise the Lord.
Praise ye the Lord." [106]

II

ADAM

II

ADAM

MAN AND THE WORLD

With ten Sayings God created the world, although a single Saying would have sufficed. God desired to make known how severe is the punishment to be meted out to the wicked, who destroy a world created with as many as ten Sayings, and how goodly the reward destined for the righteous, who preserve a world created with as many as ten Sayings.[1]

The world was made for man, though he was the last-comer among its creatures. This was design. He was to find all things ready for him. God was the host who prepared dainty dishes, set the table, and then led His guest to his seat. At the same time man's late appearance on earth is to convey an admonition to humility. Let him beware of being proud, lest he invite the retort that the gnat is older than he.[2]

The superiority of man to the other creatures is apparent in the very manner of his creation, altogether different from theirs. He is the only one who was created by the hand of God.[3] The rest sprang from the word of God. The body of man is a microcosm, the whole world in miniature, and the world in turn is a reflex of man. The hair upon his head corresponds to the woods of the earth, his tears to a river, his mouth to the ocean.[4] Also, the world resembles the ball of his eye: the ocean that encircles the earth is like unto the white of the eye, the dry land is the iris, Jerusalem the pupil, and the Temple the image mirrored in the pupil of the eye.[*]

But man is more than a mere image of this world. He unites both heavenly and earthly qualities within himself. In four he resembles the angels, in four the beasts. His power of speech, his discriminating intellect, his upright walk, the glance of his eye—they all make an angel of him. But, on the other hand, he eats and drinks, secretes the waste matter in his body, propagates his kind, and dies, like the beast of the field. Therefore God said before the creation of man: "The celestials are not propagated, but they are immortal; the beings on earth are propagated, but they die. I will create man to be the union of the two, so that when he sins, when he behaves like a beast, death shall overtake him; but if he refrains from sin, he shall live forever."[*] God now bade all beings in heaven and on earth contribute to the creation of man, and He Himself took part in it. Thus they all will love man, and if he should sin, they will be interested in his preservation.[']

The whole world naturally was created for the pious, the God-fearing man, whom Israel produces with the helpful guidance of the law of God revealed to him.[*] It was, therefore, Israel who was taken into special consideration at the time man was made. All other creatures were instructed to change their nature, if Israel should ever need their help in the course of his history. The sea was ordered to divide before Moses, and the heavens to give ear to the words of the leader; the sun and the moon were bidden to stand still

before Joshua, the ravens to feed Elijah, the fire to spare
the three youths in the furnace, the lion to do no harm to
Daniel, the fish to spew forth Jonah, and the heavens to open
before Ezekiel.'

In His modesty, God took counsel with the angels, before
the creation of the world, regarding His intention of making
man. He said: "For the sake of Israel, I will create the
world. As I shall make a division between light and darkness, so I will in time to come do for Israel in Egypt—thick
darkness shall be over the land, and the children of Israel
shall have light in their dwellings; as I shall make a separation between the waters under the firmament and the waters
above the firmament, so I will do for Israel—I will divide
the waters for him when he crosses the Red Sea; as on the
third day I shall create plants, so I will do for Israel—I will
bring forth manna for him in the wilderness; as I shall
create luminaries to divide day from night, so I will do for
Israel—I will go before him by day in a pillar of cloud and
by night in a pillar of fire; as I shall create the fowl of the
air and the fishes of the sea, so I will do for Israel—I will
bring quails for him from the sea; and as I shall breathe the
breath of life into the nostrils of man, so I will do for
Israel—I will give the Torah unto him, the tree of life."

The angels marvelled that so much love should be lav-
ished upon this people of Israel, and God told them: "On
the first day of creation, I shall make the heavens and stretch
them out; so will Israel raise up the Tabernacle as the
dwelling-place of My glory. On the second day, I shall put
a division between the terrestrial waters and the heavenly
waters; so will he hang up a veil in the Tabernacle to divide

the Holy Place and the Most Holy. On the third day, I shall
make the earth put forth grass and herb; so will he, in
obedience to My commands, eat herbs on the first night of
the Passover, and prepare showbread for Me. On the fourth
day, I shall make the luminaries; so will he make a golden
candlestick for Me. On the fifth day, I shall create the
birds; so will he fashion the cherubim with outstretched
wings. On the sixth day, I shall create man; so will Israel
set aside a man of the sons of Aaron as high priest for My
service." [10]

Accordingly, the whole of creation was conditional. God
said to the things He made on the first six days: "If Israel
accepts the Torah, you will continue and endure; otherwise,
I shall turn everything back into chaos again." The whole
world was thus kept in suspense and dread until the day
of the revelation on Sinai, when Israel received and accepted
the Torah, and so fulfilled the condition made by God at the
time when He created the universe. [11]

THE ANGELS AND THE CREATION OF MAN

God in His wisdom having resolved to create man, He
asked counsel of all around Him before He proceeded to
execute His purpose—an example to man, be he never so
great and distinguished, not to scorn the advice of the
humble and lowly. First God called upon heaven and earth,
then upon all other things He had created, and last upon the
angels.

The angels were not all of one opinion. The Angel of
Love favored the creation of man, because he would be affectionate and loving; but the Angel of Truth opposed it,

because he would be full of lies. And while the Angel of Justice favored it, because he would practice justice, the Angel of Peace opposed it, because he would be quarrelsome.

To invalidate his protest, God cast the Angel of Truth down from heaven to earth, and when the others cried out against such contemptuous treatment of their companion, He said, "Truth will spring back out of the earth."

The objections of the angels would have been much stronger, had they known the whole truth about man. God had told them only about the pious, and had concealed from them that there would be reprobates among mankind, too. And yet, though they knew but half the truth, the angels were nevertheless prompted to cry out: "What is man, that Thou art mindful of him? And the son of man, that Thou visitest him?" God replied: "The fowl of the air and the fish of the sea, what were they created for? Of what avail a larder full of appetizing dainties, and no guest to enjoy them?" And the angels could not but exclaim: "O Lord, our Lord, how excellent is Thy name in all the earth! Do as is pleasing in Thy sight." [12]

For not a few of the angels their opposition bore fatal consequences. When God summoned the band under the archangel Michael, and asked their opinion on the creation of man, they answered scornfully: "What is man, that Thou art mindful of him? And the son of man, that Thou visitest him?" God thereupon stretched forth His little finger, and all were consumed by fire except their chief Michael. And the same fate befell the band under the leadership of the archangel Gabriel; he alone of all was saved from destruction.

The third band consulted was commanded by the archangel Labbiel. Taught by the horrible fate of his predecessors, he warned his troop: "You have seen what misfortune overtook the angels who said, 'What is man, that
Thou art mindful of him?' Let us have a care not to do
likewise, lest we suffer the same dire punishment. For God
will not refrain from doing in the end what He has
planned. Therefore it is advisable for us to yield to His
wishes." Thus warned, the angels spoke: "Lord of the
world, it is well that Thou hast thought of creating man.
Do Thou create him according to Thy will. And as for us,
we will be his attendants and his ministers, and reveal unto
him all our secrets." Thereupon God changed Labbiel's
name to Raphael, the Rescuer, because his host of angels
had been rescued by his sage advice. He was appointed the
Angel of Healing, who has in his safe-keeping all the celestial
remedies, the types of the medical remedies used on earth."

The Creation of Adam

When at last the assent of the angels to the creation of
man was given, God said to Gabriel: "Go and fetch Me dust
from the four corners of the earth, and I will create man
therewith." Gabriel went forth to do the bidding of the
Lord, but the earth drove him away, and refused to let him
gather up dust from it. Gabriel remonstrated: "Why, O
Earth, dost thou not hearken unto the voice of the Lord,
who founded thee upon the waters without props or pillars?" The earth replied, and said: "I am destined to
become a curse, and to be cursed through man, and if God
Himself does not take the dust from me, no one else shall

ever do it." When God heard this, He stretched out His hand, took of the dust of the ground, and created the first man therewith.[14]

Of set purpose the dust was taken from all four corners of the earth, so that if a man from the east should happen to die in the west, or a man from the west in the east, the earth should not dare refuse to receive the dead, and tell him to go whence he was taken. Wherever a man chances to die, and wheresoever he is buried, there will he return to the earth from which he sprang. Also, the dust was of various colors—red, black, white, and green—red for the blood, black for the bowels, white for the bones and veins, and green for the pale skin.

At this early moment the Torah interfered. She addressed herself to God: " O Lord of the world! The world is Thine, Thou canst do with it as seemeth good in Thine eyes. But the man Thou art now creating will be few of days and full of trouble and sin. If it be not Thy purpose to have forbearance and patience with him, it were better not to call him into being." God replied, " Is it for naught I am called long-suffering and merciful?"[15]

The grace and lovingkindness of God revealed themselves particularly in His taking one spoonful of dust from the spot where in time to come the altar would stand, saying, " I shall take man from the place of atonement, that he may endure."[16]

THE SOUL OF MAN

The care which God exercised in fashioning every detail of the body of man is as naught in comparison with His solicitude for the human soul. The soul of man was created on the first day, for it is the spirit of God moving upon the face of the waters. Thus, instead of being the last, man is really the first work of creation.[17]

This spirit, or, to call it by its usual name, the soul of man, possesses five different powers. By means of one of them she escapes from the body every night, rises up to heaven, and fetches new life thence for man.[18]

With the soul of Adam the souls of all the generations of men were created. They are stored up in a promptuary, in the seventh of the heavens, whence they are drawn as they are needed for human body after human body.[19]

The soul and body of man are united in this way: When a woman has conceived, the Angel of the Night, Laïlah, carries the sperm before God, and God decrees what manner of human being shall become of it—whether it shall be male or female, strong or weak, rich or poor, beautiful or ugly, long or short, fat or thin, and what all its other qualities shall be. Piety and wickedness alone are left to the determination of man himself. Then God makes a sign to the angel appointed over the souls, saying, " Bring Me the soul so-and-so, which is hidden in Paradise, whose name is so-and-so, and whose form is so-and-so." The angel brings the designated soul, and she bows down when she appears in the presence of God, and prostrates herself before Him. At that moment, God issues the command, " Enter this sperm." The soul opens her mouth, and pleads: " O Lord of the world! I am well pleased with the world in which I have been living since the day on which Thou didst call me into being. Why dost Thou now desire to have me enter this impure sperm, I who am holy and pure, and a part of Thy glory?" God consoles her: "The world which I shall cause thee to enter is better than the world in which thou hast lived hitherto, and when I created thee, it was only for this purpose." The soul is then forced to enter the sperm against her will, and the angel carries her back to the womb of the mother. Two angels are detailed to watch that she shall not leave it, nor drop out of it, and a light is set above her, whereby the soul can see from one end of the world to the other. In the morning an angel carries her to Paradise, and shows her the righteous, who sit there in their glory, with crowns upon their heads. The angel then says to the soul, "Dost thou know who these are?" She replies in the negative, and the angel goes on: "These whom thou beholdest here were formed, like unto thee, in the womb of their mother. When they came into the world, they observed God's Torah and His commandments. Therefore they became the partakers of this bliss which thou seest them enjoy. Know, also thou wilt one day depart from the world below, and if thou wilt observe God's Torah, then wilt thou be found worthy of sitting with these pious ones. But if not, thou wilt be doomed to the other place."

In the evening, the angel takes the soul to hell, and there points out the sinners whom the Angels of Destruction are smiting with fiery scourges, the sinners all the while crying out Woe! Woe! but no mercy is shown unto them. The angel then questions the soul as before, "Dost thou know who these are?" and as before the reply is negative. The angel continues: "These who are consumed with fire were created like unto thee. When they were put into the world, they did not observe God's Torah and His commandments. Therefore have they come to this disgrace which thou seest them suffer. Know, thy destiny is also to depart from the world. Be just, therefore, and not wicked, that thou mayest gain the future world."

Between morning and evening the angel carries the soul around, and shows her where she will live and where she will die, and the place where she will buried, and he takes her through the whole world, and points out the just and the sinners and all things. In the evening, he replaces her in the womb of the mother, and there she remains for nine months.

When the time arrives for her to emerge from the womb into the open world, the same angel addresses the soul, "The time has come for thee to go abroad into the open world." The soul demurs, "Why dost thou want to make me go forth into the open world?" The angel replies: "Know that as thou wert formed against thy will, so now thou wilt be born against thy will, and against thy will thou shalt die, and against thy will thou shalt give account of thyself before the King of kings, the Holy One, blessed be He." But the soul is reluctant to leave her place. Then the angel fillips the babe on the nose, extinguishes the light at his head, and brings him forth into the world against his will. Immediately the child forgets all his soul has seen and learnt, and he comes into the world crying, for he loses a place of shelter and security and rest.

When the time arrives for man to quit this world, the same angel appears and asks him, "Dost thou recognize me?" And man replies, "Yes; but why dost thou come to

me to-day, and thou didst come on no other day?" The
angel says, "To take thee away from the world, for the time
of thy departure has arrived." Then man falls to weeping,
and his voice penetrates to all ends of the world, yet no
creature hears his voice, except the cock alone. Man remon-
strates with the angel, "From two worlds thou didst take
me, and into this world thou didst bring me." But the angel
reminds him: "Did I not tell thee that thou wert formed
against thy will, and thou wouldst be born against thy will,
and against thy will thou wouldst die? And against thy will
thou wilt have to give account and reckoning of thyself before the Holy One, blessed be He." [20]

The Ideal Man

Like all creatures formed on the six days of creation,
Adam came from the hands of the Creator fully and completely developed. He was not like a child, but like a man
of twenty years of age.[21] The dimensions of his body were
gigantic, reaching from heaven to earth, or, what amounts
to the same, from east to west.[22] Among later generations
of men, there were but few who in a measure resembled
Adam in his extraordinary size and physical perfections.
Samson possessed his strength, Saul his neck, Absalom his
hair, Asahel his fleetness of foot, Uzziah his forehead, Josiah
his nostrils, Zedekiah his eyes, and Zerubbabel his voice.
History shows that these physical excellencies were no blessings to many of their possessors; they invited the ruin of
almost all. Samson's extraordinary strength caused his
death; Saul killed himself by cutting his neck with his own
sword; while speeding swiftly, Asahel was pierced by

Abner's spear; Absalom was caught up by his hair in an
oak, and thus suspended met his death; Uzziah was smitten
with leprosy upon his forehead; the darts that killed Josiah
entered through his nostrils, and Zedekiah's eyes were
blinded.[23]

The generality of men inherited as little of the beauty as
of the portentous size of their first father. The fairest
women compared with Sarah are as apes compared with a
human being. Sarah's relation to Eve is the same, and,
again, Eve was but as an ape compared with Adam. His
person was so handsome that the very sole of his foot obscured the splendor of the sun.[24]

His spiritual qualities kept pace with his personal charm,
for God had fashioned his soul with particular care. She is
the image of God, and as God fills the world, so the soul fills
the human body; as God sees all things, and is seen by none,
so the soul sees, but cannot be seen; as God guides the
world, so the soul guides the body; as God in His holiness
is pure, so is the soul; and as God dwells in secret, so doth
the soul.[25]

When God was about to put a soul into Adam's clod-like
body, He said: "At which point shall I breathe the soul
into him? Into the mouth? Nay, for he will use it to speak
ill of his fellow-man. Into the eyes? With them he will
wink lustfully. Into the ears? They will hearken to slander
and blasphemy. I will breathe her into his nostrils; as they
discern the unclean and reject it, and take in the fragrant,
so the pious will shun sin, and will cleave to the words of
the Torah "[26]

The perfections of Adam's soul showed themselves as

soon as he received her, indeed, while he was still without
life. In the hour that intervened between breathing a soul
into the first man and his becoming alive, God revealed the
whole history of mankind to him. He showed him each
generation and its leaders; each generation and its prophets;
each generation and its teachers; each generation and its
scholars; each generation and its statesmen; each generation
and its judges; each generation and its pious members; each
generation and its average, commonplace members; and
each generation and its impious members. The tale of their
years, the number of their days, the reckoning of their hours,
and the measure of their steps, all were made known unto
him."

Of his own free will Adam relinquished seventy of his
allotted years. His appointed span was to be a thousand
years, one of the Lord's days. But he saw that only a single
minute of life was apportioned to the great soul of David,
and he made a gift of seventy years to her, reducing his own
years to nine hundred and thirty."

The wisdom of Adam displayed itself to greatest advantage when he gave names to the animals. Then it appeared
that God, in combating the arguments of the angels that opposed the creation of man, had spoken well, when He insisted
that man would possess more wisdom than they themselves.
When Adam was barely an hour old, God assembled the
whole world of animals before him and the angels. The
latter were called upon to name the different kinds, but they
were not equal to the task. Adam, however, spoke without
hesitation: "O Lord of the world! The proper name for
this animal is ox, for this one horse, for this one lion, for

this one camel." And so he called all in turn by name, suiting the name to the peculiarity of the animal. Then God asked him what his name was to be, and he said Adam, because he had been created out of Adamah, dust of the earth. Again, God asked him His own name, and he said: " Adonaï, Lord, because Thou art Lord over all creatures "—the very name God had given unto Himself, the name by which the angels call Him, the name that will remain immutable evermore.** But without the gift of the holy spirit, Adam could not have found names for all; he was in very truth a prophet, and his wisdom a prophetic quality.**

The names of the animals were not the only inheritance handed down by Adam to the generations after him, for mankind owes all crafts to him, especially the art of writing, and he was the inventor of all the seventy languages.** And still another task he accomplished for his descendants. God showed Adam the whole earth, and Adam designated what places were to be settled later by men, and what places were to remain waste.**

THE FALL OF SATAN

The extraordinary qualities with which Adam was blessed, physical and spiritual as well, aroused the envy of the angels. They attempted to consume him with fire, and he would have perished, had not the protecting hand of God rested upon him, and established peace between him and the heavenly host.** In particular, Satan was jealous of the first man, and his evil thoughts finally led to his fall. After Adam had been endowed with a soul, God invited all the angels to come and pay him reverence and homage. Satan,

the greatest of the angels in heaven, with twelve wings,
instead of six like all the others, refused to pay heed to the
behest of God, saying, " Thou didst create us angels from
the splendor of the Shekinah, and now Thou dost command
us to cast ourselves down before the creature which Thou
didst fashion out of the dust of the ground!" God answered, " Yet this dust of the ground has more wisdom and
understanding than thou." Satan demanded a trial of wit
with Adam, and God assented thereto, saying: " I have
created beasts, birds, and reptiles. I shall have them all
come before thee and before Adam. If thou art able to give
them names, I shall command Adam to show honor unto
thee, and thou shalt rest next to the Shekinah of My glory.
But if not, and Adam calls them by the names I have
assigned to them, then thou wilt be subject to Adam, and he
shall have a place in My garden, and cultivate it." Thus
spake God, and He betook Himself to Paradise, Satan following Him. When Adam beheld God, he said to his wife,
" O come, let us worship and bow down ; let us kneel before
the Lord our Maker." Now Satan attempted to assign
names to the animals. He failed with the first two that presented themselves, the ox and the cow. God led two others
before him, the camel and the donkey, with the same result.
Then God turned to Adam, and questioned him regarding
the names of the same animals, framing His questions in
such wise that the first letter of the first word was the same
as the first letter of the name of the animal standing before
him. Thus Adam divined the proper name, and Satan was
forced to acknowledge the superiority of the first man.
Nevertheless he broke out in wild outcries that reached the

heavens, and he refused to do homage unto Adam as he had been bidden.⁵⁴ The host of angels led by him did likewise, in spite of the urgent representations of Michael, who was the first to prostrate himself before Adam in order to show a good example to the other angels. Michael addressed Satan: "Give adoration to the image of God! But if thou doest it not, then the Lord God will break out in wrath against thee." Satan replied: "If He breaks out in wrath against me, I will exalt my throne above the stars of God, I will be like the Most High!" At once God flung Satan and his host out of heaven, down to the earth, and from that moment dates the enmity between Satan and man.⁵⁵

WOMAN

When Adam opened his eyes the first time, and beheld the world about him, he broke into praise of God, "How great are Thy works, O Lord!" But his admiration for the world surrounding him did not exceed the admiration all creatures conceived for Adam. They took him to be their creator, and they all came to offer him adoration. But he spoke: "Why do you come to worship me? Nay, you and I together will acknowledge the majesty and the might of Him who hath created us all. 'The Lord reigneth,'" he continued, "'He is apparelled with majesty.'"⁵⁶

And not alone the creatures on earth, even the angels thought Adam the lord of all, and they were about to salute him with "Holy, holy, holy, is the Lord of hosts," when God caused sleep to fall upon him, and then the angels knew that he was but a human being.⁵⁷

The purpose of the sleep that enfolded Adam was to give

him a wife, so that the human race might develop, and all
creatures recognize the difference between God and man.
When the earth heard what God had resolved to do, it began
to tremble and quake. " I have not the strength," it said,
" to provide food for the herd of Adam's descendants. "
But God pacified it with the words, " I and thou together,
we will find food for the herd." Accordingly, time was
divided between God and the earth ; God took the night, and
the earth took the day. Refreshing sleep nourishes and
strengthens man, it affords him life and rest, while the earth
brings forth produce with the help of God, who waters it.
Yet man must work the earth to earn his food.**

The Divine resolution to bestow a companion on Adam
met the wishes of man, who had been overcome by a feeling
of isolation when the animals came to him in pairs to be
named.** To banish his loneliness, Lilith was first given to
Adam as wife. Like him she had been created out of the
dust of the ground. But she remained with him only a short
time, because she insisted upon enjoying full equality with
her husband. She derived her rights from their identical
origin. With the help of the Ineffable Name, which she
pronounced, Lilith flew away from Adam, and vanished in
the air. Adam complained before God that the wife He had
given him had deserted him, and God sent forth three angels
to capture her. They found her in the Red Sea, and they
sought to make her go back with the threat that, unless she
went, she would lose a hundred of her demon children daily
by death. But Lilith preferred this punishment to living
with Adam. She takes her revenge. by injuring babes—
baby boys during the first night of their life, while baby

girls are exposed to her wicked designs until they are twenty days old. The only way to ward off the evil is to attach an amulet bearing the names of her three angel captors to the children, for such had been the agreement between them."

The woman destined to become the true companion of man was taken from Adam's body, for "only when like is joined unto like the union is indissoluble." " The creation of woman from man was possible because Adam originally had two faces, which were separated at the birth of Eve."

When God was on the point of making Eve, He said: " I will not make her from the head of man, lest she carry her head high in arrogant pride; not from the eye, lest she be wanton-eyed; not from the ear, lest she be an eavesdropper; not from the neck, lest she be insolent; not from the mouth, lest she be a tattler; not from the heart, lest she be inclined to envy; not from the hand, lest she be a meddler; not from the foot, lest she be a gadabout. I will form her from a chaste portion of the body," and to every limb and organ as He formed it, God said, " Be chaste! Be chaste! " Nevertheless, in spite of the great caution used, woman has all the faults God tried to obviate. The daughters of Zion were haughty and walked with stretched forth necks and wanton eyes; Sarah was an eavesdropper in her own tent, when the angel spoke with Abraham; Miriam was a talebearer, accusing Moses; Rachel was envious of her sister Leah; Eve put out her hand to take the forbidden fruit, and Dinah was a gadabout."

The physical formation of woman is far more complicated than that of man, as it must be for the function of child-

bearing, and likewise the intelligence of woman matures
more quickly than the intelligence of man." Many of the
physical and psychical differences between the two sexes
must be attributed to the fact that man was formed from the
ground and woman from bone. Women need perfumes,
while men do not; dust of the ground remains the same no
matter how long it is kept; flesh, however, requires salt to
keep it in good condition. The voice of women is shrill, not
so the voice of men; when soft viands are cooked, no sound
is heard, but let a bone be put in a pot, and at once it
crackles. A man is easily placated, not so a woman; a few
drops of water suffice to soften a clod of earth; a bone stays
hard, and if it were to soak in water for days. The man
must ask the woman to be his wife, and not the woman the
man to be her husband, because it is man who has sustained
the loss of his rib, and he sallies forth to make good his loss
again. The very differences between the sexes in garb and
social forms go back to the origin of man and woman for
their reasons. Woman covers her hair in token of Eve's
having brought sin into the world; she tries to hide her
shame; and women precede men in a funeral cortege, because it was woman who brought death into the world. And
the religious commands addressed to women alone are connected with the history of Eve. Adam was the heave offering of the world, and Eve defiled it. As expiation, all
women are commanded to separate a heave offering from
the dough. And because woman extinguished the light of
man's soul, she is bidden to kindle the Sabbath light."

Adam was first made to fall into a deep sleep before the
rib for Eve was taken from his side. For, had he watched

her creation, she would not have awakened love in him.   To
this day it is true that men do not appreciate the charms of
women whom they have known and observed from childhood
up.   Indeed, God had created a wife for Adam before Eve,
but he would not have her, because she had been made in
his presence.   Knowing well all the details of her formation, he was repelled by her."   But when he roused himself
from his profound sleep, and saw Eve before him in all her
surprising beauty and grace, he exclaimed, " This is she who
caused my heart to throb many a night! "   Yet he discerned
at once what the nature of woman was.   She would, he
knew, seek to carry her point with man either by entreaties
and tears, or flattery and caresses.   He said, therefore,
" This is my never-silent bell! " "

The wedding of the first couple was celebrated with pomp
never repeated in the whole course of history since.   God
Himself, before presenting her to Adam, attired and adorned
Eve as a bride.   Yea, He appealed to the angels, saying:
" Come, let us perform services of friendship for Adam
and his helpmate, for the world rests upon friendly services,
and they are more pleasing in My sight than the sacrifices
Israel will offer upon the altar."   The angels accordingly
surrounded the marriage canopy, and God pronounced the
blessings upon the bridal couple, as the Hazan does under
the Huppah.   The angels then danced and played upon
musical instruments before Adam and Eve in their ten bridal
chambers of gold, pearls, and precious stones, which God
had prepared for them.

Adam called his wife Ishah, and himself he called Ish,
abandoning the name Adam, which he had borne before the

creation of Eve, for the reason that God added His own name Yah to the names of the man and the woman—Yod to Ish and He to Ishah—to indicate that as long as they walked in the ways of God and observed His commandments, His name would shield them against all harm. But if they went astray, His name would be withdrawn, and instead of Ish there would remain Esh, fire, a fire issuing from each and consuming the other.[a]

Adam and Eve in Paradise

The Garden of Eden was the abode of the first man and woman, and the souls of all men must pass through it after death, before they reach their final destination. For the souls of the departed must go through seven portals before they arrive in the heaven 'Arabot. There the souls of the pious are transformed into angels, and there they remain forever, praising God and feasting their sight upon the glory of the Shekinah. The first portal is the Cave of Machpelah, in the vicinity of Paradise, which is under the care and supervision of Adam. If the soul that presents herself at the portal is worthy, he calls out, " Make room! Thou art welcome! " The soul then proceeds until she arrives at the gate of Paradise guarded by the cherubim and the flaming sword. If she is not found worthy, she is consumed by the sword; otherwise she receives a pass-bill, which admits her to the terrestrial Paradise. Therein is a pillar of smoke and light extending from Paradise to the gate of heaven, and it depends upon the character of the soul whether she can climb upward on it and reach heaven. The third portal, Zebul, is at the entrance of heaven. If the soul is worthy, the guard opens the portal and admits her to the heavenly Temple. Michael presents her to God, and conducts her to the seventh portal, 'Arabot, within which the souls of the pious, changed to angels, praise the Lord, and feed on the glory of the Shekinah.*

In Paradise stand the tree of life and the tree of knowledge, the latter forming a hedge about the former. Only he who has cleared a path for himself through the tree of knowledge can come close to the tree of life, which is so huge that it would take a man five hundred years to traverse a distance equal to the diameter of the trunk, and no less vast is the space shaded by its crown of branches. From beneath it flows forth the water that irrigates the whole earth,* parting thence into four streams, the Ganges, the Nile, the Tigris, and the Euphrates.* But it was only during the days of creation that the realm of plants looked to the waters of the earth for nourishment. Later on God made the plants dependent upon the rain, the upper waters. The clouds rise from earth to heaven, where water is poured into them as from a conduit.* The plants began to feel the effect of the water only after Adam was created. Although they had been brought forth on the third day, God did not permit them to sprout and appear above the surface of the earth, until Adam prayed to Him to give food unto them, for God longs for the prayers of the pious.*

Paradise being such as it was, it was, naturally, not necessary for Adam to work the land. True, the Lord God put the man into the Garden of Eden to dress it and to keep it, but that only means he is to study the Torah there and fulfil the commandments of God.* There were especially six

commandments which every human being is expected to
heed: man should not worship idols; nor blaspheme God;
nor commit murder, nor incest, nor theft and robbery; and
all generations have the duty of instituting measures of law
and order.⁵⁵ One more such command there was, but it was
a temporary injunction. Adam was to eat only the green
things of the field. But the prohibition against the
use of animals for food was revoked in Noah's time, after
the deluge. Nevertheless, Adam was not cut off from the
enjoyment of meat dishes. Though he was not permitted
to slaughter animals for the appeasing of his appetite, the
angels brought him meat and wine, serving him like attend-
ants.⁵⁶ And as the angels ministered to his wants, so also
the animals. They were wholly under his dominion, and
their food they took out of his hand and out of Eve's.⁵⁷ In
all respects, the animal world had a different relation to
Adam from their relation to his descendants. Not only did
they know the language of man,⁵⁸ but they respected the
image of God, and they feared the first human couple, all
of which changed into the opposite after the fall of man.⁵⁹

The Fall of Man

Among the animals the serpent was notable. Of all of
them he had the most excellent qualities, in some of which
he resembled man. Like man he stood upright upon two
feet, and in height he was equal to the camel. Had it not
been for the fall of man, which brought misfortune to them,
too, one pair of serpents would have sufficed to perform all
the work man has to do, and, besides, they would have supplied him with silver, gold, gems, and pearls. As a matter

of fact, it was the very ability of the serpent that led to the
ruin of man and his own ruin. His superior mental gifts
caused him to become an infidel. It likewise explains his
envy of man, especially of his conjugal relations. Envy
made him meditate ways and means of bringing about the
death of Adam." He was too well acquainted with the
character of the man to attempt to exercise tricks of persua-
sion upon him, and he approached the woman, knowing that
women are beguiled easily. The conversation with Eve was
cunningly planned, she could not but be caught in a trap.
The serpent began, " Is it true that God hath said, Ye shall
not eat of every tree in the garden? " " We may," rejoined
Eve, " eat of the fruit of all the trees in the garden, except
that which is in the midst of the garden, and that we may
not even touch, lest we be stricken with death." She spoke
thus, because in his zeal to guard her against the transgressing of the Divine command, Adam had forbidden Eve
to touch the tree, though God had mentioned only the eating
of the fruit. It remains a truth, what the proverb says,
" Better a wall ten hands high that stands, than a wall a
hundred ells high that cannot stand." It was Adam's exag-
geration that afforded the serpent the possibility of persuad-
ing Eve to taste of the forbidden fruit. The serpent pushed
Eve against the tree, and said: " Thou seest that touching
the tree has not caused thy death. As little will it hurt thee
to eat the fruit of the tree. Naught but malevolence has
prompted the prohibition, for as soon as ye eat thereof, ye
shall be as God. As He creates and destroys worlds, so will
ye have the power to create and destroy. As He doth slay
and revive, so will ye have the power to slay and revive."

He Himself ate first of the fruit of the tree, and then He created the world. Therefore doth He forbid you to eat thereof, lest you create other worlds. Everyone knows that 'artisans of the same guild hate one another.' Furthermore, have ye not observed that every creature hath dominion over the creature fashioned before itself? The heavens were made on the first day, and they are kept in place by the firmament made on the second day. The firmament, in turn, is ruled by the plants, the creation of the third day, for they take up all the water of the firmament. The sun and the other celestial bodies, which were created on the fourth day, have power over the world of plants. They can ripen their fruits and flourish only through their influence. The creation of the fifth day, the animal world, rules over the celestial spheres. Witness the ziz, which can darken the sun with its pinions. But ye are masters of the whole of creation, because ye were the last to be created. Hasten now and eat of the fruit of the tree in the midst of the garden, and become independent of God, lest He bring forth still other creatures to bear rule over you." [68]

To give due weight to these words, the serpent began to shake the tree violently and bring down its fruit. He ate thereof, saying: "As I do not die of eating the fruit, so wilt thou not die." Now Eve could not but say to herself, "All that my master"—so she called Adam—"commanded me is but lies," and she determined to follow the advice of the serpent. [69] Yet she could not bring herself to disobey the command of God utterly. She made a compromise with her conscience. First she ate only the outside skin of the fruit, and then, seeing that death did not fell her, she ate the fruit

itself." Scarce had she finished, when she saw the Angel of
Death before her. Expecting her end to come immediately,
she resolved to make Adam eat of the forbidden fruit, too,
lest he espouse another wife after her death." It required
tears and lamentations on her part to prevail upon Adam to
take the baleful step. Not yet satisfied, she gave of the fruit
to all other living beings, that they, too, might be subject to
death." All ate, and they all are mortal, with the exception
of the bird malḥam, who refused the fruit, with the words:
" Is it not enough that ye have sinned against God, and have
brought death to others? Must ye still come to me and seek
to persuade me into disobeying God's command, that I may
eat and die thereof? I will not do your bidding." A heavenly voice was heard then to say to Adam and Eve: " To
you was the command given. Ye did not heed it; ye did
transgress it, and ye did seek to persuade the bird malḥam.
He was steadfast, and he feared Me, although I gave him no
command. Therefore he shall never taste of death, neither
he nor his descendants—they all shall live forever in
Paradise." "

Adam spoke to Eve: " Didst thou give me of the tree of
which I forbade thee to eat? Thou didst give me thereof,
for my eyes are opened, and the teeth in my mouth are set
on edge." Eve made answer, " As my teeth were set on
edge, so may the teeth of all living beings be set on edge." "

The first result was that Adam and Eve became naked.
Before, their bodies had been overlaid with a horny skin,
and enveloped with the cloud of glory. No sooner had they
violated the command given them than the cloud of glory
and the horny skin dropped from them, and they stood there

in their nakedness, and ashamed." Adam tried to gather
leaves from the trees to cover part of their bodies, but he
heard one tree after the other say: " There is the thief that
deceived his Creator. Nay, the foot of pride shall not come
against me, nor the hand of the wicked touch me. Hence,
and take no leaves from me! " Only the fig-tree granted
him permission to take of its leaves. That was because the
fig was the forbidden fruit itself. Adam had the same experience as that prince who seduced one of the maid-servants in the palace. When the king, his father, chased him
out, he vainly sought a refuge with the other maid-servants,
but only she who had caused his disgrace would grant him
assistance."

THE PUNISHMENT

As long as Adam stood naked, casting about for means of
escape from his embarrassment, God did not appear unto
him, for one should not " strive to see a man in the hour of
his disgrace." He waited until Adam and Eve had covered
themselves with fig leaves." But even before God spoke to
him, Adam knew what was impending. He heard the angels
announce, " God betaketh Himself unto those that dwell in
Paradise." He heard more, too. He heard what the angels
were saying to one another about his fall, and what they
were saying to God. In astonishment the angels exclaimed:
" What! He still walks about in Paradise? He is not yet
dead? " Whereupon God: " I said to him, ' In the day that
thou eatest thereof, thou shalt surely die! ' Now, ye know
not what manner of day I meant—one of My days of a
thousand years, or one of your days. I will give him one of

My days.   He shall have nine hundred and thirty years to
live, and seventy to leave to his descendants." [72]

When Adam and Eve heard God approaching, they hid
among the trees—which would not have been possible before
the fall.   Before he committed his trespass, Adam's height
was from the heavens to the earth, but afterward it was
reduced to one hundred ells. [73]   Another consequence of his
sin was the fear Adam felt when he heard the voice of God:
before his fall it had not disquieted him in the least. [74]   Hence
it was that when Adam said, " I heard Thy voice in the
garden, and I was afraid," God replied, " Aforetime thou
wert not afraid, and now thou art afraid? " [75]

God refrained from reproaches at first.   Standing at the
gate of Paradise, He but asked, " Where art thou, Adam? "
Thus did God desire to teach man a rule of polite behavior,
never to enter the house of another without announcing himself." [76]   It cannot be denied, the words " Where art thou? "
were pregnant with meaning.   They were intended to bring
home to Adam the vast difference between his latter and
his former state—between his supernatural size then and
his shrunken size now; between the lordship of God over
him then and the lordship of the serpent over him now." [77]
At the same time, God wanted to give Adam the opportunity
of repenting of his sin, and he would have received Divine
forgiveness for it.   But so far from repenting of it, Adam
slandered God, and uttered blasphemies against Him." [78]
When God asked him, " Hast thou eaten of the tree whereof
I commanded thee thou shouldst not eat? " he did not confess his sin, but excused himself with the words: " O Lord
of the world!   As long as I was alone, I did not fall into

sin, but as soon as this woman came to me, she tempted me."
God replied: " I gave her unto thee as a help, and thou art
ungrateful when thou accusest her, saying, ' She gave me of
the tree.' Thou shouldst not have obeyed her, for thou art
the head, and not she." " God, who knows all things, had
foreseen exactly this, and He had not created Eve until
Adam had asked Him for a helpmate, so that he might not
have apparently good reason for reproaching God with
having created woman."

As Adam tried to shift the blame for his misdeed from
himself, so also Eve. She, like her husband, did not confess her transgression and pray for pardon, which would
have been granted to her." Gracious as God is, He did not
pronounce the doom upon Adam and Eve until they showed
themselves stiff-necked. Not so with the serpent. God
inflicted the curse upon the serpent without hearing his defense; for the serpent is a villain, and the wicked are good
debaters. If God had questioned him, the serpent would
have answered: " Thou didst give them a command, and I
did contradict it. Why did they obey me, and not Thee? " "
Therefore God did not enter into an argument with the serpent, but straightway decreed the following ten punish-
ments: The mouth of the serpent was closed, and his power
of speech taken away; his hands and feet were hacked off;
the earth was given him as food; he must suffer great pain
in sloughing his skin; enmity is to exist between him and
man; if he eats the choicest viands, or drinks the sweetest
beverages, they all change into dust in his mouth; the pregnancy of the female serpent lasts seven years; men shall
seek to kill him as soon as they catch sight of him; even in

the future world, where all beings will be blessed, he will **not** escape the punishment decreed for him; he will vanish **from** out of the Holy Land if Israel walks in the ways of God."

Furthermore, God spake to the serpent: " I created **thee** to be king over all animals, cattle and the beasts of the field alike; but thou wast not satisfied. Therefore thou shalt be cursed above all cattle and above every beast of the field. I created thee of upright posture; but thou wast not satisfied. Therefore thou shalt go upon thy belly. I created thee to eat the same food as man; but thou wast not satisfied. Therefore thou shalt eat dust all the days of thy life. Thou didst seek to cause the death of Adam in order to espouse his wife. Therefore I will put enmity between thee and the woman." How true it is—he who lusts after what is not his due, not only does he not attain his desire, but he also loses what he has!

As angels had been present when the doom was pronounced upon the serpent—for God had convoked a Sanhedrin of seventy-one angels when He sat in judgment upon him—so the execution of the decree against him was entrusted to angels. They descended from heaven, and chopped off his hands and feet. His suffering was so great that his agonized cries could be heard from one end of the world to the other."

The verdict against Eve also consisted of ten curses, the effect of which is noticeable to this day in the physical, spiritual, and social state of woman." It was not God Himself who announced her fate to Eve. The only woman with whom God ever spoke was Sarah. In the case of Eve, **He** made use of the services of an interpreter."

Finally, also the punishment of Adam was tenfold: he lost his celestial clothing—God stripped it off him; in sorrow he was to earn his daily bread; the food he ate was to be turned from good into bad; his children were to wander from land to land; his body was to exude sweat; he was to have an evil inclination; in death his body was to be a prey of the worms; animals were to have power over him, in that they could slay him; his days were to be few and full of trouble; in the end he was to render account of all his doings on earth.[87]

These three sinners were not the only ones to have punishment dealt out to them. The earth fared no better, for it had been guilty of various misdemeanors. In the first place, it had not entirely heeded the command of God given on the third day, to bring forth " tree of fruit." What God had desired was a tree the wood of which was to be as pleasant to the taste as the fruit thereof. The earth, however, produced a tree bearing fruit, the tree itself not being edible.[88] Again, the earth did not do its whole duty in connection with the sin of Adam. God had appointed the sun and the earth witnesses to testify against Adam in case he committed a trespass. The sun, accordingly, had grown dark the instant Adam became guilty of disobedience, but the earth, not knowing how to take notice of Adam's fall, disregarded it altogether.[89] The earth also had to suffer a tenfold punishment: independent before, she was hereafter to wait to be watered by the rain from above; sometimes the fruits of the earth fail; the grain she brings forth is stricken with blasting and mildew; she must produce all sorts of noxious vermin; thenceforth she was to be divided into val-

leys and mountains; she must grow barren trees, bearing
no fruit; thorns and thistles sprout from her; much is sown
in the earth, but little is harvested; in time to come the earth
will have to disclose her blood, and shall no more cover her
slain; and, finally, she shall, one day, "wax old like a
garment." [90]

When Adam heard the words, "Thorns and thistles shall
it bring forth," concerning the ground, a sweat broke out
on his face, and he said: "What! Shall I and my cattle
eat from the same manger?" The Lord had mercy upon
him, and spoke, "In view of the sweat of thy face, thou
shalt eat bread." [91]

The earth is not the only thing created that was made to
suffer through the sin of Adam. The same fate overtook
the moon. When the serpent seduced Adam and Eve, and
exposed their nakedness, they wept bitterly, and with them
wept the heavens, and the sun and the stars, and all created
beings and things up to the throne of God. The very
angels and the celestial beings were grieved by the transgression of Adam. The moon alone laughed, wherefore
God grew wroth, and obscured her light. Instead of shining steadily like the sun, all the length of the day, she grows
old quickly, and must be born and reborn, again and again. [92]
The callous conduct of the moon offended God, not only by
way of contrast with the compassion of all other creatures,
but because He Himself was full of pity for Adam and his
wife. He made clothes for them out of the skin stripped
from the serpent. [93] He would have done even more. He
would have permitted them to remain in Paradise, if only
they had been penitent. But they refused to repent, and

they had to leave, lest their godlike understanding urge them to ravage the tree of life, and they learn to live forever. As it was, when God dismissed them from Paradise, He did not allow the Divine quality of justice to prevail entirely. He associated mercy with it. As they left, He said: "O what a pity that Adam was not able to observe the command laid upon him for even a brief span of time!"

To guard the entrance to Paradise, God appointed the cherubim, called also the ever-turning sword of flames, because angels can turn themselves from one shape into another at need." Instead of the tree of life, God gave Adam the Torah, which likewise is a tree of life to them that lay hold upon her, and he was permitted to take up his abode in the vicinity of Paradise in the east."

Sentence pronounced upon Adam and Eve and the serpent, the Lord commanded the angels to turn the man and the woman out of Paradise. They began to weep and supplicate bitterly, and the angels took pity upon them and left the Divine command unfulfilled, until they could petition God to mitigate His severe verdict. But the Lord was inexorable, saying, "Was it I that committed a trespass, or did I pronounce a false judgment?" Also Adam's prayer, to be given of the fruit of the tree of life, was turned aside, with the promise, however, that if he would lead a pious life, he would be given of the fruit on the day of resurrection, and he would then live forever.

Seeing that God had resolved unalterably, Adam began to weep again and implore the angels to grant him at least permission to take sweet-scented spices with him out of Paradise, that outside, too, he might be able to bring offer-

ings unto God, and his prayers be accepted before the Lord.
Thereupon the angels came before God, and spake: " King
unto everlasting, command Thou us to give Adam sweet-
scented spices of Paradise," and God heard their prayer.
Thus Adam gathered saffron, nard, calamus, and cinnamon,
and all sorts of seeds besides for his sustenance. Laden with
these, Adam and Eve left Paradise, and came upon earth.^{**}

They had enjoyed the splendors of Paradise but a brief
span of time—but a few hours. It was in the first hour of the
sixth day of creation that God conceived the idea of creating
man; in the second hour, He took counsel with the angels;
in the third, He gathered the dust for the body of man; in
the fourth, He formed Adam; in the fifth, He clothed him
with skin; in the sixth, the soulless shape was complete, so
that it could stand upright; in the seventh, a soul was
breathed into it; in the eighth, man was led into Paradise;
in the ninth, the Divine command prohibiting the fruit of
the tree in the midst of the garden was issued to him; in
the tenth, he transgressed the command; in the eleventh,
he was judged; and in the twelfth hour of the day, he was
cast out of Paradise, in atonement for his sin.

This eventful day was the first of the month of Tishri.
Therefore God spoke to Adam: " Thou shalt be the proto-
type of thy children. As thou hast been judged by Me on
this day and absolved, so thy children Israel shall be judged
by Me on this New Year's Day, and they shall be
absolved." ["]

Each day of creation brought forth three things: the first,
heaven, earth, and light; the second, the firmament, Gehenna, and the angels; the third, trees, herbs, and Paradise;

the fourth, sun, moon, and stars; and the fifth, fishes, birds, and leviathan. As God intended to rest on the seventh day, the Sabbath, the sixth day had to do double duty. It brought forth six creations: Adam, Eve, cattle, reptiles, the beasts of the field, and demons. The demons were made shortly before the Sabbath came in, and they are, therefore, incorporeal spirits—the Lord had no time to create bodies for them.[96]

In the twilight, between the sixth day and the Sabbath, ten creations were brought forth: the rainbow, invisible until Noah's time; the manna; watersprings, whence Israel drew water for his thirst in the desert; the writing upon the two tables of stone given at Sinai; the pen with which the writing was written; the two tables themselves; the mouth of Balaam's she-ass; the grave of Moses; the cave in which Moses and Elijah dwelt; and the rod of Aaron, with its blossoms and its ripe almonds.[99]

SABBATH IN HEAVEN

Before the world was created, there was none to praise God and know Him. Therefore He created the angels and the holy Ḥayyot, the heavens and their host, and Adam as well. They all were to praise and glorify their Creator. During the week of creation, however, there was no suitable time to proclaim the splendor and praise of the Lord. Only on the Sabbath, when all creation rested, the beings on earth and in heaven, all together, broke into song and adoration when God ascended His throne and sate upon it.[100] It was the Throne of Joy upon which He sate, and He had all the angels pass before Him—the angel of the water, the angel of the rivers, the angel of the mountains, the angel of the hills, the angel of the abysses, the angel of the deserts, the angel of the sun, the angel of the moon, the angel of the Pleiades, the angel of Orion, the angel of the herbs, the angel of Paradise, the angel of Gehenna, the angel of the trees, the angel of the reptiles, the angel of the wild beasts, the angel of the domestic animals, the angel of the fishes, the angel of the locusts, the angel of the birds, the chief angel of the angels, the angel of each heaven, the chief angel of each division of the heavenly hosts, the chief angel of the holy Ḥayyot, the chief angel of the cherubim, the chief angel of the ofanim, and all the other splendid, terrible, and mighty angel chiefs. They all appeared before God with great joy, laved in a stream of joy, and they rejoiced and danced and sang, and extolled the Lord with many praises and many instruments. The ministering angels began, " Let the glory of the Lord endure forever! " And the rest of the angels took up the song with the words, " Let the Lord rejoice in His works! " 'Arabot, the seventh heaven, was filled with joy and glory, splendor and strength, power and might and pride and magnificence and grandeur, praise and jubilation, song and gladness, steadfastness and righteousness, honor and adoration.

Then God bade the Angel of the Sabbath seat himself upon a throne of glory, and He brought before him the chiefs of the angels of all the heavens and all the abysses, and bade them dance and rejoice, saying, " Sabbath it is unto the Lord! " and the exalted princes of the heavens responded, " Unto the Lord it is Sabbath! " Even Adam was permitted to ascend to the highest heaven, to take part in the rejoicing over the Sabbath.

By bestowing Sabbath joy upon all beings, not excepting Adam, thus did the Lord dedicate His creation. Seeing the majesty of the Sabbath, its honor and greatness, and the joy it conferred upon all, being the fount of all joy, Adam intoned a song of praise for the Sabbath day. Then God said to him, "Thou singest a song of praise to the Sabbath day, and singest none to Me, the God of the Sabbath?" Thereupon the Sabbath rose from his seat, and prostrated himself before God, saying, "It is a good thing to give thanks unto the Lord," and the whole of creation added, "And to sing praises unto Thy Name, O Most High!"[101]

This was the first Sabbath, and this its celebration in heaven by God and the angels. The angels were informed at the same time that in days to come Israel would hallow the day in similar manner. God told them: "I will set aside for Myself a people from among all the peoples. This people will observe the Sabbath, and I will sanctify it to be My people, and I will be God unto it. From all that I have seen, I have chosen the seed of Israel wholly, and I have inscribed him as My first-born son, and I sanctified him unto Myself unto all eternity, him and the Sabbath, that he keep the Sabbath and hallow it from all work."[102]

For Adam the Sabbath had a peculiar significance. When he was made to depart out of Paradise in the twilight of the Sabbath eve, the angels called after him, "Adam did not abide in his glory overnight!" Then the Sabbath appeared before God as Adam's defender, and he spoke: "O Lord of the world! During the six working days no creature was slain. If Thou wilt begin now by slaying Adam, what will become of the sanctity and the blessing of the Sabbath?"

In this way Adam was rescued from the fires of hell, the meet punishment for his sins, and in gratitude he composed a psalm in honor of the Sabbath, which David later embodied in his Psalter.[103]

Still another opportunity was given to Adam to learn and appreciate the value of the Sabbath. The celestial light, whereby Adam could survey the world from end to end, should properly have been made to disappear immediately after his sin. But out of consideration for the Sabbath, God had let this light continue to shine, and the angels, at sundown on the sixth day, intoned a song of praise and thanksgiving to God, for the radiant light shining through the night. Only with the going out of the Sabbath day the celestial light ceased, to the consternation of Adam, who feared that the serpent would attack him in the dark. But God illumined his understanding, and he learned to rub two stones against each other and produce light for his needs.[104]

The celestial light was but one of the seven precious gifts enjoyed by Adam before the fall and to be granted to man again only in the Messianic time. The others are the resplendence of his countenance; life eternal; his tall stature; the fruits of the soil; the fruits of the tree; and the luminaries of the sky, the sun and the moon, for in the world to come the light of the moon shall be as the light of the sun, and the light of the sun shall be sevenfold.[105]

Adam's Repentance

Cast out of Paradise, Adam and Eve built a hut for themselves, and for seven days they sat in it in great distress, mourning and lamenting. At the end of the seven days, tor-

mented by hunger, they came forth and sought food. For
seven other days, Adam journeyed up and down in the land,
looking for such dainties as he had enjoyed in Paradise. In
vain; he found nothing. Then Eve spoke to her husband:
" My lord, if it please thee, slay me. Mayhap God will then
take thee back into Paradise, for the Lord God became
wroth with thee only on account of me." But Adam rejected her plan with abhorrence, and both went forth again
on the search for food. Nine days passed, and still they
found naught resembling what they had had in Paradise.
They saw only food fit for cattle and beasts. Then Adam
proposed: " Let us do penance, mayhap the Lord God will
forgive us and have pity on us, and give us something to sustain our life." Knowing that Eve was not vigorous enough
to undergo the mortification of the flesh which he purposed
to inflict upon himself, he prescribed a penance for her different from his own. He said to her: " Arise, and go to the
Tigris, take a stone and stand upon it in the deepest part of
the river, where the water will reach as high as thy neck.
And let no speech issue forth from thy mouth, for we are unworthy to supplicate God, our lips are unclean by reason of
the forbidden fruit of the tree. Remain in the water for
thirty-seven days."

For himself Adam ordained forty days of fasting, while
he stood in the river Jordan in the same way as Eve was
to take up her stand in the waters of the Tigris. After he
had adjusted the stone in the middle of the Jordan, and
mounted it, with the waters surging up to his neck, he said:
" I adjure thee, O thou water of the Jordan! Afflict thyself
with me, and gather unto me all swimming creatures that

live in thee. Let them surround me and sorrow with me, and let them not beat their own breasts with grief, but let them beat me. Not they have sinned, only I alone!" Very soon they all came, the dwellers in the Jordan, and they encompassed him, and from that moment the water of the Jordan stood still and ceased from flowing.

The penance which Adam and Eve laid upon themselves awakened misgivings in Satan. He feared God might forgive their sin, and therefore essayed to hinder Eve in her purpose. After a lapse of eighteen days he appeared unto her in the guise of an angel. As though in distress on account of her, he began to cry, saying: "Step up out of the river, and weep no longer. The Lord God hath heard your mourning, and your penitence hath been accepted by Him. All the angels supplicated the Lord in your behalf, and He hath sent me to fetch you out of the water and give you the sustenance that you enjoyed in Paradise, and for which you have been mourning." Enfeebled as she was by her penances and mortifications, Eve yielded to the solicitations of Satan, and he led her to where her husband was. Adam recognized him at once, and amid tears he cried out: "O Eve, Eve, where now is thy penitence? How couldst thou let our adversary seduce thee again—him who robbed us of our sojourn in Paradise and all spiritual joy?" Thereupon Eve, too, began to weep and cry out: "Woe unto thee, O Satan! Why strivest thou against us without any reason? What have we done unto thee that thou shouldst pursue us so craftily?" With a deep-fetched sigh, Satan told them how that Adam, of whom he had been jealous, had been the real reason of his fall. Having lost his glory through him, he had intrigued to have him driven from Paradise.

When Adam heard the confession of Satan, he prayed to God: "O Lord my God! In Thy hands is my life. Remove from me this adversary, who seeks to deliver my soul to destruction, and grant me the glory he has forfeited." Satan disappeared forthwith, but Adam continued his penance, standing in the waters of the Jordan for forty days.[106]

While Adam stood in the river, he noticed that the days were growing shorter, and he feared the world might be darkened on account of his sin, and go under soon. To avert the doom, he spent eight days in prayer and fasting. But after the winter solstice, when he saw that the days grew longer again, he spent eight days in rejoicing, and in the following year he celebrated both periods, the one before and the one after the solstice. This is why the heathen celebrate the calends and the saturnalia in honor of their gods, though Adam had consecrated those days to the honor of God.[107]

The first time Adam witnessed the sinking of the sun he was also seized with anxious fears. It happened at the conclusion of the Sabbath, and Adam said, "Woe is me! For my sake, because I sinned, the world is darkened, and it will again become void and without form. Thus will be executed the punishment of death which God has pronounced against me!" All the night he spent in tears, and Eve, too, wept as she sat opposite to him. When day began to dawn, he understood that what he had deplored was but the course of nature, and he brought an offering unto God, a unicorn whose horn was created before his hoofs,[108] and he sacrificed it on the spot on which later the altar was to stand in Jerusalem.[109]

THE BOOK OF RAZIEL

After Adam's expulsion from Paradise, he prayed to God in these words: "O God, Lord of the world! Thou didst create the whole world unto the honor and glory of the Mighty One, and Thou didst as was pleasing unto Thee. Thy kingdom is unto all eternity, and Thy reign unto all generations. Naught is hidden from Thee, and naught is concealed from Thine eyes. Thou didst create me as Thy handiwork, and didst make me the ruler over Thy creatures, that I might be the chief of Thy works. But the cunning, accursed serpent seduced me with the tree of desire and lusts, yea, he seduced the wife of my bosom. But Thou didst not make known unto me what shall befall my children and the generations after me. I know well that no human being can be righteous in Thine eyes, and what is my strength that I should step before Thee with an impudent face? I have no mouth wherewith to speak and no eye wherewith to see, for I did sin and commit a trespass, and, by reason of my sins, I was driven forth from Paradise. I must plough the earth whence I was taken, and the other inhabitants of the earth, the beasts, no longer, as once, stand in awe and fear of me. From the time I ate of the tree of knowledge of good and evil, wisdom departed from me, and I am a fool that knoweth naught, an ignorant man that understandeth not. Now, O merciful and gracious God, I pray to Thee to turn again Thy compassion to the head of Thy works, to the spirit which Thou didst instil into him, and the soul Thou didst breathe into him. Meet me with Thy grace, for Thou art gracious, slow to anger, and full of love. O that my prayer would reach unto the throne of

Thy glory, and my supplication unto the throne of Thy mercy, and Thou wouldst incline to me with lovingkindness. May the words of my mouth be acceptable, that Thou turn not away from my petition. Thou wert from everlasting, and Thou wilt be unto everlasting; Thou wert king, and Thou wilt ever be king. Now, have Thou mercy upon the work of Thy hands. Grant me knowledge and understanding, that I may know what shall befall me, and my posterity, and all the generations that come after me, and what shall befall me on every day and in every month, and mayest Thou not withhold from me the help of Thy servants and of Thy angels."

On the third day after he had offered up this prayer, while he was sitting on the banks of the river that flows forth out of Paradise, there appeared to him, in the heat of the day, the angel Raziel, bearing a book in his hand. The angel addressed Adam thus: "O Adam, why art thou so faint-hearted? Why art thou distressed and anxious? Thy words were heard at the moment when thou didst utter thy supplication and entreaties, and I have received the charge to teach thee pure words and deep understanding, to make thee wise through the contents of the sacred book in my hand, to know what will happen to thee until the day of thy death. And all thy descendants and all the later generations, if they will but read this book in purity, with a devout heart and an humble mind, and obey its precepts, will become like unto thee. They, too, will foreknow what things shall happen, and in what month and on what day or in what night. All will be manifest to them—they will know and understand whether a calamity will come, a famine or wild

beasts, floods or drought; whether there will be abundance
of grain or dearth; whether the wicked will rule the world;
whether locusts will devastate the land; whether the fruits
will drop from the trees unripe; whether boils will afflict
men; whether wars will prevail, or diseases or plagues
among men and cattle; whether good is resolved upon in
heaven, or evil; whether blood will flow, and the death-rattle
of the slain be heard in the city. And now, Adam, come and
give heed unto what I shall tell thee regarding the manner
of this book and its holiness."

Raziel, the angel, then read from the book, and when
Adam heard the words of the holy volume as they issued
from the mouth of the angel, he fell down affrighted. But
the angel encouraged him. "Arise, Adam," he said, "be of
good courage, be not afraid, take the book from me and keep
it, for thou wilt draw knowledge from it thyself and become
wise, and thou wilt also teach its contents to all those who
shall be found worthy of knowing what it contains."

In the moment when Adam took the book, a flame of fire
shot up from near the river, and the angel rose heavenward
with it. Then Adam knew that he who had spoken to him
was an angel of God, and it was from the Holy King Himself that the book had come, and he used it in holiness and
purity. It is the book out of which all things worth knowing
can be learnt, and all mysteries, and it teaches also how to
call upon the angels and make them appear before men, and
answer all their questions. But not all alike can use the
book, only he who is wise and God-fearing, and resorts to
it in holiness. Such an one is secure against all wicked
counsels, his life is serene, and when death takes him from

this world, he finds repose in a place where there are neither demons nor evil spirits, and out of the hands of the wicked he is quickly rescued.[110]

THE SICKNESS OF ADAM

When Adam had lived to be nine hundred and thirty years old, a sickness seized him, and he felt that his days were drawing to an end. He summoned all his descendants, and assembled them before the door of the house of worship in which he had always offered his prayers to God, to give them his last blessing. His family were astonished to find him stretched out on the bed of sickness, for they did not know what pain and suffering were.[111] They thought he was overcome with longing after the fruits of Paradise, and for lack of them was depressed. Seth announced his willingness to go to the gates of Paradise and beg God to let one of His angels give him of its fruits. But Adam explained to them what sickness and pain are, and that God had inflicted them upon him as a punishment for his sin.[112] Adam suffered violently ; tears and groans were wrung from him. Eve sobbed, and said, " Adam, my lord, give me the half of thy sickness, I will gladly bear it. Is it not on account of me that this hath come upon thee? On account of me thou undergoest pain and anguish."

Adam bade Eve go with Seth to the gates of Paradise and entreat God to have mercy upon him, and send His angel to catch up some of the oil of life flowing from the tree of His mercy and give it to his messengers. The ointment would bring him rest, and banish the pain consuming him. On his way to Paradise, Seth was attacked by a wild beast.

Eve called out to the assailant, "How durst thou lay hand on the image of God?" The ready answer came: "It is thine own fault. Hadst thou not opened thy mouth to eat of the forbidden fruit, my mouth would not be opened now to destroy a human being." But Seth remonstrated: "Hold thy tongue! Desist from the image of God until the day of judgment." And the beast gave way, saying, "See, I refrain myself from the image of God," and it slunk away to its covert.[118]

Arrived at the gates of Paradise, Eve and Seth began to cry bitterly, and they besought God with many lamentations to give them oil from the tree of His mercy. For hours they prayed thus. At last the archangel Michael appeared, and informed them that he came as the messenger of God to tell them that their petition could not be granted. Adam would die in a few days, and as he was subject to death, so would be all his descendants. Only at the time of the resurrection, and then only to the pious, the oil of life would be dispensed, together with all the bliss and all the delights of Paradise.[114] Returned to Adam, they reported what had happened, and he said to Eve: "What misfortune didst thou bring upon us when thou didst arouse great wrath! See, death is the portion of all our race! Call hither our children and our children's children, and tell them the manner of our sinning." And while Adam lay prostrate upon the bed of pain, Eve told them the story of their fall.[115]

EVE'S STORY OF THE FALL

After I was created, God divided Paradise and all the animals therein between Adam and me. The east and the north were assigned to Adam, together with the male animals. I was mistress of the west and the south and all the female animals. Satan, smarting under the disgrace of having been dismissed from the heavenly host,[118] resolved to bring about our ruin and avenge himself upon the cause of his discomfiture. He won the serpent over to his side, and pointed out to him that before the creation of Adam the animals could enjoy all that grew in Paradise, and now they were restricted to the weeds. To drive Adam from Paradise would therefore be for the good of all. The serpent demurred, for he stood in awe of the wrath of God. But Satan calmed his fears, and said, " Do thou but become my vessel,[119] and I shall speak a word through thy mouth wherewith thou wilt succeed in seducing man."

The serpent thereupon suspended himself from the wall surrounding Paradise, to carry on his conversation with me from without. And this happened at the very moment when my two guardian angels had betaken themselves to heaven to supplicate the Lord. I was quite alone therefore, and when Satan assumed the appearance of an angel, bent over the wall of Paradise, and intoned seraphic songs of praise, I was deceived, and thought him an angel. A conversation was held between us, Satan speaking through the mouth of the serpent:

" Art thou Eve? "

" Yes, it is I."

" What art thou doing in Paradise? "

" The Lord has put us here to cultivate it and eat of its fruits."

" That is good. Yet you eat not of all the trees."

"That we do, excepting a single one, the tree that stands in the midst of Paradise. Concerning it alone, God has forbidden us to eat of it, else, the Lord said, ye will die."

The serpent made every effort to persuade me that I had naught to fear—that God knew that in the day that Adam and I ate of the fruit of the tree, we should be as He Himself. It was jealousy that had made Him say,[118] "Ye shall not eat of it." In spite of all his urging, I remained steadfast and refused to touch the tree. Then the serpent engaged to pluck the fruit for me. Thereupon I opened the gate of Paradise, and he slipped in. Scarcely was he within, when he said to me, "I repent of my words, I would rather not give thee of the fruit of the forbidden tree." It was but a cunning device to tempt me more. He consented to give me of the fruit only after I swore to make my husband eat of it, too. This is the oath he made me take: "By the throne of God, by the cherubim, and by the tree of life, I shall give my husband of this fruit, that he may eat, too." Thereupon the serpent ascended the tree and injected his poison, the poison of the evil inclination, into the fruit,[119] and bent the branch on which it grew to the ground. I took hold of it, but I knew at once that I was stripped of the righteousness in which I had been clothed.[120] I began to weep, because of it and because of the oath the serpent had forced from me.

The serpent disappeared from the tree, while I sought leaves wherewith to cover my nakedness, but all the trees within my reach had cast off their leaves at the moment when I ate of the forbidden fruit.[121] There was only one that retained its leaves, the fig-tree, the very tree the fruit of which

had been forbidden to me.[122] I summoned Adam, and by
means of blasphemous words I prevailed upon him to eat of
the fruit. As soon as it had passed his lips, he knew his
true condition, and he exclaimed against me: " Thou wicked
woman, what hast thou brought down upon me? Thou
hast removed me from the glory of God."

At the same time Adam and I heard the archangel
Michael[123] blow his trumpet, and all the angels cried out:
" Thus saith the Lord, Come ye with Me to Paradise and
hearken unto the sentence which I will pronounce upon
Adam."[124]

We hid ourselves because we feared the judgment of God.
Sitting in his chariot drawn by cherubim, the Lord, accom-
panied by angels uttering His praise, appeared in Paradise.
At His coming the bare trees again put forth leaves.[125] His
throne was erected by the tree of life, and God addressed
Adam: " Adam, where dost thou keep thyself in hiding?
Thinkest thou I cannot find thee? Can a house conceal itself
from its architect? "[126]

Adam tried to put the blame on me, who had promised to
hold him harmless before God. And I in turn accused the
serpent. But God dealt out justice to all three of us. To
Adam He said: " Because thou didst not obey My commands, but didst hearken unto the voice of thy wife, cursed
is the ground in spite of thy work. When thou dost cultivate
it, it will not yield thee its strength. Thorns and thistles
shall it bring forth to thee, and in the sweat of thy face shalt
thou eat bread. Thou wilt suffer many a hardship, thou wilt
grow weary, and yet find no rest. Bitterly oppressed, thou
shalt never taste of any sweetness. Thou shalt be scourged

by heat, and yet pinched by cold. Thou shalt toil greatly, and yet not gain wealth. Thou shalt grow fat, and yet cease to live. And the animals over which thou art the master will rise up against thee, because thou didst not keep my command." [127]

Upon me God pronounced this sentence: " Thou shalt suffer anguish in childbirth and grievous torture. In sorrow shalt thou bring forth children, and in the hour of travail, when thou art near to lose thy life, thou wilt confess and cry, ' Lord, Lord, save me this time, and I will never again indulge in carnal pleasure,' and yet thy desire shall ever and ever be unto thy husband." [128]

At the same time all sorts of diseases were decreed upon us. God said to Adam: " Because thou didst turn aside from My covenant, I will inflict seventy plagues upon thy flesh. The pain of the first plague shall lay hold on thy eyes; the pain of the second plague upon thy hearing, and one after the other all the plagues shall come upon thee." [129]

The serpent God addressed thus: " Because thou becamest the vessel of the Evil One, [130] deceiving the innocent, cursed art thou above all cattle and above every beast of the field. Thou shalt be robbed of the food thou wast wont to eat, and dust shalt thou eat all the days of thy life. Upon thy breast and thy belly shalt thou go, and of thy hands and thy feet thou shalt be deprived. Thou shalt not remain in possession of thy ears, nor of thy wings, nor of any of thy limbs wherewith thou didst seduce the woman and her husband, bringing them to such a pass that they must be driven forth from Paradise. And I will put enmity between thee and the seed of man. It shall bruise thy head, and thou shalt bruise his heel until the day of judgment." [131]

The Death of Adam

On the last day of Adam's life, Eve said to him, " Why should I go on living, when thou art no more? How long shall I have to linger on after thy death? Tell me this!" Adam assured her she would not tarry long. They would die together, and be buried together in the same place. He commanded her not to touch his corpse until an angel from God had made provision regarding it, and she was to begin at once to pray to God until his soul escaped from his body.

While Eve was on her knees in prayer, an angel came,[132] and bade her rise. " Eve, arise from thy penance," he commanded. " Behold, thy husband hath left his mortal coil. Arise, and see his spirit go up to his Creator, to appear before Him." And, lo, she beheld a chariot of light, drawn by four shining eagles, and preceded by angels. In this chariot lay the soul of Adam, which the angels were taking to heaven. Arrived there, they burnt incense until the clouds of smoke enveloped the heavens. Then they prayed to God to have mercy upon His image and the work of His holy hands. In her awe and fright, Eve summoned Seth, and she bade him look upon the vision and explain the celestial sights beyond her understanding. She asked, " Who may the two Ethiopians be, who are adding their prayers to thy father's?" Seth told her, they were the sun and the moon, turned so black because they could not shine in the face of the Father of light.[133] Scarcely had he spoken, when an angel blew a trumpet, and all the angels cried out with awful voices, " Blessed be the glory of the Lord by His creatures, for He has shown mercy unto Adam, the work of His hands!" A seraph then seized Adam, and carried him off to the river Acheron, washed him three times, and brought him before the presence of God, who sat upon His throne, and, stretching out His hand, lifted Adam up and gave him over to the archangel Michael, with the words, "Raise him to the Paradise of the third heaven, and there thou shalt leave him until the great and fearful day ordained by Me." Michael executed the Divine behest, and all the angels sang a song of praise, extolling God for the pardon He had accorded Adam.

Michael now entreated God to let him attend to the preparation of Adam's body for the grave. Permission being given, Michael repaired to earth, accompanied by all the angels. When they entered the terrestrial Paradise, all the trees blossomed forth, and the perfume wafted thence lulled all men into slumber except Seth alone. Then God said to Adam, as his body lay on the ground: "If thou hadst kept My commandment, they would not rejoice who brought thee hither. But I tell thee, I will turn the joy of Satan and his consorts into sorrow, and thy sorrow shall be turned into joy. I will restore thee to thy dominion, and thou shalt sit upon the throne of thy seducer, while he shall be damned, with those who hearken unto him." [184]

Thereupon, at the bidding of God, the three great arch-angels [185] covered the body of Adam with linen, and poured sweet-smelling oil upon it. With it they interred also the body of Abel, which had lain unburied since Cain had slain him, for all the murderer's efforts to hide it had been in vain. The corpse again and again sprang forth from the earth, and a voice issued thence, proclaiming, "No creature shall rest in the earth until the first one of all has returned the

dust to me of which it was formed." [184] The angels carried
the two bodies to Paradise, Adam's and Abel's—the latter
had all this time been lying on a stone on which angels had
placed it—and they buried them both on the spot whence
God had taken the dust wherewith to make Adam. [187]

God called unto the body of Adam, "Adam! Adam!" and
it answered, "Lord, here am I!" Then God said: "I told
thee once, Dust thou art, and unto dust shalt thou return.
Now I promise thee resurrection. I will awaken thee on
the day of judgment, when all the generations of men that
spring from thy loins shall arise from the grave." God
then sealed up the grave, that none might do him harm
during the six days to elapse until his rib should be restored
to him through the death of Eve. [188]

The Death of Eve

The interval between Adam's death and her own Eve
spent in weeping. She was distressed in particular that she
knew not what had become of Adam's body, for none except
Seth had been awake while the angel interred it. When the
hour of her death drew nigh, Eve supplicated to be buried in
the selfsame spot in which the remains of her husband
rested. She prayed to God: "Lord of all powers! Remove
not Thy maid-servant from the body of Adam, from which
Thou didst take me, from whose limbs Thou didst form me.
Permit me, who am an unworthy and sinning woman, to
enter into his habitation. As we were together in Paradise,
neither separated from the other; as together we were
tempted to transgress Thy law, neither separated from the
other, so, O Lord, separate us not now." To the end of her

prayer she added the petition, raising her eyes heavenward, "Lord of the world! Receive my spirit!" and she gave up her soul to God.

The archangel Michael came and taught Seth how to prepare Eve for burial, and three angels descended and interred her body in the grave with Adam and Abel. Then Michael spoke to Seth, "Thus shalt thou bury all men that die until the resurrection day." And again, having given him this command, he spoke: "Longer than six days ye shall not mourn.[139] The repose of the seventh day is the token of the resurrection in the latter day, for on the seventh day the Lord rested from all the work which He had created and made." [140]

Though death was brought into the world through Adam, yet he cannot be held responsible for the death of men. Once on a time he said to God: "I am not concerned about the death of the wicked, but I should not like the pious to reproach me and lay the blame for their death upon me. I pray Thee, make no mention of my guilt." And God promised to fulfil his wish. Therefore, when a man is about to die, God appears to him, and bids him set down in writing all he has done during his life, for, He tells him, "Thou art dying by reason of thy evil deeds." The record finished, God orders him to seal it with his seal. This is the writing God will bring out on the judgment day, and to each will be made known his deeds.[141] As soon as life is extinct in a man, he is presented to Adam, whom he accuses of having caused his death. But Adam repudiates the charge: "I committed but one trespass. Is there any among you, and be he the most pious, who has not been guilty of more than one?" [142]

III

THE TEN GENERATIONS

THE TEN GENERATIONS

THE BIRTH OF CAIN

There were ten generations from Adam to Noah, to show how long-suffering is the Lord, for all the generations provoked Him unto wrath, until He brought the deluge upon them.[1] By reason of their impiousness God changed His plan of calling one thousand generations into being between the creation of the world and the revelation of the law at Mount Sinai; nine hundred and seventy-four He suppressed before the flood.[2]

Wickedness came into the world with the first being born of woman, Cain, the oldest son of Adam. When God bestowed Paradise upon the first pair of mankind, He warned them particularly against carnal intercourse with each other. But after the fall of Eve, Satan, in the guise of the serpent, approached her, and the fruit of their union was Cain, the ancestor of all the impious generations that were rebellious toward God, and rose up against Him. Cain's descent from Satan, who is the angel Samael, was revealed in his seraphic appearance. At his birth, the exclamation was wrung from Eve, "I have gotten a man through an angel of the Lord."[3]

Adam was not in the company of Eve during the time of her pregnancy with Cain. After she had succumbed a second time to the temptations of Satan, and permitted herself to be interrupted in her penance,⁴ she left her husband and journeyed westward, because she feared her presence might continue to bring him misery.   Adam remained in the east. When the days of Eve to be delivered were fulfilled, and she began to feel the pangs of travailing, she prayed to God for help.   But He hearkened not unto her supplications. "Who will carry the report to my lord Adam?" she asked herself.   "Ye luminaries in the sky, I beg you, tell it to my master Adam when ye return to the east!"   In that self-same hour, Adam cried out: "The lamentation of Eve has pierced to my ear! Mayhap the serpent has again assaulted her," and he hastened to his wife.   Finding her in grievous pain, he besought God in her behalf, and twelve angels appeared, together with two heavenly powers.⁵   All these took up their post to right of her and to left of her, while Michael, also standing on her right side, passed his hand over her, from her face downward to her breast, and said to her, "Be thou blessed, Eve, for the sake of Adam.   Because of his solicitations and his prayers I was sent to grant thee our assistance.   Make ready to give birth to thy child!"   Immediately her son was born, a radiant figure.⁶   A little while and the babe stood upon his feet, ran off, and returned holding in his hands a stalk of straw, which he gave to his mother.   For this reason he **was named** Cain, the Hebrew word for stalk of straw.

Now Adam took Eve and the boy to his home in the east. God sent him various kinds of seeds by the hand of the angel Michael, and he was taught how to cultivate the ground and make it yield produce and fruits, to sustain himself and his family and his posterity.⁷

After a while, Eve bore her second son, whom she named Hebel, because, she said, he was born but to die.

FRATRICIDE

The slaying of Abel by Cain did not come as a wholly unexpected event to his parents. In a dream Eve had seen the blood of Abel flow into the mouth of Cain, who drank it with avidity, though his brother entreated him not to take all. When she told her dream to Adam, he said, lamenting, " O that this may not portend the death of Abel at the hand of Cain! " He separated the two lads, assigning to each an abode of his own, and to each he taught a different occupation. Cain became a tiller of the ground, and Abel a keeper of sheep. It was all in vain. In spite of these precautions, Cain slew his brother.[9]

His hostility toward Abel had more than one reason. It began when God had respect unto the offering of Abel, and accepted it by sending heavenly fire down to consume it, while the offering of Cain was rejected.[10] They brought their sacrifices on the fourteenth day of Nisan, at the instance of their father, who had spoken thus to his sons: " This is the day on which, in times to come, Israel will offer sacrifices. Therefore, do ye, too, bring sacrifices to your Creator on this day, that He may take pleasure in you." The place of offering which they chose was the spot whereon the altar of the Temple at Jerusalem stood later.[11] Abel selected the best of his flocks for his sacrifice, but Cain ate his meal first, and after he had satisfied his appetite, he offered unto God what was left over, a few grains of flax seed. As though his offense had not been great enough in offering unto God fruit of the ground which had been cursed by God![¹²] What wonder that his sacrifice was not received with favor! Besides, a chastisement was inflicted upon him. His face turned black as smoke.[¹³] Nevertheless, his disposition underwent no change, even when God spoke to him thus: "If thou wilt amend thy ways, thy guilt will be forgiven thee; if not, thou wilt be delivered into the power of the evil inclination. It coucheth at the door of thy heart, yet it depends upon thee whether thou shalt be master over it, or it shall be master over thee."[¹⁴]

Cain thought he had been wronged, and a dispute followed between him and Abel. "I believed," he said, "that the world was created through goodness,[¹⁵] but I see that good deeds bear no fruit. God rules the world with arbitrary power, else why had He respect unto thy offering, and not unto mine also?" Abel opposed him; he maintained that God rewards good deeds, without having respect unto persons. If his sacrifice had been accepted graciously by God, and Cain's not, it was because his deeds were good, and his brother's wicked.[¹⁶]

But this was not the only cause of Cain's hatred toward Abel. Partly love for a woman brought about the crime. To ensure the propagation of the human race, a girl, destined to be his wife, was born together with each of the sons of Adam. Abel's twin sister was of exquisite beauty, and Cain desired her.[¹⁷] Therefore he was constantly brooding over ways and means of ridding himself of his brother.

The opportunity presented itself ere long. One day a sheep belonging to Abel tramped over a field that had been planted by Cain. In a rage, the latter called out, "What right hast thou to live upon my land and let thy sheep pasture yonder?" Abel retorted: "What right hast thou to use the products of my sheep, to make garments for thyself from their wool? If thou wilt take off the wool of my sheep wherein thou art arrayed, and wilt pay me for the flesh of the flocks which thou hast eaten, then I will quit thy land as thou desirest, and fly into the air, if I can do it." Cain thereupon said, "And if I were to kill thee, who is there to demand thy blood of me?" Abel replied: "God, who brought us into the world, will avenge me. He will require my blood at thine hand, if thou shouldst slay me. God is the Judge, who will visit their wicked deeds upon the wicked, and their evil deeds upon the evil. Shouldst thou slay me, God will know thy secret, and He will deal out punishment unto thee."

These words but added to the anger of Cain, and he threw himself upon his brother.[18] Abel was stronger than he, and he would have got the worst of it, but at the last moment he begged for mercy, and the gentle Abel released his hold upon him. Scarcely did he feel himself free, when he turned against Abel once more, and slew him. So true is the saying, " Do the evil no good, lest evil fall upon thee."[19]

The Punishment of Cain

The manner of Abel's death was the most cruel conceivable. Not knowing what injury was fatal, Cain pelted all parts of his body with stones, until one struck him on the neck and inflicted death.

After committing the murder, Cain resolved to flee, saying, " My parents will demand account of me concerning

Abel, for there is no other human being on earth." This
thought had but passed through his mind when God appeared unto him, and addressed him in these words: "Before thy parents thou canst flee, but canst thou go out from
My presence, too? 'Can any hide himself in secret places
that I shall not see him?' Alas for Abel that he showed
thee mercy, and refrained from killing thee, when he had
thee in his power! Alas that he granted thee the opportunity of slaying him!"

Questioned by God, "Where is Abel thy brother?" Cain
answered: "Am I my brother's keeper? Thou art He who
holdest watch over all creatures, and yet Thou demandest
account of me! True, I slew him, but Thou didst create
the evil inclination in me. Thou guardest all things; why,
then, didst Thou permit me to slay him? Thou didst Thyself slay him, for hadst Thou looked with a favorable countenance toward my offering as toward his, I had had no
reason for envying him, and I had not slain him." But God
said, "The voice of thy brother's blood issuing from his
many wounds crieth out against thee," and likewise the blood
of all the pious who might have sprung from the loins of
Abel."

Also the soul of Abel denounced the murderer, for she
could find rest nowhere. She could neither soar heavenward, nor abide in the grave with her body, for no human
soul had done either before." But Cain still refused to confess his guilt. He insisted that he had never seen a man
killed, and how was he to suppose that the stones which he
threw at Abel would take his life? Then, on account of
Cain. God cursed the ground, that it might not yield fruit

unto him.[22] With a single punishment both Cain and the earth were chastised, the earth because it retained the corpse of Abel, and did not cast it above ground.[23]

In the obduracy of his heart, Cain spake: "O Lord of the world! Are there informers who denounce men before Thee? My parents are the only living human beings, and they know naught of my deed. Thou abidest in the heavens, and how shouldst Thou know what things happen on earth?" God said in reply: "Thou fool! I carry the whole world. I have made it, and I will bear it"—a reply that gave Cain the opportunity of feigning repentance. "Thou bearest the whole world," he said, "and my sin Thou canst not bear?[24] Verily, mine iniquity is too great to be borne! Yet, yesterday Thou didst banish my father from Thy presence, to-day Thou dost banish me. In sooth, it will be said, it is Thy way to banish."[25]

Although this was but dissimulation, and not true repentance, yet God granted Cain pardon, and removed the half of his chastisement from him. Originally, the decree had condemned him to be a fugitive and a wanderer on the earth. Now he was no longer to roam about forever, but a fugitive he was to remain. And so much was hard enough to have to suffer, for the earth quaked under Cain, and all the animals, the wild and the tame, among them the accursed serpent, gathered together and essayed to devour him in order to avenge the innocent blood of Abel. Finally Cain could bear it no longer, and, breaking out in tears, he cried: "Whither shall I go from Thy spirit? Or whither shall I flee from Thy presence?"[26] To protect him from the onslaught of the beasts, God inscribed one letter of His Holy

Name upon his forehead," and furthermore He addressed the animals: " Cain's punishment shall not be like unto the punishment of future murderers. He has shed blood, but there was none to give him instruction. Henceforth, however, he who slays another shall himself be slain." Then God gave him the dog as a protection against the wild beasts, and to mark him as a sinner, He afflicted him with leprosy.

Cain's repentance, insincere though it was, bore a good result. When Adam met him, and inquired what doom had been decreed against him, Cain told how his repentance had propitiated God, and Adam exclaimed, " So potent is repentance, and I knew it not!" Thereupon he composed a hymn of praise to God, beginning with the words, " It is a good thing to confess thy sins unto the Lord!"

The crime committed by Cain had baneful consequences, not for himself alone, but for the whole of nature also. Before, the fruits which the earth bore unto him when he tilled the ground had tasted like the fruits of Paradise. Now his labor produced naught but thorns and thistles." The ground changed and deteriorated at the very moment of Abel's violent end. The trees and the plants in the part of the earth whereon the victim lived refused to yield their fruits, on account of their grief over him, and only at the birth of Seth those that grew in the portion belonging to Abel began to flourish and bear again. But never did they resume their former powers. While, before, the vine had borne nine hundred and twenty-six different varieties of fruit, it now brought forth but one kind. And so it was with all other species. They will regain their pristine powers only in the world to come."

Nature was modified also by the burial of the corpse of
Abel. For a long time it lay there exposed, above ground,
because Adam and Eve knew not what to do with it. They
sat beside it and wept, while the faithful dog of Abel kept
guard that birds and beasts did it no harm. On a
sudden, the mourning parents observed how a raven
scratched the earth away in one spot, and then hid a dead
bird of his own kind in the ground. Adam, following the
example of the raven, buried the body of Abel, and the raven
was rewarded by God. His young are born with white
feathers, wherefore the old birds desert them, not recognizing them as their offspring. They take them for serpents. God feeds them until their plumage turns black, and
the parent birds return to them. As an additional reward,
God grants their petition when the ravens pray for rain.[n]

THE INHABITANTS OF THE SEVEN EARTHS

When Adam was cast out of Paradise, he first reached the
lowest of the seven earths, the Erez, which is dark, without
a ray of light, and utterly void. Adam was terrified, particularly by the flames of the ever-turning sword, which is
on this earth. After he had done penance, God led him to
the second earth, the Adamah, where there is light reflected
from its own sky and from its phantom-like stars and constellations. Here dwell the phantom-like beings that issued
from the union of Adam with the spirits.[13] They are always
sad ; the emotion of joy is not known to them. They leave
their own earth and repair to the one inhabited by men,
where they are changed into evil spirits. Then they return
to their abode for good, repent of their wicked deeds, and till

the ground, which, however, bears neither wheat nor any
other of the seven species.⁸⁰ In this Adamah, Cain, Abel,
and Seth were born. After the murder of Abel, Cain was
sent back to the Erez, where he was frightened into repentance by its darkness and by the flames of the ever-turning
sword. Accepting his penitence, God permitted him to ascend to the third earth, the Arḳa, which receives some light
from the sun. The Arḳa was surrendered to the Cainites
forever, as their perpetual domain. They till the ground,
and plant trees, but they have neither wheat nor any other
of the seven species.

Some of the Cainites are giants, some of them are dwarfs.
They have two heads, wherefore they can never arrive at a
decision; they are always at loggerheads with themselves.⁸⁴
It may happen that they are pious now, only to be inclined
to do evil the next moment.

In the Ge, the fourth earth, live the generation of the
Tower of Babel and their descendants. God banished them
thither because the fourth earth is not far from Gehenna,
and therefore close to the flaming fire.⁸⁵ The inhabitants of
the Ge are skilful in all arts, and accomplished in all depart-
ments of science and knowledge, and their abode overflows
with wealth. When an inhabitant of our earth visits them,
they give him the most precious thing in their possession,
but then they lead him to the Neshiah, the fifth earth, where
he becomes oblivious of his origin and his home. The
Neshiah is inhabited by dwarfs without noses; they breathe
through two holes instead. They have no memory; once a
thing has happened, they forget it completely, whence their
earth is called Neshiah, " forgetting." The fourth and fifth

earths are like the Arḳa; they have trees, but neither wheat nor any other of the seven species.

The sixth earth, the Ẓiah, is inhabited by handsome men, who are the owners of abundant wealth, and live in palatial residences, but they lack water, as the name of their territory, Ẓiah, "drought," indicates. Hence vegetation is sparse with them, and their tree culture meets with indifferent success. They hasten to any waterspring that is discovered, and sometimes they succeed in slipping through it up to our earth, where they satisfy their sharp appetite for the food eaten by the inhabitants of our earth. For the rest, they are men of steadfast faith, more than any other class of mankind.[36]

Adam remained in the Adamah until after the birth of Seth. Then, passing the third earth, the Arḳa, the abiding-place of the Cainites, and the next three earths as well, the Ge, the Neshiah, and the Ziah, God transported him to the Tebel, the seventh earth, the earth inhabited by men.

THE DESCENDANTS OF CAIN

Cain knew only too well that his blood-guiltiness would be visited upon him in the seventh generation. Thus had God decreed against him.[37] He endeavored, therefore, to immortalize his name by means of monuments,[38] and he became a builder of cities. The first of them he called Enoch, after his son, because it was at the birth of Enoch that he began to enjoy a measure of rest and peace.[39] Besides, he founded six other cities.[40] This building of cities was a godless deed, for he surrounded them with a wall, forcing his family to remain within. All his other doings were equally impious. The punishment God had ordained for him did not effect any improvement. He sinned in order to secure his own pleasure, though his neighbors suffered injury thereby. He augmented his household substance by rapine and violence; he excited his acquaintances to procure pleasures and spoils by robbery, and he became a great leader of men into wicked courses. He also introduced a change in the ways of simplicity wherein men had lived before, and he was the author of measures and weights. And whereas men lived innocently and generously while they knew nothing of such arts, he changed the world into cunning craftiness."

Like unto Cain were all his descendants, impious and godless, wherefore God resolved to destroy them."

The end of Cain overtook him in the seventh generation of men, and it was inflicted upon him by the hand of his great-grandson Lamech. This Lamech was blind, and when he went a-hunting, he was led by his young son, who would apprise his father when game came in sight, and Lamech would then shoot at it with his bow and arrow. Once upon a time he and his son went on the chase, and the lad discerned something horned in the distance. He naturally took it to be a beast of one kind or another, and he told the blind Lamech to let his arrow fly. The aim was good, and the quarry dropped to the ground. When they came close to the victim, the lad exclaimed: " Father, thou hast killed something that resembles a human being in all respects, except it carries a horn on, its forehead! " Lamech knew at once what had happened—he had killed his ancestor Cain, who had been marked by God with a horn." In despair he smote his hands together, inadvertently killing his son as he clasped them. Misfortune still followed upon misfortune. The earth opened her mouth and swallowed up the four generations sprung from Cain—Enoch, Irad, Mehujael, and Methushael. Lamech, sightless as he was, could not go home; he had to remain by the side of Cain's corpse and his son's. Toward evening, his wives, seeking him, found him there. When they heard what he had done, they wanted to separate from him, all the more as they knew that whoever was descended from Cain was doomed to annihilation. But Lamech argued, "If Cain, who committed murder of malice aforethought, was punished only in the seventh generation, then I, who had no intention of killing a human being, may hope that retribution will be averted for seventy and seven generations." With his wives, Lamech repaired to Adam, who heard both parties, and decided the case in favor of Lamech."

The corruptness of the times, and especially the depravity of Cain's stock, appears in the fact that Lamech, as well as all the men in the generation of the deluge, married two wives, one with the purpose of rearing children, the other in order to pursue carnal indulgences, for which reason the latter was rendered sterile by artificial means. As the men of the time were intent upon pleasure rather than desirous of doing their duty to the human race, they gave all their love and attention to the barren women, while their other wives spent their days like widows, joyless and in gloom.

The two wives of Lamech, Adah and Zillah, bore him each two children, Adah two sons, Jabal and Jubal, and Zillah a son, Tubal-cain, and a daughter, Naamah. Jabal was the first among men to erect temples to idols, and Jubal invented the music sung and played therein. Tubal-cain was rightly

named, for he completed the work of his ancestor Cain.
Cain committed murder, and Tubal-cain, the first who knew
how to sharpen iron and copper, furnished the instruments
used in wars and combats. Naamah, " the lovely," earned her
name from the sweet sounds which she drew from her cymbals when she called the worshippers to pay homage to idols."

THE DESCENDANTS OF ADAM AND LILITH

When the wives of Lamech heard the decision of Adam,
that they were to continue to live with their husband, they
turned upon him, saying, " O physician, heal thine own
lameness ! " They were alluding to the fact that he himself
had been living apart from his wife since the death of Abel,
for he had said, " Why should I beget children, if it is but
to expose them to death ? " "

Though he avoided intercourse with Eve, he was visited
in his sleep by female spirits, and from his union with them
sprang shades and demons of various kinds," and they were
endowed with peculiar gifts.

Once upon a time there lived in Palestine a very rich and
pious man, who had a son named Rabbi Ḥanina. He knew
the whole of the Torah by heart. When he was at the point
of death, he sent for his son, Rabbi Ḥanina, and bade him,
as his last request, to study the Torah day and night, fulfil
the commands of the law, and be a faithful friend to the
poor. He also told him that he and his wife, the mother of
Rabbi Ḥanina, would die on the selfsame day, and the seven
days of mourning for the two would end on the eve of the
Passover. He enjoined him not to grieve excessively, but
to go to market on that day, and buy the first article offered

to him, no matter how costly it might be. If it happened to
be an edible, he was to prepare it and serve it with much
ceremony. His expense and trouble would receive their
recompense. All happened as foretold: the man and his
wife died upon the same day, and the end of the week of
mourning coincided with the eve of the Passover. The son
in turn carried out his father's behest: he repaired to market, and there he met an old man who offered a silver dish
for sale. Although the price asked was exorbitant, yet he
bought it, as his father had bidden. The dish was set upon
the Seder table, and when Rabbi Ḥanina opened it, he found
a second dish within, and inside of this a live frog, jumping
and hopping around gleefully. He gave the frog food and
drink, and by the end of the festival he was grown so big
that Rabbi Ḥanina made a cabinet for him, in which he ate
and lived. In the course of time, the cabinet became too
small, and the Rabbi built a chamber, put the frog within,
and gave him abundant food and drink. All this he did
that he might not violate his father's last wish. But the frog
waxed and grew; he consumed all his host owned, until,
finally, Rabbi Ḥanina was stripped bare of all his possessions. Then the frog opened his mouth and began to speak.
"My dear Rabbi Ḥanina," he said, "do not worry! Seeing
thou didst raise me and care for me, thou mayest ask of me
whatever thy heart desireth, and it shall be granted thee."
Rabbi Ḥanina made reply, "I desire naught but that thou
shouldst teach me the whole of the Torah." The frog assented, and he did, indeed, teach him the whole of the Torah,
and the seventy languages of men besides.[48] His method
was to write a few words upon a scrap of paper, which he

had his pupil swallow. Thus he acquired not alone the
Torah and the seventy tongues, but also the language of
beasts and birds. Thereupon the frog spoke to the wife of
Rabbi Ḥanina: "Thou didst tend me well, and I have
given thee no recompense. But thy reward will be paid
thee before I depart from you, only you must both accompany me to the woods. There you shall see what I shall do
for you." Accordingly, they went to the woods with him.
Arrived there, the frog began to cry aloud, and at the sound
all sorts of beasts and birds assembled. These he commanded to produce precious stones, as many as they could
carry. Also they were to bring herbs and roots for the wife
of Rabbi Ḥanina, and he taught her how to use them as
remedies for all varieties of disease. All this they were
bidden to take home with them. When they were about to
return, the frog addressed them thus: "May the Holy One,
blessed be He, have mercy upon you, and requite you for all
the trouble you took on my account, without so much as
inquiring who I am. Now I shall make my origin known to
you. I am the son of Adam, a son whom he begot during
the hundred and thirty years of his separation from Eve.
God has endowed me with the power of assuming any form
or guise I desire." Rabbi Ḥanina and his wife departed
for their home, and they became very rich, and enjoyed the
respect and confidence of the king."

SETH AND HIS DESCENDANTS

The exhortations of the wives of Lamech took effect upon
Adam. After a separation of one hundred and thirty years,
he returned to Eve, and the love he now bore her was

stronger by far than in the former time. She was in his thoughts even when she was not present to him bodily. The fruit of their reunion was Seth, who was destined to be the ancestor of the Messiah."

Seth was so formed from birth that the rite of circumcision could be dispensed with. He was thus one of the thirteen men born perfect in a way." Adam begot him in his likeness and image, different from Cain, who had not been in his likeness and image. Thus Seth became, in a genuine sense, the father of the human race, especially the father of the pious, while the depraved and godless are descended from Cain."

Even during the lifetime of Adam the descendants of Cain became exceedingly wicked, dying successively, one after another, each more wicked than the former. They were intolerable in war, and vehement in robberies, and if any one were slow to murder people, yet was he bold in his profligate behavior in acting unjustly and doing injury for gain.

Now as to Seth. When he was brought up, and came to those years in which he could discern what was good, he became a virtuous man, and as he was himself of excellent character, so he left children behind him who imitated his virtues. All these proved to be of good disposition. They also inhabited one and the same country without dissensions, and in a happy condition, without any misfortune's falling upon them, until they died. They also were the inventors of that peculiar sort of wisdom which is concerned with the heavenly bodies and their order. And that their inventions might not be lost before they were sufficiently known, they made two pillars, upon Adam's prediction that the world was to be destroyed at one time by the force of fire and at another time by the violence and quantity of water. The one was of brick, the other of stone, and they inscribed their discoveries on both, that in case the pillar of brick should be destroyed by the flood, the pillar of stone might remain, and exhibit these discoveries to man- kind, and also inform them that there was another pillar, of brick, erected by them.⁸

ENOSH

Enosh was asked who his father was, and he named Seth. The questioners, the people of his time, continued: " Who was the father of Seth? " Enosh: " Adam."—" And who was the father of Adam? "—" He had neither father nor mother, God formed him from the dust of the earth."—" But man has not the appearance of dust! "—" After death man returns to dust, as God said, ' And man shall turn again unto dust;' but on the day of his creation, man was made in the image of God."—" How was the woman created? "— " Male and female He created them."—" But how? "—" God took water and earth, and moulded them together in the form of man."—" But how? " pursued the questioners.

Enosh took six clods of earth, mixed them, and moulded them, and formed an image of dust and clay. " But," said the people, " this image does not walk, nor does it possess any breath of life." He then essayed to show them how God breathed the breath of life into the nostrils of Adam, but when he began to blow his breath into the image he had formed, Satan entered it, and the figure walked, and the people of his time who had been inquiring these matters of Enosh went astray after it, saying, " What is the difference between bowing down before this image and paying homage to a man ? " [54]

The generation of Enosh were thus the first idol worshippers, and the punishment for their folly was not delayed long. God caused the sea to transgress its bounds, and a portion of the earth was flooded. This was the time also when the mountains became rocks, and the dead bodies of men began to decay. And still another consequence of the sin of idolatry was that the countenances of the men of the following generations were no longer in the likeness and image of God, as the countenances of Adam, Seth, and Enosh had been. They resembled centaurs and apes, and the demons lost their fear of men. [55]

But there was a still more serious consequence from the idolatrous practices introduced in the time of Enosh. When God drove Adam forth from Paradise, the Shekinah remained behind, enthroned above a cherub under the tree of life. The angels descended from heaven and repaired thither in hosts, to receive their instructions, and Adam and his descendants sat by the gate to bask in the splendor of the Shekinah, sixty-five thousand times more radiant than the splendor of the sun. This brightness of the Shekinah makes all upon whom it falls exempt from disease, and neither insects nor demons can come nigh unto them to do them harm.

Thus it was until the time of Enosh, when men began to gather gold, silver, gems, and pearls from all parts of the earth, and made idols thereof a thousand parasangs high.

What was worse, by means of the magic arts taught them by the angels Uzza and Azzael, they set themselves as masters over the heavenly spheres, and forced the sun, the moon, and the stars to be subservient to themselves instead of the Lord. This impelled the angels to ask God: " ' What is man, that Thou art mindful of him?' Why didst Thou abandon the highest of the heavens, the seat of Thy glory and Thy exalted Throne in 'Arabot, and descend to men, who pay worship to idols, putting Thee upon a level with them?" The Shekinah was induced to leave the earth and ascend to heaven, amid the blare and flourish of the trumpets of the myriads of angel hosts.⁸⁸

The Fall of the Angels

The depravity of mankind, which began to show itself in the time of Enosh, had increased monstrously in the time of his grandson Jared, by reason of the fallen angels. When the angels saw the beautiful, attractive daughters of men, they lusted after them, and spoke: " We will choose wives for ourselves only from among the daughters of men, and beget children with them." Their chief Shemhazai said, " I fear me, ye will not put this plan of yours into execution, and I alone shall have to suffer the consequences of a great sin." Then they answered him, and said: " We will all swear an oath, and we will bind ourselves, separately and together, not to abandon the plan, but to carry it through to the end."

Two hundred angels descended to the summit of Mount Hermon, which owes its name to this very occurrence, because they bound themselves there to fulfil their purpose,

on the penalty of Ḥerem, anathema. Under the leadership
of twenty captains they defiled themselves with the daughters of men, unto whom they taught charms, conjuring
formulas, how to cut roots, and the efficacy of plants. The
issue from these mixed marriages was a race of giants, three
thousand ells tall, who consumed the possessions of men.
When all had vanished, and they could obtain nothing more
from them, the giants turned against men and devoured
many of them, and the remnant of men began to trespass
against the birds, beasts, reptiles, and fishes, eating their
flesh and drinking their blood.

Then the earth complained about the impious evil-doers.
But the fallen angels continued to corrupt mankind. Azazel
taught men how to make slaughtering knives, arms, shields,
and coats of mail. He showed them metals and how to
work them, and armlets and all sorts of trinkets, and the
use of rouge for the eyes, and how to beautify the eyelids,
and how to ornament themselves with the rarest and most
precious jewels and all sorts of paints. The chief of the
fallen angels, Shemḥazai, instructed them in exorcisms and
how to cut roots; Armaros taught them how to raise spells;
Barakel, divination from the stars; Kawkabel, astrology;
Ezekeel, augury from the clouds; Arakiel, the signs of the
earth; Samsaweel, the signs of the sun; and Seriel, the signs
of the moon."

While all these abominations defiled the earth, the pious
Enoch lived in a secret place. None among men knew his
abode, or what had become of him, for he was sojourning
with the angel watchers and holy ones. Once he heard the
call addressed to him: " Enoch, thou scribe of justice, go

unto the watchers of the heavens, who have left the high heavens, the eternal place of holiness, defiling themselves with women, doing as men do, taking wives unto themselves, and casting themselves into the arms of destruction upon earth. Go and proclaim unto them that they shall find neither peace nor pardon. For every time they take joy in their offspring, they shall see the violent death of their sons, and sigh over the ruin of their children. They will pray and supplicate evermore, but never shall they attain to mercy or peace."

Enoch repaired to Azazel and the other fallen angels, to announce the doom uttered against them. They all were filled with fear. Trembling seized upon them, and they implored Enoch to set up a petition for them and read it to the Lord of heaven, for they could not speak with God as aforetime, nor even raise their eyes heavenward, for shame on account of their sins. Enoch granted their request, and in a vision he was vouchsafed the answer which he was to carry back to the angels. It appeared to Enoch that he was wafted into heaven upon clouds, and was set down before the throne of God. God spake: "Go forth and say to the watchers of heaven who have sent thee hither to intercede for them: Verily, it is you who ought to plead in behalf of men, not men in behalf of you! Why did ye forsake the high, holy, and eternal heavens, to pollute yourselves with the daughters of men, taking wives unto yourselves, doing like the races of the earth, and begetting giant sons? Giants begotten by flesh and spirits will be called evil spirits on earth, and on the earth will be their dwelling-place. Evil spirits proceed from their bodies, because they are created from above, and from the holy watchers is their beginning and primal origin; they will be evil spirits on earth, and evil spirits they will be named. And the spirits of heaven have their dwelling in heaven, but the spirits of the earth, which were born upon the earth, have their dwelling on the earth. And the spirits of the giants will devour, oppress, destroy, attack, do battle, and cause destruction on the earth, and work affliction. They will take no kind of food, nor will they thirst, and they will be invisible. And these spirits will rise up against the children of men and against the women, because they have proceeded from them. Since the days of murder and destruction and the death of the giants, when the spirits went forth from the soul of their flesh, in order to destroy without incurring judgment—thus will they destroy until the day when the great consummation of the great world be consummated. And now as to the watchers who have sent thee to intercede for them, who had been aforetime in heaven, say to them: You have been in heaven, and though the hidden things had not yet been revealed to you, you know worthless mysteries, and in the hardness of your hearts you have recounted these to the women, and through these mysteries women and men work much evil on earth. Say to them therefore: You have no peace!"[⁵⁸]

ENOCH, RULER AND TEACHER

After Enoch had lived a long time secluded from men, he once heard the voice of an angel calling to him: "Enoch, Enoch, make thyself ready and leave the house and the secret place wherein thou hast kept thyself hidden, and assume dominion over men, to teach them the ways in which they shall walk, and the deeds which they shall do, in order that they may walk in the ways of God."

Enoch left his retreat and betook himself to the haunts of men. He gathered them about him, and instructed them in the conduct pleasing to God. He sent messengers all over to announce, " Ye who desire to know the ways of God and righteous conduct, come ye to Enoch! " Thereupon a vast concourse of people thronged about him, to hear the wisdom he would teach and learn from his mouth what is good and right. Even kings and princes, no less than one hundred and thirty in number, assembled about him, and submitted themselves to his dominion, to be taught and guided by him, as he taught and guided all the others. Peace reigned thus over the whole world all the two hundred and forty-three years during which the influence of Enoch prevailed.

At the expiration of this period, in the year in which Adam died, and was buried with great honors by Seth, Enosh, Enoch, and Methuselah, Enoch resolved to retire again from intercourse with men, and devote himself wholly to the service of God. But he withdrew gradually. First he would spend three days in prayer and praise of God, and on the fourth day he would return to his disciples and grant them instruction. Many years passed thus, then he appeared among them but once a week, later, once a month, and, finally, once a year. The kings, princes, and all others who were desirous of seeing Enoch and hearkening to his words did not venture to come close to him during the times of his retirement. Such awful majesty sat upon his countenance, they feared for their very life if they but looked at him.

They therefore resolved that all men should prefer their requests before Enoch on the day he showed himself unto them.

The impression made by the teachings of Enoch upon all who heard them was powerful. They prostrated themselves before him, and cried "Long live the king! Long live the king!" On a certain day, while Enoch was giving audience to his followers, an angel appeared and made known unto him that God had resolved to install him as king over the angels in heaven, as until then he had reigned over men. He called together all the inhabitants of the earth, and addressed them thus: "I have been summoned to ascend into heaven, and I know not on what day I shall go thither. Therefore I will teach you wisdom and righteousness before I go hence." A few days yet Enoch spent among men, and all the time left to him he gave instruction in wisdom, knowledge, God-fearing conduct, and piety, and established law and order, for the regulation of the affairs of men. Then those gathered near him saw a gigantic steed descend from the skies, and they told Enoch of it, who said, "The steed is for me, for the time has come and the day when I leave you, never to be seen again." So it was. The steed approached Enoch, and he mounted upon its back, all the time instructing the people, exhorting them, enjoining them to serve God and walk in His ways. Eight hundred thousand of the people followed a day's journey after him. But on the second day Enoch urged his retinue to turn back: "Go ye home, lest death overtake you, if you follow me farther." Most of them heeded his words and went back, but a number remained with him for six days, though he admonished them daily to return and not bring death down upon themselves. On the sixth day of the journey, he said to those still accompanying him, " Go ye home, for on the morrow I shall ascend to heaven, and whoever will then be near me, he will die." Nevertheless, some of his companions remained with him, saying: " Whithersoever thou goest, we will go. By the living God, death alone shall part us."

On the seventh day Enoch was carried into the heavens in a fiery chariot drawn by fiery chargers. The day thereafter, the kings who had turned back in good time sent messengers to inquire into the fate of the men who had refused to separate themselves from Enoch, for they had noted the number of them. They found snow and great hailstones upon the spot whence Enoch had risen, and, when they searched beneath, they discovered the bodies of all who had remained behind with Enoch. He alone was not among them ; he was on high in heaven.⁸

THE ASCENSION OF ENOCH

This was not the first time Enoch had been in heaven. Once before, while he sojourned among men, he had been permitted to see all there is on earth and in the heavens. On a time when he was sleeping, a great grief came upon his heart, and he wept in his dream, not knowing what the grief meant, nor what would happen to him. And there appeared to him two men, very tall. Their faces shone like the sun, and their eyes were like burning lamps, and fire came forth from their lips ; their wings were brighter than gold, their hands whiter than snow. They stood at the head of

Enoch's bed, and called him by his name. He awoke from his sleep, and hastened and made obeisance to them, and was terrified. And these men said to him: " Be of good cheer, Enoch, be not afraid; the everlasting God hath sent us to thee, and lo! to-day thou shalt ascend with us into heaven. And tell thy sons and thy servants, and let none seek thee, till the Lord bring thee back to them."

Enoch did as he was told, and after he had spoken to his sons, and instructed them not to turn aside from God, and to keep His judgment, these two men summoned him, and took him on their wings, and placed him on the clouds, which moved higher and higher, till they set him down in the first heaven. Here they showed him the two hundred angels who rule the stars, and their heavenly service. Here he saw also the treasuries of snow and ice, of clouds and dew.

From there they took him to the second heaven, where he saw the fallen angels imprisoned, they who obeyed not the commandments of God, and took counsel of their own will. The fallen angels said to Enoch, " O man of God! Pray for us to the Lord," and he answered: " Who am I, a mortal man, that I should pray for angels? Who knows whither I go, or what awaits me? "

They took him from thence to the third heaven, where they showed him Paradise, with all the trees of beautiful colors, and their fruits, ripe and luscious, and all kinds of food which they produced, springing up with delightful fragrance. In the midst of Paradise he saw the tree of life, in that place in which God rests when He comes into Paradise. This tree cannot be described for its excellence and sweet fragrance, and it is beautiful, more than any created

thing, and on all its sides it is like gold and crimson in appearance, and transparent as fire, and it covers everything.
From its root in the garden there go forth four streams,
which pour out honey, milk, oil, and wine, and they go down
to the Paradise of Eden, that lies on the confines between
the earthly region of corruptibility and the heavenly region
of incorruptibility, and thence they go along the earth. He
also saw the three hundred angels who keep the garden, and
with never-ceasing voices and blessed singing they serve the
Lord every day. The angels leading Enoch explained to
him that this place is prepared for the righteous, while the
terrible place prepared for the sinners is in the northern
regions of the third heaven. He saw there all sorts of tortures, and impenetrable gloom, and there is no light there,
but a gloomy fire is always burning. And all that place has
fire on all sides, and on all sides cold and ice, thus it burns
and freezes. And the angels, terrible and without pity, carry
savage weapons, and their torture is unmerciful.

The angels took him then to the fourth heaven, and
showed him all the comings in and goings forth, and all the
rays of the light of the sun and the moon. He saw the fifteen myriads of angels who go out with the sun, and attend
him during the day, and the thousand angels who attend him
by night. Each angel has six wings, and they go before the
chariot of the sun, while one hundred angels keep the sun
warm, and light it up. He saw also the wonderful and
strange creatures named phœnixes and chalkidri, who
attend the chariot of the sun, and go with him, bringing heat
and dew. They showed him also the six gates in the east
of the fourth heaven, by which the sun goes forth, and the

six gates in the west where he sets, and also the gates by
which the moon goes out, and those by which she enters.
In the middle of the fourth heaven he saw an armed host,
serving the Lord with cymbals and organs and unceasing
voices.

In the fifth heaven he saw many hosts of the angels called
Grigori. Their appearance was like men, and their size was
greater than the size of the giants, their countenances were
withered, and their lips silent. On his question who they
were, the angels leading him answered, "These are the
Grigori, who with their prince Salamiel rejected the holy
Lord." Enoch then said to the Grigori, "Why wait ye,
brethren, and serve ye not before the face of the Lord, and
why perform ye not your duties before the face of the Lord,
and anger not your Lord to the end?" The Grigori listened
to the rebuke, and when the trumpets resounded together
with a loud call, they also began to sing with one voice,
and their voices went forth before the Lord with sadness
and tenderness.

In the seventh heaven he saw the seven bands of archangels who arrange and study the revolutions of the stars
and the changes of the moon and the revolution of the sun,
and superintend the good or evil conditions of the world.
And they arrange teachings and instructions and sweet
speaking and singing and all kinds of glorious praise. They
hold in subjection all living things, both in heaven and on
earth. In the midst of them are seven phœnixes, and seven
cherubim, and seven six-winged creatures, singing with one
voice.

When Enoch reached the seventh heaven, and saw all the

fiery hosts of great archangels and incorporeal powers and lordships and principalities and powers, he was afraid and trembled with a great terror. Those leading him took hold of him, and brought him into the midst of them, and said to him, " Be of good cheer, Enoch, be not afraid," and they showed him the Lord from afar, sitting on His lofty throne, while all the heavenly hosts, divided in ten classes, having approached, stood on the ten steps according to their rank, and made obeisance to the Lord. And so they proceeded to their places in joy and mirth and boundless light, singing songs with low and gentle voices, and gloriously serving Him. They leave not nor depart day or night, standing before the face of the Lord, working His will, cherubim and seraphim, standing around His throne. And the six-winged creatures overshadow all His throne, singing with a soft voice before the face of the Lord, " Holy, holy, holy, is the Lord of hosts; heaven and earth are full of His glory." When he had seen all these, the angels leading him said to him, " Enoch, up to this time we were ordered to accompany thee." They departed, and he saw them no more. Enoch remained at the extremity of the seventh heaven, in great terror, saying to himself, " Woe is me! What has come upon me!" But then Gabriel came and said unto him, " Enoch, be not afraid, stand up and come with me, and stand up before the face of the Lord forever." And Enoch answered: " O my lord, my spirit has departed from me with fear and trembling. Call the men to me who have brought me to the place! Upon them I have relied, and with them I would go before the face of the Lord." And Gabriel hurried him away like a leaf carried off by the wind, and set him before the face of the Lord. Enoch fell down and worshipped the Lord, who said to him: "Enoch, be not afraid! Rise up and stand before My face forever." And Michael lifted him up, and at the command of the Lord took his earthly robe from him, and anointed him with the holy oil, and clothed him, and when he gazed upon himself, he looked like one of God's glorious ones, and fear and trembling departed from him. God called then one of His archangels who was more wise than all the others, and wrote down all the doings of the Lord, and He said to him, "Bring forth the books from My store-place, and give a reed to Enoch, and interpret the books to him." The angel did as he was commanded, and he instructed Enoch thirty days and thirty nights, and his lips never ceased speaking, while Enoch was writing down all the things about heaven and earth, angels and men, and all that is suitable to be instructed in. He also wrote down all about the souls of men, those of them which are not born, and the places prepared for them forever. He copied all accurately, and he wrote three hundred and sixty-six books. After he had received all the instructions from the archangel, God revealed unto him great secrets, which even the angels do not know. He told him how, out of the lowest darkness, the visible and the invisible were created, how He formed heaven, light, water, and earth, and also the fall of Satan and the creation and sin of Adam He narrated to him, and further revealed to him that the duration of the world will be seven thousand years, and the eighth millennium will be a time when there is no computation, no end, neither years. nor months, nor weeks, nor days, nor hours.

The Lord finished this revelation to Enoch with the words: "And now I give thee Samuil and Raguil, who brought thee to Me. Go with them upon the earth, and tell thy sons what things I have said to thee, and what thou hast seen from the lowest heaven up to My throne. Give them the works written out by thee, and they shall read them, and shall distribute the books to their children's children and from generation to generation and from nation to nation. And I will give thee My messenger Michael for thy writings and for the writings of thy fathers, Adam, Seth, Enosh, Kenan, Mahalalel, and Jared thy father. And I shall not require them till the last age, for I have instructed My two angels, Ariuk and Mariuk, whom I have put upon the earth as their guardians, and I have ordered them in time to guard them, that the account of what I shall do in thy family may not be lost in the deluge to come. For on account of the wickedness and iniquity of men, I will bring a deluge upon the earth, and I will destroy all, but I will leave a righteous man of thy race with all his house, who shall act according to My will. From their seed will be raised up a numerous generation, and on the extinction of that family, I will show them the books of thy writings and of thy father, and the guardians of them on earth will show them to the men who are true and please Me. And they shall tell to another generation, and they, having read them, shall be glorified at last more than before."

Enoch was then sent to earth to remain there for thirty days to instruct his sons, but before he left heaven, God sent an angel to him whose appearance was like snow, and his hands were like ice. Enoch looked at him, and his face

was chilled, that men might be able to endure the sight of
him. The angels who took him to heaven put him upon his
bed, in the place where his son Methuselah was expecting
him by day and by night. Enoch assembled his sons and all
his household, and instructed them faithfully about all
things he had seen, heard, and written down, and he gave
his books to his sons, to keep them and read them, admonishing them not to conceal the books, but tell them to all
desiring to know. When the thirty days had been completed, the Lord sent darkness upon the earth, and there
was gloom, and it hid the men standing with Enoch. And
the angels hasted and took Enoch, and carried him to the
highest heaven, where the Lord received him and set him
before His face, and the darkness departed from the earth,
and there was light. And the people saw, and did not understand how Enoch was taken, and they glorified God.

Enoch was born on the sixth day of the month of Siwan,
and he was taken to heaven in the same month, Siwan, on
the same day and in the same hour when he was born.
And Methuselah hasted and all his brethren, the sons of
Enoch, and built an altar in the place called Achuzan,
whence Enoch was taken up to heaven. The elders and all the
people came to the festivity and brought their gifts to the sons
of Enoch, and made a great festivity, rejoicing and being
merry for three days, praising God, who had given such a
sign by means of Enoch, who had found favor with them.**

THE TRANSLATION OF ENOCH

The sinfulness of men was the reason why Enoch was
translated to heaven. Thus Enoch himself told Rabbi Ish-

mael. When the generation of the deluge transgressed, and
spoke to God, saying, " Depart from us, for we do not desire
to know Thy ways," Enoch was carried to heaven, to serve
there as a witness that God was not a cruel God in spite of
the destruction decreed upon all living beings on earth.

When Enoch, under the guidance of the angel 'Anpiel,
was carried from earth to heaven, the holy beings, the
ofanim, the seraphim, the cherubim, all those who move the
throne of God, and the ministering spirits whose substance
is of consuming fire, they all, at a distance of six hundred
and fifty million and three hundred parasangs, noticed the
presence of a human being, and they exclaimed: " Whence
the odor of one born of woman? How comes he into the
highest heaven of the fire-coruscating angels? " But God
replied: " O My servants and hosts, ye, My cherubim, ofanim, and seraphim, let this not be an offense unto you, for
all the children of men denied Me and My mighty dominion,
and they paid homage to the idols, so that I transferred the
Shekinah from earth to heaven. But this man Enoch is the
elect of men. He has more faith, justice, and righteousness
than all the rest, and he is the only reward I have derived
from the terrestrial world."

Before Enoch could be admitted to service near the Divine
throne, the gates of wisdom were opened unto him, and the
gates of understanding, and of discernment, of life, peace,
and the Shekinah, of strength and power, of might, loveli-
ness, and grace, of humility and fear of sin. Equipped by
God with extraordinary wisdom, sagacity, judgment, knowledge, learning, compassionateness, love, kindness, grace,
humility, strength, power, might, splendor, beauty, shapeli-

ness, and all other excellent qualities, beyond the endowment of any of the celestial beings, Enoch received, besides, many thousand blessings from God, and his height and his breadth became equal to the height and the breadth of the world, and thirty-six wings were attached to his body, to the right and to the left, each as large as the world, and three hundred and sixty-five thousand eyes were bestowed upon him, each brilliant as the sun. A magnificent throne was erected for him beside the gates of the seventh celestial palace, and a herald proclaimed throughout the heavens concerning him, who was henceforth to be called Metatron in the celestial regions: " I have appointed My servant Metatron as prince and chief over all the princes in My realm, with the exception only of the eight august and exalted princes that bear My name. Whatever angel has a request to prefer to Me, shall appear before Metatron, and what he will command at My bidding, ye must observe and do, for the prince of wisdom and the prince of understanding are at his service, and they will reveal unto him the sciences of the celestials and the terrestrials, the knowledge of the present order of the world and the knowledge of the future order of the world. Furthermore, I have made him the guardian of the treasures of the palaces in the heaven 'Arabot, and of the treasures of life that are in the highest heaven."

Out of the love He bore Enoch, God arrayed him in a magnificent garment, to which every kind of luminary in existence was attached, and a crown gleaming with forty-nine jewels, the splendor of which pierced to all parts of the seven heavens and to the four corners of the earth. In the presence of the heavenly family, He set this crown upon the head of Enoch, and called him "the little Lord." It bears also the letters by means of which heaven and earth were created, and seas and rivers, mountains and valleys, planets and constellations, lightning and thunder, snow and hail, storm and whirlwind—these and also all things needed in the world, and the mysteries of creation. Even the princes of the heavens, when they see Metatron, tremble before him, and prostrate themselves; his magnificence and majesty, the splendor and beauty radiating from him overwhelm them, even the wicked Samael, the greatest of them, even Gabriel the angel of the fire, Bardiel the angel of the hail, Ruḥiel the angel of the wind, Barḳiel the angel of the lightning, Za'miel the angel of the hurricane, Zaḳḳiel the angel of the storm, Sui'el the angel of the earthquake, Za'fiel the angel of the showers, Ra'miel the angel of the thunder, Ra'shiel the angel of the whirlwind, Shalgiel the angel of the snow, Maṭriel the angel of the rain, Shamshiel the angel of the day, Leliel the angel of the night, Galgliel the angel of the solar system, Ofaniel the angel of the wheel of the moon, Kokabiel the angel of the stars, and Rahtiel the angel of the constellations.

When Enoch was transformed into Metatron, his body was turned into celestial fire—his flesh became flame, his veins fire, his bones glimmering coals, the light of his eyes heavenly brightness, his eyeballs torches of fire, his hair a flaring blaze, all his limbs and organs burning sparks, and his frame a consuming fire. To right of him sparkled flames of fire, to left of him burnt torches of fire, and on all sides he was engirdled by storm and whirlwind, hurricane and thundering.[n]

Methuselah

After the translation of Enoch, Methuselah was proclaimed ruler of the earth by all the kings. He walked in the footsteps of his father, teaching truth, knowledge, and fear of God to the children of men all his life, and deviating from the path of rectitude neither to the right nor the left." He delivered the world from thousands of demons, the posterity of Adam which he had begotten with Lilith, that she-devil of she-devils. These demons and evil spirits, as often as they encountered a man, had sought to injure and even slay him, until Methuselah appeared, and supplicated the mercy of God. He spent three days in fasting, and then God gave him permission to write the Ineffable Name upon his sword, wherewith he slew ninety-four myriads of the demons in a minute, until Agrimus, the first-born of them, came to him and entreated him to desist, at the same time handing the names of the demons and imps over to him. And so Methuselah placed their kings in iron fetters, while the remainder fled away and hid themselves in the innermost chambers and recesses of the ocean. And it is on account of the wonderful sword by means of which the demons were killed that he was called Methuselah."

He was so pious a man that he composed two hundred and thirty parables in praise of God for every word he uttered. When he died, the people heard a great commotion in the heavens, and they saw nine hundred rows of mourners corresponding to the nine hundred orders of the Mishnah which he had studied, and tears flowed from the eyes of the holy beings down upon the spot where he died. Seeing the grief of the celestials, the people on earth also mourned over the demise of Methuselah, and God rewarded them therefor. He added seven days to the time of grace which He had ordained before bringing destruction upon the earth by a flood of waters."

IV

NOAH

IV

NOAH

The Birth of Noah

Methuselah took a wife for his son Lamech, and she bore him a man child. The body of the babe was white as snow and red as a blooming rose, and the hair of his head and his long locks were white as wool, and his eyes like the rays of the sun. When he opened his eyes, he lighted up the whole house, like the sun, and the whole house was very full of light.[1] And when he was taken from the hand of the midwife, he opened his mouth and praised the Lord of righteousness.[2] His father Lamech was afraid of him, and fled, and came to his own father Methuselah. And he said to him: " I have begotten a strange son; he is not like a human being, but resembles the children of the angels of heaven, and his nature is different, and he is not like us, and his eyes are as the rays of the sun, and his countenance is glorious.[3] And it seems to me that he is not sprung from me, but from the angels, and I fear that in his days a wonder may be wrought on the earth. And now, my father, I am here to petition thee and implore thee, that thou mayest go to Enoch, our father, and learn from him the truth, for his dwellingplace is among the angels."

And when Methuselah heard the words of his son, he went to Enoch, to the ends of the earth, and he cried aloud, and Enoch heard his voice, and appeared before him, and asked

him the reason of his coming. Methuselah told him the
cause of his anxiety, and requested him to make the truth
known to him. Enoch answered, and said: " The Lord will
do a new thing in the earth. There will come a great destruction on the earth, and a deluge for one year. This son
who is born unto thee will be left on the earth, and his three
children will be saved with him, when all mankind that are
on the earth shall die. And there will be a great punishment on the earth, and the earth will be cleansed from all
impurity. And now make known to thy son Lamech that
he who was born is in truth his son, and call his name Noah,
for he will be left to you, and he and his children will be
saved from the destruction which will come upon the earth."
When Methuselah had heard the words of his father, who
showed him all the secret things, he returned home, and
he called the child Noah, for he would cause the earth to
rejoice in compensation for all destruction.*

By the name Noah he was called only by his grandfather
Methuselah; his father and all others called him Menahem.
His generation was addicted to sorcery, and Methuselah
apprehended that his grandson might be bewitched if his
true name were known, wherefore he kept it a secret.
Menahem, Comforter, suited him as well as Noah; it indicated that he would be a consoler, if but the evil-doers of his
time would repent of their misdeeds.* At his very birth it
was felt that he would bring consolation and deliverance.
When the Lord said to Adam, " Cursed is the ground for thy
sake," he asked, " For how long a time?" and the answer
made by God was, " Until a man child shall be born whose
conformation is such that the rite of circumcision need not

be practiced upon him." This was fulfilled in Noah, he was circumcised from his mother's womb.

Noah had scarcely come into the world when a marked change was noticeable. Since the curse brought upon the earth by the sin of Adam, it happened that wheat being sown, yet oats would sprout and grow. This ceased with the appearance of Noah: the earth bore the products planted in it. And it was Noah who, when he was grown to manhood, invented the plough, the scythe, the hoe, and other implements for cultivating the ground. Before him men had worked the land with their bare hands.'

There was another token to indicate that the child born unto Lamech was appointed for an extraordinary destiny. When God created Adam, He gave him dominion over all things: the cow obeyed the ploughman, and the furrow was willing to be drawn. But after the fall of Adam all things rebelled against him: the cow refused obedience to the ploughman, and also the furrow was refractory. Noah was born, and all returned to its state preceding the fall of man.

Before the birth of Noah, the sea was in the habit of transgressing its bounds twice daily, morning and evening, and flooding the land up to the graves. After his birth it kept within its confines. And the famine that afflicted the world in the time of Lamech, the second of the ten great famines appointed to come upon it, ceased its ravages with the birth of Noah.'

THE PUNISHMENT OF THE FALLEN ANGELS

Grown to manhood, Noah followed in the ways of his grandfather Methuselah, while all other men of the time rose up against this pious king. So far from observing his precepts, they pursued the evil inclination of their hearts, and perpetrated all sorts of abominable deeds.⁸ Chiefly the fallen angels and their giant posterity caused the depravity of mankind. The blood spilled by the giants cried unto heaven from the ground, and the four archangels accused the fallen angels and their sons before God, whereupon He gave the following orders to them: Uriel was sent to Noah to announce to him that the earth would be destroyed by a flood, and to teach him how to save his own life. Raphael was told to put the fallen angel Azazel into chains, cast him into a pit of sharp and pointed stones in the desert Dudael, and cover him with darkness, and so was he to remain until the great day of judgment, when he would be thrown into the fiery pit of hell, and the earth would be healed of the corruption he had contrived upon it. Gabriel was charged to proceed against the bastards and the reprobates, the sons of the angels begotten with the daughters of men, and plunge them into deadly conflicts with one another. Shemhazai's ilk were handed over to Michael, who first caused them to witness the death of their children in their bloody combat with each other, and then he bound them and pinned them under the hills of the earth, where they will remain for seventy generations, until the day of judgment, to be carried thence to the fiery pit of hell.⁹

The fall of Azazel and Shemhazai came about in this way. When the generation of the deluge began to practice idolatry, God was deeply grieved. The two angels Shemhazai and Azazel arose, and said: " O Lord of the world! It has happened, that which we foretold at the creation of the

world and of man, saying, 'What is man, that Thou art
mindful of him?'" And God said, "And what will become
of the world now without man?" Whereupon the angels:
"We will occupy ourselves with it." Then said God: "I
am well aware of it, and I know that if you inhabit the earth,
the evil inclination will overpower you, and you will be more
iniquitous than ever men." The angels pleaded, "Grant
us but permission to dwell among men, and Thou shalt see
how we will sanctify Thy Name." God yielded to their
wish, saying, "Descend and sojourn among men!"

When the angels came to earth, and beheld the daughters
of men in all their grace and beauty, they could not restrain
their passion. Shemhazai saw a maiden named Istehar, and
he lost his heart to her. She promised to surrender herself
to him, if first he taught her the Ineffable Name, by means
of which he raised himself to heaven. He assented to her
condition. But once she knew it, she pronounced the Name,
and herself ascended to heaven, without fulfilling her promise to the angel. God said, "Because she kept herself aloof
from sin, we will place her among the seven stars, that men
may never forget her," and she was put in the constellation
of the Pleiades.

Shemhazai and Azazel, however, were not deterred from
entering into alliances with the daughters of men, and to
the first two sons were born. Azazel began to devise the
finery and the ornaments by means of which women allure
men. Thereupon God sent Metatron to tell Shemhazai that
He had resolved to destroy the world and bring on a deluge.
The fallen angel began to weep and grieve over the fate of
the world and the fate of his two sons. If the world went

under, what would they have to eat, they who needed daily a
thousand camels, a thousand horses, and a thousand steers?

These two sons of Shemhazai, Hiwwa and Hiyya by
name, dreamed dreams. The one saw a great stone which
covered the earth, and the earth was marked all over with
lines upon lines of writing. An angel came, and with a
knife obliterated all the lines, leaving but four letters upon
the stone. The other son saw a large pleasure grove planted
with all sorts of trees. But angels approached bearing axes,
and they felled the trees, sparing a single one with three of
its branches.

When Hiwwa and Hiyya awoke, they repaired to their
father, who interpreted the dreams for them, saying, " God
will bring a deluge, and none will escape with his life, excepting only Noah and his sons." When they heard this,
the two began to cry and scream, but their father consoled
them: " Soft, soft! Do not grieve. As often as men
cut or haul stones, or launch vessels, they shall invoke your
names, Hiwwa! Hiyya! " This prophecy soothed them.

Shemhazai then did penance. He suspended himself between heaven and earth, and in this position of a penitent
sinner he hangs to this day. But Azazel persisted obdurately
in his sin of leading mankind astray by means of sensual
allurements. For this reason two he-goats were sacrificed
in the Temple on the Day of Atonement, the one for God,
that He pardon the sins of Israel, the other for Azazel, that
he bear the sins of Israel."

Unlike Istehar, the pious maiden, Naamah, the lovely
sister of Tubal-cain, led the angels astray with her beauty,
and from her union with Shamdon sprang the devil Asmo-

deus.[11] She was as shameless as all the other descendants of
Cain, and as prone to bestial indulgences. Cainite women
and Cainite men alike were in the habit of walking abroad
naked, and they gave themselves up to every conceivable
manner of lewd practices. Of such were the women whose
beauty and sensual charms tempted the angels from the path
of virtue. The angels, on the other hand, no sooner had
they rebelled against God and descended to earth than they
lost their transcendental qualities, and were invested with
sublunary bodies, so that a union with the daughters of men
became possible. The offspring of these alliances between
the angels and the Cainite women were the giants,[12] known
for their strength and their sinfulness; as their very name,
the Emim, indicates, they inspired fear. They have many
other names. Sometimes they go by the name Rephaim,
because one glance at them made one's heart grow weak; or
by the name Gibborim, simply giants, because their size was
so enormous that their thigh measured eighteen ells; or by
the name Zamzummmim, because they were great masters in
war; or by the name Anakim, because they touched the sun
with their neck; or by the name Ivvim, because, like the
snake, they could judge of the qualities of the soil; or finally,
by the name Nephilim, because, bringing the world to its fall,
they themselves fell.[13]

THE GENERATION OF THE DELUGE

While the descendants of Cain resembled their father in
his sinfulness and depravity, the descendants of Seth led a
pious, well-regulated life, and the difference between the
conduct of the two stocks was reflected in their habitations.

The family of Seth was settled upon the mountains in the vicinity of Paradise, while the family of Cain resided in the field of Damascus, the spot whereon Abel was slain by Cain.

Unfortunately, at the time of Methuselah, following the death of Adam, the family of Seth became corrupted after the manner of the Cainites. The two strains united with each other to execute all kinds of iniquitous deeds. The result of the marriages between them were the Nephilim, whose sins brought the deluge upon the world. In their arrogance they claimed the same pedigree as the posterity of Seth, and they compared themselves with princes and men of noble descent.[14]

The wantonness of this generation was in a measure due to the ideal conditions under which mankind lived before the flood. They knew neither toil nor care, and as a consequence of their extraordinary prosperity they grew insolent. In their arrogance they rose up against God. A single sowing bore a harvest sufficient for the needs of forty years, and by means of magic arts they could compel the very sun and moon to stand ready to do their service.[15] The raising of children gave them no trouble. They were born after a few days' pregnancy, and immediately after birth they could walk and talk; they themselves aided the mother in severing the navel string. Not even demons could do them harm. Once a new-born babe, running to fetch a light whereby his mother might cut the navel string, met the chief of the demons, and a combat ensued between the two. Suddenly the crowing of a cock was heard, and the demon made off, crying out to the child, " Go and report unto thy mother, if it had not been for the crowing of the cock, I had killed thee!" Whereupon the child retorted, "Go and report unto thy mother, if it had not been for my uncut navel string, I had killed thee!"[16]

It was their care-free life that gave them space and leisure for their infamies. For a time God, in His long-suffering kindness, passed by the iniquities of men, but His forbearance ceased when once they began to lead unchaste lives, for "God is patient with all sins save only an immoral life."[17]

The other sin that hastened the end of the iniquitous generation was their rapacity. So cunningly were their depredations planned that the law could not touch them. If a countryman brought a basket of vegetables to market, they would edge up to it, one after the other, and abstract a bit, each in itself of petty value, but in a little while the dealer would have none left to sell.[18]

Even after God had resolved upon the destruction of the sinners, He still permitted His mercy to prevail, in that He sent Noah unto them, who exhorted them for one hundred and twenty years to amend their ways, always holding the flood over them as a threat. As for them, they but derided him. When they saw him occupying himself with the building of the ark, they asked, "Wherefore this ark?"

Noah: "God will bring a flood upon you."

The sinners: "What sort of flood? If He sends a fire flood, against that we know how to protect ourselves. If it is a flood of waters, then, if the waters bubble up from the earth, we will cover them with iron rods, and if they descend from above, we know a remedy against that, too."

Noah: "The waters will ooze out from under your feet, and you will not be able to ward them off."

Partly they persisted in their obduracy of heart because Noah had made known to them that the flood would not descend so long as the pious Methuselah sojourned among them. The period of one hundred and twenty years which God had appointed as the term of their probation having expired, Methuselah died, but out of regard for the memory of this pious man God gave them another week's respite, the week of mourning for him. During this time of grace, the laws of nature were suspended, the sun rose in the west and set in the east. To the sinners God gave the dainties that await man in the future world, for the purpose of showing them what they were forfeiting.[19] But all this proved unavailing, and, Methuselah and the other pious men of the generation having departed this life, God brought the deluge upon the earth.[20]

THE HOLY BOOK

Great wisdom was needed for building the ark, which was to have space for all beings on earth, even the spirits. Only the fishes did not have to be provided for.[21] Noah acquired the necessary wisdom from the book given to Adam by the angel Raziel, in which all celestial and all earthly knowledge is recorded.

While the first human pair were still in Paradise, it once happened that Samael, accompanied by a lad, approached Eve and requested her to keep a watchful eye upon his little son until he should return. Eve gave him the promise. When Adam came back from a walk in Paradise, he found a howling, screaming child with Eve, who, in reply to his question, told him it was Samael's. Adam was annoyed, and

his annoyance **grew** as the boy cried and screamed more
and more violently. In his vexation he dealt the little one a
blow that killed him. But the corpse did not cease to wail
and weep, nor did it cease when Adam cut it up into bits.
To rid himself of the plague, Adam cooked the remains, and
he and Eve ate them. Scarcely had they finished, when
Samael appeared and demanded his son. The two malefac-
tors tried to deny everything; they pretended they had no
knowledge of his son. But Samael said to them: "What!
You dare tell lies, and God in times to come will give Israel
the Torah in which it is said, 'Keep thee far from a false
word'?"

While they were speaking thus, suddenly the voice of the
slain lad was heard proceeding from the heart of Adam and
Eve, and it addressed these words to Samael: "Go
hence! I have penetrated to the heart of Adam and the
heart of Eve, and never again shall I quit their hearts, nor
the hearts of their children, or their children's children, unto
the end of all generations."

Samael departed, but Adam was sore grieved, and he put
on sackcloth and ashes, and he fasted many, many days,
until God appeared unto him, and said: "My son, have no
fear of Samael. I will give thee a remedy that will help
thee against him, for it was at My instance that he went to
thee." Adam asked, "And what is this remedy?" God:
"The Torah." Adam: "And where is the Torah?" God
then gave him the book of the angel Raziel, which he studied
day and night. After some time had passed, the angels
visited Adam, and, envious of the wisdom he had drawn
from the book, they sought to destroy him cunningly by

calling him a god and prostrating themselves before him, in spite of his remonstrance, "Do not prostrate yourselves before me, but magnify the Lord with me, and let us exalt His Name together." However, the envy of the angels was so great that they stole the book God had given Adam from him, and threw it in the sea. Adam searched for it everywhere in vain, and the loss distressed him sorely. Again he fasted many days, until God appeared unto him, and said: "Fear not! I will give the book back to thee," and He called Rahab, the Angel of the Sea, and ordered him to recover the book from the sea and restore it to Adam. And so he did.[a]

Upon the death of Adam, the holy book disappeared, but later the cave in which it was hidden was revealed to Enoch in a dream. It was from this book that Enoch drew his knowledge of nature, of the earth and of the heavens, and he became so wise through it that his wisdom exceeded the wisdom of Adam. Once he had committed it to memory, Enoch hid the book again.

Now, when God resolved upon bringing the flood on the earth, He sent the archangel Raphael to Noah, as the bearer of the following message: "I give thee herewith the holy book, that all the secrets and mysteries written therein may be made manifest unto thee, and that thou mayest know how to fulfil its injunction in holiness, purity, modesty, and humbleness. Thou wilt learn from it how to build an ark of the wood of the gopher tree, wherein thou, and thy sons, and thy wife shall find protection."

Noah took the book, and when he studied it, the holy spirit came upon him, and he knew all things needful for the building of the ark and the gathering together of the animals. The book, which was made of sapphires, he took with him into the ark, having first enclosed it in a golden casket. All the time he spent in the ark it served him as a time-piece, to distinguish night from day. Before his death, he entrusted it to Shem, and he in turn to Abraham. From Abraham it descended through Jacob, Levi, Moses, and Joshua to Solomon, who learnt all his wisdom from it, and his skill in the healing art, and also his mastery over the demons.

The Inmates of the Ark

The ark was completed according to the instructions laid down in the Book of Raziel. Noah's next task was gathering in the animals. No less than thirty-two species of birds and three hundred and sixty-five of reptiles he had to take along with him. But God ordered the animals to repair to the ark, and they trooped thither, and Noah did not have to do so much as stretch out a finger. Indeed, more appeared than were required to come, and God instructed him to sit at the door of the ark and note which of the animals lay down as they reached the entrance and which stood. The former belonged in the ark, but not the latter. Taking up his post as he had been commanded, Noah observed a lioness with her two cubs. All three beasts crouched. But the two young ones began to struggle with the mother, and she arose and stood up next to them. Then Noah led the two cubs into the ark. The wild beasts, and the cattle, and the birds which were not accepted remained standing about the ark all of seven days, for the assembling of the animals happened one week before the flood began to descend. On the day whereon they came to the ark, the sun was darkened, and the foundations of the earth trembled, and lightning flashed, and the thunder boomed, as never before. And yet the sinners remained impenitent. In naught did they change their wicked doings during those last seven days.

When finally the flood broke loose, seven hundred thousand of the children of men gathered around the ark, and implored Noah to grant them protection. With a loud voice he replied, and said: "Are ye not those who were rebellious toward God, saying, 'There is no God'? Therefore He has brought ruin upon you, to annihilate you and destroy you from the face of the earth. Have I not been prophesying this unto you these hundred and twenty years, and you would not give heed unto the voice of God? Yet now you desire to be kept alive!" Then the sinners cried out: "So be it! We all are ready now to turn back to God, if only thou wilt open the door of thy ark to receive us, that we may live and not die." Noah made answer, and said: "That ye do now, when your need presses hard upon you. Why did you not turn to God during all the hundred and twenty years which the Lord appointed unto you as the term of repentance? Now do ye come, and ye speak thus, because distress besets your lives. Therefore God will not hearken unto you and give you ear; naught will you accomplish!"

The crowd of sinners tried to take the entrance to the ark by storm, but the wild beasts keeping watch around the ark set upon them, and many were slain, while the rest escaped, only to meet death in the waters of the flood." The water alone could not have made an end of them, for they were giants in stature and strength. When Noah threat-

ened them with the scourge of God, they would make reply:
"If the waters of the flood come from above, they will
never reach up to our necks; and if they come from below,
the soles of our feet are large enough to dam up the
springs." But God bade each drop pass through Gehenna
before it fell to earth, and the hot rain scalded the skin of
the sinners. The punishment that overtook them was be-
fitting their crime. As their sensual desires had made them
hot, and inflamed them to immoral excesses, so they were
chastised by means of heated water.[26]

Not even in the hour of the death struggle could the
sinners suppress their vile instincts. When the water began
to stream up out of the springs, they threw their little children into them, to choke the flood.[27]

It was by the grace of God, not on account of his merits,
that Noah found shelter in the ark before the overwhelming
force of the waters.[28] Although he was better than his contemporaries, he was yet not worthy of having wonders done
for his sake. He had so little faith that he did not enter the
ark until the waters had risen to his knees. With him his
pious wife Naamah, the daughter of Enosh, escaped the
peril, and his three sons, and the wives of his three sons.[29]

Noah had not married until he was four hundred and
ninety-eight years old. Then the Lord had bidden him to
take a wife unto himself. He had not desired to bring children
into the world, seeing that they would all have to perish in
the flood, and he had only three sons, born unto him shortly
before the deluge came.[30] God had given him so small a
number of offspring that he might be spared the necessity
of building the ark on an overlarge scale in case they turned

out to be pious. And if not, if they, too, were depraved like the rest of their generation, sorrow over their destruction would but be increased in proportion to their number.[51]

As Noah and his family were the only ones not to have a share in the corruptness of the age, so the animals received into the ark were such as had led a natural life. For the animals of the time were as immoral as the men: the dog united with the wolf, the cock with the pea-fowl, and many others paid no heed to sexual purity. Those that were saved were such as had kept themselves untainted.[52]

·Before the flood the number of unclean animals had been greater than the number of the clean. Afterward the ratio was reversed, because while seven pairs of clean animals were preserved in the ark, but two pairs of the unclean were preserved.[53]

One animal, the reëm, Noah could not take into the ark. On account of its huge size it could not find room therein. Noah therefore tied it to the ark, and it ran on behind.[54] Also, he could not make space for the giant Og, the king of Bashan. He sat on top of the ark securely, and in this way escaped the flood of waters. Noah doled out his food to him daily, through a hole, because Og had promised that he and his descendants would serve him as slaves in perpetuity.[55]

Two creatures of a most peculiar kind also found refuge in the ark. Among the beings that came to Noah there was Falsehood asking for shelter. He was denied admission, because he had no companion, and Noah was taking in the animals only by pairs. Falsehood went off to seek a partner, and he met Misfortune, whom he associated with himself on the condition that she might appropriate what Falsehood earned. The pair were then accepted in the ark. When they left it, Falsehood noticed that whatever he gathered together disappeared at once, and he betook himself to his companion to seek an explanation, which she gave him in the following words, " Did we not agree to the condition that I might take what you earn? " and Falsehood had to depart empty-handed.⁸⁶

THE FLOOD

The assembling of the animals in the ark was but the smaller part of the task imposed upon Noah. His chief difficulty was to provide food for a year and accommodations for them. Long afterward Shem, the son of Noah, related to Eliezer, the servant of Abraham, the tale of their experiences with the animals in the ark. This is what he said: " We had sore troubles in the ark. The day animals had to be fed by day, and the night animals by night. My father knew not what food to give to the little ziḳta. Once he cut a pomegranate in half, and a worm dropped out of the fruit, and was devoured by the ziḳta. Thenceforth my father would knead bran, and let it stand until it bred worms, which were fed to the animal. The lion suffered with a fever all the time, and therefore he did not annoy the others, because he did not relish dry food. The animal urshana my father found sleeping in a corner of the vessel, and he asked him whether he needed nothing to eat. He answered, and said: ' I saw thou wast very busy, and I did not wish to add to thy cares.' Whereupon my father said, ' May it be the will of the Lord to keep thee alive forever,' and the blessing was realized." ⁸⁷

The difficulties were increased when the flood began to toss the ark from side to side. All inside of it were shaken up like lentils in a pot. The lions began to roar, the oxen lowed, the wolves howled, and all the animals gave vent to their agony, each through the sounds it had the power to utter.

Also Noah and his sons, thinking that death was nigh, broke into tears. Noah prayed to God: " O Lord, help us, for we are not able to bear the evil that encompasses us. The billows surge about us, the streams of destruction make us afraid, and death stares us in the face. O hear our prayer, deliver us, incline Thyself unto us, and be gracious unto us! Redeem us and save us! " [58]

The flood was produced by a union of the male waters, which are above the firmament, and the female waters issuing from the earth.[59] The upper waters rushed through the space left when God removed two stars out of the constellation Pleiades. Afterward, to put a stop to the flood, God had to transfer two stars from the constellation of the Bear to the constellation of the Pleiades. That is why the Bear runs after the Pleiades. She wants her two children back, but they will be restored to her only in the future world.[60]

There were other changes among the celestial spheres during the year of the flood. All the time it lasted, the sun and the moon shed no light, whence Noah was called by his name, " the resting one," for in his life the sun and the moon rested. The ark was illuminated by a precious stone, the light of which was more brilliant by night than by day, so enabling Noah to distinguish between day and night.[61]

The duration of the flood was a whole year. It began on the seventeenth day of Heshwan, and the rain continued for forty days, until the twenty-seventh of Kislew. The punishment corresponded to the crime of the sinful generation. They had led immoral lives, and begotten bastard children, whose embryonic state lasts forty days. From the twenty-seventh of Kislew until the first of Siwan, a period of one hundred and fifty days, the water stood at one and the same height, fifteen ells above the earth. During that time all the wicked were destroyed, each one receiving the punishment due to him. Cain was among those that perished, and thus the death of Abel was avenged. So powerful were the waters in working havoc that the corpse of Adam was not spared in its grave.

On the first of Siwan the waters began to abate, a quarter of an ell a day, and at the end of sixty days, on the tenth day of Ab, the summits of the mountains showed themselves. But many days before, on the tenth of Tammuz, Noah had sent forth the raven, and a week later the dove, on the first of her three sallies, repeated at intervals of a week. It took from the first of Ab until the first of Tishri for the waters to subside wholly from the face of the earth. Even then the soil was so miry that the dwellers in the ark had to remain within until the twenty-seventh day of Heshwan, completing a full sun year, consisting of twelve moons and eleven days.

Noah had experienced difficulty all along in ascertaining the state of the waters. When he desired to dispatch the raven, the bird said: "The Lord, thy Master, hates me, and thou dost hate me, too. Thy Master hates me, for He bade thee take seven pairs of the clean animals into the ark, and but two pairs of the unclean animals, to which I belong. Thou hatest me, for thou dost not choose, as a messenger, a bird of one of the kinds of which there are seven pairs in the ark, but thou sendest me, and of my kind there is but one pair. Suppose, now, I should perish by reason of heat or cold, would not the world be the poorer by a whole species of animals? Or can it be that thou hast cast a lustful eye upon my mate, and desirest to rid thyself of me?" Whereunto Noah made answer, and said: "Wretch! I must live apart from my own wife in the ark. How much less would such thoughts occur to my mind as thou imputest to me!" "

The raven's errand had no success, for when he saw the body of a dead man, he set to work to devour it, and did not execute the orders given to him by Noah. Thereupon the dove was sent out. Toward evening she returned with an olive leaf in her bill, plucked upon the Mount of Olives at Jerusalem, for the Holy Land had not been ravaged by the deluge. As she plucked it, she said to God: "O Lord of the world, let my food be as bitter as the olive, but do Thou give it to me from Thy hand, rather than it should be sweet, and I be delivered into the power of men." "

NOAH LEAVES THE ARK

Though the earth assumed its old form at the end of the year of punishment, Noah did not abandon the ark until he received the command of God to leave it. He said to himself, " As I entered the ark at the bidding of God, so I will leave it only at His bidding." Yet, when God bade Noah go out of the ark, he refused, because he feared that after he had lived upon the dry land for some time, and begotten children, God would bring another flood. He therefore would not leave the ark until God swore He would never visit the earth with a flood again.⁴⁸

When he stepped out from the ark into the open, he began to weep bitterly at sight of the enormous ravages wrought by the flood, and he said to God: "O Lord of the world! Thou art called the Merciful, and Thou shouldst have had mercy upon Thy creatures." God answered, and said: "O thou foolish shepherd, now thou speakest to Me. Thou didst not so when I addressed kind words to thee, saying: 'I saw thee as a righteous man and perfect in thy generation, and I will bring the flood upon the earth to destroy all flesh. Make an ark for thyself of gopher wood.' Thus spake I to thee, telling thee all these circumstances, that thou mightest entreat mercy for the earth. But thou, as soon as thou didst hear that thou wouldst be rescued in the ark, thou didst not concern thyself about the ruin that would strike the earth. Thou didst but build an ark for thyself, in which thou wast saved. Now that the earth is wasted, thou openest thy mouth to supplicate and pray."

Noah realized that he had been guilty of folly. To propitiate God and acknowledge his sin, he brought a sacrifice.⁴⁹ God accepted the offering with favor, whence he is called by his name Noah.⁵⁰ The sacrifice was not offered by Noah with his own hands; the priestly services connected with it were performed by his son Shem. There was a reason for this. One day in the ark Noah forgot to give his ration to the lion, and the hungry beast struck him so violent a blow with his paw that he was lame forever after, and, having a bodily defect, he was not permitted to do the offices of a priest.[1]

The sacrifices consisted of an ox, a sheep, a goat, two turtle doves, and two young pigeons. Noah had chosen these kinds because he supposed they were appointed for sacrifices, seeing that God had commanded him to take seven pairs of them into the ark with him. The altar was erected in the same place on which Adam and Cain and Abel had brought their sacrifices, and on which later the altar was to be in the sanctuary at Jerusalem.[2]

After the sacrifice was completed, God blessed Noah and his sons. He made them to be rulers of the world as Adam had been,[3] and He gave them a command, saying, " Be fruitful and multiply upon the earth," for during their so-journ in the ark, the two sexes, of men and animals alike, had lived apart from each other, because while a public calamity rages continence is becoming even to those who are left unscathed. This law of conduct had been violated by none in the ark except by Ham, by the dog, and by the raven. They all received a punishment. Ham's was that his descendants were men of dark-hued skin.[4]

As a token that He would destroy the earth no more, God set His bow in the cloud. Even if men should be steeped in sin again, the bow proclaims to them that their sins will cause no harm to the world. Times came in the course of the ages when men were pious enough not to have to live in dread of punishment. In such times the bow was not visible.[5]

God accorded permission to Noah and his descendants to use the flesh of animals for food, which had been forbidden from the time of Adam until then. But they were to abstain from the use of blood. He ordained the seven Noachian laws, the observance of which is incumbent upon all men, not upon Israel alone. God enjoined particularly the command against the shedding of human blood. Whoso would shed man's blood, his blood would be shed. Even if human judges let the guilty man go free, his punishment would overtake him. He would die an unnatural death, such as he had inflicted upon his fellow-man. Yea, even beasts that slew men, even of them would the life of men be required."

THE CURSE OF DRUNKENNESS

Noah lost his epithet "the pious" when he began to occupy himself with the growing of the vine. He became a "man of the ground," and this first attempt to produce wine at the same time produced the first to drink to excess, the first to utter curses upon his associates, and the first to introduce slavery. This is the way it all came about. Noah found the vine which Adam had taken with him from Paradise, when he was driven forth. He tasted the grapes upon it, and, finding them palatable, he resolved to plant the vine and tend it." On the selfsame day on which he planted it, it bore fruit, he put it in the wine-press, drew off the juice, drank it, became drunken, and was dishonored—all on one day. His assistant in the work of cultivating the vine was Satan, who had happened along at the very moment when he was engaged in planting the slip he had found. Satan asked him: "What is it thou art planting here?"

Noah: "A vineyard."

Satan: "And what may be the qualities of what it produces?"

Noah: "The fruit it bears is sweet, be it dry or moist. It yields wine that rejoiceth the heart of man."

Satan: "Let us go into partnership in this business of planting a vineyard."

Noah: "Agreed!"

Satan thereupon slaughtered a lamb, and then, in succession, a lion, a pig, and a monkey. The blood of each as it was killed he made to flow under the vine. Thus he conveyed to Noah what the qualities of wine are: before man drinks of it, he is innocent as a lamb; if he drinks of it moderately, he feels as strong as a lion; if he drinks more of it than he can bear, he resembles the pig; and if he drinks to the point of intoxication, then he behaves like a monkey, he dances around, sings, talks obscenely, and knows not what he is doing.[58]

This deterred Noah no more than did the example of Adam, whose fall had also been due to wine, for the forbidden fruit had been the grape, with which he had made himself drunk.[59]

In his drunken condition Noah betook himself to the tent of his wife. His son Ham saw him there, and he told his brothers what he had noticed, and said: "The first man had but two sons, and one slew the other; this man Noah has three sons, yet he desires to beget a fourth besides." Nor did Ham rest satisfied with these disrespectful words against his father. He added to this sin of irreverence the still greater outrage of attempting to perform an operation upon his father designed to prevent procreation.

When Noah awoke from his wine and became sober, he pronounced a curse upon Ham in the person of his youngest

son Canaan. To Ham himself he could do no harm, for God
had conferred a blessing upon Noah and his three sons as
they departed from the ark. Therefore he put the curse
upon the last-born son of the son that had prevented him
from begetting a younger son than the three he had.[**]
The descendants of Ham through Canaan therefore have red
eyes, because Ham looked upon the nakedness of his father;
they have misshapen lips, because Ham spoke with his lips
to his brothers about the unseemly condition of his father;
they have twisted curly hair, because Ham turned and
twisted his head round to see the nakedness of his father; and
they go about naked, because Ham did not cover the nakedness of his father. Thus he was requited, for it is the way
of God to mete out punishment measure for measure.

Canaan had to suffer vicariously for his father's sin. Yet
some of the punishment was inflicted upon him on his own
account, for it had been Canaan who had drawn the attention
of Ham to Noah's revolting condition. Ham, it appears,
was but the worthy father of such a son.[a] The last will
and testament of Canaan addressed to his children read as
follows: "Speak not the truth; hold not yourselves aloof
from theft; lead a dissolute life; hate your master with an
exceeding great hate; and love one another."[b]

As Ham was made to suffer requital for his irreverence,
so Shem and Japheth received a reward for the filial, deferential way in which they took a garment and laid it upon
both their shoulders, and walking backward, with averted
faces, covered the nakedness of their father. Naked the
descendants of Ham, the Egyptians and Ethiopians, were
led away captive and into exile by the king of Assyria, while

the descendants of Shem, the Assyrians, even when the angel of the Lord burnt them in the camp, were not exposed, their garments remained upon their corpses unsinged. And in time to come, when Gog shall suffer his defeat, God will provide both shrouds and a place of burial for him and all his multitude, the posterity of Japheth.

Though Shem and Japheth both showed themselves to be dutiful and deferential, yet it was Shem who deserved the larger meed of praise. He was the first to set about covering his father. Japheth joined him after the good deed had been begun. Therefore the descendants of Shem received as their special reward the tallit, the garment worn by them, while the Japhethites have only the toga.⁴⁰ A further distinction accorded to Shem was the mention of his name in connection with God's in the blessing of Noah. "Blessed be the Lord, the God of Shem," he said, though as a rule the name of God is not joined to the name of a living person, only to the name of one who has departed this life.⁴⁴

The relation of Shem to Japheth was expressed in the blessing their father pronounced upon them: God will grant a land of beauty to Japheth, and his sons will be proselytes dwelling in the academies of Shem.⁴⁵ At the same time Noah conveyed by his words that the Shekinah would dwell only in the first Temple, erected by Solomon, a son of Shem, and not in the second Temple, the builder of which would be Cyrus, a descendant of Japheth.⁴⁶

NOAH'S DESCENDANTS SPREAD ABROAD

When it became known to Ham that his father had cursed him, he fled ashamed, and with his family he settled in the

city built by him, and named Neelatamauk for his wife.
Jealous of his brother, Japheth followed his example. He
likewise built a city which he named for his wife, Ada-
taneses. Shem was the only one of the sons of Noah who
did not abandon him. In the vicinity of his father's home,
by the mountain, he built his city, to which he also gave his
wife's name, Zedeketelbab. The three cities are all near
Mount Lubar, the eminence upon which the ark rested. The
first lies to the south of it, the second to the west, and the
third to the east.

Noah endeavored to inculcate the ordinances and the commands known to him upon his children and his children's
children. In particular he admonished them against the fornication, the uncleanness, and all the iniquity which had
brought the flood down upon the earth. He reproached
them with living apart from one another, and with their
jealousies, for he feared that, after his death, they might go
so far as to shed human blood. Against this he warned
them impressively, that they be not annihilated from the
earth like those that went before. Another law which he
enjoined upon them, to observe it, was the law ordaining that
the fruit of a tree shall not be used the first three years it
bears, and even in the fourth year it shall be the portion of
the priests alone, after a part thereof has been offered upon
the altar of God. And having made an end of giving his
teachings and injunctions, Noah said: " For thus did Enoch,
your ancestor, exhort his son Methuselah, and Methuselah
his son Lamech, and Lamech delivered all unto me as his
father had bidden him, and now I do exhort you, my children, as Enoch exhorted his son. When he lived, in his

generation, which was the seventh generation of man, he commanded it and testified it unto his children and his children's children, until the day of his death." [*]

In the year 1569 after the creation of the world, Noah divided the earth by lot among his three sons, in the presence of an angel. Each one stretched forth his hand and took a slip from the bosom of Noah. Shem's slip was inscribed with the middle of the earth, and this portion became the inheritance of his descendants unto all eternity. Noah rejoiced that the lot had assigned it to Shem. Thus was fulfilled his blessing upon him, " And God in the habitation of Shem," for three holy places fell within his precincts—the Holy of Holies in the Temple, Mount Sinai, the middle point of the desert, and Mount Zion, the middle point of the navel of the earth.

The south fell to the lot of Ham, and the north became the inheritance of Japheth. The land of Ham is hot, Japheth's cold, but Shem's is neither hot nor cold, its temperature is hot and cold mixed. [*]

This division of the earth took place toward the end of the life of Peleg, the name given to him by his father Eber, who, being a prophet, knew that the division of the earth would take place in the time of his son. [*] The brother of Peleg was called Joktan, because the duration of the life of man was shortened in his time. [*]

In turn, the three sons of Noah, while they were still standing in the presence of their father, divided each his portion among his children, Noah threatening with his curse any who should stretch out his hand to take a portion not assigned to him by lot. And they all cried, " So be it ! So be it ! " [*]

Thus were divided one hundred and four lands and ninety-nine islands among seventy-two nations, each with a language of its own, using sixteen different sets of characters for writing. To Japheth were allotted forty-four lands, thirty-three islands, twenty-two languages, and five kinds of writing; Ham received thirty-four lands, thirty-three islands, twenty-four languages, and five kinds of writing; and Shem twenty-six lands, thirty-three islands, twenty-six languages, and six kinds of writing—one set of written characters more to Shem than to either of his brothers, the extra set being the Hebrew."

The land appointed as the inheritance of the twelve sons of Jacob was provisionally granted to Canaan, Zidon, Heth, the Jebusites, the Amorites, the Girgashites, the Hivites, the Arkites, the Sinites, the Arvadites, the Zemarites, and the Hamathites. It was the duty of these nations to take care of the land until the rightful owners should come."

No sooner had the children of Noah and their children's children taken possession of the habitations apportioned to them, than the unclean spirits began to seduce men and torment them with pain and all sorts of suffering leading to spiritual and physical death. Upon the entreaties of Noah God sent down the angel Raphael, who banished nine-tenths of the unclean spirits from the earth, leaving but one-tenth for Mastema, to punish sinners through them. Raphael, supported by the chief of the unclean spirits, at that time revealed to Noah all the remedies residing in plants, that he might resort to them at need. Noah recorded them in a book, which he transmitted to his son Shem." This is the source to which go back all the medical books whence the

wise men of India, Aram, Macedonia, and Egypt draw their
knowledge. The sages of India devoted themselves particularly to the study of curative trees and spices; the Ara-
means were well versed in the knowledge of the properties
of grains and seeds, and they translated the old medical
books into their language. The wise men of Macedonia
were the first to apply medical knowledge practically, while
the Egyptians sought to effect cures by means of magic arts
and by means of astrology, and they taught the Midrash of
the Chaldees, composed by Kangar, the son of Ur, the son
of Kesed. Medical skill spread further and further until
the time of Æsculapius. This Macedonian sage, accompanied by forty learned magicians, journeyed from country
to country, until they came to the land beyond India, in the
direction of Paradise. They hoped there to find some wood
of the tree of life, and thus spread their fame abroad over
the whole world. Their hope was frustrated. When they
arrived at the spot, they found healing trees and wood of the
tree of life, but when they were in the act of stretching forth
their hands to gather what they desired, lightning darted
out of the ever-turning sword, smote them to the ground,
and they were all burnt. With them disappeared all knowledge of medicine, and it did not revive until the time of the
first Artaxerxes, under the Macedonian sage Hippocrates,
Dioscorides of Baala, Galen of Caphtor, and the Hebrew
Asaph."

THE DEPRAVITY OF MANKIND

With the spread of mankind corruption increased. While
Noah was still alive, the descendants of Shem, Ham, and

Japheth appointed princes over each of the three groups—
Nimrod for the descendants of Ham, Joktan for the descendants of Shem, and Phenech for the descendants of
Japheth. Ten years before Noah's death, the number of
those subject to the three princes amounted to millions.
When this great concourse of men came to Babylonia upon
their journeyings, they said to one another: "Behold, the
time is coming when, at the end of days, neighbor will be
separated from neighbor, and brother from brother, and one
will carry on war against the other. Go to, let us build us
a city, and a tower, whose top may reach unto heaven, and
let us make us a great name upon the earth. And now let
us make bricks, and each one write his name upon his brick."
All agreed to this proposal, with the exception of twelve
pious men, Abraham among them. They refused to join
the others. They were seized by the people, and brought
before the three princes, to whom they gave the following
reason for their refusal: "We will not make bricks, nor
remain with you, for we know but one God, and Him we
serve; even if you burn us in the fire together with the
bricks, we will not walk in your ways." Nimrod and Phenech
flew into such a passion over the twelve men that they resolved to throw them into the fire. Joktan, however, besides
being a God-fearing man, was of close kin to the men on
trial, and he essayed to save them. He proposed to his two
colleagues to grant them a seven days' respite. His plan was
accepted, such deference being paid him as the primate
among the three. The twelve were incarcerated in the
house of Joktan. In the night he charged fifty of his attendants to mount the prisoners upon mules and take them to the

mountains. Thus they would escape the threatened punishment. Joktan provided them with food for a month. He
was sure that in the meantime either a change of sentiment
would come about, and the people desist from their purpose,
or God would help the fugitives. Eleven of the prisoners
assented to the plan with gratitude. Abraham alone rejected
it, saying: "Behold, to-day we flee to the mountains to
escape from the fire, but if wild beasts rush out from the
mountains and devour us, or if food is lacking, so that we
die by famine, we shall be found fleeing before the people
of the land and dying in our sins. Now, as the Lord liveth,
in whom I trust, I will not depart from this place wherein
they have imprisoned me, and if I am to die through my
sins, then will I die by the will of God, according to His
desire."

In vain Joktan endeavored to persuade Abraham to flee.
He persisted in his refusal. He remained behind alone in
the prison house, while the other eleven made their escape.
At the expiration of the set term, when the people returned
and demanded the death of the twelve captives, Joktan could
produce only Abraham. His excuse was that the rest had
broken loose during the night. The people were about to
throw themselves upon Abraham and cast him into the lime-
kiln. Suddenly an earthquake was felt, the fire darted from
the furnace, and all who were standing round about, eighty-
four thousand of the people, were consumed, while Abraham
remained untouched. Thereupon he repaired to his eleven
friends in the mountains, and told them of the miracle that
had befallen for his sake. They all returned with him, and,
unmolested by the people, they gave praise and thanks to
God.ˣ

NIMROD

The first among the leaders of the corrupt men was Nimrod." His father Cush had married his mother at an advanced age, and Nimrod, the offspring of this belated union, was particularly dear to him as the son of his old age. He gave him the clothes made of skins with which God had furnished Adam and Eve at the time of their leaving Paradise. Cush himself had gained possession of them through Ham. From Adam and Eve they had descended to Enoch, and from him to Methuselah, and to Noah, and the last had taken them with him into the ark. When the inmates of the ark were about to leave their refuge, Ham stole the garments and kept them concealed, finally passing them on to his first-born son Cush. Cush in turn hid them for many years. When his son Nimrod reached his twentieth year, he gave them to him." These garments had a wonderful property. He who wore them was both invincible and irresistible. The beasts and birds of the woods fell down before Nimrod as soon as they caught sight of him arrayed in them," and he was equally victorious in his combats with men." The source of his unconquerable strength was not known to them. They attributed it to his personal prowess, and therefore they appointed him king over themselves." This was done after a conflict between the descendants of Cush and the descendants of Japheth, from which Nimrod emerged triumphant, having routed the enemy utterly with the assistance of a handful of warriors. He chose Shinar as his capital. Thence he extended his dominion farther and farther, until he rose by cunning and force to be the sole ruler of the whole world. the first mortal to hold universal sway, as the ninth ruler to possess the same power will be the Messiah.[82]

His impiousness kept pace with his growing power. Since the flood there had been no such sinner as Nimrod. He fashioned idols of wood and stone, and paid worship to them. But not satisfied to lead a godless life himself, he did all he could to tempt his subjects into evil ways, wherein he was aided and abetted by his son Mardon. This son of his outstripped his father in iniquity. It was their time and their life that gave rise to the proverb, " Out of the wicked cometh forth wickedness." [83]

The great success that attended all of Nimrod's undertakings produced a sinister effect. Men no longer trusted in God, but rather in their own prowess and ability,[84] an attitude to which Nimrod tried to convert the whole world.[85] Therefore people said, " Since the creation of the world there has been none like Nimrod, a mighty hunter of men and beasts, and a sinner before God." [86]

And not all this sufficed unto Nimrod's evil desire. Not enough that he turned men away from God, he did all he could to make them pay Divine honors unto himself. He set himself up as a god, and made a seat for himself in imitation of the seat of God. It was a tower built out of a round rock, and on it he placed a throne of cedar wood, upon which arose, one above the other, four thrones, of iron, copper, silver, and gold. Crowning all, upon the golden throne, lay a precious stone, round in shape and gigantic in size. This served him as a seat, and as he sate upon it, all nations came and paid him Divine homage.[87]

THE TOWER OF BABEL

The iniquity and godlessness of Nimrod reached their climax in the building of the Tower of Babel. His counsellors had proposed the plan of erecting such a tower, Nimrod had agreed to it, and it was executed in Shinar by a mob of six hundred thousand men. The enterprise was neither more nor less than rebellion against God, and there were three sorts of rebels among the builders. The first party spoke, Let us ascend into the heavens and wage warfare with Him; the second party spoke, Let us ascend into the heavens, set up our idols, and pay worship unto them there; and the third party spoke, Let us ascend into the heavens, and ruin them with our bows and spears.

Many, many years were passed in building the tower. It reached so great a height that it took a year to mount to the top. A brick was, therefore, more precious in the sight of the builders than a human being. If a man fell down, and met his death, none took notice of it, but if a brick dropped, they wept, because it would take a year to replace it. So intent were they upon accomplishing their purpose that they would not permit a woman to interrupt herself in her work of brick-making when the hour of travail came upon her. Moulding bricks she gave birth to her child, and, tying it round her body in a sheet, she went on moulding bricks.

They never slackened in their work, and from their dizzy height they constantly shot arrows toward heaven, which, returning, were seen to be covered with blood. They were thus fortified in their delusion, and they cried, " We have slain all who are in heaven." Thereupon God turned to the seventy angels who encompass His throne, and He spake:

" Go to, let us go down, and there confound their language, that they may not understand one another's speech." Thus it happened. Thenceforth none knew what the other spoke. One would ask for the mortar, and the other handed him a brick; in a rage, he would throw the brick at his partner and kill him. Many perished in this manner, and the rest were punished according to the nature of their rebellious conduct. Those who had spoken, " Let us ascend into the heavens, set up our idols, and pay worship unto them there," God transformed into apes and phantoms; those who had proposed to assault the heavens with their arms, God set against each other so that they fell in the combat; and those who had resolved to carry on a combat with God in heaven were scattered broadcast over the earth. As for the unfinished tower, a part sank into the earth, and another part was consumed by fire; only one-third of it remained standing.[88] The place of the tower has never lost its peculiar quality. Whoever passes it forgets all he knows.[89]

The punishment inflicted upon the sinful generation of the tower is comparatively lenient. On account of rapine the generation of the flood were utterly destroyed, while the generation of the tower were preserved in spite of their blasphemies and all their other acts offensive to God. The reason is that God sets a high value upon peace and harmony. Therefore the generation of the deluge, who gave themselves up to depredation, and bore hatred to one another, were extirpated, root and branch, while the generation of the Tower of Babel dwelling amicably together, and loving one another, were spared alive, at least a remnant of them.[90]

Beside the chastisement of sin and sinners by the con-
founding of speech, another notable circumstance was connected with the descent of God upon earth—one of only ten
such descents to occur between the creation of the world and
the day of judgment. It was on this occasion that God and
the seventy angels that surround His throne cast lots concerning the various nations. Each angel received a nation,
and Israel fell to the lot of God. To every nation a peculiar
language was assigned, Hebrew being reserved for Israel—
the language made use of by God at the creation of the
world.[α]

V

ABRAHAM

V

ABRAHAM

The Wicked Generations

Ten generations there were from Noah to Abraham, to show how great is the clemency of God, for all the generations provoked His wrath, until Abraham our father came and received the reward of all of them.[1] For the sake of Abraham God had shown himself long-suffering and patient during the lives of these ten generations. Yea, more, the world itself had been created for the sake of his merits.[2] His advent had been made manifest to his ancestor Reu, who uttered the following prophecy at the birth of his son Serug: "From this child he shall be born in the fourth generation that shall set his dwelling over the highest, and he shall be called perfect and spotless, and shall be the father of nations, and his covenant shall not be dissolved, and his seed shall be multiplied forever."[3]

It was, indeed, high time that the "friend of God"[4] should make his appearance upon earth. The descendants of Noah were sinking from depravity to lower and lower depths of depravity. They were beginning to quarrel and slay, eat blood, build fortified cities and walls and towers, and set one man over the whole nation as king, and wage wars, people against people, and nations against nations, and cities against cities, and do all manner of evil, and acquire weapons, and teach warfare unto their children. And they began also to take captives and sell them as slaves. And they made unto themselves molten images, which they worshipped, each one the idol he had molten for himself, for the evil spirits under their leader Mastema led them astray into sin and uncleanness. For this reason Reu called his son Serug, because all mankind had turned aside unto sin and transgression. When he grew to manhood, the name was seen to have been chosen fittingly, for he, too, worshipped idols, and when he himself had a son, Nahor by name, he taught him the arts of the Chaldees, how to be a soothsayer and practice magic according to signs in the heavens. When, in time, a son was born to Nahor, Mastema sent ravens and other birds to despoil the earth and rob men of the proceeds of their work. As soon as they had dropped the seed in the furrows, and before they could cover it over with earth, the birds picked it up from the surface of the ground, and Nahor called his son Terah, because the ravens and the other birds plagued men, devoured their seed, and reduced them to destitution.[']

THE BIRTH OF ABRAHAM

Terah married Emtelai, the daughter of Karnabo,['] and the offspring of their union was Abraham. His birth had been read in the stars by Nimrod,['] for this impious king was a cunning astrologer, and it was manifest to him that a man would be born in his day who would rise up against him and triumphantly give the lie to his religion. In his terror at the fate foretold him in the stars, he sent for his princes and governors, and asked them to advise him in the matter. They answered, and said: " Our unanimous advice is that thou shouldst build a great house, station a guard at the entrance thereof, and make known in the whole of thy realm that all pregnant women shall repair thither together with their midwives, who are to remain with them when they are delivered. When the days of a woman to be delivered are fulfilled, and the child is born, it shall be the duty of the midwife to kill it, if it be a boy. But if the child be a girl, it shall be kept alive, and the mother shall receive gifts and costly garments, and a herald shall proclaim, ' Thus is done unto the woman who bears a daughter ! ' "

The king was pleased with this counsel, and he had a proclamation published throughout his whole kingdom, summoning all the architects to build a great house for him, sixty ells high and eighty wide. After it was completed, he issued a second proclamation, summoning all pregnant women thither, and there they were to remain until their confinement. Officers were appointed to take the women to the house, and guards were stationed in it and about it, to prevent the women from escaping thence. He furthermore sent midwives to the house, and commanded them to slay the men children at their mothers' breasts. But if a woman bore a girl, she was to be arrayed in byssus, silk, and embroidered garments, and led forth from the house of detention amid great honors. No less than seventy thousand children were slaughtered thus. Then the angels appeared before God, and spoke, " Seest Thou not what he doth, yon sinner and blasphemer, Nimrod son of Canaan, who slays so many innocent babes that have done no harm? " God answered, and said: " Ye holy angels, I know it and I see it, for I neither slumber nor sleep. I behold and I know the secret things and the things that are revealed, and ye shall witness what I will do unto this sinner and blasphemer, for I will turn My hand against him to chastise him." [*]

It was about this time that Terah espoused the mother of Abraham, and she was with child. When her body grew large at the end of three months of pregnancy, [*] and her countenance became pale, Terah said unto her, "What ails thee, my wife, that thy countenance is so pale and thy body so swollen?" She answered, and said, "Every year I suffer with this malady." [10] But Terah would not be put off thus. He insisted: "Show me thy body. It seems to me thou art big with child. If that be so, it behooves us not to violate the command of our god Nimrod." [11] When he passed his hand over her body, there happened a miracle. The child rose until it lay beneath her breasts, and Terah could feel nothing with his hands. He said to his wife, "Thou didst speak truly," and naught became visible until the day of her delivery.

When her time approached, she left the city in great terror and wandered toward the desert, walking along the edge of a valley, [12] until she happened across a cave. She entered this refuge, and on the next day she was seized with throes, and she gave birth to a son. The whole cave was filled with the light of the child's countenance as with the splendor of the sun, and the mother rejoiced exceedingly. The babe she bore was our father Abraham.

His mother lamented, and said to her son: "Alas that I bore thee at a time when Nimrod is king. For thy sake seventy thousand men children were slaughtered, and I am seized with terror on account of thee, that he hear of thy

existence, and slay thee. Better thou shouldst perish here
in this cave than my eye should behold thee dead at my
breast." She took the garment in which she was clothed,
and wrapped it about the boy. Then she abandoned him in
the cave, saying, " May the Lord be with thee, may He not
fail thee nor forsake thee." [13]

THE BABE PROCLAIMS GOD

Thus Abraham was deserted in the cave, without a nurse,
and he began to wail. God sent Gabriel down to give him
milk to drink, and the angel made it to flow from the little
finger of the baby's right hand, and he sucked at it until he
was ten days old.[14] Then he arose and walked about, and
he left the cave, and went along the edge of the valley.[15]
When the sun sank, and the stars came forth, he said,
" These are the gods!" But the dawn came, and the stars
could be seen no longer, and then he said, " I will not pay
worship to these, for they are no gods." Thereupon the sun
came forth, and he spoke, "This is my god, him will I
extol." But again the sun set, and he said, " He is no god,"
and beholding the moon, he called her his god to whom he
would pay Divine homage. Then the moon was obscured,
and he cried out : " This, too, is no god! There is One who
sets them all in motion." [16]

He was still communing with himself when the angel
Gabriel approached him and met him with the greeting,
" Peace be with thee," and Abraham returned, " With thee
be peace," and asked, " Who art thou?" And Gabriel
answered, and said, " I am the angel Gabriel, the messenger
of God," and he led Abraham to a spring of water near by,

and Abraham washed his face and his hands and feet, and he prayed to God, bowing down and prostrating himself.

Meantime the mother of Abraham thought of him in sorrow and tears, and she went forth from the city to seek him in the cave in which she had abandoned him. Not finding her son, she wept bitterly, and said, "Woe unto me that I bore thee but to become a prey of wild beasts, the bears and the lions and the wolves!" She went to the edge of the valley, and there she found her son. But she did not recognize him, for he had grown very large. She addressed the lad, "Peace be with thee!" and he returned, "With thee be peace!" and he continued, "Unto what purpose didst thou come to the desert?" She replied, "I went forth from the city to seek my son." Abraham questioned further, "Who brought thy son hither?" and the mother replied thereto: "I had become pregnant from my husband Terah, and when the days of my delivery were fulfilled, I was in anxiety about my son in my womb, lest our king come, the son of Canaan, and slay him as he had slain the seventy thousand other men children. Scarcely had I reached the cave in this valley when the throes of travailing seized me, and I bore a son, whom I left behind in the cave, and I went home again. Now am I come to seek him, but I find him not."

Abraham then spoke, "As to this child thou tellest of, how old was it?"

The mother: "It was about twenty days old."

Abraham: "Is there a woman in the world who would forsake her new-born son in the desert, and come to seek him after twenty days?"

The mother: "Peradventure God will show Himself a merciful God!"

Abraham: "I am the son whom thou hast come to seek in this valley!"

The mother: "My son, how thou art grown! But twenty days old, and thou canst already walk, and talk with thy mouth!""

Abraham: "So it is, and thus, O my mother, it is made known unto thee that there is in the world a great, terrible, living, and ever-existing God, who doth see, but who cannot be seen. He is in the heavens above, and the whole earth is full of His glory."

The mother: "My son, is there a God beside Nimrod?"

Abraham: "Yes, mother, the God of the heavens and the God of the earth, He is also the God of Nimrod son of Canaan. Go, therefore, and carry this message unto Nimrod."

The mother of Abraham returned to the city and told her husband Terah how she had found their son. Terah, who was a prince and a magnate in the house of the king, betook himself to the royal palace, and cast himself down before the king upon his face. It was the rule that one who prostrated himself before the king was not permitted to lift up his head until the king bade him lift it up. Nimrod gave permission to Terah to rise and state his request. Thereupon Terah related all that had happened with his wife and his son. When Nimrod heard his tale, abject fear seized upon him, and he asked his counsellors and princes what to do with the lad. They answered, and said: "Our king and our god! Wherefore art thou in fear by reason of a little child?

There are myriads upon myriads of princes in thy realm,[20] rulers of thousands, rulers of hundreds, rulers of fifties, and rulers of tens, and overseers without number. Let the pettiest of the princes go and fetch the boy and put him in prison." But the king interposed, " Have ye ever seen a baby of twenty days walking with his feet, speaking with his mouth, and proclaiming with his tongue that there is a God in heaven, who is One, and none beside Him, who sees and is not seen? " All the assembled princes were horror-struck at these words.[21]

At this time Satan in human form appeared, clad in black silk garb, and he cast himself down before the king. Nimrod said, " Raise thy head and state thy request." Satan asked the king: " Why art thou terrified, and why are ye all in fear on account of a little lad? I will counsel thee what thou shalt do: Open thy arsenal and give weapons unto all the princes, chiefs, and governors, and unto all the warriors, and send them to fetch him unto thy service and to be under thy dominion."

This advice given by Satan the king accepted and followed. He sent a great armed host to bring Abraham to him. When the boy saw the army approach him, he was sore afraid, and amid tears he implored God for help. In answer to his prayer, God sent the angel Gabriel to him, and he said: " Be not afraid and disquieted, for God is with thee. He will rescue thee out of the hands of all thine adversaries." God commanded Gabriel to put thick, dark clouds between Abraham and his assailants. Dismayed by the heavy clouds, they fled, returning to Nimrod, their king, and they said to him, " Let us depart and leave this realm," and the king gave money unto all his princes and his servants, and together with the king they departed and journeyed to Babylon."

ABRAHAM'S FIRST APPEARANCE IN PUBLIC

Now Abraham, at the command of God, was ordered by the angel Gabriel to follow Nimrod to Babylon. He objected that he was in no wise equipped to undertake a campaign against the king, but Gabriel calmed him with the words: " Thou needest no provision for the way, no horse to ride upon, no warriors to carry on war with Nimrod, no chariots, nor riders. Do thou but sit thyself upon my shoulder, and I shall bear thee to Babylon."

Abraham did as he was bidden, and in the twinkling of an eye he found himself before the gates of the city of Babylon." At the behest of the angel, he entered the city, and he called unto the dwellers therein with a loud voice: " The Eternal, He is the One Only God, and there is none beside. He is the God of the heavens, and the God of the gods, and the God of Nimrod. Acknowledge this as the truth, all ye men, women, and children. Acknowledge also that I am Abraham His servant, the trusted steward of His house."

Abraham met his parents in Babylon, and also he saw the angel Gabriel, who bade him proclaim the true faith to his father and his mother. Therefore Abraham spake to them, and said: " Ye serve a man of your own kind, and you pay worship to an image of Nimrod. Know ye not that it has a mouth, but it speaks not; an eye, but it sees not; an ear, but it hears not; nor does it walk upon its feet, and there is no profit in it, either unto itself or unto others? "

When Terah heard these words, he persuaded Abraham to follow him into the house, where his son told him all that had happened—how in one day he had completed a forty days' journey. Terah thereupon went to Nimrod and reported to him that his son Abraham had suddenly appeared in Babylon.²² The king sent for Abraham, and he came before him with his father. Abraham passed the magnates and the dignitaries until he reached the royal throne, upon which he seized hold, shaking it and crying out with a loud voice: "O Nimrod, thou contemptible wretch, that deniest the essence of faith, that deniest the living and immutable God, and Abraham His servant, the trusted steward of His house. Acknowledge Him, and repeat after me the words: The Eternal is God, the Only One, and there is none beside; He is incorporeal, living, ever-existing; He slumbers not and sleeps not, who hath created the world that men might believe in Him. And confess also concerning me, and say that I am the servant of God and the trusted steward of His house." ²³

While Abraham proclaimed this with a loud voice, the idols fell upon their faces, and with them also King Nimrod.²⁴ For a space of two hours and a half the king lay lifeless, and when his soul returned upon him, he spoke and said, " Is it thy voice, O Abraham, or the voice of thy God ? " And Abraham answered, and said, " This voice is the voice of the least of all creatures called into existence by God." Thereupon Nimrod said, " Verily, the God of Abraham is a great and powerful God, the King of all kings," and he commanded Terah to take his son and remove him, and return again unto his own city, and father and son did as the king had ordered.²⁵

THE PREACHER OF THE TRUE FAITH

When Abraham attained the age of twenty years, his father Terah fell ill. He spoke as follows to his sons Haran and Abraham, " I adjure you by your lives, my sons, sell these two idols for me, for I have not enough money to meet our expenses." Haran executed the wish of his father, but if any one accosted Abraham, to buy an idol from him, and asked him the price, he would answer, " Three manehs," and then question in turn, " How old art thou? " " Thirty years," the reply would be. " Thou art thirty years of age, and yet thou wouldst worship this idol which I made but to-day? " The man would depart and go his way, and another would approach Abraham, and ask, " How much is this idol? " and " Five manehs " would be the reply, and again Abraham would put the question, " How old art thou? "—" Fifty years."—" And dost thou who art fifty years of age bow down before this idol which was made but to-day? " Thereupon the man would depart and go his way. Abraham then took two idols, put a rope about their necks, and, with their faces turned downward, he dragged them along the ground, crying aloud all the time : " Who will buy an idol wherein there is no profit, either unto itself or unto him that buys it in order to worship it? It has a mouth, but it speaketh not ; eyes, but it seeth not ; feet, but it walketh not ; ears, but it heareth not."

The people who heard Abraham were amazed exceedingly at his words. As he went through the streets, he met an old woman who approached him with the purpose of buying an idol, good and big, to be worshipped and loved. " Old woman, old woman," said Abraham, " I know no profit therein, either in the big ones or in the little ones, either unto themselves or unto others. And," he continued to speak to her, " what has become of the big image thou didst buy from my brother Haran, to worship it?" " Thieves," she replied, " came in the night and stole it, while I was still at the bath." "If it be thus," Abraham went on questioning her, "how canst thou pay homage to an idol that cannot save itself from thieves, let alone save others, like thyself, thou silly old woman, out of misfortune? How is it possible for thee to say that the image thou worshippest is a god? If it be a god, why did it not save itself out of the hands of those thieves? Nay, in the idol there is no profit, either unto itself or unto him that adores it." [36]

The old woman rejoined, " If what thou sayest be true, whom shall I serve?" " Serve the God of all gods," returned Abraham, "the Lord of lords, who hath created heaven and earth, the sea and all therein—the God of Nimrod and the God of Terah, the God of the east, the west, the south, and the north. Who is Nimrod, the dog, who calleth himself a god, that worship be offered unto him?"

Abraham succeeded in opening the eyes of the old woman, and she became a zealous missionary for the true God. When she discovered the thieves who had carried off her idol, and they restored it to her, she broke it in pieces with a stone, and as she wended her way through the streets, she cried aloud, " Who would save his soul from destruction, and be prosperous in all his doings, let him serve the God of Abraham." Thus she converted many men and women to the true belief.

Rumors of the words and deeds of the old woman reached

the king, and he sent for her. When she appeared before him, he rebuked her harshly, asking her how she dared serve any god but himself. The old woman replied: "Thou art a liar, thou deniest the essence of faith, the One Only God, beside whom there is no other god. Thou livest upon His bounty, but thou payest worship to another, and thou dost repudiate Him, and His teachings, and Abraham His servant."

The old woman had to pay for her zeal for the faith with her life. Nevertheless great fear and terror took possession of Nimrod, because the people became more and more attached to the teachings of Abraham, and he knew not how to deal with the man who was undermining the old faith. At the advice of his princes, he arranged a seven days' festival, at which all the people were bidden to appear in their robes of state, their gold and silver apparel. By such display of wealth and power he expected to intimidate Abraham and bring him back to the faith of the king. Through his father Terah, Nimrod invited Abraham to come before him, that he might have the opportunity of seeing his greatness and wealth, and the glory of his dominion, and the multitude of his princes and attendants. But Abraham refused to appear before the king. On the other hand, he granted his father's request that in his absence he sit by his idols and the king's, and take care of them.

Alone with the idols, and while he repeated the words, "The Eternal He is God, the Eternal He is God!" he struck the king's idols from their thrones, and began to belabor them with an axe. With the biggest he started, and with the smallest he ended. He hacked off the feet of one, and the other he beheaded. This one had his eyes struck out, the other had his hands crushed.⁷⁷ After all were mutilated, he went away, having first put the axe into the hand of the largest idol.

The feast ended, the king returned, and when he saw all his idols shivered in pieces, he inquired who had perpetrated the mischief. Abraham was named as the one who had been guilty of the outrage, and the king summoned him and questioned him as to his motive for the deed. Abraham replied: " I did not do it; it was the largest of the idols who shattered all the rest. Seest thou not that he still has the axe in his hand? And if thou wilt not believe my words, ask him and he will tell thee."

IN THE FIERY FURNACE

Now the king was exceedingly wroth at Abraham, and ordered him to be cast into prison, where he commanded the warden not to give him bread or water.⁷⁸ But God hearkened unto the prayer of Abraham, and sent Gabriel to him in his dungeon. For a year the angel dwelt with him, and provided him with all sorts of food, and a spring of fresh water welled up before him, and he drank of it. At the end of a year, the magnates of the realm presented themselves before the king, and advised him to cast Abraham into the fire, that the people might believe in Nimrod forever. Thereupon the king issued a decree that all the subjects of the king in all his provinces, men and women, young and old, should bring wood within forty days, and he caused it to be thrown into a great furnace and set afire.⁷⁹ The flames shot up to the skies, and the people were sore afraid of the fire.

Now the warden of the prison was ordered to bring Abraham forth and cast him in the flames. The warden reminded the king that Abraham had not had food or drink a whole year, and therefore must be dead, but Nimrod nevertheless desired him to step in front of the prison and call his name. If he made reply, he was to be hauled out to the pyre. If he had perished, his remains were to receive burial, and his memory was to be wiped out henceforth.

Greatly amazed the warden was when his cry, "Abraham, art thou alive?" was answered with "I am living." He questioned further, "Who has been bringing thee food and drink all these many days?" and Abraham replied: "Food and drink have been bestowed upon me by Him who is over all things, the God of all gods and the Lord of all lords, who alone doeth wonders, He who is the God of Nimrod and the God of Terah and the God of the whole world. He dispenseth food and drink unto all beings. He sees, but He cannot be seen, He is in the heavens above, and He is present in all places, for He Himself superviseth all things and provideth for all."

The miraculous rescue of Abraham from death by starvation and thirst convinced the prison-keeper of the truth of God and His prophet Abraham, and he acknowledged his belief in both publicly. The king's threat of death unless he recanted could not turn him away from his new and true faith. When the hangman raised his sword and set it at his throat to kill him, he exclaimed, "The Eternal He is God, the God of the whole world as well as of the blasphemer Nimrod." But the sword could not cut his flesh. The harder it was pressed against his throat. the more it broke into pieces."

Nimrod, however, was not to be turned aside from his purpose, to make Abraham suffer death by fire. One of the princes was dispatched to fetch him forth. But scarcely did the messenger set about the task of throwing him into the fire, when the flame leapt forth from the furnace and consumed him. Many more attempts were made to cast Abraham into the furnace, but always with the same success—whoever seized him to pitch him in was himself burnt, and a large number lost their lives. Satan appeared in human shape, and advised the king to place Abraham in a catapult and sling him into the fire. Thus no one would be required to come near the flame. Satan himself constructed the catapult. Having proved it fit three times by means of stones put in the machine, they bound Abraham, hand and foot, and were about to consign him to the flames. At that moment Satan, still disguised in human shape, approached Abraham, and said, " If thou desirest to deliver thyself from the fire of Nimrod, bow down before him and believe in him." But Abraham rejected the tempter with the words, " May the Eternal rebuke thee, thou vile, contemptible, accursed blasphemer!" and Satan departed from him.

Then the mother of Abraham came to him and implored him to pay homage to Nimrod and escape the impending misfortune. But he said to her: " O mother, water can extinguish Nimrod's fire, but the fire of God will not die out for evermore. Water cannot quench it." [11] When his mother heard these words, she spake, " May the God whom thou servest rescue thee from the fire of Nimrod!"

Abraham was finally placed in the catapult, and he raised his eyes heavenward, and spoke, " O Lord my God, Thou

seest what this sinner purposes to do unto me!"¹² His
confidence in God was unshakable. When the angels received the Divine permission to save him, and Gabriel approached him, and asked, "Abraham, shall I save thee from
the fire?" he replied, "God in whom I trust, the God of
heaven and earth, will rescue me," and God, seeing the sub-
missive spirit of Abraham, commanded the fire, "Cool off
and bring tranquillity to my servant Abraham."¹³

No water was needed to extinguish the fire. The logs
burst into buds, and all the different kinds of wood put forth
fruit, each tree bearing its own kind. The furnace was
transformed into a royal pleasance, and the angels sat
therein with Abraham. When the king saw the miracle, he
said: "Great witchcraft! Thou makest it known that fire
hath no power over thee, and at the same time thou showest
thyself unto the people sitting in a pleasure garden." But
the princes of Nimrod interposed all with one voice, "Nay,
our lord, this is not witchcraft, it is the power of the great
God, the God of Abraham, beside whom there is no other
god, and we acknowledge that He is God, and Abraham is
His servant." All the princes and all the people believed in
God at this hour, in the Eternal, the God of Abraham, and
they all cried out, "The Lord He is God in heaven above
and upon the earth beneath; there is none else."¹⁴

Abraham was the superior, not only of the impious king
Nimrod and his attendants, but also of the pious men of his
time, Noah, Shem, Eber, and Asshur.¹⁵ Noah gave himself no concern whatsoever in the matter of spreading the
pure faith in God. He took an interest in planting his vineyard, and was immersed in material pleasures. Shem and

Eber kept in hiding, and as for Asshur, he said, " How can
I live among such sinners? " and departed out of the land."
The only one who remained unshaken was Abraham. " I
will not forsake God," he said, and therefore God did not
forsake him, who had hearkened neither unto his father nor
unto his mother.

The miraculous deliverance of Abraham from the fiery
furnace, together with his later fortunes, was the fulfilment
and explanation of what his father Terah had read in the
stars. He had seen the star of Haran consumed by fire, and
at the same time fill and rule the whole world. The meaning was plain now. Haran was irresolute in his faith, he
could not decide whether to adhere to Abraham or the
idolaters. When it befell that those who would not serve
idols were cast into the fiery furnace, Haran reasoned in
this manner: "Abraham, being my elder, will be called
upon before me. If he comes forth out of the fiery trial
triumphant, I will declare my allegiance to him; otherwise
I will take sides against him." After God Himself had
rescued Abraham from death, and Haran's turn came to
make his confession of faith, he announced his adherence
to Abraham. But scarcely had he come near the furnace,"
when he was seized by the flames and consumed, because
he was lacking in firm faith in God. Terah had read the
stars well, it now appeared: Haran was burnt, and his
daughter Sarah " became the wife of Abraham, whose descendants fill the earth." In another way the death of Haran
was noteworthy. It was the first instance, since the creation
of the world, of a son's dying while his father was still
alive."

The king, the princes, and all the people, who had been witnesses of the wonders done for Abraham, came to him, and prostrated themselves before him. But Abraham said: " Do not bow down before me, but before God, the Master of the universe, who hath created you. Serve Him and walk in His ways, for He it was who delivered me from the flames, and He it is who hath created the soul and the spirit of every human being, who formeth man in the womb of his mother, and bringeth him into the world. He saveth from all sickness those who put their trust in Him."

The king then dismissed Abraham, after loading him down with an abundance of precious gifts, among them two slaves who had been raised in the royal palace. 'Ogi was the name of the one, Eliezer the name of the other. The princes followed the example of the king, and they gave him silver, and gold, and gems. But all these gifts did not rejoice **the heart** of Abraham so much as the three hundred followers that joined him and became adherents of his religion.

Abraham Emigrates to Haran

For a period of two years Abraham could devote himself undisturbed to his chosen task of turning the hearts of men to God and His teachings.⁴¹ In his pious undertaking he was aided by his wife Sarah, whom he had married in the meantime. While he exhorted the men and sought to convert them, Sarah addressed herself to the women.⁴² She was a helpmeet worthy of Abraham. Indeed, in prophetical powers she ranked higher than her husband.⁴³ She was sometimes called Iscah, " the seer," on that account.⁴⁴

At the expiration of two years it happened that Nimrod dreamed a dream. In his dream he found himself with his army near the fiery furnace in the valley into which Abraham had been cast. A man resembling Abraham stepped out of the furnace, and he ran after the king with drawn sword, the king fleeing before him in terror. While running, the pursuer threw an egg at Nimrod's head, and a mighty stream issued therefrom, wherein the king's whole host was drowned. The king alone survived, with three men. When Nimrod examined his companions, he observed that they wore royal attiré, and in form and stature they resembled himself. The stream changed back into an egg again, and a little chick broke forth from it, and it flew up, settled upon the head of the king, and put out one of his eyes.

The king was confounded in his sleep, and when he awoke, his heart beat like a trip-hammer, and his fear was exceeding great. In the morning, when he arose, he sent and called for his wise men and his magicians, and told them his dream. One of his wise men, Anoko by name, stood up, and said: " Know, O king, this dream points to the misfortune which Abraham and his descendants will bring upon thee. A time will come when he and his followers will make war upon thy army, and they will annihilate it. Thou and the three kings, thy allies, will be the only ones to escape death. But later thou wilt lose thy life at the hands of one of the descendants of Abraham. Consider, O king, that thy wise men read this fate of thine in the stars, fifty-two years ago, at the birth of Abraham. As long as Abraham liveth upon the ground, thou shalt not be stablished, nor thy kingdom."

Nimrod took Anoko's words to heart, and dispatched some
of his servants to seize Abraham and kill him. It happened
that Eliezer, the slave whom Abraham had received as a
present from Nimrod, was at that time at the royal court.
With great haste he sped to Abraham to induce him to flee
before the king's bailiffs. His master accepted his advice,
and took refuge in the house of Noah and Shem, where he
lay in hiding a whole month. The king's officers reported
that despite zealous efforts Abraham was nowhere to be
found. Thenceforth the king did not concern himself about
Abraham.

When Terah visited his son in his hiding-place, Abraham
proposed that they leave the land and take up their abode in
Canaan, in order to escape the pursuit of Nimrod. He said:
"Consider that it was not for thy sake that Nimrod over-
loaded thee with honors, but for his own profit. Though he
continue to confer the greatest of benefactions upon thee,
what are they but earthly vanity? for riches and possessions
profit not in the day of wrath and fury. Hearken unto my
voice, O my father, let us depart for the land of Canaan,
and serve the God that hath created thee, that it may be
well with thee."

Noah and Shem aided and abetted the efforts of Abraham
to persuade Terah, whereupon Terah consented to leave his
country, and he, and Abraham, and Lot, the son of Haran,
departed for Haran with their households. They found
the land pleasant, and also the inhabitants thereof, who
readily yielded to the influence of Abraham's humane spirit
and his piety. Many of them obeyed his precepts and became God-fearing and good."

Terah's resolve to quit his native land for the sake of Abraham and take up his abode in strange parts, and his impulse to do it before even the Divine call visited Abraham himself—this the Lord accounted a great merit unto Terah, and he was permitted to see his son Abraham rule as king over the whole world. For when the miracle happened, and Isaac was born unto his aged parents, the whole world repaired to Abraham and Sarah, and demanded to know what they had done that so great a thing should be accomplished for them. Abraham told them all that had happened between Nimrod and himself, how he had been ready to be burnt for the glory of God, and how the Lord had rescued him from the flames. In token of their admiration for Abraham and his teachings, they appointed him to be their king, and in commemoration of Isaac's wondrous birth, the money coined by Abraham bore the figures of an aged husband and wife on the obverse side, and of a young man and his wife on the reverse side, for Abraham and Sarah both were rejuvenated at the birth of Isaac, Abraham's white hair turned black, and the lines in Sarah's face were smoothed out.

For many years Terah continued to live a witness of his son's glory, for his death did not occur until Isaac was a youth of thirty-five.⁴⁶ And a still greater reward waited upon his good deed. God accepted his repentance, and when he departed this life, he entered into Paradise, and not into hell, though he had passed the larger number of his days in sin. Indeed, it had been his fault that Abraham came near losing his life at the hands of Nimrod.⁴⁷

THE STAR IN THE EAST

Terah had been a high official at the court of Nimrod, and he was held in great consideration by the king and his suite. A son was born unto him whom he called Abram, because the king had raised him to an exalted place. In the night of Abraham's birth, the astrologers and the wise men of Nimrod came to the house of Terah, and ate and drank, and rejoiced with him that night. When they left the house, they lifted up their eyes toward heaven to look at the stars, and they saw, and, behold, one great star came from the east and ran athwart the heavens and swallowed up the four stars at the four corners. They all were astonished at the sight, but they understood this matter, and knew its import. They said to one another: " This only betokens that the child that hath been born unto Terah this night will grow up and be fruitful, and he will multiply and possess all the earth, he and his children forever, and he and his seed will slay great kings and inherit their lands."

They went home that night, and in the morning they rose up early, and assembled in their meeting-house. They spake, and said to one another: "Lo, the sight that we saw last night is hidden from the king, it has not been made known to him, and should this thing become known to him in the latter days, he will say to us, Why did you conceal this matter from me? and then we shall all suffer death. Now, let us go and tell the king the sight which we saw, and the interpretation thereof, and we shall be clear from this thing." And they went to the king and told him the sight they had seen, and their interpretation thereof, and they added the advice that he pay the value of the child to Terah, and slay the babe.

Accordingly, the king sent for Terah, and when he came, he spake to him: "It hath been told unto me that a son was born to thee yesternight, and a wondrous sign was observed in the heavens at his birth. Now give me the boy, that we may slay him before evil comes upon us from him, and I will give thee thy house full of silver and gold in exchange for him." Terah answered: "This thing which thou promisest unto me is like the words which a man spoke to a mule, saying, 'I will give thee a great heap of barley, a houseful thereof, on condition that I cut off thy head!' The mule replied, 'Of what use will all the barley be to me, if thou cuttest off my head? Who will eat it when thou givest it to me?' Thus also do I say: What shall I do with silver and gold after the death of my son? Who shall inherit me?" But when Terah saw how the king's anger burned within him at these words, he added, "Whatever the king desireth to do unto his servant, that let him do, even my son is at the king's disposal, without value or exchange, he and his two older brethren."

The king spake, however, saying, "I will purchase thy youngest son for a price." And Terah made answer, "Let my king give me three days' time to consider the matter and consult about it with my family." The king agreed to this condition, and on the third day he sent to Terah, saying, "Give me thy son for a price, as I spoke unto thee, and if thou wilt not do this, I will send and slay all thou hast in thy house, there shall not be a dog left unto thee."

Then Terah took a child which his handmaid had borne unto him that day, and he brought the babe to the king, and received value for him, and the king took the child and dashed his head against the ground, for he thought it was Abraham. But Terah took his son Abraham, together with the child's mother and his nurse, and concealed them in a cave, and thither he carried provisions to them once a month, and the Lord was with Abraham in the cave, and he grew up, but the king and all his servants thought that Abraham was dead.

And when Abraham was ten years old, he and his mother and his nurse went out from the cave, for the king and his servants had forgotten the affair of Abraham.

In that time all the inhabitants of the earth, with the exception of Noah and his household, transgressed against the Lord, and they made unto themselves every man his god, gods of wood and stone, which could neither speak, nor hear, nor deliver from distress. The king and all his servants, and Terah with his household, were the first to worship images of wood and stone. Terah made twelve gods of large size, of wood and of stone, corresponding to the twelve months of the year, and he paid homage to them monthly in turn.⁴⁸

The True Believer

Once Abraham went into the temple of the idols in his father's house, to bring sacrifices to them, and he found one of them, Marumath by name, hewn out of stone, lying prostrate on his face before the iron god of Nahor. The idol was too heavy for him to raise it alone, and he called his father to help him put Marumath back in his place. While they were handling the image, its head dropped off, and Terah took a stone, and chiselled another Marumath, setting the head of the first upon the new body. Then Terah continued and made five more gods, and all these he delivered to Abraham, and bade him sell them in the streets of the city.

Abraham saddled his mule, and went to the inn where merchants from Fandana in Syria put up on their way to Egypt. He hoped to dispose of his wares there. When he reached the inn, one of the camels belonging to the merchants belched, and the sound frightened his mule so that it ran off pell-mell and broke three of the idols. The merchants not only bought the two sound idols from him, they also gave him the price of the broken ones, for Abraham had told them how distressed he was to appear before his father with less money than he had expected to receive for his handiwork.

This incident made Abraham reflect upon the worthlessness of idols, and he said to himself: " What are these evil things done by my father? Is not he the god of his gods, for do they not come into being by reason of his carving and chiselling and contriving? Were it not more seemly that they should pay worship to him than he to them, seeing they are the work of his hands?" Meditating thus, he reached his father's house, and he entered and handed his father the money for the five images, and Terah rejoiced, and said, " Blessed art thou unto my gods, because thou didst bring me the price of the idols, and my labor was not in vain." But Abraham made reply: " Hear, my father Terah, blessed are thy gods through thee, for thou art their god, since thou didst fashion them, and their blessing is destruction and their help is vanity. They that help not themselves, how can they help thee or bless me?"

Terah grew very wrathful at Abraham, that he uttered such speech against his gods, and Abraham, thinking upon his father's anger, left him and went from the house. But Terah called him back, and said, " Gather together the chips of the oak wood from which I made images before thou didst return, and prepare my dinner for me." Abraham made ready to do his father's bidding, and as he took up the chips he found a little god among them, whose forehead bore the inscription " God Barisat." He threw the chips upon the fire, and set Barisat up next to it, saying : " Attention ! Take care, Barisat, that the fire go not out until I come back. If it burns low, blow into it, and make it flame up again." Speaking thus, he went out. When he came in again, he found Barisat lying prone upon his back, badly burnt. Smiling, he said to himself, " In truth, Barisat, thou canst keep the fire alive and prepare food," and while he spoke, the idol was consumed to ashes. Then he took the dishes to his father, and he ate and drank and was glad and blessed his god Marumath. But Abraham said to his father, " Bless not thy god Marumath, but rather thy god Barisat, for he it was who, out of his great love for thee, threw himself into the fire that thy meal might be cooked." " Where is he now ? " exclaimed Terah, and Abraham answered, " He hath become ashes in the fierceness of the fire." Terah said, " Great is the power of Barisat ! I will make me another this day, and to-morrow he will prepare my food for me."

These words of his father made Abraham laugh in his mind, but his soul was grieved at his obduracy, and he proceeded to make clear his views upon the idols, saying : " Father, no matter which of the two idols thou blessest, thy behavior is senseless, for the images that stand in the holy temple are more to be worshipped than thine. Zucheus, the god of my brother Nahor, is more venerable than Marumath, because he is made cunningly of gold, and when he grows old, he will be worked over again. But when thy Marumath becomes dim, or is shivered in pieces, he will not be renewed, for he is of stone. And the god Joauv, who stands above the other gods with Zucheus, is more venerable than Barisat, made of wood, because he is hammered out of silver, and ornamented by men, to show his magnificence. But thy Barisat, before thou didst fashion him into a god with thy axe, was rooted in the earth, standing there great and wonderful, with the glory of branches and blossoms. Now he is dry, and gone is his sap. From his height he has fallen to the earth, from grandeur he came to pettiness, and the appearance of his face has paled away, and he himself was burnt in the fire, and he was consumed unto ashes, and he is no more. And thou didst then say, ' I will make me another this day, and to-morrow he will prepare my food for me.' Father," Abraham continued, and said, " the fire is more to be worshipped than thy gods of gold and silver and wood and stone, because it consumes them. But also the fire I call not god, because it is subject to the water, which quenches it. But also the water I call not god, because it is sucked up by the earth, and I call the earth more venerable, because it conquers the water. But also the earth I call not god, because it is dried out by the sun, and I call the sun more venerable than the earth, because he illumines the whole world with his rays. But also the sun I call not god, because his light is obscured when darkness cometh up. Nor do I call the moon and the stars gods, because their light, too, is extinguished when their time to shine is past. But hearken unto this, my father Terah, which I will declare unto thee, The God who hath created all things, He is the true God, He hath empurpled the heavens, and gilded the sun, and given radiance to the moon and also the stars, and He drieth out the earth in the midst of many waters, and also thee hath He put upon the earth, and me hath He sought out in the confusion of my thoughts." **

THE ICONOCLAST

But Terah could not be convinced, and in reply to Abraham's question, who the God was that had created heaven and earth and the children of men, he took him to the hall wherein stood twelve great idols and a large number of little idols, and pointing to them he said, "Here are they who have made all thou seest on earth, they who have created also me and thee and all men on the earth," and he bowed down before his gods, and left the hall with his son.

Abraham went thence to his mother, and he spoke to her, saying: "Behold, my father has shown those unto me who made heaven and earth and all the sons of men. Now, therefore, hasten and fetch a kid from the flock, and make of it savory meat, that I may bring it to my father's gods, perhaps I may thereby become acceptable to them." His mother did according to his request, but when Abraham brought the offering to the gods, he saw that they had no voice, no hearing, no motion, and not one of them stretched forth his hand to eat. Abraham mocked them, and said, "Surely, the savory meat that I prepared doth not please you, or perhaps

it is too little for you! Therefore I will prepare fresh
savory meat to-morrow, better and more plentiful than this,
that I may see what cometh therefrom." But the gods remained mute and without motion before the second offering
of excellent savory meat as before the first offering, and
the spirit of God came over Abraham, and he cried out, and
said: "Woe unto my father and his wicked generation,
whose hearts are all inclined to vanity, who serve these idols
of wood and stone, which cannot eat, nor smell, nor hear,
nor speak, which have mouths without speech, eyes without
sight, ears without hearing, hands without feeling, and legs
without motion!"

Abraham then took a hatchet in his hand, and broke all
his father's gods, and when he had done breaking them he
placed the hatchet in the hand of the biggest god among
them all, and he went out. Terah, having heard the crash
of the hatchet on the stone, ran to the room of the idols, and
he reached it at the moment when Abraham was leaving it,
and when he saw what had happened, he hastened after
Abraham, and he said to him, "What is this mischief thou
hast done to my gods?" Abraham answered: "I set savory
meat before them, and when I came nigh unto them, that
they might eat, they all stretched out their hands to take of
the meat, before the big one had put forth his hand to eat.
This one, enraged against them on account of their behavior,
took the hatchet and broke them all, and, behold, the hatchet
is yet in his hands, as thou mayest see."

Then Terah turned in wrath upon Abraham, and he said:
"Thou speakest lies unto me! Is there spirit, soul, or power
in these gods to do all thou hast told me? Are they not

wood and stone? and have I not myself made them? It is thou that didst place the hatchet in the hand of the big god, and thou sayest he smote them all." Abraham answered his father, and said: "How, then, canst thou serve these idols in whom there is no power to do anything? Can these idols in which thou trustest deliver thee? Can they hear thy prayers when thou callest upon them?" After having spoken these and similar words, admonishing his father to mend his ways and refrain from worshipping idols, he leapt up before Terah, took the hatchet from the big idol, broke it therewith, and ran away.

Terah hastened to Nimrod, bowed down before him, and besought him to hear his story, about his son who had been born to him fifty years back, and how he had done to his gods, and how he had spoken. "Now, therefore, my lord and king," he said, " send for him that he may come before thee, and do thou judge him according to the law, that we may be delivered from his evil." When Abraham was brought before the king, he told him the same story as he had told Terah, about the big god who broke the smaller ones, but the king replied, " Idols do neither speak, nor eat, nor move." Then Abraham reproached him for worshipping gods that can do nothing, and admonished him to serve the God of the universe. His last words were, " If thy wicked heart will not hearken to my words, to cause thee to forsake thy evil ways and serve the Eternal God, then wilt thou die in shame in the latter days, thou, thy people, and all that are connected with thee, who hear thy words, and walk in thy evil ways."

The king ordered Abraham to be put into prison, and at

the end of ten days he caused all the princes and great men of the realm to appear before him, and to them he put the case of Abraham. Their verdict was that he should be burnt, and, accordingly, the king had a fire prepared for three days and three nights, in his furnace at Kasdim, and Abraham was to be carried thither from prison to be burnt.

All the inhabitants of the land, about nine hundred thousand men, and the women and the children besides, came to see what would be done with Abraham. And when he was brought forth, the astrologers recognized him, and they said to the king, "Surely, this is the man whom we knew as a child, at whose birth the great star swallowed the four stars. Behold, his father did transgress thy command, and he made a mockery of thee, for he did bring thee another child, and him didst thou kill."

Terah was greatly terrified, for he was afraid of the king's wrath, and he admitted that he had deceived the king, and when the king said, "Tell me who advised thee to do this. Hide naught, and thou shalt not die," he falsely accused Haran, who had been thirty-two years old at the time of Abraham's birth, of having advised him to deceive the king. At the command of the king, Abraham and Haran, stripped of all their clothes except their hosen, and their hands and feet bound with linen cords, were cast into the furnace. Haran, because his heart was not perfect with the Lord, perished in the fire, and also the men who cast them into the furnace were burnt by the flames which leapt out over them, and Abraham alone was saved by the Lord, and he was not burnt, though the cords with which he was bound were consumed. For three days and three nights Abraham walked in the midst of the fire, and all the servants of the king came and told him, " Behold, we have seen Abraham walking about in the midst of the fire." [50]

At first the king would not believe them, but when some of his faithful princes corroborated the words of his servants, he rose up and went to see for himself. He then commanded his servants to take Abraham from the fire, but they could not, because the flames leapt toward them from the furnace, and when they tried again, at the king's command, to approach the furnace, the flames shot out and burnt their faces, so that eight of their number died. The king then called unto Abraham, and said: " O servant of the God who is in heaven, go forth from the midst of the fire, and come hither and stand before me," and Abraham came and stood before the king. And the king spoke to Abraham, and said, " How cometh it that thou wast not burnt in the fire?" And Abraham made answer, " The God of heaven and earth in whom I trust, and who hath all things in His power, He did deliver me from the fire into which thou didst cast me." [51]

ABRAHAM IN CANAAN

With ten temptations Abraham was tempted, and he withstood them all, showing how great was the love of Abraham. [52] The first test to which he was subjected was the departure from his native land. The hardships were many and severe which he encountered, and he was loth to leave his home, besides. He spoke to God, and said, " Will not the people talk about me, and say, ' He is endeavoring to bring the nations under the wings of the Shekinah, yet he leaves his old father in Haran, and he goes away.' " But God answered him, and said: "Dismiss all care concerning thy father and thy kinsmen from thy thoughts. Though they speak words of kindness to thee, yet are they all of one mind, to ruin thee." [63]

Then Abraham forsook his father in Haran, and journeyed to Canaan, accompanied by the blessing of God, who said unto him, "I will make of thee a great nation, and I will bless thee, and make thy name great." These three blessings were to counteract the evil consequences which, he feared, would follow emigration, for travelling from place to place interferes with the growth of the family, it lessens one's substance, and it diminishes the consideration one enjoys. [64] The greatest of all blessings, however, was the word of God, "And be thou a blessing." The meaning of this was that whoever came in contact with Abraham was blessed. Even the mariners on the sea were indebted to him for prosperous voyages. [65] Besides, God held out the promise to him that in time to come his name would be mentioned in the Benedictions, God would be praised as the Shield of Abraham, a distinction accorded to no other mortal except David. [66] But the words, "And be thou a blessing," will be fulfilled only in the future world, when the seed of Abraham shall be known among the nations and his offspring among the peoples as "the seed which the Lord hath blessed." [67]

When Abraham first was bidden to leave his home, he was not told to what land he was to journey—all the greater would be his reward for executing the command of God. [68] And Abraham showed his trust in God, for he said, "I am ready to go whithersoever Thou sendest me." The Lord then bade him go to a land wherein He would reveal Him-

self, and when he went to Canaan later, God appeared to
him, and he knew that it was the promised land."

On entering Canaan, Abraham did not yet know that it
was the land appointed as his inheritance. Nevertheless he
rejoiced when he reached it. In Mesopotamia and in Aram-
naharaim, the inhabitants of which he had seen eating, drinking, and acting wantonly, he had always wished, " O that
my portion may not be in this land," but when he came to
Canaan, he observed that the people devoted themselves in-
dustriously to the cultivation of the land, and he said, " O
that my portion may be in this land! " God then spoke to
him, and said, " Unto thy seed will I give this land." "
Happy in these joyous tidings, Abraham erected an altar to
the Lord to give thanks unto Him for the promise, and then
he journeyed on, southward, in the direction of the spot
whereon the Temple was once to stand. In Hebron he
again erected an altar, thus taking possession of the land in
a measure. And likewise he raised an altar in Ai, because
he foresaw that a misfortune would befall his offspring
there, at the conquest of the land under Joshua. The altar,
he hoped, would obviate the evil results that might follow.

Each altar raised by him was a centre for his activities as
a missionary. As soon as he came to a place in which he
desired to sojourn, he would stretch a tent first for Sarah,
and next for himself, and then he would proceed at once
to make proselytes and bring them under the wings of the
Shekinah. Thus he accomplished his purpose of inducing
all men to proclaim the Name of God."

For the present Abraham was but a stranger in his promised land. After the partition of the earth among the sons

of Noah, when all had gone to their allotted portions, it happened that Canaan son of Ham saw that the land extending from the Lebanon to the River of Egypt was fair to look upon, and he refused to go to his own allotment, westward by the sea. He settled in the land upon Lebanon, eastward and westward from the border of the Jordan and the border of the sea. And Ham, his father, and his brothers Cush and Mizraim spoke to him, and said: " Thou livest in a land that is not thine, for it was not assigned unto us when the lots were drawn. Do not thus! But if thou persistest, ye, thou and thy children, will fall, accursed, in the land, in a rebellion. Thy settling here was rebellion, and through rebellion thy children will be felled down, and thy seed will be destroyed unto all eternity. Sojourn not in the land of Shem, for unto Shem and unto the children of Shem was it apportioned by lot. Accursed art thou, and accursed wilt thou be before all the children of Noah on account of the curse, for we took an oath before the holy Judge and before our father Noah."

But Canaan hearkened not unto the words of his father and his brothers. He dwelt in the land of the Lebanon from Hamath even unto the entrance of Egypt, he and his sons.⁶² Though the Canaanites had taken unlawful possession of the land, yet Abraham respected their rights; he provided his camels with muzzles, to prevent them from pasturing upon the property of others.⁶³

His Sojourn in Egypt

Scarcely had Abraham established himself in Canaan when a devastating famine broke out—one of the ten God.

appointed famines for the chastisement of men. The first of them came in the time of Adam, when God cursed the ground for his sake; the second was this one in the time of Abraham; the third compelled Isaac to take up his abode among the Philistines; the ravages of the fourth drove the sons of Jacob into Egypt to buy grain for food; the fifth came in the time of the Judges, when Elimelech and his family had to seek refuge in the land of Moab; the sixth occurred during the reign of David, and it lasted three years; the seventh happened in the day of Elijah, who had sworn that neither rain nor dew should fall upon the earth; the eighth was the one in the time of Elisha, when an ass's head was sold for fourscore pieces of silver; the ninth is the famine that comes upon men piecemeal, from time to time; and the tenth will scourge men before the advent of Messiah, and this last will be " not a famine of bread, nor a thirst for water, but of hearing the words of the Lord." [44]

The famine in the time of Abraham prevailed only in Canaan, and it had been inflicted upon the land in order to test his faith. He stood this second temptation as he had the first. He murmured not, and he showed no sign of impatience toward God, who had bidden him shortly before to abandon his native land for a land of starvation. [45] The famine compelled him to leave Canaan for a time, and he repaired to Egypt, to become acquainted there with the wisdom of the priests and, if necessary, give them instruction in the truth. [46]

On this journey from Canaan to Egypt, Abraham first observed the beauty of Sarah. Chaste as he was, he had never before looked at her, but now, when they were wading through a stream, he saw the reflection of her beauty in the water like the brilliance of the sun.[67] Wherefore he spoke to her thus, " The Egyptians are very sensual, and I will put thee in a casket that no harm befall me on account of thee." At the Egyptian boundary, the tax collectors asked him about the contents of the casket, and Abraham told them he had barley in it. " No," they said, " it contains wheat." " Very well," replied Abraham, " I am prepared to pay the tax on wheat." The officers then hazarded the guess, " It contains pepper ! " Abraham agreed to pay the tax on pepper, and when they charged him with concealing gold in the casket, he did not refuse to pay the tax on gold, and finally on precious stones. Seeing that he demurred to no charge, however high, the tax collectors, made thoroughly suspicious, insisted upon his unfastening the casket and letting them examine the contents. When it was forced open, the whole of Egypt was resplendent with the beauty of Sarah. In comparison with her, all other beauties were like apes compared with men. She excelled Eve herself.[68] The servants of Pharaoh outbid one another in seeking to obtain possession of her, though they were of opinion that so radiant a beauty ought not to remain the property of a private individual. They reported the matter to the king,[69] and Pharaoh sent a powerful armed force to bring Sarah to the palace,[70] and so bewitched was he by her charms that those who had brought him the news of her coming into Egypt were loaded down with bountiful gifts.[71]

Amid tears, Abraham offered up a prayer. He entreated God in these words: " Is this the reward for my confidence in Thee ? For the sake of Thy grace and Thy lovingkindness, let not my hope be put to shame." " Sarah also implored God, saying: " O God, Thou didst bid my lord Abraham leave his home, the land of his fathers, and journey to Canaan, and Thou didst promise him to do good unto him if he fulfilled Thy commands. And now we have done as Thou didst command us to do. We left our country and our kindred, and we journeyed to a strange land, unto a people which we knew not heretofore. We came hither to save our people from starvation, and now hath this terrible misfortune befallen. O Lord, help me and save me from the hand of this enemy, and for the sake of Thy grace show me good."

An angel appeared unto Sarah while she was in the presence of the king, to whom he was not visible, and he bade her take courage, saying, " Fear naught, Sarah, for God hath heard thy prayer." The king questioned Sarah as to the man in the company of whom she had come to Egypt, and Sarah called Abraham her brother. Pharaoh pledged himself to make Abraham great and powerful, to do for him whatever she wished. He sent much gold and silver to Abraham, and diamonds and pearls, sheep and oxen, and men slaves and women slaves, and he assigned a residence to him within the precincts of the royal palace." In the love he bore Sarah, he wrote out a marriage contract, deeding to her all he owned in the way of gold and silver, and men slaves and women slaves, and the province of Goshen besides, the province occupied in later days by the descendants of Sarah, because it was their property. Most remarkable of all, he gave her his own daughter Hagar as slave, for he preferred to see his daughter the servant of Sarah to reigning as mistress in another harem."

His free-handed generosity availed naught. During the night, when he was about to approach Sarah, an angel appeared armed with a stick, and if Pharaoh but touched Sarah's shoe to remove it from her foot, the angel planted a blow upon his hand, and when he grasped her dress, a second blow followed. At each blow he was about to deal, the angel asked Sarah whether he was to let it descend, and if she bade him give Pharaoh a moment to recover himself, he waited and did as she desired. And another great miracle came to pass. Pharaoh, and his nobles, and his servants, the very walls of his house and his bed were afflicted with leprosy, and he could not indulge his carnal desires.[15] This night in which Pharaoh and his court suffered their well-deserved punishment was the night of the fifteenth of Nisan, the same night wherein God visited the Egyptians in a later time in order to redeem Israel, the descendants of Sarah.[16]

Horrified by the plague sent upon him, Pharaoh inquired how he could rid himself thereof. He applied to the priests, from whom he found out the true cause of his affliction, which was corroborated by Sarah. He then sent for Abraham and returned his wife to him, pure and untouched, and excused himself for what had happened, saying that he had had the intention of connecting himself in marriage with him, whom he had thought to be the brother of Sarah.[17] He bestowed rich gifts upon the husband and the wife, and they departed for Canaan, after a three months' sojourn in Egypt.[18]

Arrived in Canaan they sought the same night-shelters at which they had rested before, in order to pay their accounts, and also to teach by their example that it is not proper to seek new quarters unless one is forced to it.[19]

Abraham's sojourn in Egypt was of great service to the inhabitants of the country, because he demonstrated to the wise men of the land how empty and vain their views were, and also he taught them astronomy and astrology, unknown in Egypt before his time.[80]

THE FIRST PHARAOH

The Egyptian ruler, whose meeting with Abraham had proved so untoward an event, was the first to bear the name Pharaoh. The succeeding kings were named thus after him. The origin of the name is connected with the life and adventures of Rakyon, Have-naught, a man wise, handsome, and poor, who lived in the land of Shinar. Finding himself unable to support himself in Shinar, he resolved to depart for Egypt, where he expected to display his wisdom before the king, Ashwerosh, the son of 'Anam. Perhaps he would find grace in the eyes of the king, who would give Rakyon the opportunity of supporting himself and rising to be a great man. When he reached Egypt, he learnt that it was the custom of the country for the king to remain in retirement in his palace, removed from the sight of the people. Only on one day of the year he showed himself in public, and received all who had a petition to submit to him. Richer by a disappointment, Rakyon knew not how he was to earn a livelihood in the strange country. He was forced to spend the night in a ruin, hungry as he was. The next day he decided to try to earn something by selling vegetables. By a lucky chance he fell in with some dealers in vegetables, but as he did not know the customs of the country, his new undertaking was not favored with good fortune.

Ruffians assaulted him, snatched his wares from him, and made a laughing-stock of him. The second night, which he was compelled to spend in the ruin again, a sly plan ripened in his mind. He arose and gathered together a crew of thirty lusty fellows. He took them to the graveyard, and bade them, in the name of the king, charge two hundred pieces of silver for every body they buried. Otherwise interment was to be prevented. In this way he succeeded in amassing great wealth within eight months. Not only did he acquire silver, gold, and precious gems, but also he attached a considerable force, armed and mounted, to his person.

On the day on which the king appeared among the people, they began to complain of this tax upon the dead. They said: " What is this thou art inflicting upon thy servants— permitting none to be buried unless they pay thee silver and gold! Has a thing like this come to pass in the world since the days of Adam, that the dead should not be interred unless money be paid therefor! We know well that it is the privilege of the king to take an annual tax from the living. But thou takest tribute from the dead, too, and thou exactest it day by day. O king, we cannot endure this any longer, for the whole of the city is ruined thereby."

The king, who had had no suspicion of Rakyon's doings, fell into a great rage when the people gave him information about them. He ordered him and his armed force to appear before him. Rakyon did not come empty-handed. He was preceded by a thousand youths and maidens, mounted upon steeds and arrayed in state apparel. These were a present to the king. When he himself stepped before the king, he delivered gold, silver, and diamonds to him in great abundance, and a magnificent charger. These gifts and the display of splendor did not fail of taking effect upon the king, and when Rakyon, in well-considered words and with a pliant tongue, described the undertaking, he won not only the king to his side, but also the whole court, and the king said to him, " No longer shalt thou be called Rakyon, Havenaught, but Pharaoh, Paymaster, for thou didst collect taxes from the dead."

So profound was the impression made by Rakyon that the king, the grandees, and the people, all together resolved to put the guidance of the realm in the hands of Pharaoh. Under the suzerainty of Ashwerosh he administered law and justice throughout the year; only on the one day when he showed himself to the people did the king himself give judgment and decide cases. Through the power thus conferred upon him and through cunning practices, Pharaoh succeeded in usurping royal authority, and he collected taxes from all the inhabitants of Egypt. Nevertheless he was beloved of the people, and it was decreed that every ruler of Egypt should thenceforth bear the name Pharaoh.[n]

THE WAR OF THE KINGS

On his return from Egypt Abraham's relations to his own family were disturbed by annoying circumstances. Strife developed between the herdmen of his cattle and the herdmen of Lot's cattle. Abraham furnished his herds with muzzles, but Lot made no such provision, and when the shepherds that pastured Abraham's flocks took Lot's shepherds to task on account of the omission, the latter replied: " It is known of a surety that God said unto Abraham, 'To thy seed will I give the land.' But Abraham is a sterile mule. Never will he have children. On the morrow he will die, and Lot will be his heir. Thus the flocks of Lot are but consuming what belongs to them or their master." But God spoke: "Verily, I said unto Abraham I would give the land unto his seed, but only after the seven nations shall have been destroyed from out of the land. To-day the Canaanites are therein, and the Perizzites. They still have the right of habitation."

Now, when the strife extended from the servants to the masters, and Abraham vainly called his nephew Lot to account for his unbecoming behavior, Abraham decided he would have to part from his kinsman, though he should have to compel Lot thereto by force. Lot thereupon separated himself not from Abraham alone, but from the God of Abraham also, and he betook himself to a district in which immorality and sin reigned supreme, wherefore punishment overtook him, for his own flesh seduced him later unto sin.

God was displeased with Abraham for not living in peace and harmony with his own kindred, as he lived with all the world beside. On the other hand, God also took it in ill part that Abraham was accepting Lot tacitly as his heir, though He had promised him, in clear, unmistakable words, "To thy seed will I give the land." After Abraham had separated himself from Lot, he received the assurance again that Canaan should once belong to his seed, which God would multiply as the sand which is upon the sea-shore. As the sand fills the whole earth, so the offspring of Abraham would be scattered over the whole earth, from end to end; and as the earth is blessed only when it is moistened with water, so his offspring would be blessed through the Torah, which is likened unto water; and as the earth endures longer than metal, so his offspring would endure forever, while the heathen would vanish; and as the earth is trodden upon, so his offspring would be trodden upon by the four kingdoms."

The departure of Lot had a serious consequence, for the war waged by Abraham against the four kings is intimately connected with it. Lot desired to settle in the well-watered circle of the Jordan, but the only city of the plain that would receive him was Sodom, the king of which admitted the nephew of Abraham out of consideration for the latter." The five impious kings planned first to make war upon Sodom on account of Lot and then advance upon Abraham." For one of the five, Amraphel, was none other than Nimrod, Abraham's enemy from of old. The immediate occasion for the war was this: Chedorlaomer, one of Nimrod's generals, rebelled against him after the builders of the tower were dispersed, and he set himself up as king of Elam. Then he subjugated the Hamitic tribes living in the five cities of the plain of the Jordan, and made them tributary. For twelve years they were faithful to their sovereign ruler Chedorlaomer, but then they refused to pay the tribute, and they persisted in their insubordination for thirteen years. Making the most of Chedorlaomer's embarrassment, Nimrod led a host of seven thousand warriors against his former general. In the battle fought between Elam and Shinar, Nimrod suffered a disastrous defeat, he lost six hundred of his army, and among the slain was the king's son Mardon. Humiliated and abased, he returned to his country, and he

was forced to acknowledge the suzerainty of Chedorlaomer,
who now proceeded to form an alliance with Arioch king of
Ellasar, and Tidal, the king of several nations, the purpose
of which was to crush the cities of the circle of the Jordan.
The united forces of these kings, numbering eight hundred
thousand, marched upon the five cities, subduing whatever
they encountered in their course,[85] and annihilating the descendants of the giants. Fortified places, unwalled cities,
and flat, open country, all fell in their hands.[86] They pushed
on through the desert as far as the spring issuing from the
rock at Kadesh, the spot appointed by God as the place of
pronouncing judgment against Moses and Aaron on account
of the waters of strife. Thence they turned toward the
central portion of Palestine, the country of dates, where they
encountered the five godless kings, Bera, the villain, king of
Sodom; Birsha, the sinner, king of Gomorrah; Shinab, the
father-hater, king of Admah; Shemeber, the voluptuary,
king of Zeboiim; and the king of Bela, the city that devours
its inhabitants. The five were routed in the fruitful Vale of
Siddim, the canals of which later formed the Dead Sea.
They that remained of the rank and file fled to the mountains, but the kings fell into the slime pits and stuck there.
Only the king of Sodom was rescued, miraculously, for the
purpose that he might convert those heathen to faith in God
that had not believed in the wonderful deliverance of Abraham from the fiery furnace.[87]

The victors despoiled Sodom of all its goods and victuals,
and took Lot, boasting, "We have taken the son of Abraham's brother captive," so betraying the real object of their
undertaking; their innermost desire was to strike at
Abraham.[89]

It was on the first evening of the Passover, and Abraham was eating of the unleavened bread,[89] when the archangel Michael brought him the report of Lot's captivity. This angel bears another name besides, Palit, the escaped, because when God threw Samael and his host from their holy place in heaven, the rebellious leader held on to Michael and tried to drag him along downward, and Michael escaped falling from heaven only through the help of God.[90]

When the report of his nephew's evil state reached Abraham, he straightway dismissed all thought of his dissensions with Lot from his mind, and only considered ways and means of deliverance.[91] He convoked his disciples to whom he had taught the true faith, and who all called themselves by the name Abraham.[92] He gave them gold and silver, saying at the same time: " Know that we go to war for the purpose of saving human lives. Therefore, do ye not direct your eyes upon money, here lie gold and silver before you." Furthermore he admonished them in these words: " We are preparing to go to war. Let none join us who hath committed a trespass, and fears that Divine punishment will descend upon him." Alarmed by his warning, not one would obey his call to arms, they were fearful on account of their sins. Eliezer alone remained with him, wherefore God spake, and said: " All forsook thee save only Eliezer. Verily, I shall invest him with the strength of the three hundred and eighteen men whose aid thou didst seek in vain." [93]

The battle fought with the mighty hosts of the kings, from which Abraham emerged victorious, happened on the fifteenth of Nisan, the night appointed for miraculous deeds.[94]

The arrows and stones hurled at him effected naught,[95] but the dust of the ground, the chaff, and the stubble which he threw at the enemy were transformed into death-dealing javelins and swords.[96] Abraham, as tall as seventy men set on end, and requiring as much food and drink as seventy men, marched forward with giant strides, each of his steps measuring four miles, until he overtook the kings, and annihilated their troops. Further he could not go, for he had reached Dan, where Jeroboam would once raise the golden calves, and on this ominous spot Abraham's strength diminished.[97]

His victory was possible only because the celestial powers espoused his side. The planet Jupiter made the night bright for him, and an angel, Laïlah by name, fought for him.[98] In a true sense, it was a victory of God. All the nations acknowledged his more than human achievement, and they fashioned a throne for Abraham, and erected it on the field of battle. When they attempted to seat him upon it, amid exclamations of " Thou art our king! Thou art our prince! Thou art our god!" Abraham warded them off, and said, " The universe has its King, and it has its God!" He declined all honors, and returned his property unto each man. Only the little children he kept by himself. He reared them in the knowledge of God, and later they atoned for the disgrace of their parents.

Somewhat arrogantly the king of Sodom set out to meet Abraham. He was proud that a great miracle, his rescue from the slime pit, had been performed for him, too. He made Abraham the proposition that he keep the despoiled goods for himself.[99] But Abraham refused them, and said:

" I have lift up mine hand unto the Lord, God Most High, who hath created the world for the sake of the pious, that I will not take a thread nor a shoe-latchet nor aught that is thine. I have no right upon any goods taken as spoils,[100] save only that which the young men have eaten, and the portion of the men who tarried by the stuff, though they went not down to the battle itself." The example of Abraham in giving a share in the spoils even unto the men not concerned directly in the battle, was followed later by David, who heeded not the protest of the wicked men and the base fellows with him, that the watchers who staid by the stuff were not entitled to share alike with the warriors that had gone down to the battle.[101]

In spite of his great success, Abraham nevertheless was concerned about the issue of the war. He feared that the prohibition against shedding the blood of man had been transgressed, and he also dreaded the resentment of Shem, whose descendants had perished in the encounter. But God reassured him, and said: " Be not afraid! Thou hast but extirpated the thorns, and as to Shem, he will bless thee rather than curse thee." So it was. When Abraham returned from the war, Shem, or, as he is sometimes called, Melchizedek, the king of righteousness, priest of God Most High, and king of Jerusalem, came forth to meet him with bread and wine.[102] And this high priest instructed Abraham in the laws of the priesthood and in the Torah, and to prove his friendship for him he blessed him, and called him the partner of God in the possession of the world, seeing that through him the Name of God had first been made known among men.[103] But Melchizedek arranged the words of his blessing in an unseemly way. He named Abraham first and then God. As a punishment, he was deposed by God from the priestly dignity, and instead it was passed over to Abraham, with whose descendants it remained forever.[104]

As a reward for the sanctification of the Holy Name, which Abraham had brought about when he refused to keep aught of the goods taken in battle,[105] his descendants received two commands, the command of the threads in the borders of their garments, and the command of the latchets to be bound upon their hands and to be used as frontlets between their eyes. Thus they commemorate that their ancestor refused to take so much as a thread or a latchet. And because he would not touch a shoe-latchet of the spoils, his descendants cast their shoe upon Edom.[106]

THE COVENANT OF THE PIECES

Shortly after the war, God revealed Himself unto Abraham, to soothe his conscience as to the spilling of innocent blood, for it was a scruple that gave him much anguish of spirit. God assured him at the same time that He would cause pious men to arise among his descendants, who, like himself, would be a shield unto their generation.[107] As a further distinction, God gave him leave to ask what he would have, rare grace accorded to none beside, except Jacob, Solomon, Ahaz, and the Messiah. Abraham spoke, and said: "O Lord of the world, if in time to come my descendants should provoke Thy wrath, it were better I remained childless. Lot, for the sake of whom I journeyed as far as Damascus, where God was my protection, would be well pleased to be my heir. Moreover, I have read in

the stars, ' Abraham, thou wilt beget no children.' " Thereupon God raised Abraham above the vault of the skies, and
He said, " Thou art a prophet, not an astrologer! " " [108]   Now
Abraham demanded no sign that he would be blessed with
offspring. Without losing another word, he believed in the
Lord, and he was rewarded for his simple faith by a share
in this world and a share in the world to come as well, and,
besides, the redemption of Israel from the exile will take
place as a recompense for his firm trust.[109]

But though he believed the promise made him with a full
and abiding faith, he yet desired to know by what merit of
theirs his descendants would maintain themselves. Therefore God bade him bring Him a sacrifice of three heifers,
three she-goats, three rams, a turtle dove, and a young
pigeon, thus indicating to Abraham the various sacrifices
that should once be brought in the Temple, to atone for the
sins of Israel and further his welfare.[110]   " But what will become of my descendants," asked Abraham, " after the
Temple is destroyed? " God replied, and said, " If they read
the order of sacrifices as they will be set down in the Scriptures, I will account it unto them as though they had offered
the sacrifices, and I will forgive all their sins." [111]   And God
continued and revealed to Abraham the course of Israel's
history and the history of the whole world: The heifer of
three years indicates the dominion of Babylon, the she-goat
of three years stands for the empire of the Greeks, the ram
of three years for the Medo-Persian power, the rule of Ishmael is represented by the ram, and Israel is the innocent
dove.

Abraham took him these animals and divided them in the

midst. Had he not done so, Israel would not have been able to resist the power of the four kingdoms. But the birds he divided not, to indicate that Israel will remain whole. And the birds of prey came down upon the carcasses, and Abraham drove them away. Thus was announced the advent of the Messiah, who will cut the heathen in pieces, but Abraham bade Messiah wait until the time appointed unto him.[113] And as the Messianic time was made known unto Abraham, so also the time of the resurrection of the dead. When he laid the halves of the pieces over against each other, the animals became alive again, as the bird flew over them.[114]

While he was preparing these sacrifices, a vision of great import was granted to Abraham. The sun sank, and a deep sleep fell upon him, and he beheld a smoking furnace, Gehenna, the furnace that God prepares for the sinner; and he beheld a flaming torch, the revelation on Sinai, where all the people saw flaming torches; and he beheld the sacrifices to be brought by Israel; and an horror of great darkness fell upon him, the dominion of the four kingdoms. And God spake to him: " Abraham, as long as thy children fulfil the two duties of studying the Torah and performing the service in the Temple, the two visitations, Gehenna and alien rule, will be spared them. But if they neglect the two duties, they will have to suffer the two chastisements; only thou mayest choose whether they shall be punished by means of Gehenna or by means of the dominion of the stranger." All the day long Abraham wavered, until God called unto him: " How long wilt thou halt between two opinions? Decide for one of the two, and let it be for the dominion of the stranger!" Then God made known to him the four hundred

years' bondage of Israel in Egypt, reckoning from the birth
of Isaac, for unto Abraham himself was the promise given
that he should go to his fathers in peace, and feel naught of
the arrogance of the stranger oppressor. At the same time,
it was made known to Abraham that his father Terah would
have a share in the world to come, for he had done penance
for his sinful deeds. Furthermore it was revealed to him
that his son Ishmael would turn into the path of righteousness while yet his father was alive, and his grandson Esau
would not begin his impious way of life until he himself had
passed away. And as he received the promise of their deliverance together with the announcement of the slavery of his
seed, in a land not theirs, so it was made known to him that
God would judge the four kingdoms and destroy them.[114]

THE BIRTH OF ISHMAEL

The covenant of the pieces, whereby the fortunes of his
descendants were revealed to Abraham, was made at a time
when he was still childless.[115] As long as Abraham and
Sarah dwelt outside of the Holy Land, they looked upon
their childlessness as a punishment for not abiding within it.
But when a ten years' sojourn in Palestine found her barren
as before, Sarah perceived that the fault lay with her.[116]
Without a trace of jealousy she was ready to give her slave
Hagar to Abraham as wife,[117] first making her a freed
woman.[118] For Hagar was Sarah's property, not her husband's. She had received her from Pharaoh, the father of
Hagar. Taught and bred by Sarah, she walked in the same
path of righteousness as her mistress,[119] and thus was a suitable companion for Abraham, and, instructed by the holy
spirit, he acceded to Sarah's proposal.

No sooner had Hagar's union with Abraham been consummated, and she felt that she was with child, than she began to treat her former mistress contemptuously, though Sarah was particularly tender toward her in the state in which she was. When noble matrons came to see Sarah, she was in the habit of urging them to pay a visit to " poor Hagar," too. The dames would comply with her suggestion, but Hagar would use the opportunity to disparage Sarah. " My lady Sarah," she would say, " is not inwardly what she appears to be outwardly. She makes the impression of a righteous, pious woman, but she is not, for if she were, how could her childlessness be explained after so many years of marriage, while I became pregnant at once? "

Sarah scorned to bicker with her slave, yet the rage she felt found vent in these words to Abraham:[120] " It is thou who art doing me wrong. Thou hearest the words of Hagar, and thou sayest naught to oppose them, and I hoped that thou wouldst take my part. For thy sake did I leave my native land and the house of my father, and I followed thee into a strange land with trust in God. In Egypt I pretended to be thy sister, that no harm might befall thee. When I saw that I should bear no children, I took the Egyptian woman, my slave Hagar, and gave her unto thee for wife, contenting myself with the thought that I would rear the children she would bear. Now she treats me disdainfully in thy presence. O that God might look upon the injustice which hath been done unto me, to judge between thee and me, and have mercy upon us, restore peace to our home, and grant us offspring, that we have no need of children from Hagar, the Egyptian bondwoman of the generation of the heathen that cast thee in the fiery furnace! "[121]

Abraham, modest and unassuming as he was, was ready to do justice to Sarah, and he conferred full power upon her to dispose of Hagar according to her pleasure. He added but one caution, " Having once made her a mistress, we cannot again reduce her to the state of a bondwoman." Unmindful of this warning, Sarah exacted the services of a slave from Hagar. Not alone this, she tormented her, and finally she cast an evil eye upon her, so that the unborn child dropped from her, and she ran away. On her flight she was met by several angels, and they bade her return, at the same time making known to her that she would bear a son who should be called Ishmael—one of the six men who have been given a name by God before their birth, the others being Isaac, Moses, Solomon, Josiah, and the Messiah.[12]

Thirteen years after the birth of Ishmael the command was issued to Abraham that he put the sign of the covenant upon his body and upon the bodies of the male members of his household. Abraham was reluctant at first to do the bidding of God, for he feared that the circumcision of his flesh would raise a barrier between himself and the rest of mankind. But God said unto him, " Let it suffice thee that I am thy God and thy Lord, as it sufficeth the world that I am its God and its Lord."[13]

Abraham then consulted with his three true friends, Aner, Eshcol, and Mamre, regarding the command of the circumcision. The first one spoke, and said, " Thou art nigh unto a hundred years old, and thou considerest inflicting such pain upon thyself?" The advice of the second was also against it. " What," said Eshcol, " thou choosest to mark thyself so that thy enemies may recognize thee without fail?"

Mamre, the third, was the only one to advise obedience to the command of God. "God succored thee from the fiery furnace," he said, "He helped thee in the combat with the kings, He provided for thee during the famine, and thou dost hesitate to execute His behest concerning the circumcision?"[124] Accordingly, Abraham did as God had commanded, in bright daylight, bidding defiance to all, that none might say, "Had we seen him attempt it, we should have prevented him."[125]

The circumcision was performed on the tenth day of Tishri, the Day of Atonement, and upon the spot on which the altar was later to be erected in the Temple, for the act of Abraham remains a never-ceasing atonement for Israel.[126]

THE VISIT OF THE ANGELS

On the third day after his circumcision, when Abraham was suffering dire pain,[127] God spoke to the angels, saying, "Go to, let us pay a visit to the sick." The angels refused, and said: "What is man, that Thou art mindful of him? And the son of man, that Thou visitest him? And Thou desirest to betake Thyself to a place of uncleanness, a place of blood and filth?" But God replied unto them, "Thus do ye speak. As ye live, the savor of this blood is sweeter to me than myrrh and incense, and if you do not desire to visit Abraham, I will go alone."[128]

The day whereon God visited him was exceedingly hot, for He had bored a hole in hell, so that its heat might reach as far as the earth, and no wayfarer venture abroad on the highways, and Abraham be left undisturbed in his pain.[129]

But the absence of strangers caused Abraham great vexation, and he sent his servant Eliezer forth to keep a lookout for travellers. When the servant returned from his fruitless search, Abraham himself, in spite of his illness and the scorching heat, prepared to go forth on the highway and see whether he would not succeed where failure had attended Eliezer, whom he did not wholly trust at any rate, bearing in mind the well-known saying, " No truth among slaves." [180] At this moment God appeared to him, surrounded by the angels. Quickly Abraham attempted to rise from his seat, but God checked every demonstration of respect, and when Abraham protested that it was unbecoming to sit in the presence of the Lord, God said, " As thou livest, thy descendants at the age of four and five will sit in days to come in the schools and in the synagogues while I reside therein." [181]

Meantime Abraham beheld three men. They were the angels Michael, Gabriel, and Raphael. They had assumed the form of human beings to fulfil his wish for guests toward whom to exercise hospitality. Each of them had been charged by God with a special mission, besides, to be executed on earth. Raphael was to heal the wound of Abraham, Michael was to bring Sarah the glad tidings that she would bear a son, and Gabriel was to deal destruction to Sodom and Gomorrah. Arrived at the tent of Abraham, the three angels noticed that he was occupied in nursing himself, and they withdrew. [182] Abraham, however, hastened after them through another door of the tent, which had wide open entrances on all sides. [183] He considered the duty of hospitality more important than the duty of receiving the

Shekinah. Turning to God, he said, " O Lord, may it please Thee not to leave Thy servant while he provides for the entertainment of his guests." [184] Then he addressed himself to the stranger walking in the middle between the other two, whom by this token he considered the most distinguished,— it was the archangel Michael—and he bade him and his companions turn aside into his tent. The manner of his guests, who treated one another politely, made a good impression upon Abraham. He was assured that they were men of worth whom he was entertaining.[185] But as they appeared outwardly like Arabs, and the people worshipped the dust of their feet, he bade them first wash their feet, that they might not defile his tent.[186]

He did not depend upon his own judgment in reading the character of his guests. By his tent a tree was planted, which spread its branches out over all who believed in God, and afforded them shade. But if idolaters went under the tree, the branches turned upward, and cast no shade upon the ground. Whenever Abraham saw this sign, he would at once set about the task of converting the worshippers of the false gods. And as the tree made a distinction between the pious and the impious, so also between the clean and the unclean. Its shade was denied them as long as they refrained from taking the prescribed ritual bath in the spring that flowed out from its roots, the waters of which rose at once for those whose uncleanness was of a venial character and could be removed forthwith, while others had to wait seven days for the water to come up. Accordingly, Abraham bade the three men lean against the trunk of the tree. Thus he would soon learn their worth or their unworthiness.[187]

Being of the truly pious, " who promise little, but perform
much," [138] Abraham said only: " I will fetch a morsel of
bread, and comfort ye your heart, seeing that ye chanced to
pass my tent at dinner time. Then, after ye have given thanks
to God, ye may pass on." [139] But when the meal was served
to the guests, it was a royal banquet, exceeding Solomon's
at the time of his most splendid magnificence. Abraham
himself ran unto the herd, to fetch cattle for meat. He
slaughtered three calves, that he might be able to set a
" tongue with mustard " before each of his guests. [140] In
order to accustom Ishmael to God-pleasing deeds, he had
him dress the calves, [141] and he bade Sarah bake the bread.
But as he knew that women are apt to treat guests niggardly,
he was explicit in his request to her. He said, " Make ready
quickly three measures of meal, yea, fine meal." As it happened, the bread was not brought to the table, because it had
accidentally become unclean, and our father Abraham was
accustomed to eat his daily bread only in a clean state. [142]
Abraham himself served his guests, and it appeared to him
that the three men ate. But this was an illusion. In reality
the angels did not eat, [143] only Abraham, his three friends,
Aner, Eshcol, and Mamre, and his son Ishmael partook of
the banquet, and the portions set before the angels were
devoured by a heavenly fire. [144]

Although the angels remained angels even in their human
disguise, nevertheless the personality of Abraham was so
exalted that in his presence the archangels felt insignifi-
cant. [145]

After the meal the angels asked after Sarah, though they
knew that she was in retirement in her tent, but it was

proper for them to pay their respects to the lady of the house and send her the cup of wine over which the blessing had been said.[146] Michael, the greatest of the angels, thereupon announced the birth of Isaac. He drew a line upon the wall, saying, " When the sun crosses this point, Sarah will be with child, and when he crosses the next point, she will give birth to a child." This communication, which was intended for Sarah and not for Abraham, to whom the promise had been revealed long before,[147] the angels made at the entrance to her tent, but Ishmael stood between the angel and Sarah, for it would not have been seemly to deliver the message in secret, with none other by. Yet, so radiant was the beauty of Sarah that a beam of it struck the angel, and made him look up. In the act of turning toward her, he heard her laugh within herself:[148] " Is it possible that these bowels can yet bring forth a child, these shrivelled breasts give suck? And though I should be able to bear, yet is not my lord Abraham old? "[149]

And the Lord said unto Abraham: " Am I too old to do wonders? And wherefore doth Sarah laugh, saying, Shall I of a surety bear a child, which am old? "[150] The reproach made by God was directed against Abraham as well as against Sarah, for he, too, had showed himself of little faith when he was told that a son would be born unto him. But God mentioned only Sarah's incredulity, leaving Abraham to become conscious of his defect himself.[151]

Regardful of the peace of their family life, God had not repeated Sarah's words accurately to Abraham. Abraham might have taken amiss what his wife had said about his advanced years, and so precious is the peace between hus-

band and wife that even the Holy One, blessed be He, preserved it at the expense of truth.[152]

After Abraham had entertained his guests, he went with
them to bring them on their way, for, important as the duty
of hospitality is, the duty of speeding the parting guest is
even more important.[153] Their way lay in the direction of
Sodom, whither two of the angels were going, the one to
destroy it, and the second to save Lot, while the third, his
errand to Abraham fulfilled, returned to heaven.[154]

THE CITIES OF SIN

The inhabitants of Sodom and Gomorrah and the three
other cities of the plain were sinful and godless. In their
country there was an extensive vale, where they foregathered
annually with their wives and their children and all
belonging to them, to celebrate a feast lasting several days
and consisting of the most revolting orgies. If a stranger
merchant passed through their territory, he was besieged by
them all, big and little alike, and robbed of whatever he possessed. Each one appropriated a bagatelle, until the traveller was stripped bare. If the victim ventured to remon-
strate with one or another, he would show him that he had
taken a mere trifle, not worth talking about. And the end
was that they hounded him from the city.

Once upon a time it happened that a man journeying from
Elam arrived in Sodom toward evening. No one could be
found to grant him shelter for the night. Finally a sly fox
named Hedor invited him cordially to follow him to his
house. The Sodomite had been attracted by a rarely magnificent carpet, strapped to the stranger's ass by means of a

rope. He meant to secure it for himself. The friendly persuasions of Hedor induced the stranger to remain with him two days, though he had expected to stay only overnight. When the time came for him to continue on his journey, he asked his host for the carpet and the rope. Hedor said: "Thou hast dreamed a dream, and this is the interpretation of thy dream: the rope signifies that thou wilt have a long life, as long as a rope; the varicolored carpet indicates that thou wilt own an orchard wherein thou wilt plant all sorts of fruit trees." The stranger insisted that his carpet was a reality, not a dream fancy, and he continued to demand its return. Not only did Hedor deny having taken anything from his guest, he even insisted upon pay for having interpreted his dream to him. His usual price for such services, he said, was four silver pieces, but in view of the fact that he was his guest, he would, as a favor to him, content himself with three pieces of silver.

After much wrangling, they put their case before one of the judges of Sodom, Sherek by name, and he said to the plaintiff, "Hedor is known in this city as a trustworthy interpreter of dreams, and what he tells thee is true." The stranger declared himself not satisfied with the verdict, and continued to urge his side of the case. Then Sherek drove both the plaintiff and the defendant from the court room. Seeing this, the inhabitants gathered together and chased the stranger from the city, and lamenting the loss of his carpet, he had to pursue his way.

As Sodom had a judge worthy of itself, so also had the other cities—Sharkar in Gomorrah, Zabnak in Admah, and Manon in Zeboiim. Eliezer, the bondman of Abraham, made

slight changes in the names of these judges, in accordance
with the nature of what they did: the first he called Shakkara, Liar; the second Shakrura, Arch-deceiver; the third
Kazban, Falsifier; and the fourth, Mazle-Din, Perverter of
Judgment. At the suggestion of these judges, the cities set
up beds on their commons. When a stranger arrived, three
men seized him by his head, and three by his feet, and they
forced him upon one of the beds. If he was too short to
fit into it exactly, his six attendants pulled and wrenched his
limbs until he filled it out; if he was too long for it, they
tried to jam him in with all their combined strength, until
the victim was on the verge of death. His outcries were
met with the words, "Thus will be done to any man that
comes into our land."

After a while travellers avoided these cities, but if some
poor devil was betrayed occasionally into entering them,
they would give him gold and silver, but never any bread,
so that he was bound to die of starvation. Once he was
dead, the residents of the city came and took back the
marked gold and silver which they had given him, and they
would quarrel about the distribution of his clothes, for they
would bury him naked.

Once Eliezer, the bondman of Abraham, went to Sodom,
at the bidding of Sarah, to inquire after the welfare of Lot.
He happened to enter the city at the moment when the
people were robbing a stranger of his garments. Eliezer
espoused the cause of the poor wretch, and the Sodomites
turned against him; one threw a stone at his forehead and
caused considerable loss of blood. Instantly, the assailant,
seeing the blood gush forth, demanded payment for having

performed the operation of cupping. Eliezer refused to pay
for the infliction of a wound upon him, and he was haled before the judge Shakkara. The decision went against him,
for the law of the land gave the assailant the right to demand
payment. Eliezer quickly picked up a stone and threw it at
the judge's forehead. When he saw that the blood was
flowing profusely, he said to the judge, " Pay my debt to
the man and give me the balance."

The cause of their cruelty was their exceeding great
wealth. Their soil was gold, and in their miserliness and
their greed for more and more gold, they wanted to prevent
strangers from enjoying aught of their riches. Accordingly,
they flooded the highways with streams of water, so that
the roads to their city were obliterated, and none could find
the way thither. They were as heartless toward beasts as
toward men. They begrudged the birds what they ate, and
therefore extirpated them.[155] They behaved impiously
toward one another, too, not shrinking back from murder to
gain possession of more gold. If they observed that a man
owned great riches, two of them would conspire against him.
They would beguile him to the vicinity of ruins, and while
the one kept him on the spot by pleasant converse, the other
would undermine the wall near which he stood, until it suddenly crashed down upon him and killed him. Then the two
plotters would divide his wealth between them.

Another method of enriching themselves with the property
of others was in vogue among them. They were adroit
thieves. When they made up their minds to commit theft,
they would first ask their victim to take care of a sum of
money for them, which they smeared with strongly scented

oil before handing it over to him. The following night they
would break into his house, and rob him of his secret treasures, led to the place of concealment by the smell of the oil.

Their laws were calculated to do injury to the poor. The
richer a man, the more was he favored before the law. The
owner of two oxen was obliged to render one day's shepherd
service, but if he had but one ox, he had to give two days'
service. A poor orphan, who was thus forced to tend the
flocks a longer time than those who were blessed with large
herds, killed all the cattle entrusted to him in order to take
revenge upon his oppressors, and he insisted, when the skins
were assigned, that the owner of two head of cattle should
have but one skin, but the owner of one head should receive
two skins, in correspondence to the method pursued in
assigning the work. For the use of the ferry, a traveller
had to pay four zuz, but if he waded through the water, he
had to pay eight zuz.¹⁴⁰

The cruelty of the Sodomites went still further. Lot had
a daughter, Paltit, so named because she had been born to
him shortly after he escaped captivity through the help of
Abraham. Paltit lived in Sodom, where she had married.
Once a beggar came to town, and the court issued a proclamation that none should give him anything to eat, in order
that he might die of starvation. But Paltit had pity upon
the unfortunate wretch, and every day when she went to the
well to draw water, she supplied him with a piece of bread,
which she hid in her water pitcher. The inhabitants of the
two sinful cities, Sodom and Gomorrah, could not understand why the beggar did not perish, and they suspected that
some one was giving him food in secret. Three men con-

cealed themselves near the beggar, and caught Paltit in the act of giving him something to eat. She had to pay for her humanity with death; she was burnt upon a pyre.

The people of Admah were no better than those of Sodom. Once a stranger came to Admah, intending to stay overnight and continue his journey the next morning. The daughter of a rich man met the stranger, and gave him water to drink and bread to eat at his request. When the people of Admah heard of this infraction of the law of the land, they seized the girl and arraigned her before the judge, who condemned her to death. The people smeared her with honey from top to toe, and exposed her where bees would be attracted to her. The insects stung her to death, and the callous people paid no heed to her heartrending cries. Then it was that God resolved upon the destruction of these sinners.[157]

Abraham Pleads for the Sinners

When God saw that there was no righteous man among the inhabitants of the sinful cities, and there would be none among their descendants, for the sake of whose merits the rest might be treated with lenient consideration, He resolved to annihilate them one and all.[158] But before judgment was executed, the Lord made known unto Abraham what He would do to Sodom, Gomorrah, and the other cities of the plain, for they formed a part of Canaan, the land promised unto Abraham, and therefore did God say, "I will not destroy them without the consent of Abraham."[159]

Like a compassionate father, Abraham importuned the grace of God in behalf of the sinners. He spoke to God, and said: "Thou didst take an oath that no more should all

flesh be cut off by the waters of a flood. Is it meet that
Thou shouldst evade Thy oath and destroy cities by fire?
Shall the Judge of all the earth not do right Himself?
Verily, if Thou desirest to maintain the world, Thou must
give up the strict line of justice. If Thou insistest upon the
right alone, there can be no world." Whereupon God said
to Abraham: "Thou takest delight in defending My creatures, and thou wouldst not call them guilty. Therefore I
spoke with none but thee during the ten generations since
Noah."[100] Abraham ventured to use still stronger words
in order to secure the safety of the godless. "That be far
from Thee," he said, "to slay the righteous with the wicked,
that the dwellers on the earth say not, 'It is His trade to
destroy the generations of men in a cruel manner; for He
destroyed the generation of Enosh, then the generation of
the flood, and then He sent the confusion of tongues. He
sticks ever to His trade.'"

God made reply: "I will let all the generations I have
destroyed pass before thee, that thou mayest see they have
not suffered the extreme punishment they deserved. But if
thou thinkest that I did not act justly, then instruct thou Me
in what I must do, and I will endeavor to act in accordance
with thy words." And Abraham had to admit that God had
not diminished in aught the justice due to every creature in
this world or the other world.[101] Nevertheless he continued
to speak, and he said: "Wilt Thou consume the cities, if
there be ten righteous men in each?" And God said, "No,
if I find fifty righteous therein, I will not destroy the
cities."[102]

Abraham: "I have taken upon me to speak unto the Lord,

I who would have been turned long since into dust of the
ground by Amraphel and into ashes by Nimrod, had it not
been for Thy grace.[188] Peradventure there shall lack five of
the fifty righteous for Zoar, the smallest of the five cities.
Wilt Thou destroy all the city for lack of five?"

God: "I will not destroy it, if I find there forty and five."

Abraham: "Peradventure there be ten pious in each of
the four cities, then forgive Zoar in Thy grace, for its sins
are not so great in number as the sins of the others."

God granted his petition, yet Abraham continued to plead,
and he asked whether God would not be satisfied if there
were but thirty righteous, ten in each of the three larger
cities, and would pardon the two smaller ones, even though
there were no righteous therein, whose merits would intercede for them. This, too, the Lord granted, and furthermore He promised not to destroy the cities if but twenty
righteous were found therein; yes, God conceded that He
would preserve the five cities for the sake of ten righteous
therein.[184] More than this Abraham did not ask, for he knew
that eight righteous ones, Noah and his wife, and his three
sons and their wives, had not sufficed to avert the doom of
the generation of the flood, and furthermore he hoped that
Lot, his wife, and their four daughters, together with the
husbands of their daughters, would make up the number
ten. What he did not know was that even the righteous in
these sin-laden cities, though better than the rest, were far
from good.[185]

Abraham did not cease to pray for the deliverance of the
sinners even after the Shekinah had removed from him.
But his supplications and his intercessions were in vain.[186]

For fifty-two years God had warned the godless; He had
made mountains to quake and tremble. But they hearkened
not unto the voice of admonition. They persisted in their
sins, and their well-merited punishment overtook them.[157]
God forgives all sins, only not an immoral life. And as all
these sinners led a life of debauchery, they were burnt with
fire.[158]

THE DESTRUCTION OF THE SINFUL CITIES

The angels left Abraham at noon time, and they reached
Sodom at the approach of evening. As a rule, angels proclaim their errand with the swiftness of lightning, but these
were angels of mercy, and they hesitated to execute their
work of destruction, ever hoping that the evil would be
turned aside from Sodom.[159] With nightfall, the fate of
Sodom was sealed irrevocably, and the angels arrived
there.[160]

Bred in the house of Abraham, Lot had learnt from him
the beautiful custom of extending hospitality, and when he
saw the angels before him in human form, thinking they
were wayfarers, he bade them turn aside and tarry all night
in his house. But as the entertainment of strangers was forbidden in Sodom on penalty of death, he dared invite them
only under cover of the darkness of night,[161] and even then
he had to use every manner of precaution, bidding the angels
to follow him by devious ways.

The angels, who had accepted Abraham's hospitality without delay, first refused to comply with Lot's request, for it
is a rule of good breeding to show reluctance when an ordinary man invites one, but to accept the invitation of a great

man at once. Lot, however, was insistent, and carried them into his house by main force.[171] At home he had to overcome the opposition of his wife, for she said, " If the inhabitants of Sodom hear of this, they will slay thee."

Lot divided his dwelling in two parts, one for himself and his guests, the other for his wife, so that, if aught happened, his wife would be spared.[172] Nevertheless it was she who betrayed him. She went to a neighbor and borrowed some salt, and to the question, whether she could not have supplied herself with salt during daylight hours, she replied, " We had enough salt, until some guests came to us; for them we needed more." In this way the presence of strangers was bruited abroad in the city.[173]

In the beginning the angels were inclined to hearken to the petition of Lot in behalf of the sinners, but when all the people of the city, big and little, crowded around the house of Lot with the purpose of committing a monstrous crime, the angels warded off his prayers, saying, " Hitherto thou couldst intercede for them, but now no longer." It was not the first time that the inhabitants of Sodom wanted to perpetrate a crime of this sort. They had made a law some time before that all strangers were to be treated in this horrible way. Lot, who was appointed chief judge on the very day of the angels' coming, tried to induce the people to desist from their purpose, saying to them, " My brethren, the generation of the deluge was extirpated in consequence of such sins as you desire to commit, and you would revert to them ? " But they replied: " Back! And though Abraham himself came hither, we should have no consideration for him. Is it possible that thou wouldst set aside a law which thy predecessors administered ? " [174]

Even Lot's moral sense was no better than it should have been. It is the duty of a man to venture his life for the honor of his wife and his daughters, but Lot was ready to sacrifice the honor of his daughters, wherefor he was punished severely later on.[176]

The angels told Lot who they were, and what the mission that had brought them to Sodom, and they charged him to flee from the city with his wife and his four daughters, two of them married, and two betrothed.[177] Lot communicated their bidding to his sons-in-law, and they mocked at him, and said: "O thou fool! Violins, cymbals, and flutes resound in the city, and thou sayest Sodom will be destroyed!" Such scoffing but hastened the execution of the doom of Sodom.[178] The angel Michael laid hold upon the hand of Lot, and his wife and his daughters, while with his little finger the angel Gabriel touched the rock whereon the sinful cities were built, and overturned them. At the same time the rain that was streaming down upon the two cities was changed into brimstone.[179]

When the angels had brought forth Lot and his family and set them without the city, he bade them run for their lives, and not look behind, lest they behold the Shekinah, which had descended to work the destruction of the cities. The wife of Lot could not control herself. Her mother love made her look behind to see if her married daughters were following. She beheld the Shekinah, and she became a pillar of salt. This pillar exists unto this day. The cattle lick it all day long, and in the evening it seems to have disappeared, but when morning comes it stands there as large as before.[180]

The savior angel had urged Lot himself to take refuge with Abraham. But he refused, and said: "As long as I dwelt apart from Abraham, God compared my deeds with the deeds of my fellow-citizens, and among them I appeared as a righteous man. If I should return to Abraham, God will see that his good deeds outweigh mine by far." [181] The angel then granted his plea that Zoar be left undestroyed. This city had been founded a year later than the other four; it was only fifty-one years old, and therefore the measure of its sins was not so full as the measure of the sins of the neighboring cities. [182]

The destruction of the cities of the plain took place at dawn of the sixteenth day of Nisan, for the reason that there were moon and sun worshippers among the inhabitants. God said: "If I destroy them by day, the moon worshippers will say, Were the moon here, she would prove herself our savior; and if I destroy them by night, the sun worshippers will say, Were the sun here, he would prove himself our savior. I will therefore let their chastisement overtake them on the sixteenth day of Nisan at an hour at which the moon and the sun are both in the skies." [183]

The sinful inhabitants of the cities of the plain not only lost their life in this world, but also their share in the future world. As for the cities themselves, however, they will be restored in the Messianic time. [184]

The destruction of Sodom happened at the time at which Abraham was performing his morning devotions, and for his sake it was established as the proper hour for the morning prayer unto all times. [185] When he turned his eyes toward Sodom and beheld the rising smoke, he prayed for the de-

liverance of Lot, and God granted his petition—the fourth
time that Lot became deeply indebted to Abraham. Abraham had taken him with him to Palestine, he had made him
rich in flocks, herds, and tents, he had rescued him from captivity, and by his prayer he saved him from the destruction
of Sodom. The descendants of Lot, the Ammonites and the
Moabites, instead of showing gratitude to the Israelites, the
posterity of Abraham, committed four acts of hostility
against them. They sought to compass the destruction of
Israel by means of Balaam's curses, they waged open war
against him at the time of Jephthah, and also at the time of
Jehoshaphat, and finally they manifested their hatred against
Israel at the destruction of the Temple. Hence it is that
God appointed four prophets, Isaiah, Jeremiah, Ezekiel, and
Zephaniah, to proclaim punishment unto the descendants of
Lot, and four times their sin is recorded in Holy Writ.[188]

Though Lot owed his deliverance to the petition of Abraham, yet it was at the same time his reward for not having
betrayed Abraham in Egypt, when he pretended to be the
brother of Sarah.[187] But a greater reward still awaits him.
The Messiah will be a descendant of his, for the Moabitess
Ruth is the great-grandmother of David, and the Am-
monitess Naamah is the mother of Rehoboam, and the Messiah is of the line of these two kings.[188]

AMONG THE PHILISTINES

The destruction of Sodom induced Abraham to journey
to Gerar. Accustomed to extend hospitality to travellers
and wayfarers, he no longer felt comfortable in a district in
which all traffic had ceased by reason of the ruined cities.

There was another reason for Abraham's leaving his place; the people spoke too much about the ugly incident with Lot's daughters.[189]

Arrived in the land of the Philistines, he again, as aforetime in Egypt, came to an understanding with Sarah, that she was to call herself his sister. When the report of her beauty reached the king, he ordered her to be brought before him, and he asked her who her companion was, and she told him that Abraham was her brother. Entranced by her beauty, Abimelech the king took Sarah to wife, and heaped marks of honor upon Abraham in accordance with the just claims of a brother of the queen. Toward evening, before retiring, while he was still seated upon his throne, Abimelech fell into a sleep, and he slept until the morning, and in the dream he dreamed he saw an angel of the Lord raising his sword to deal him a death blow. Sore frightened, he asked the cause, and the angel replied, and said: " Thou wilt die on account of the woman thou didst take into thy house this day, for she is the wife of Abraham, the man whom thou didst cite before thee. Return his wife unto him! But if thou restore her not, thou shalt surely die, thou and all that are thine."

In that night the voice of a great crying was heard in the whole land of the Philistines, for they saw the figure of a man walking about, with sword in hand, slaying all that came in his way. At the same time it happened that in men and beasts alike all the apertures of the body closed up, and the land was seized with indescribable excitement. In the morning, when the king awoke, in agony and terror, he called all his servants and told his dream in their ears. One

of their number said: "O lord and king! Restore this
woman unto the man, for he is her husband. It is but his
way in a strange land to pretend that she is his sister. Thus
did he with the king of Egypt, too, and God sent heavy
afflictions upon Pharaoh when he took the woman unto himself. Consider, also, O lord and king, what hath befallen
this night in the land; great pain, wailing, and confusion
there was, and we know that it came upon us only because
of this woman." [190]

There were some among his servants who spake: "Be
not afraid of dreams! What dreams make known to man
is but falsehood." Then God appeared unto Abimelech
again and commanded him to let Sarah go free, otherwise
he would be a dead man.[191] Abimelech replied: "Is this
Thy way? Then, I ween, the generation of the flood and
the generation of the confusion of tongues were innocent,
too! The man himself did say unto me, She is my sister,
and she, even she herself said, He is my brother, and all
the people of their household said the same words." And
God said unto him: "Yea, I know that thou hast not yet
committed a trespass, for I withheld thee from sinning.
Thou didst not know that Sarah was a man's wife.[192] But is
it becoming to question a stranger, no sooner does he set
foot upon thy territory, about the woman accompanying him,
whether she be his wife or his sister? Abraham, who is a
prophet, knew beforehand the danger to himself if he revealed the whole truth.[193] But, being a prophet, he also
knows that thou didst not touch his wife, and he shall pray
for thee, and thou shalt live."

The smoke was still rising from the ruins of Sodom, and

Abimelech and his people, seeing it, feared that a like fate might overtake them.[184] The king called Abraham and reproached him for having caused such great misfortune through his false statements concerning Sarah. Abraham excused his conduct by his apprehension that, the fear of God not being in the place, the inhabitants of the land slay him for his wife.[185] Abraham went on and told the history of his whole life, and he said: "When I dwelt in the house of my father, the nations of the world sought to do me harm, but God proved Himself my Redeemer. When the nations of the world tried to lead me astray to idolatry, God revealed Himself to me, and He said, 'Get thee out of thy country, and from thy kindred, and from thy father's house.' And when the nations of the world were about to go astray, God sent two prophets, my kinsmen Shem and Eber, to admonish them."[186]

Abimelech gave rich gifts to Abraham, wherein he acted otherwise than Pharaoh in similar circumstances. The Egyptian king gave gifts to Sarah, but Abimelech was God-fearing, and desired that Abraham pray for him.[187] To Sarah he gave a costly robe that covered her whole person, hiding her seductive charms from the view of beholders. At the same time it was a reproach to Abraham, that he had not fitted Sarah out with the splendor due to his wife.[188]

Though Abimelech had done him great injury, Abraham not only granted him the forgiveness he craved, but also he prayed for him to God. Thus he is an exemplar unto all. "Man should be pliant as a reed, not hard like the cedar." He should be easily appeased, and slow to anger, and as soon as he who has sinned against him asks for pardon, he should forgive him with all his heart. Even if deep and serious injury has been done to him, he should not be vengeful, nor bear his brother a grudge in his heart."[199]

Abraham prayed thus for Abimelech: " O Lord of the world! Thou hast created man that he may increase and propagate his kind. Grant that Abimelech and his house may multiply and increase!"[200] God fulfilled Abraham's petition in behalf of Abimelech and his people, and it was the first time it happened in the history of mankind that God fulfilled the prayer of one human being for the benefit of another.[201] Abimelech and his subjects were healed of all their diseases, and so efficacious was the prayer offered by Abraham that the wife of Abimelech, barren hitherto, bore a child.[202]

THE BIRTH OF ISAAC

When the prayer of Abraham for Abimelech was heard, and the king of the Philistines recovered, the angels raised a loud cry, and spoke to God thus: " O Lord of the world! All these years hath Sarah been barren, as the wife of Abimelech was. Now Abraham prayed to Thee, and the wife of Abimelech hath been granted a child. It is just and fair that Sarah should be remembered and granted a child." These words of the angels, spoken on the New Year's Day, when the fortunes of men are determined in heaven for the whole year, bore a result. Barely seven months later, on the first day of the Passover, Isaac was born.

The birth of Isaac was a happy event, and not in the house of Abraham alone. The whole world rejoiced, for God remembered all barren women at the same time with Sarah.

They all bore children. And all the blind were made to see, all the lame were made whole, the dumb were made to speak, and the mad were restored to reason. And a still greater miracle happened: on the day of Isaac's birth the sun shone with such splendor as had not been seen since the fall of man, and as he will shine again only in the future world.[208]

To silence those who asked significantly, " Can one a hundred years old beget a son? " God commanded the angel who has charge over the embryos, to give them form and shape, that he fashion Isaac precisely according to the model of Abraham, so that all seeing Isaac might exclaim, " Abraham begot Isaac." [204]

That Abraham and Sarah were blessed with offspring only after they had attained so great an age, had an important reason. It was necessary that Abraham should bear the sign of the covenant upon his body before he begot the son who was appointed to be the father of Israel.[205] And as Isaac was the first child born to Abraham after he was marked with the sign, he did not fail to celebrate his circumcision with much pomp and ceremony on the eighth day.[206] Shem, Eber, Abimelech king of the Philistines, and his whole retinue, Phicol the captain of his host in it—they all were present, and also Terah and his son Nahor, in a word, all the great ones round about.[207] On this occasion Abraham could at last put a stop to the talk of the people, who said, " Look at this old couple! They picked up a foundling on the highway, and they pretend he is their own son, and to make their statement seem credible, they arrange a feast in his honor." Abraham had invited not only men to the celebration, but also the wives of the magnates with their infants, and God permitted a miracle to be done. Sarah had enough milk in her breasts to suckle all the babes there,[208] and they who drew from her breasts had much to thank her for. Those whose mothers had harbored only pious thoughts in their minds when they let them drink the milk that flowed from the breasts of the pious Sarah, they became proselytes when they grew up; and those whose mothers let Sarah nurse them only in order to test her, they grew up to be powerful rulers, losing their dominion only at the revelation on Mount Sinai, because they would not accept the Torah. All proselytes and pious heathen are the descendants of these infants.[209]

Among the guests of Abraham were the thirty-one kings and thirty-one viceroys of Palestine who were vanquished by Joshua at the conquest of the Holy Land. Even Og king of Bashan was present, and he had to suffer the teasing of the other guests, who rallied him upon having called Abraham a sterile mule, who would never have offspring. Og, on his part, pointed at the little boy with contempt, and said, "Were I to lay my finger upon him, he would be crushed." Whereupon God said to him: "Thou makest mock of the gift given to Abraham! As thou livest, thou shalt look upon millions and myriads of his descendants, and in the end thou shalt fall into their hands."[210]

Ishmael Cast Off

When Isaac grew up, quarrels broke out between him and Ishmael, on account of the rights of the first-born. Ishmael insisted he should receive a double portion of the inheritance after the death of Abraham, and Isaac should receive only one portion. Ishmael, who had been accustomed from his youth to use the bow and arrow, was in the habit of aiming his missiles in the direction of Isaac, saying at the same time that he was but jesting.[211] Sarah, however, insisted that Abraham make over to Isaac all he owned, that no disputes might arise after his death,[212] " for," she said, " Ishmael is not worthy of being heir with my son, nor with a man like Isaac, and certainly not with my son Isaac."[213] Furthermore, Sarah insisted that Abraham divorce himself from Hagar, the mother of Ishmael, and send away the woman and her son, so that there be naught in common between them and her own son, either in this world or in the future world.

Of all the trials Abraham had to undergo, none was so hard to bear as this, for it grieved him sorely to separate himself from his son. God appeared to him in the following night, and said to him: " Abraham, knowest thou not that Sarah was appointed to be thy wife from her mother's womb? She is thy companion and the wife of thy youth, and I named not Hagar as thy wife, nor Sarah as thy bond-woman. What Sarah spoke unto thee was naught but truth, and let it not be grievous in thy sight because of the lad, and because of thy bondwoman." The next morning Abraham rose up early, gave Hagar her bill of divorcement, and sent her away with her son, first binding a rope about her loins that all might see she was a bondwoman.[214]

The evil glance cast upon her stepson by Sarah made him sick and feverish, so that Hagar had to carry him, grown-up as he was. In his fever he drank often of the water in the bottle given her by Abraham as she left his house, and the water was quickly spent. That she might not look upon the

death of her child, Hagar cast Ishmael under the willow
shrubs growing on the selfsame spot whereon the angels
had once spoken with her and made known to her that she
would bear a son. In the bitterness of her heart, she spoke
to God, and said, " Yesterday Thou didst say to me, I will
greatly multiply thy seed, that it shall not be numbered for
multitude, and to-day my son dies of thirst." Ishmael himself cried unto God, and his prayer and the merits of Abraham brought them help in their need, though the angels
appeared against Ishmael before God. They said, " Wilt
Thou cause a well of water to spring up for him whose
descendants will let Thy children of Israel perish with
thirst? " But God replied, and said, " What is Ishmael at
this moment—righteous or wicked? " and when the angels
called him righteous, God continued, " I treat man according to his deserts at each moment." [218]

At that moment Ishmael was pious indeed, for he was
praying to God in the following words: " O Lord of the
world! If it be Thy will that I shall perish, then let me die
in some other way, not by thirst, for the tortures of thirst
are great beyond all others." Hagar, instead of praying to
God, addressed her supplications to the idols of her youth.
The prayer of Ishmael was acceptable before God, and He
bade Miriam's well spring up, the well created in the twilight of the sixth day of creation.[219] Even after this miracle
Hagar's faith was no stronger than before. She filled the
bottle with water, because she feared it might again be
spent, and no other would be nigh. Thereupon she journeyed to Egypt with her son, for " Throw the stick into the
air as thou wilt, it will always land on its point." Hagar

had come from Egypt, and to Egypt she returned, to choose a wife for her son.²¹

THE TWO WIVES OF ISHMAEL

The wife of Ishmael bore four sons and a daughter, and afterward Ishmael, his mother, and his wife and children went and returned to the wilderness. They made themselves tents in the wilderness in which they dwelt, and they continued to encamp and journey, month by month and year by year. And God gave Ishmael flocks, and herds, and tents, on account of Abraham his father, and the man increased in cattle. And some time after, Abraham said to Sarah, his wife, " I will go and see my son Ishmael; I yearn to look upon him, for I have not seen him for a long time." And Abraham rode upon one of his camels to the wilderness, to seek his son Ishmael, for he heard that he was dwelling in a tent in the wilderness with all belonging to him. And Abraham went to the wilderness, and he reached the tent of Ishmael about noon, and he asked after him. He found the wife of Ishmael sitting in the tent with her children, and her husband and his mother were not with them. And Abraham asked the wife of Ishmael, saying, " Where has Ishmael gone? " And she said, " He has gone to the field to hunt game." And Abraham was still mounted upon the camel, for he would not alight upon the ground, as he had sworn to his wife Sarah that he would not get off from the camel. And Abraham said to Ishmael's wife, " My daughter, give me a little water, that I may drink, for I am fatigued and tired from the journey." And Ishmael's wife answered and said to Abraham, " We have neither water

nor bread," and she was sitting in the tent, and did not take
any notice of Abraham. She did not even ask him who he
was. But all the while she was beating her children in the
tent, and she was cursing them, and she also cursed her husband Ishmael, and spoke evil of him, and Abraham heard
the words of Ishmael's wife to her children, and it was an
evil thing in his eyes. And Abraham called to the woman to
come out to him from the tent, and the woman came out, and
stood face to face with Abraham, while Abraham was still
mounted upon the camel. And Abraham said to Ishmael's
wife, "When thy husband Ishmael returns home, say these
words to him: A very old man from the land of the Philistines came hither to seek thee, and his appearance was thus
and so, and thus was his figure. I did not ask him who he
was, and seeing thou wast not here, he spoke unto me, and
said, When Ishmael thy husband returns, tell him, Thus did
the man say, When thou comest home, put away this tent-
pin which thou hast placed here, and place another tent-pin
in its stead." And Abraham finished his instructions to the
woman, and he turned and went off on the camel homeward.
And when Ishmael returned to the tent, he heard the words
of his wife, and he knew that it was his father, and that his
wife had not honored him. And Ishmael understood his
father's words that he had spoken to his wife, and he
hearkened to the voice of his father, and he divorced
his wife, and she went away. And Ishmael afterward went
to the land of Canaan, and he took another wife, and he
brought her to his tent, to the place where he dwelt.

And at the end of three years, Abraham said, "I will go
again and see Ishmael my son, for I have not seen him for a

long time." And he rode upon his camel, and went to the wilderness, and he reached the tent of Ishmael about noon. And he asked after Ishmael, and his wife came out of the tent, and she said, " He is not here, my lord, for he has gone to hunt in the fields and feed the camels," and the woman said to Abraham, " Turn in, my lord, into the tent, and eat a morsel of bread, for thy soul must be wearied on account of the journey." And Abraham said to her, " I will not stop, for I am in haste to continue my journey, but give me a little water to drink, for I am thirsty," and the woman hastened and ran into the tent, and she brought out water and bread to Abraham, which she placed before him, urging him to eat and drink, and he ate and drank, and his heart was merry, and he blessed his son Ishmael. And he finished his meal, and he blessed the Lord, and he said to Ishmael's wife: " When Ishmael comes home, say these words to him: A very old man from the land of the Philistines came hither, and asked after thee, and thou wast not here, and I brought him out bread and water, and he ate and drank, and his heart was merry. And he spoke these words to me, When Ishmael thy husband comes home, say unto him, The tent-pin which thou hast is very good, do not put it away from the tent." And Abraham finished commanding the woman, and he rode off to his home, to the land of the Philistines, and when Ishmael came to his tent, his wife went forth to meet him with joy and a cheerful heart, and she told him the words of the old man. Ishmael knew that it was his father, and that his wife had honored him, and he praised the Lord. And Ishmael then took his wife and his children and his cattle and all belonging to him, and he journeyed from there, and he went to his father in the land of the Philistines. And Abraham related to Ishmael all that had happened between him and the first wife that Ishmael had taken, according to what she had done. And Ishmael and his children dwelt with Abraham many days in that land, and Abraham dwelt in the land of the Philistines a long time.[218]

THE COVENANT WITH ABIMELECH

After a sojourn of twenty-six years in the land of the Philistines, Abraham departed thence, and he settled in the neighborhood of Hebron. There he was visited by Abimelech with twenty of his grandees,[219] who requested him to make an alliance with the Philistines.

As long as Abraham was childless, the heathen did not believe in his piety, but when Isaac was born, they said to him, " God is with thee." But again they entertained doubt of his piety when he cast off Ishmael. They said, " Were he a righteous man, he would not drive his first-born forth from his house." But when they observed the impious deeds of Ishmael, they said, " God is with thee in all thou doest." That Abraham was the favorite of God, they saw in this, too, that although Sodom was destroyed and all traffic had come to a standstill in that region, yet Abraham's treasure chambers were filled. For these reasons, the Philistines sought to form an alliance with him, to remain in force for three generations to come, for it is to the third generation that the love of a father extends.

Before Abraham concluded the covenant with Abimelech, king of the Philistines, he reproved him on account of a well, for " Correction leads to love," and " There is no peace

without correction." The herdmen of Abraham and those
of Abimelech had left their dispute about the well to decision
by ordeal: the well was to belong to the party for whose
sheep the waters would rise so that they could drink of them.
But the shepherds of Abimelech disregarded the agreement,
and they wrested the well for their own use.[320] As a witness
and a perpetual sign that the well belonged to him, Abraham
set aside seven sheep, corresponding to the seven Noachian
laws binding upon all men alike.[321] But God said, " Thou
didst give him seven sheep. As thou livest, the Philistines
shall one day slay seven righteous men, Samson, Hophni,
Phinehas, and Saul with his three sons, and they will destroy
seven holy places, and they will keep the holy Ark in their
country as booty of war for a period of seven months, and
furthermore only the seventh generation of thy descendants
will be able to rejoice in the possession of the land promised
to them." [322] After concluding the alliance with Abimelech,
who acknowledged Abraham's right upon the well, Abraham
called the place Beer-sheba, because there they swore both
of them unto a covenant of friendship.

In Beer-sheba Abraham dwelt many years, and thence he
endeavored to spread the law of God. He planted a large
grove there, and he made four gates for it, facing the four
sides of the earth, east, west, north, and south, and he
planted a vineyard therein. If a traveller came that way, he
entered by the gate that faced him, and he sat in the grove,
and ate, and drank, until he was satisfied, and then he departed. For the house of Abraham was always open for all
passers-by, and they came daily to eat and drink there. If
one was hungry, and he came to Abraham, he would give

him what he needed, so that he might eat and drink and be
satisfied; and if one was naked, and he came to Abraham,
he would clothe him with the garments of the poor man's
choice, and give him silver and gold, and make known to
him the Lord, who had created him and set him on earth.[22]
After the wayfarers had eaten, they were in the habit of
thanking Abraham for his kind entertainment of them,
whereto he would reply: "What, ye give thanks unto me!
Rather return thanks to your host, He who alone provides
food and drink for all creatures." Then the people would
ask, "Where is He?" and Abraham would answer them,
and say: "He is the Ruler of heaven and earth. He
woundeth and He healeth, He formeth the embryo in the
womb of the mother and bringeth it forth into the world,
He causeth the plants and the trees to grow, He killeth and
He maketh alive, He bringeth down to Sheol and bringeth
up." When the people heard such words, they would ask,
"How shall we return thanks to God and manifest our
gratitude unto Him?" And Abraham would instruct them
in these words: "Say, Blessed be the Lord who is blessed!
Blessed be He that giveth bread and food unto all flesh!"
In this manner did Abraham teach those who had enjoyed
his hospitality how to praise and thank God.[24] Abraham's
house thus became not only a lodging-place for the hungry
and thirsty, but also a place of instruction where the knowledge of God and His law were taught.[25]

SATAN ACCUSES ABRAHAM

In spite of the lavish hospitality practiced in the house of
Abraham, it happened once that a poor man, or rather an

alleged poor man, was turned away empty-handed, and this was the immediate reason for the last of Abraham's temptations, the sacrifice of his favorite son Isaac. It was the day on which Abraham celebrated the birth of Isaac with a great banquet, to which all the magnates of the time were bidden with their wives. Satan, who always appears at a feast in which no poor people participate, and keeps aloof from those to which poor guests are invited, turned up at Abraham's banquet in the guise of a beggar asking alms at the door. He had noticed that Abraham had invited no poor man, and he knew that his house was the right place for him.

Abraham was occupied with the entertainment of his distinguished guests, and Sarah was endeavoring to convince their wives, the matrons, that Isaac was her child in very truth, and not a spurious child. No one concerned himself about the beggar at the door, who thereupon accused Abraham before God.[226]

Now, there was a day when the sons of God came to present themselves before the Lord, and Satan came also among them.[227] And the Lord said unto Satan, "From whence comest thou?" and Satan answered the Lord, and said, "From going to and fro on the earth, and from walking up and down in it." And the Lord said unto Satan, "What hast thou to say concerning all the children of the earth?" and Satan answered the Lord, and said: "I have seen all the children of the earth serving Thee and remembering Thee, when they require aught from Thee. And when Thou givest them what they require from Thee, then they forsake Thee, and they remember Thee no more. Hast Thou seen

Abraham, the son of Terah, who at first had no children, and he served Thee and erected altars to Thee wherever he came, and he brought offerings upon them, and he proclaimed Thy name continually to all the children of the earth? And now his son Isaac is born to him, he has forsaken Thee. He made a great feast for all the inhabitants of the land, and the Lord he has forgotten. For amidst all that he has done, he brought Thee no offering, neither burnt offering nor peace offering, neither one lamb nor goat of all that he had killed in the day that his son was weaned. Even from the time of his son's birth till now, being thirty-seven years, he built no altar before Thee, nor brought up any offering to Thee, for he saw that Thou didst give what he requested before Thee, and he therefore forsook Thee." And the Lord said to Satan: "Hast thou considered My servant Abraham? For there is none like him in the earth, a perfect and an upright man before Me for a burnt offering, and that feareth God and escheweth evil. As I live, were I to say unto him, Bring up Isaac thy son before Me, he would not withhold him from Me, much less if I told him to bring up a burnt offering before Me from his flocks or herds." And Satan answered the Lord, and said, "Speak now unto Abraham as Thou hast said, and Thou wilt see whether he will not transgress and cast aside Thy words this day." [128]

God wished to try Isaac also. Ishmael once boasted to Isaac, saying, "I was thirteen years old when the Lord spoke to my father to circumcise us, and I did not transgress His word, which He commanded my father." And Isaac answered Ishmael, saying, "What dost thou boast to me about this, about a little bit of thy flesh which thou didst take from thy body, concerning which the Lord commanded thee? As the Lord liveth, the God of my father Abraham, if the Lord should say unto my father, Take now thy son Isaac and bring him up as an offering before Me, I would not refrain, but I would joyfully accede to it."

THE JOURNEY TO MORIAH

And the Lord thought to try Abraham and Isaac in this matter.[289] And He said to Abraham, " Take now thy son."

Abraham: " I have two sons, and I do not know which of them Thou commandest me to take."

God: " Thine only son."

Abraham: " The one is the only son of his mother, and the other is the only son of his mother."

God: " Whom thou lovest."

Abraham: " I love this one and I love that one."

God: " Even Isaac." [290]

Abraham: " And where shall I go? "

God: " To the land I will show thee, and offer Isaac there for a burnt offering."

Abraham: " Am I fit to perform the sacrifice, am I a priest? Ought not rather the high priest Shem to do it? "

God: " When thou wilt arrive at that place, I will consecrate thee and make thee a priest." [291]

And Abraham said within himself, " How shall I separate my son Isaac from Sarah his mother? " And he came into the tent, and he sate before Sarah his wife, and he spake these words to her: " My son Isaac is grown up, and he has not yet studied the service of God. Now, to-morrow I will go and bring him to Shem and Eber his son, and there he

will learn the ways of the Lord, for they will teach him to
know the Lord, and to know how to pray unto the Lord
that He may answer him, and to know the way of serving
the Lord his God." And Sarah said, " Thou hast spoken
well. Go, my lord, and do unto him as thou hast said,
but remove him not far from me, neither let him remain
there too long, for my soul is bound within his soul." And
Abraham said unto Sarah, " My daughter, let us pray to the
Lord our God that He may do good with us." And Sarah
took her son Isaac, and he abode with her all that night, and
she kissed and embraced him, and she laid injunctions upon
him till morning, and she said to Abraham: " O my lord,
I pray thee, take heed of thy son, and place thine eyes over
him, for I have no other son nor daughter but him. O neglect him not. If he be hungry, give him bread, and if he be
thirsty, give him water to drink; do not let him go on foot,
neither let him sit in the sun, neither let him go by himself
on the road, neither turn him from whatever he may desire,
but do unto him as he may say to thee."

After spending the whole night in weeping on account of
Isaac, she got up in the morning and selected a very fine
and beautiful garment from those that Abimelech had given
to her. And she dressed Isaac therewith, and she put a
turban upon his head, and she fastened a precious stone in
the top of the turban, and she gave them provisions for the
road. And Sarah went out with them, and she accompanied
them upon the road to see them off, and they said to her,
" Return to the tent." And when Sarah heard the words of
her son Isaac, she wept bitterly, and Abraham wept with
her, and their son wept with them, a great weeping, also

those of their servants who went with them wept greatly. And Sarah caught hold of Isaac, and she held him in her arms, and she embraced him, and continued to weep with him, and Sarah said, " Who knoweth if I shall ever see thee again after this day? "

Abraham departed with Isaac amid great weeping, while Sarah and the servants returned to the tent.[233] He took two of his young men with him, Ishmael and Eliezer, and while they were walking in the road, the young men spoke these words to each other. Said Ishmael to Eliezer: " Now my father Abraham is going with Isaac to bring him up for a burnt offering to the Lord, and when he returneth, he will give unto me all that he possesses, to inherit after him, for I am his first-born." Eliezer answered: " Surely, Abraham did cast thee off with thy mother, and swear that thou shouldst not inherit anything of all he possesses. And to whom will he give all that he has, all his precious things, but unto his servant, who has been faithful in his house, to me, who have served him night and day, and have done all that he desired me? " The holy spirit answered, " Neither this one nor that one will inherit Abraham." [233]

And while Abraham and Isaac were proceeding along the road, Satan came and appeared to Abraham in the figure of a very aged man, humble and of contrite spirit, and said to him: " Art thou silly or foolish, that thou goest to do this thing to thine only son? God gave thee a son in thy latter days, in thine old age, and wilt thou go and slaughter him, who did not commit any violence; and wilt thou cause the soul of thine only son to perish from the earth? Dost thou not know and understand that this thing cannot be from the

Lord? For the Lord would not do unto man such evil, to command him, Go and slaughter thy son." Abraham, hearing these words, knew that it was Satan, who endeavored to turn him astray from the way of the Lord, and he rebuked him that he went away. And Satan returned and came to Isaac, and he appeared unto him in the figure of a young man, comely and well-favored, saying unto him: "Dost thou not know that thy silly old father bringeth thee to the slaughter this day for naught? Now, my son, do not listen to him, for he is a silly old man, and let not thy precious soul and beautiful figure be lost from the earth." And Isaac told these words to his father, but Abraham said to him, "Take heed of him, and do not listen to his words, for he is Satan endeavoring to lead us astray from the commands of our God." And Abraham rebuked Satan again, and Satan went from them, and, seeing he could not prevail over them, he transformed himself into a large brook of water in the road, and when Abraham, Isaac, and the two young men reached that place, they saw a brook large and powerful as the mighty waters. And they entered the brook, trying to pass it, but the further they went, the deeper the brook, so that the water reached up to their necks, and they were all terrified on account of the water. But Abraham recognized the place, and he knew that there had been no water there before, and he said to his son: "I know this place, on which there was no brook nor water. Now, surely, it is Satan who doth all this to us, to draw us aside this day from the commands of God." And Abraham rebuked Satan, saying unto him: "The Lord rebuke thee, O Satan. Begone from us, for we go by the command of God." And Satan was terrified at the voice of Abraham, and he went away from them, and the place became dry land again as it was at first. And Abraham went with Isaac toward the place that God had told him.[236]

Satan then appeared unto Sarah in the figure of an old man, and said unto her, "Where did thine husband go?" She said, "To his work." "And where did thy son Isaac go?" he inquired further, and she answered, "He went with his father to a place of study of the Torah." Satan said: "O thou poor old woman, thy teeth will be set on edge on account of thy son, as thou knowest not that Abraham took his son with him on the road to sacrifice him." In this hour Sarah's loins trembled, and all her limbs shook. She was no more of this world. Nevertheless she aroused herself, and said, "All that God hath told Abraham, may he do it unto life and unto peace."[235]

On the third day of his journey, Abraham lifted up his eyes and saw the place at a distance, which God had told him. He noticed upon the mountain a pillar of fire reaching from the earth to heaven, and a heavy cloud in which the glory of God was seen. Abraham said to Isaac, "My son, dost thou see on that mountain which we perceive at a distance that which I see upon it?" And Isaac answered, and said unto his father, "I see, and, lo, a pillar of fire and a cloud, and the glory of the Lord is seen upon the cloud." Abraham knew then that Isaac was accepted before the Lord for an offering. He asked Ishmael and Eliezer, "Do you also see that which we see upon the mountain?" They answered, "We see nothing more than like the other mountains," and Abraham knew that they were not accepted be-

fore the Lord to go with them.³³⁰   Abraham said to them,
" Abide ye here with the ass, you are like the ass—as little
as it sees, so little do you see."³³¹   I and Isaac my son go
to yonder mount, and worship there before the Lord, and
this eve we will return to you."³³²   An unconscious prophecy
had come to Abraham, for he prophesied that he and Isaac
would both return from the mountain.³³³   Eliezer and Ishmael remained in that place, as Abraham had commanded,
while he and Isaac went further.

The 'Aḳedah

And while they were walking along, Isaac spake unto his
father, " Behold, the fire and the wood, but where then is
the lamb for a burnt offering before the Lord? "   And
Abraham answered Isaac, saying, " The Lord hath chosen
thee, my son, for a perfect burnt offering, instead of the
lamb."   And Isaac said unto his father, " I will do all that
the Lord hath spoken to thee with joy and cheerfulness of
heart."   And Abraham again said unto Isaac his son, " Is
there in thy heart any thought or counsel concerning this
which is not proper?   Tell me, my son, I pray thee !   O my
son, conceal it not from me."   And Isaac answered, " As
the Lord liveth, and as thy soul liveth, there is nothing in
my heart to cause me to deviate either to the right or the left
from the word that He hath spoken unto thee.   Neither limb
nor muscle hath moved or stirred on account of this, nor is
there in my heart any thought or evil counsel concerning
this.   But I am joyful and cheerful of heart in this matter,
and I say, Blessed is the Lord who has this day chosen me
to be a burnt offering before Him."

Abraham greatly rejoiced at the words of Isaac, and they went on and came together to that place that the Lord had spoken of. And Abraham approached to build the altar in that place, and Abraham did build, while Isaac handed him stones and mortar, until they finished erecting the altar. And Abraham took the wood and arranged it upon the altar, and he bound Isaac, to place him upon the wood which was upon the altar, to slay him for a burnt offering before the Lord. Isaac spake hereupon: " Father, make haste, bare thine arm, and bind my hands and feet securely, for I am a young man, but thirty-seven years of age, and thou art an old man. When I behold the slaughtering knife in thy hand, I may perchance begin to tremble at the sight and push against thee, for the desire unto life is bold. Also I may do myself an injury and make myself unfit to be sacrificed. I adjure thee, therefore, my father, make haste, execute the will of thy Creator, delay not. Turn up thy garment, gird thy loins, and after that thou hast slaughtered me, burn me unto fine ashes. Then gather the ashes, and bring them to Sarah, my mother, and place them in a casket in her chamber. At all hours, whenever she enters her chamber, she will remember her son Isaac and weep for him."

And again Isaac spoke: " As soon as thou hast slaughtered me, and hast separated thyself from me, and returnest to Sarah my mother, and she asketh thee, Where is my son Isaac? what wilt thou answer her, and what will you two do in your old age? " Abraham answered, and said, " We know we can survive thee by a few days only. He who was our Comfort before thou wast born, will comfort us now and henceforth."

After he had laid the wood in order, and bound Isaac on the altar, upon the wood, Abraham braced his arms, rolled up his garments, and leaned his knees upon Isaac with all his strength. And God, sitting upon His throne, high and exalted, saw how the hearts of the two were the same, and tears were rolling down from the eyes of Abraham upon Isaac, and from Isaac down upon the wood, so that it was submerged in tears. When Abraham stretched forth his hand, and took the knife to slay his son, God spoke to the angels: "Do you see how Abraham my friend proclaims the unity of My Name in the world? Had I hearkened unto you at the time of the creation of the world, when ye spake, What is man, that Thou art mindful of him? And the son of man, that Thou visitest him? who would there have been to make known the unity of My Name in this world?" The angels then broke into loud weeping, and they exclaimed: "The highways lie waste, the wayfaring man ceaseth, he hath broken the covenant. Where is the reward of Abraham, he who took the wayfarers into his house, gave them food and drink, and went with them to bring them on the way? The covenant is broken, whereof Thou didst speak to him, saying, 'For in Isaac shall thy seed be called,' and saying, 'My covenant will I establish with Isaac,' for the slaughtering knife is set upon his throat."

The tears of the angels fell upon the knife, so that it could not cut Isaac's throat, but from terror his soul escaped from him. Then God spoke to the archangel Michael, and said: "Why standest thou here? Let him not be slaughtered." Without delay, Michael, anguish in his voice, cried out: "Abraham! Abraham! Lay not thine hand upon the lad, neither do thou any thing unto him!" Abraham made answer, and he said: "God did command me to slaughter Isaac, and thou dost command me not to slaughter him! The words of the Teacher and the words of the disciple—unto whose words doth one hearken?"[342] Then Abraham heard it said: "By Myself have I sworn, saith the Lord, because thou hast done this thing, and hast not withheld thy son, thine only son, that in blessing I will bless thee, and in multiplying I will multiply thy seed as the stars of the heaven, and as the sand which is upon the sea-shore; and thy seed shall possess the gate of his enemies, and in thy seed shall all the nations of the earth be blessed, because thou hast obeyed My voice."

At once Abraham left off from Isaac, who returned to life, revived by the heavenly voice admonishing Abraham not to slaughter his son. Abraham loosed his bonds, and Isaac stood upon his feet, and spoke the benediction, "Blessed art Thou, O Lord, who quickenest the dead."[343]

Then spake Abraham to God, "Shall I go hence without having offered up a sacrifice?" Whereunto God replied, and said, "Lift up thine eyes, and behold the sacrifice behind thee."[344] And Abraham lifted up his eyes, and, behold, behind him a ram caught in the thicket, which God had created in the twilight of Sabbath eve in the week of creation, and prepared since then as a burnt offering instead of Isaac. And the ram had been running toward Abraham, when Satan caught hold of him and entangled his horns in the thicket, that he might not advance to Abraham. And Abraham, seeing this, fetched him from the thicket, and brought him upon the altar as an offering in the place of his

son Isaac. And Abraham sprinkled the blood of the ram
upon the altar, and he exclaimed, and said, " This is instead
of my son, and may this be considered as the blood of my
son before the Lord." And whatsoever Abraham did by
the altar, he exclaimed, and said, " This is instead of my
son, and may it be considered before the Lord in place of
my son." And God accepted the sacrifice of the ram, and
it was accounted as though it had been Isaac.[245]

As the creation of this ram had been extraordinary, so
also was the use to which all parts of his carcass were put.
Not one thing went to waste. The ashes of the parts burnt
upon the altar formed the foundation of the inner altar,
whereon the expiatory sacrifice was brought once a year,
on the Day of Atonement, the day on which the offering of
Isaac took place. Of the sinews of the ram, David made ten
strings for his harp upon which he played. The skin served
Elijah for his girdle, and of his two horns, the one was
blown at the end of the revelation on Mount Sinai, and the
other will be used to proclaim the end of the Exile, when the
" great horn shall be blown, and they shall come which were
ready to perish in the land of Assyria, and they that were
outcasts in the land of Egypt, and they shall worship the
Lord in the holy mountain at Jerusalem." [246]

When God commanded the father to desist from sacri-
ficing Isaac, Abraham said: " One man tempts another,
because he knoweth not what is in the heart of his neighbor. But Thou surely didst know that I was ready to sacrifice my son ! "

God: " It was manifest to Me, and I foreknew it, that
thou wouldst withhold not even thy soul from Me."

Abraham: "And why, then, didst Thou afflict me thus?"

God: "It was My wish that the world should become acquainted with thee, and should know that it is not without good reason that I have chosen thee from all the nations. Now it hath been witnessed unto men that thou fearest God." [247]

Hereupon God opened the heavens, and Abraham heard the words, "By Myself I swear!"

Abraham: "Thou swearest, and also I swear, I will not leave this altar until I have said what I have to say."

God: "Speak whatsoever thou hast to speak!"

Abraham: "Didst Thou not promise me Thou wouldst let one come forth out of mine own bowels, whose seed should fill the whole world?"

God: "Yes."

Abraham: "Whom didst Thou mean?"

God: "Isaac."

Abraham: "Didst Thou not promise me to make my seed as numerous as the sand of the sea-shore?"

God: "Yes."

Abraham: "Through which one of my children?"

God: "Through Isaac."

Abraham: "I might have reproached Thee, and said, O Lord of the world, yesterday Thou didst tell me, In Isaac shall Thy seed be called, and now Thou sayest, Take thy son, thine only son, even Isaac, and offer him for a burnt offering. But I refrained myself, and I said nothing. Thus mayest Thou, when the children of Isaac commit trespasses and because of them fall upon evil times, be mindful of the offering of their father Isaac, and forgive their sins and deliver them from their suffering."

God: "Thou hast said what thou hadst to say, and I will now say what I have to say. Thy children will sin before me in time to come, and I will sit in judgment upon them on the New Year's Day. If they desire that I should grant them pardon, they shall blow the ram's horn on that day, and I, mindful of the ram that was substituted for Isaac as a sacrifice, will forgive them for their sins." [248]

Furthermore, the Lord revealed unto Abraham that the Temple, to be erected on the spot of Isaac's offering, would be destroyed,[249] and as the ram substituted for Isaac extricated himself from one tree but to be caught in another, so his children would pass from kingdom to kingdom—delivered from Babylonia they would be subjugated by Media, rescued from Media they would be enslaved by Greece, escaped from Greece they would serve Rome—yet in the end they would be redeemed in a final redemption, at the sound of the ram's horn, when "the Lord God shall blow the trumpet, and shall go with whirlwinds of the south." [250]

The place on which Abraham had erected the altar was the same whereon Adam had brought the first sacrifice, and Cain and Abel had offered their gifts to God—the same whereon Noah raised an altar to God after he left the ark ;[251] and Abraham, who knew that it was the place appointed for the Temple, called it Yireh, for it would be the abiding-place of the fear and the service of God.[252] But as Shem had given it the name Shalem, Place of Peace, and God would not give offence to either Abraham or Shem, He united the two names, and called the city by the name Jerusalem.[253]

After the sacrifice on Mount Moriah, Abraham returned to Beer-sheba, the scene of so many of his joys.[254] Isaac was carried to Paradise by angels, and there he sojourned for three years. Thus Abraham returned home alone, and when Sarah beheld him, she exclaimed, " Satan spoke truth when he said that Isaac was sacrificed," and so grieved was her soul that it fled from her body.[385]

THE DEATH AND BURIAL OF SARAH

While Abraham was engaged in the sacrifice, Satan went to Sarah, and appeared to her in the figure of an old man, very humble and meek, and said to her: " Dost thou not know all that Abraham has done unto thine only son this day? He took Isaac, and built an altar, slaughtered him, and brought him up as a sacrifice. Isaac cried and wept before his father, but he looked not at him, neither did he have compassion upon him." After saying these words to Sarah, Satan went away from her, and she thought him to be an old man from amongst the sons of men who had been with her son. Sarah lifted up her voice, and cried bitterly, saying: " O my son, Isaac, my son, O that I had this day died instead of thee! It grieves me for thee! After that I have reared thee and have brought thee up, my joy is turned into mourning over thee. In my longing for a child, I cried and prayed, till I bore thee at ninety. Now hast thou served this day for the knife and the fire. But I console myself, it being the word of God, and thou didst perform the command of thy God, for who can transgress the word of our God, in whose hands is the soul of every living creature? Thou art just, O Lord our God, for all Thy works are good and righteous, for I also rejoice with the word which Thou didst command, and while mine eye weepeth bitterly, my

heart rejoiceth." And Sarah laid her head upon the bosom
of one of her handmaids, and she became as still as a stone.

She rose up afterward and went about making inquiries
concerning her son, till she came to Hebron, and no one
could tell her what had happened to her son. Her servants
went to seek him in the house of Shem and Eber, and they
could not find him, and they sought throughout the land, and
he was not there. And, behold, Satan came to Sarah in the
shape of an old man, and said unto her, "I spoke falsely
unto thee, for Abraham did not kill his son, and he is not
dead," and when she heard the word, her joy was so exceedingly violent that her soul went out through joy.

When Abraham with Isaac returned to Beer-sheba, they
sought for Sarah and could not find her, and when they
made inquiries concerning her, they were told that she had
gone as far as Hebron to seek them. Abraham and Isaac
went to her to Hebron, and when they found that she was
dead, they cried bitterly over her, and Isaac said: "O my
mother, my mother, how hast thou left me, and whither hast
thou gone? O whither hast thou gone, and how hast thou
left me?" And Abraham and all his servants wept and
mourned over her a great and heavy mourning,[206] even that
Abraham did not pray, but spent his time in mourning and
weeping over Sarah.[207] And, indeed, he had great reason to
mourn his loss, for even in her old age Sarah had retained
the beauty of her youth and the innocence of her childhood.[208]

The death of Sarah was a loss not only for Abraham and
his family, but for the whole country. So long as she was
alive, all went well in the land. After her death confusion
ensued. The weeping, lamenting, and wailing over her

going hence was universal, and Abraham, instead of receiving consolation, had to offer consolation to others. He spoke to the mourning people, and said: " My children, take not the going hence of Sarah too much to heart. There is one event unto all, to the pious and the impious alike. I pray you now, give me a burying-place with you, not as a gift, but for money." [259]

In these last few words Abraham's unassuming modesty was expressed. God had promised him the whole land, yet when he came to bury his dead, he had to pay for the grave, and it did not enter his heart to cast aspersions upon the ways of God. In all humility he spake to the people of Hebron, saying, " I am a stranger and a sojourner with you." Therefore spake God to him, and said, " Thou didst bear thyself modestly. As thou livest, I will appoint thee lord and prince over them." [260]

To the people themselves he appeared an angel, and they answered his words, saying: " Thou art a prince of God among us. In the choice of our sepulchres bury thy dead, among the rich if thou wilt, or among the poor if thou wilt." [261]

Abraham first of all gave thanks to God for the friendly feeling shown to him by the children of Heth, and then he continued his negotiations for the Cave of Machpelah. [262] He had long known the peculiar value of this spot. Adam had chosen it as a burial-place for himself. He had feared his body might be used for idolatrous purposes after his death; he therefore designated the Cave of Machpelah as the place of his burial, and in the depths his corpse was laid, so that none might find it. [263] When he interred Eve there, he

wanted to dig deeper, because he scented the sweet fragrance
of Paradise, near the entrance to which it lay, but a heavenly voice called to him, Enough! Adam himself was buried
there by Seth, and until the time of Abraham the place was
guarded by angels, who kept a fire burning near it per-
petually, so that none dared approach it and bury his dead
therein.[264] Now, it happened on the day when Abraham
received the angels in his house, and he wanted to slaughter
an ox for their entertainment, that the ox ran away, and in
his pursuit of him Abraham entered the Cave of Machpelah.
There he saw Adam and Eve stretched out upon couches,
candles burning at the head of their resting-places, while a
sweet scent pervaded the cave.

Therefore Abraham wished to acquire the Cave of Machpelah from the children of Heth, the inhabitants of the city
of Jebus. They said to him, " We know that in time to come
God will give these lands unto thy seed, and now do thou
swear a covenant with us that Israel shall not wrest the city
of Jebus from its inhabitants without their consent." Abraham agreed to the condition, and he acquired the field from
Ephron, in whose possession it lay.[265]

This happened the very day on which Ephron had been
made the chief of the children of Heth, and he had been
raised to the position so that Abraham might not have to
have dealings with a man of low rank. It was of advantage
to Abraham, too, for Ephron at first refused to sell his field,
and only the threat of the children of Heth to depose him
from his office, unless he fulfilled the desire of Abraham,
could induce him to change his disposition.[266]

Dissembling deceitfully, Ephron then offered to give

Abraham the field without compensation, but when Abraham insisted upon paying for it, Ephron said: "My lord, hearken unto me. A piece of land worth four hundred shekels of silver, what is that betwixt me and thee?" showing only too well that the money was of the greatest consequence to him. Abraham understood his words, and when he came to pay for the field, he weighed out the sum agreed upon between them in the best of current coin.[287] A deed, signed by four witnesses, was drawn up, and the field of Ephron, which was in Machpelah, the field, and the cave which was therein, were made sure unto Abraham and his descendants for all times.

The burial of Sarah then took place, amid great magnificence and the sympathy of all. Shem and his son Eber, Abimelech king of the Philistines, Aner, Eshcol, and Mamre, as well as all the great of the land, followed her bier. A seven days' mourning was kept for her, and all the inhabitants of the land came to condole with Abraham and Isaac.[288]

When Abraham entered the cave to place the body of Sarah within, Adam and Eve refused to remain there, " because," they said, " as it is, we are ashamed in the presence of God on account of the sin we committed, and now we shall be even more ashamed on account of your good deeds." Abraham soothed Adam. He promised to pray to God for him, that the need for shame be removed from him. Adam resumed his place, and Abraham entombed Sarah, and at the same time he carried Eve, resisting, back to her place.[289]

One year after the death of Sarah, Abimelech king of the Philistines died, too, at the age of one hundred and ninety-three years. His successor upon the throne was his twelve

year old son Benmelek, who took the name of his father
after his accession. Abraham did not fail to pay a visit of
condolence at the court of Abimelech.

Lot also died about this time, at the age of one hundred
and forty-two. His sons, Moab and Ammon, both married
Canaanitish wives. Moab begot a son, and Ammon had
six sons, and the descendants of both were numerous
exceedingly.

Abraham suffered a severe loss at the same time in the
death of his brother Nahor, whose days ended at Haran,
when he had reached the age of one hundred and seventy-
two years.[270]

ELIEZER'S MISSION

The death of Sarah dealt Abraham a blow from which
he did not recover. So long as she was alive, he felt himself young and vigorous, but after she had passed away, old
age suddenly overtook him.[271] It was he himself who made
the plea that age be betrayed by suitable signs and tokens.
Before the time of Abraham an old man was not distin
guishable externally from a young man, and as Isaac was
the image of his father, it happened frequently that father
and son were mistaken for each other, and a request meant
for the one was preferred to the other. Abraham prayed
therefore that old age might have marks to distinguish it
from youth, and God granted his petition, and since the time
of Abraham the appearance of men changes in old age.
This is one of the seven great wonders that have occurred
in the course of history.[272]

The blessing of God did not forsake Abraham in old age,

either. That it might not be said it had been granted to him only for the sake of Sarah, God prospered him after her death, too. Hagar bore him a daughter, and Ishmael repented of his evil ways and subordinated himself to Isaac. And as Abraham enjoyed undisturbed happiness in his family, so also outside, in the world. The kings of the east and the west eagerly besieged the door of his house in order to derive benefit from his wisdom. From his neck a precious stone was suspended, which possessed the power of healing the sick who looked upon it. On the death of Abraham, God attached it to the wheel of the sun. The greatest blessing enjoyed by him, and by none beside except his son Isaac and Jacob the son of Isaac, was that the evil inclination had no power over him, so that in this life he had a foretaste of the future world.[373]

But all these Divine blessings showered upon Abraham were not undeserved. He was clean of hand, and pure of heart, one that did not lift up his soul unto vanity.[374]

He fulfilled all the commands that were revealed later, even the Rabbinical injunctions, as, for instance, the one relating to the limits of a Sabbath day's journey, wherefor his reward was that God disclosed to him the new teachings which He expounded daily in the heavenly academy.[375]

But one thing lacked to complete the happiness of Abraham, the marriage of Isaac. He therefore called his old servant Eliezer unto himself. Eliezer resembled his master not only externally, in his appearance, but also spiritually. Like Abraham he possessed full power over the evil inclination,[376] and like the master, the servant was an adept in the law.[377] Abraham spake the following words to Eliezer: " I

am stricken in age, and I know not the day of my death.
Therefore prepare thyself, and go unto my country, and to
my kindred, and fetch hither a wife for my son." [278] Thus
he spake by reason of the resolution he had taken immediately after the sacrifice of Isaac on Moriah, for he had there
said within himself, that if the sacrifice had been executed,
Isaac would have gone hence childless. He was even ready
to choose a wife for his son from among the daughters of
his three friends, Aner, Eshcol, and Mamre, because he
knew them to be pious, and he did not attach much importance to aristocratic stock. Then spake God to him, and
said: "Concern thyself not about a wife for Isaac." [279] One
has already been provided for him," and it was made known
to Abraham that Milcah, the wife of his brother Nahor,
childless until the birth of Isaac, had then been remembered
by God and made fruitful. She bore Bethuel, and he in turn,
at the time of Isaac's sacrifice, begot the daughter destined
to be the wife of Isaac. [280]

Mindful of the proverb, "Even if the wheat of thine own
place be darnel, use it for seed," Abraham determined to
take a wife for Isaac from his own family. He argued that
as any wife he chose would have to become a proselyte, it
would be best to use his own stock, which had the first claim
upon him. [281]

Eliezer now said to his master: "Peradventure no woman
will be willing to follow me unto this land. May I then
marry my own daughter to Isaac?" "No," replied Abraham, "thou art of the accursed race, and my son is of the
blessed race, and curse and blessing cannot be united. [282] But
beware thou that thou bring not my son again unto the land

from whence I came, for if thou broughtest him thither
again, it were as though thou tookest him to hell. God who
sets the heavens in motion, He will set this matter right,
too,[283] and He that took me from my father's house, and that
spake unto me, and that swore unto me in Haran, and at the
covenant of the pieces, that He would give this land unto
my seed, He shall send His excellent angel before thee, and
thou shalt take a wife for my son from thence." Eliezer
then swore to his master concerning the matter, and Abraham made him take the oath by the sign of the covenant.[284]

The Wooing of Rebekah

Attended by ten men,[285] mounted upon ten camels laden
with jewels and trinkets, Eliezer betook himself to Haran
under the convoy of two angels, the one appointed to keep
guard over Eliezer, the other over Rebekah.[286]

The journey to Haran took but a few hours, at evening
of the same day he reached there, because the earth hastened
to meet him in a wonderful way.[287] He made a halt at the
well of water, and he prayed to God to permit him to distinguish the wife appointed for Isaac among the damsels
that came to draw water, by this token, that she alone, and
not the others, would give him drink.[288] Strictly speaking,
this wish of his was unseemly, for suppose a bondwoman
had given him water to drink![289] But God granted his request. All the damsels said they could not give him of their
water, because they had to take it home. Then appeared
Rebekah, coming to the well contrary to her wont, for she
was the daughter of a king, Bethuel her father being king
of Haran. When Eliezer addressed his request for water

to drink to this young innocent child, not only was she ready
to do his bidding, but she rebuked the other maidens on
account of their discourtesy to a stranger.²⁰⁰ Eliezer noticed,
too, how the water rose up to her of its own accord from the
bottom of the well, so that she needed not to exert herself
to draw it. Having scrutinized her carefully, he felt certain
that she was the wife chosen for Isaac. He gave her a nose
ring, wherein was set a precious stone, half a shekel in
weight, foreshadowing the half-shekel which her descendants would once bring to the sanctuary year by year. He
gave her also two bracelets for her hands, of ten shekels
weight in gold, in token of the two tables of stone and the
Ten Commandments upon them.²⁰¹

When Rebekah, bearing the jewels, came to her mother
and to her brother Laban, this one hastened to Eliezer in
order to slay him and take possession of his goods. Laban
soon learnt that he would not be able to do much harm to a
giant like Eliezer. He met him at the moment when Eliezer
seized two camels and bore them across the stream.²⁰² Besides, on account of Eliezer's close resemblance to Abraham,
Laban thought he saw Abraham before him, and he said:
" Come in, thou blessed of the Lord! It is not becoming
that thou shouldst stand without, I have cleansed my house
of idols." ²⁰³

But when Eliezer arrived at the house of Bethuel, they
tried to kill him with cunning. They set poisoned food before him. Luckily, he refused to eat before he had dis-
charged himself of his errand. While he was telling his
story, it was ordained by God that the dish intended for him
should come to stand in front of Bethuel, who ate of it and
died.²⁰⁴

Eliezer showed the document he had in which Abraham deeded all his possessions to Isaac, and he made it known to the kindred of Abraham, how deeply attached to them his master was, in spite of the long years of separation.[296] Yet he let them know at the same time that Abraham was not dependent wholly upon them. He might seek a wife for his son among the daughters of Ishmael or Lot. At first the kindred of Abraham consented to let Rebekah go with Eliezer, but as Bethuel had died in the meantime, they did not want to give Rebekah in marriage without consulting her. Besides, they deemed it proper that she should remain at home at least during the week of mourning for her father.[296] But Eliezer, seeing the angel wait for him, would brook no delay, and he said, " The man who came with me and prospered my way, waits for me without," and as Rebekah professed herself ready to go at once with Eliezer, her mother and brother granted her wish and dismissed her with their blessings.[297] But their blessings did not come from the bottom of their hearts. Indeed, as a rule, the blessing of the impious is a curse, wherefore Rebekah remained barren for years.[298]

Eliezer's return to Canaan was as wonderful as his going to Haran had been. A seventeen days' journey he accomplished in three hours. He left Haran at noon, and he arrived at Hebron[299] at three o'clock in the afternoon, the time for the Minḥah Prayer, which had been introduced by Isaac. He was in the posture of praying when Rebekah first laid eyes upon him, wherefore she asked Eliezer what man this was. She saw he was not an ordinary individual. She noticed the unusual beauty of Isaac, and also that an

angel accompanied him. Thus her question was not dic-
tated by mere curiosity.[300] At this moment she learnt
through the holy spirit, that she was destined to be the
mother of the godless Esau. Terror seized her at the knowledge, and, trembling, she fell from the camel and inflicted an
injury upon herself.[301]

After Isaac had heard the wonderful adventures of
Eliezer, he took Rebekah to the tent of his mother Sarah,
and she showed herself worthy to be her successor. The
cloud appeared again that had been visible over the tent
during the life of Sarah, and had vanished at her death; the
light shone again in the tent of Rebekah that Sarah had
kindled at the coming in of the Sabbath, and that had burnt
miraculously throughout the week; the blessing returned
with Rebekah that had hovered over the dough kneaded by
Sarah; and the gates of the tent were opened for the needy,
wide and spacious, as they had been during the lifetime of
Sarah.[302]

For three years Isaac had mourned for his mother, and
he could find no consolation in the academy of Shem and
Eber, his abiding-place during that period. But Rebekah
comforted him after his mother's death,[303] for she was the
counterpart of Sarah in person and in spirit.[304]

As a reward for having executed to his full satisfaction
the mission with which he had charged him, Abraham set
his bondman free.[305] The curse resting upon Eliezer, as
upon all the descendants of Canaan, was transformed into a
blessing, because he ministered unto Abraham loyally.[306]
Greatest reward of all, God found him worthy of entering
Paradise alive, a distinction that fell to the lot of very few.[307]

THE LAST YEARS OF ABRAHAM

Rebekah first saw Isaac as he was coming from the way of Beer-lahai-roi, the dwelling-place of Hagar, whither he had gone after the death of his mother, for the purpose of reuniting his father with Hagar,³⁰⁸ or, as she is also called, Keturah.³⁰⁹

Hagar bore him six sons, who, however, did scant honor to their father, for they all were idolaters.³¹⁰ Abraham, therefore, during his own lifetime, sent them away from the presence of Isaac, that they might not be singed by Isaac's flame, and gave them the instruction to journey eastward as far as possible.³¹¹ There he built a city for them, surrounded by an iron wall, so high that the sun could not shine into the city. But Abraham provided them with huge gems and pearls, their lustre more brilliant than the light of the sun, which will be used in the Messianic time when "the moon shall be confounded and the sun ashamed."³¹² Also Abraham taught them the black art, wherewith they held sway over demons and spirits. It is from this city in the east that Laban, Balaam, and Balaam's father Beor derived their sorceries.³¹³

Epher, one of the grandsons of Abraham and Keturah, invaded Lybia with an armed force, and took possession of the country. From this Epher the whole land of Africa has its name.³¹⁴ Aram is also a country made habitable by a kinsman of Abraham. In his old age Terah contracted a new marriage with Pelilah, and from this union sprang a son Zoba, who was the father in turn of three sons. The oldest of these, Aram, was exceedingly rich and powerful, and the old home in Haran sufficed not for him and his kinsmen, the sons of Nahor, the brother of Abraham. Aram and his brethren and all that belonged to him therefore departed from Haran, and they settled in a vale, and they built themselves a city there which they called Aram-Zoba, to perpetuate the name of the father and his first-born son. Another Aram, Aram-naharaim, on the Euphrates, was built by Aram son of Kemuel, a nephew of Abraham. Its real name was Petor, after the son of Aram, but it is better known as Aram-naharaim. The descendants of Kesed, another nephew of Abraham, a son of his brother Nahor, established themselves opposite to Shinar, where they founded the city of Kesed, the city whence the Chaldees are called Kasdim.[215]

Though Abraham knew full well that Isaac deserved his paternal blessing beyond all his sons, yet he withheld it from him, that no hostile feelings be aroused among his descendants. He spake, and said : " I am but flesh and blood, here to-day, to-morrow in the grave. What I was able to do for my children I have done. Henceforth let come what God desires to do in His world," and it happened that immediately after the death of Abraham God Himself appeared unto Isaac, and gave him His blessing.[216]

A HERALD OF DEATH

When the day of the death of Abraham drew near, the Lord said to Michael, " Arise and go to Abraham and say to him, Thou shalt depart from life ! " so that he might set his house in order before he died. And Michael went and came to Abraham and found him sitting before his oxen for ploughing. Abraham, seeing Michael, but not knowing who he was, saluted him and said to him, "Sit down a little while, and I will order a beast to be brought, and we will go to my house, that thou mayest rest with me, for it is toward evening, and arise in the morning and go whithersoever thou wilt." And Abraham called one of his servants, and said to him: "Go and bring me a beast, that the stranger may sit upon it, for he is wearied with his journey." But Michael said, "I abstain from ever sitting upon any four-footed beast, let us walk therefore, till we reach the house."

On their way to the house they passed a huge tree, and Abraham heard a voice from its branches, singing, "Holy art thou, because thou hast kept the purpose for which thou wast sent." Abraham hid the mystery in his heart, thinking that the stranger did not hear it. Arrived at his house, he ordered the servants to prepare a meal, and while they were busy with their work, he called his son Isaac, and said to him, "Arise and put water in the vessel, that we may wash the feet of the stranger." And he brought it as he was commanded, and Abraham said, "I perceive that in this basin I shall never again wash the feet of any man coming to us as a guest." Hearing this, Isaac began to weep, and Abraham, seeing his son weep, also wept, and Michael, seeing them weep, wept also, and the tears of Michael fell into the water, and became precious stones.

Before sitting down to the table, Michael arose, went out for a moment, as if to ease nature, and ascended to heaven in the twinkling of an eye, and stood before the Lord, and said to Him: "Lord and Master, let Thy power know that I am unable to remind that righteous man of his death, for I have not seen upon the earth a man like him, compas-

stonate, hospitable, righteous, truthful, devout, refraining
from every evil deed." Then the Lord said to Michael, "Go
down to My friend Abraham, and whatever he may say to
thee, that do thou also, and whatever he may eat, eat thou also
with him, and I will cast the thought of the death of Abraham into the heart of Isaac, his son, in a dream, and Isaac
will relate the dream, and thou shalt interpret it, and he
himself will know his end." And Michael said, "Lord, all
the heavenly spirits are incorporeal, and neither eat nor
drink, and this man has set before me a table with an abundance of all good things earthly and corruptible. Now,
Lord, what shall I do?" The Lord answered him, "Go
down to him and take no thought for this, for when thou
sittest down with him, I will send upon thee a devouring
spirit, and it will consume out of thy hands and through thy
mouth all that is on the table."

Then Michael went into the house of Abraham, and they
ate and drank and were merry. And when the supper was
ended, Abraham prayed after his custom, and Michael
prayed with him, and each lay down to sleep upon his couch
in one room, while Isaac went to his chamber, lest he be
troublesome to the guest. About the seventh hour of the
night, Isaac awoke and came to the door of his father's
chamber, crying out and saying, "Open, father, that I may
touch thee before they take thee away from me." And Abraham wept together with his son, and when Michael saw
them weep, he wept likewise. And Sarah, hearing the weeping, called forth from her bedchamber, saying: "My lord
Abraham, why this weeping? Has the stranger told thee
of thy brother's son Lot, that he is dead? or has aught

befallen us?" Michael answered, and said to her, "Nay, my sister Sarah, it is not as thou sayest, but thy son Isaac, methinks, beheld a dream, and came to us weeping, and we, seeing him, were moved in our hearts and wept." Sarah, hearing Michael speak, knew straightway that it was an angel of the Lord, one of the three angels whom they had entertained in their house once before, and therefore she made a sign to Abraham to come out toward the door, to inform him of what she knew. Abraham said: "Thou hast perceived well, for I, too, when I washed his feet, knew in my heart that they were the feet that I had washed at the oak of Mamre, and that went to save Lot." Abraham, returning to his chamber, made Isaac relate his dream, which Michael interpreted to them, saying: "Thy son Isaac has spoken truth, for thou shalt go and be taken up into the heavens, but thy body shall remain on earth, until seven thousand ages are fulfilled, for then all flesh shall arise. Now, therefore, Abraham, set thy house in order, for thou hast heard what is decreed concerning thee." Abraham answered, "Now I know thou art an angel of the Lord, and wast sent to take my soul, but I will not go with thee, but do thou whatever thou art commanded." Michael returned to heaven and told God of Abraham's refusal to obey his summons, and he was again commanded to go down and admonish Abraham not to rebel against God, who had bestowed many blessings upon him, and he reminded him that no one who has come from Adam and Eve can escape death, and that God in His great kindness toward him did not permit the sickle of death to meet him, but sent His chief captain, Michael, to him. "Wherefore, then," he ended, "hast thou said to the chief captain, I will not go with thee?" When Michael delivered these exhortations to Abraham, he saw that it was futile to oppose the will of God, and he consented to die, but wished to have one desire of his fulfilled while still alive. He said to Michael: "I beseech thee, lord, if I must depart from my body, I desire to be taken up in my body, that I may see the creatures that the Lord has created in heaven and on earth." Michael went up into heaven, and spake before the Lord concerning Abraham, and the Lord answered Michael, "Go and take up Abraham in the body and show him all things, and whatever he shall say to thee, do to him as to My friend."

ABRAHAM VIEWS EARTH AND HEAVEN

The archangel Michael went down, and took Abraham upon a chariot of the cherubim, and lifted him up into the air of heaven, and led him upon the cloud, together with sixty angels, and Abraham ascended upon the chariot over all the earth, and saw all things that are below on the earth, both good and bad. Looking down upon the earth, he saw a man committing adultery with a wedded woman, and turning to Michael he said, "Send fire from heaven to consume them." Straightway there came down fire and consumed them, for God had commanded Michael to do whatsoever Abraham should ask him to do. He looked again, and he saw thieves digging through a house, and Abraham said, "Let wild beasts come out of the desert, and tear them in pieces," and immediately wild beasts came out of the desert and devoured them. Again he looked down, and he saw people preparing to commit murder, and he said,

"Let the earth open and swallow them," and, as he spoke, the earth swallowed them alive. Then God spoke to Michael: "Turn away Abraham to his own house and let nim not go round the whole earth, because he has no compassion on sinners, but I have compassion on sinners, that they may turn and live and repent of their sins, and be saved."

So Michael turned the chariot, and brought Abraham to the place of judgment of all souls. Here he saw two gates, the one broad and the other narrow, the narrow gate that of the just, which leads to life, they that enter through it go into Paradise. The broad gate is that of sinners, which leads to destruction and eternal punishment. Then Abraham wept, saying, "Woe is me, what shall I do? for I am a man big of body, and how shall I be able to enter by the narrow gate?" Michael answered, and said to Abraham, "Fear not, nor grieve, for thou shalt enter by it unhindered, and all they who are like thee." Abraham, perceiving that a soul was adjudged to be set in the midst, asked Michael the reason for it, and Michael answered, "Because the judge found its sins and its righteousness equal, he neither committed it to judgment nor to be saved." Abraham said to Michael, "Let us pray for this soul, and see whether God will hear us," and when they rose up from their prayer, Michael informed Abraham that the soul was saved by the prayer, and was taken by an angel and carried up to Paradise. Abraham said to Michael, "Let us yet call upon the Lord and supplicate His compassion and entreat His mercy for the souls of the sinners whom I formerly, in my anger, cursed and destroyed, whom the earth devoured, and the wild beasts tore in pieces, and the fire consumed, through my words. Now I know that I have sinned before the Lord our God."

After the joint prayer of the archangel and Abraham, there came a voice from heaven, saying, " Abraham, Abraham, I have hearkened to thy voice and thy prayer, and I forgive thee thy sin, and those whom thou thinkest that I destroyed, I have called up and brought them into life by My exceeding kindness, because for a season I have requited them in judgment, and those whom I destroy living upon earth, I will not requite in death."

When Michael brought Abraham back to his house, they found Sarah dead. Not seeing what had become of Abraham, she was consumed with grief and gave up her soul. Though Michael had fulfilled Abraham's wish, and had shown him all the earth and the judgment and recompense, he still refused to surrender his soul to Michael, and the archangel again ascended to heaven, and said unto the Lord : " Thus speaks Abraham, I will not go with thee, and I refrain from laying my hands on him, because from the beginning he was Thy friend, and he has done all things pleasing in Thy sight. There is no man like him on earth, not even Job, the wondrous man." But when the day of the death of Abraham drew nigh, God commanded Michael to adorn Death with great beauty and send him thus to Abraham, that he might see him with his eyes.

While sitting under the oak of Mamre, Abraham perceived a flashing of light and a smell of sweet odor, and turning around he saw Death coming toward him in great glory and beauty. And Death said unto Abraham : " Think not, Abraham, that this beauty is mine, or that I come thus to every man. Nay, but if any one is righteous like thee, I thus take a crown and come to him, but if he is a sinner, I come in great corruption, and out of their sins I make a crown for my head, and I shake them with great fear, so that they are dismayed." Abraham said to him, " And art thou, indeed, he that is called Death?" He answered, and said, " I am the bitter name," but Abraham answered, " I will not go with thee." And Abraham said to Death, " Show us thy corruption." And Death revealed his corruption, showing two heads, the one had the face of a serpent, the other head was like a sword. All the servants of Abraham, looking at the fierce mien of Death, died, but Abraham prayed to the Lord, and he raised them up. As the looks of Death were not able to cause Abraham's soul to depart from him, God removed the soul of Abraham as in a dream, and the archangel Michael took it up into heaven. After great praise and glory had been given to the Lord by the angels who brought Abraham's soul, and after Abraham bowed down to worship, then came the voice of God, saying thus: " Take My friend Abraham into Paradise, where are the tabernacles of My righteous ones and the abodes of My saints Isaac and Jacob in his bosom, where there is no trouble, nor grief, nor sighing, but peace and rejoicing and life unending." [217]

Abraham's activity did not cease with his death, and as he interceded in this world for the sinners, so will he intercede for them in the world to come. On the day of judgment he will sit at the gate of hell, and he will not suffer those who kept the law of circumcision to enter therein. [218]

THE PATRON OF HEBRON

Once upon a time some Jews lived in Hebron, few in number, but pious and good, and particularly hospitable. When strangers came to the Cave of Machpelah to pray there, the inhabitants of the place fairly quarrelled with each other for the privilege of entertaining the guests, and the one who carried off the victory rejoiced as though he had found great spoil.

On the eve of the Day of Atonement, it appeared that, in spite of all their efforts, the dwellers at Hebron could not secure the tenth man needed for public Divine service, and they feared they would have none on the holy day. Toward evening, when the sun was about to sink, they descried an old man with silver white beard, bearing a sack upon his shoulder, his raiment tattered, and his feet badly swollen from much walking. They ran to meet him, took him to one of the houses, gave him food and drink, and, after supplying him with new white garments, they all together went to the synagogue for worship. Asked what his name was, the stranger replied, Abraham.

At the end of the fast, the residents of Hebron cast lots for the privilege of entertaining the guest. Fortune favored the beadle, who, the envy of the rest, bore his guest away to his house. On the way, he suddenly disappeared, and the beadle could not find him anywhere. In vain all the Jews of the place went on a quest for him. Their sleepless night, spent in searching, had no result. The stranger could not be found. But no sooner had the beadle lain down, toward morning, weary and anxious, to snatch some sleep, than he saw the lost guest before him, his face luminous as lightning, and his garments magnificent and studded with

gems radiant as the sun.   Before the beadle, stunned by
fright, could open his mouth, the stranger spake, and said:
" I am Abraham the Hebrew, your ancestor, who rests here
in the Cave of Machpelah.   When I saw how grieved you
were at not having the number of men prescribed for a
public service, I came forth to you.   Have no fear!   Rejoice
and be merry of heart! " [319]

On another occasion Abraham granted his assistance to
the people of Hebron.   The lord of the city was a heartless
man, who oppressed the Jews sorely.   One day he commanded them to pay a large sum of money into his coffers,
the whole sum in uniform coins, all stamped with the same
year.   It was but a pretext to kill the Jews.   He knew that
his demand was impossible of fulfilment.

The Jews proclaimed a fast and day of public prayer, on
which to supplicate God that He turn aside the sword suspended above them.   The night following, the beadle in a
dream saw an awe-inspiring old man, who addressed him in
the following words: " Up, quickly!   Hasten to the gate of
the court, where lies the money you need.   I am your father
Abraham.   I have beheld the affliction wherewith the Gentiles oppress you, but God has heard your groans."   In
great terror the beadle arose, but he saw no one, yet he went
to the spot designated by the vision, and he found the money
and took it to the congregation, telling his dream at the same
time.   Amazed, they counted the gold, precisely the amount
required of them by the prince, no more and no less.   They
surrendered the sum to him, and he who had considered
compliance with his demand impossible, recognized now that
God is with the Jews, and thenceforth they found favor in
his eyes. [320]

VI

JACOB

VI

JACOB

Isaac was the counterpart of his father in body and soul. He resembled him in every particular—" in beauty, wisdom, strength, wealth, and noble deeds."[1] It was, therefore, as great an honor for Isaac to be called the son of his father as for Abraham to be called the father of his son, and though Abraham was the progenitor of thirty nations, he is always designated as the father of Isaac.[2]

Despite his many excellent qualities, Isaac married late in life. God permitted him to meet the wife suitable to him only after he had successfully disproved the mocking charges of Ishmael, who was in the habit of taunting him with having been circumcised at the early age of eight days, while Ishmael had submitted himself voluntarily to the operation when he was thirteen years old. For this reason God demanded Isaac as a sacrifice when he had attained to full manhood, at the age of thirty-seven, and Isaac was ready to give up his life. Ishmael's jibes were thus robbed of their sting, and Isaac was permitted to marry. But another delay occurred before his marriage could take place. Directly after the sacrifice on Mount Moriah, his mother died, and he mourned her for three years.[3] Finally he married Rebekah, who was then a maiden of fourteen.[4]

Rebekah was " a rose between thorns." Her father was

the Aramean Bethuel, and her brother was Laban, but she did not walk in their ways.' Her piety was equal to Isaac's.' Nevertheless their marriage was not entirely happy, for they lived together no less than twenty years without begetting children.' Rebekah besought her husband to entreat God for the gift of children, as his father Abraham had done. At first Isaac would not do her bidding. God had promised Abraham a numerous progeny, and he thought their child-lessness was probably Rebekah's fault, and it was her duty to supplicate God, and not his. But Rebekah would not de-sist, and husband and wife repaired to Mount Moriah to-gether to pray to God there. And Isaac said: " O Lord God of heaven and earth, whose goodness and mercies fill the earth, Thou who didst take my father from his father's house and from his birthplace, and didst bring him unto this land, and didst say unto him, To thee and thy seed will I give the land, and didst promise him and declare unto him, I will multiply thy seed as the stars of heaven and as the sand of the sea, now may Thy words be verified which Thou didst speak unto my father. For Thou art the Lord our God, our eyes are toward Thee, to give us seed of men as Thou didst promise us, for Thou art the Lord our God, and our eyes are upon Thee."' Isaac prayed furthermore that all chil-dren destined for him might be born unto him from this pious wife of his, and Rebekah made the same petition re-garding her husband Isaac and the children destined for her.

Their united prayer was heard.' Yet it was chiefly for the sake of Isaac that God gave them children. It is true, Rebekah's piety equalled her husband's, but the prayer of a pious man who is the son of a pious man is far more efficacious than the prayer of one who, though pious himself, is descended from a godless father.

The prayer wrought a great miracle, for Isaac's physique was such that he could not have been expected to beget children, and equally it was not in the course of nature that Rebekah should bear children.[10]

When Rebekah had been pregnant seven months,[11] she began to wish that the curse of childlessness had not been removed from her.[12] She suffered torturous pain, because her twin sons began their lifelong quarrels in her womb. They strove to kill each other. If Rebekah walked in the vicinity of a temple erected to idols, Esau moved in her body, and if she passed a synagogue or a Bet ha-Midrash, Jacob essayed to break forth from her womb.[13] The quarrels of the children turned upon such differences as these. Esau would insist that there was no life except the earthly life of material pleasures, and Jacob would reply: " My brother, there are two worlds before us, this world and the world to come. In this world, men eat and drink, and traffic and marry, and bring up sons and daughters, but all this does not take place in the world to come. If it please thee, do thou take this world, and I will take the other."[14] Esau had Samael as his ally, who desired to slay Jacob in his mother's womb. But the archangel Michael hastened to Jacob's aid. He tried to burn Samael, and the Lord saw it was necessary to constitute a heavenly court for the purpose of arbitrating the case of Michael and Samael.[15] Even the quarrel between the two brothers regarding the birthright had its beginning before they emerged from the womb of their mother. Each desired to be the first to come into the world. It was only when Esau threatened to carry his point at the expense of his mother's life that Jacob gave way.[16]

Rebekah asked other women whether they, too, had suffered such pain during their pregnancy, and when they told her they had not heard of a case like hers, except the pregnancy of Nimrod's mother, she betook herself to Mount Moriah, whereon Shem and Eber had their Bet ha-Midrash. She requested them as well as Abraham to inquire of God what the cause of her dire suffering was.[17] And Shem replied: " My daughter, I confide a secret to thee. See to it that none finds it out. Two nations are in thy womb, and how should thy body contain them, seeing that the whole world will not be large enough for them to exist in it together peaceably? Two nations they are, each owning a world of its own, the one the Torah, the other sin. From the one will spring Solomon, the builder of the Temple, from the other Vespasian, the destroyer thereof. These two are what are needed to raise the number of nations to seventy. They will never be in the same estate. Esau will vaunt lords, while Jacob will bring forth prophets, and if Esau has princes, Jacob will have kings.[18] They, Israel and Rome, are the two nations destined to be hated by all the world.[19] One will exceed the other in strength. First Esau will subjugate the whole world, but in the end Jacob will rule over all.[20] The older of the two will serve the younger, provided this one is pure of heart, otherwise the younger will be enslaved by the older." [21]

The circumstances connected with the birth of her twin sons were as remarkable as those during the period of Rebekah's pregnancy. Esau was the first to see the light, and

with him all impurity came from the womb; [22] Jacob was born
clean and sweet of body. Esau was brought forth with hair,
beard, and teeth, both front and back,[23] and he was blood-red,
a sign of his future sanguinary nature.[24] On account of his
ruddy appearance he remained uncircumcised. Isaac, his
father, feared that it was due to poor circulation of the blood,
and he hesitated to perform the circumcision. He decided to
wait until Esau should attain his thirteenth year, the age at
which Ishmael had received the sign of the covenant. But
when Esau grew up, he refused to give heed to his father's
wish, and so he was left uncircumcised.[25] The opposite of
his brother in this as in all respects, Jacob was born with
the sign of .he covenant upon his body, a rare distinction.[26]
But Esau also bore a mark upon him at birth, the figure of a
serpent, the symbol of all that is wicked and hated of God.[27]

The names conferred upon the brothers are pregnant with
meaning. The older was called Esau, because he was 'Asui,
fully developed when he was born, and the name of the
younger was given to him by God, to point to some important events in the future of Israel by the numerical value of
each letter. The first letter in *Ya'akob* Yod, with the value
of ten, stands for the decalogue; the second, 'Ayin, equal to
seventy, for the seventy elders, the leaders of Israel; the
third, Kof, a hundred, for the Temple, a hundred ells in
height; and the last, Bet, for the two tables of stone.[28]

THE FAVORITE OF ABRAHAM

While Esau and Jacob were little, their characters could
not be judged properly. They were like the myrtle and the
thorn-bush, which look alike in the early stages of their

growth. After they have attained full size, the myrtle is known by its fragrance, and the thorn-bush by its thorns.

In their childhood, both brothers went to school, but when they reached their thirteenth year, and were of age, their ways parted. Jacob continued his studies in the Bet ha-Midrash of Shem and Eber, and Esau abandoned himself to idolatry and an immoral life.²⁹ Both were hunters of men, Esau tried to capture them in order to turn them away from God, and Jacob, to turn them toward God.³⁰ In spite of his impious deeds, Esau possessed the art of winning his father's love. His hypocritical conduct made Isaac believe that his first-born son was extremely pious. "Father," he would ask Isaac, "what is the tithe on straw and salt?" The question made him appear God-fearing in the eyes of his father, because these two products are the very ones that are exempt from tithing.³¹ Isaac failed to notice, too, that his older son gave him forbidden food to eat. What he took for the flesh of young goats was dog's meat.³²

Rebekah was more clear-sighted. She knew her sons as they really were, and therefore her love for Jacob was exceeding great. The oftener she heard his voice, the deeper grew her affection for him.³³ Abraham agreed with her. He also loved his grandson Jacob, for he knew that in him his name and his seed would be called. And he said unto Rebekah, "My daughter, watch over my son Jacob, for he shall be in my stead on the earth and for a blessing in the midst of the children of men, and for the glory of the whole seed of Shem." Having admonished Rebekah thus to keep guard over Jacob, who was destined to be the bearer of the blessing given to Abraham by God, he called for his grandson, and in the presence of Rebekah he blessed him, and said: "Jacob, my beloved son, whom my soul loveth, may God bless thee from above the firmament, and may He give thee all the blessing wherewith He blessed Adam, and Enoch, and Noah, and Shem, and all the things of which He told me, and all the things which He promised to give me may He cause to cleave to thee and to thy seed forever, according to the days of the heavens above the earth. And the spirit of Masṭema shall not rule over thee or over thy seed, to turn thee from the Lord, who is thy God from henceforth and forever. And may the Lord God be a father to thee, and mayest thou be His first-born son, and may He be a father to thy people always. Go in peace, my son." [84]

And Abraham had good reason to be particularly fond of Jacob, for it was due to the merits of his grandson that he had been rescued from the fiery furnace. [85]

Isaac and Rebekah, knowing of Abraham's love for their young son, sent their father a meal by Jacob on the last Feast of Pentecost which Abraham was permitted to celebrate on earth, that he might eat and bless the Creator of all things before he died. Abraham knew that his end was approaching, and he thanked the Lord for all the good He had granted him during the days of his life, and blessed Jacob and bade him walk in the ways of the Lord, and especially he was not to marry a daughter of the Canaanites. Then Abraham prepared for death. He placed two of Jacob's fingers upon his eyes, and thus holding them closed he fell into his eternal sleep, while Jacob lay beside him on the bed. The lad did not know of his grandfather's death, until he called him, on awakening next morning, "Father, father," and received no answer. [86]

THE SALE OF THE BIRTHRIGHT

Though Abraham reached a good old age, beyond the limit of years vouchsafed later generations, he yet died five years before his allotted time. The intention was to let him live to be one hundred and eighty years old, the same age as Isaac's at his death, but on account of Esau God brought his life to an abrupt close. For some time Esau had been pursuing his evil inclinations in secret. Finally he dropped his mask, and on the day of Abraham's death he was guilty of five crimes: he ravished a betrothed maiden, committed murder, doubted the resurrection of the dead, scorned the birthright, and denied God. Then the Lord said: " I promised Abraham that he should go to his fathers in peace. Can I now permit him to be a witness of his grandson's rebellion against God, his violation of the laws of chastity, and his shedding of blood? It is better for him to die now in peace." [87]

The men slain by Esau on this day were Nimrod and two of his adjutants. A long-standing feud had existed between Esau and Nimrod, because the mighty hunter before the Lord was jealous of Esau, who also devoted himself assiduously to the chase. Once when he was hunting it happened that Nimrod was separated from his people, only two men were with him. Esau, who lay in ambush, noticed his isolation, and waited until he should pass his covert. Then he threw himself upon Nimrod suddenly, and felled him and his two companions, who hastened to his succor. The outcries of the latter brought the attendants of Nimrod to the spot where he lay dead, but not before Esau had stripped him of his garments, and fled to the city with them. [88]

These garments of Nimrod had an extraordinary effect upon cattle, beasts, and birds. Of their own accord they would come and prostrate themselves before him who was arrayed in them. Thus Nimrod and Esau after him were able to rule over men and beasts.³⁹

After slaying Nimrod, Esau hastened cityward in great fear of his victim's followers. Tired and exhausted he arrived at home to find Jacob busy preparing a dish of lentils. Numerous male and female slaves were in Isaac's household. Nevertheless Jacob was so simple and modest in his demeanor that, if he came home late from the Bet ha-Midrash, he would disturb none to prepare his meal, but would do it himself.⁴⁰ On this occasion he was cooking lentils for his father, to serve to him as his mourner's meal after the death of Abraham. Adam and Eve had eaten lentils after the murder of Abel, and so had the parents of Haran, when he perished in the fiery furnace. The reason they are used for the mourner's meal is that the round lentil symbolizes death: as the lentil rolls, so death, sorrow, and mourning constantly roll about among men, from one to the other.⁴¹

Esau accosted Jacob thus, "Why art thou preparing lentils?"

Jacob: "Because our grandfather passed away; they shall be a sign of my grief and mourning, that he may love me in the days to come."

Esau: "Thou fool! Dost thou really think it possible that man should come to life again after he has been dead and has mouldered in the grave?"⁴² He continued to taunt Jacob. "Why dost thou give thyself so much trouble?" he said. "Lift up thine eyes, and thou wilt see that all men

eat whatever comes to hand—fish, creeping and crawling
creatures, swine's flesh, and all sorts of things like these, and
thou vexest thyself about a dish of lentils."

Jacob: "If we act like other men, what shall we do on
the day of the Lord, the day on which the pious will receive their reward, when a herald will proclaim: Where is
He that weigheth the deeds of men, where is He that
counteth?"

Esau: "Is there a future world? Or will the dead be
called back to life? If it were so, why hath not Adam returned? Hast thou heard that Noah, through whom the
world was raised anew, hath reappeared? Yea, Abraham,
the friend of God, more beloved of Him than any man, hath
he come to life again?"

Jacob: "If thou art of opinion that there is no future
world, and that the dead do not rise to new life, then why
dost thou want thy birthright? Sell it to me, now, while it
is yet possible to do so. Once the Torah is revealed, it cannot be done. Verily, there is a future world, in which the
righteous receive their reward. I tell thee this, lest thou
say later I deceived thee."

Jacob was little concerned about the double share of the
inheritance that went with the birthright. What he thought
of was the priestly service, which was the prerogative of the
first-born in ancient times, and Jacob was loth to have his
impious brother Esau play the priest, he who despised all
Divine service.

The scorn manifested by Esau for the resurrection of the
dead he felt also for the promise of God to give the Holy
Land to the seed of Abraham. He did not believe in it, and

therefore he was willing to cede his birthright and the blessing attached thereto in exchange for a mess of pottage." In
addition, Jacob paid him in coin," and, besides, he gave him
what was more than money, the wonderful sword of Methuselah, which Isaac had inherited from Abraham and
bestowed upon Jacob."

Esau made game of Jacob. He invited his associates to
feast at his brother's table, saying, " Know ye what I did to
this Jacob? I ate his lentils, drank his wine, amused myself
at his expense, and sold my birthright to him." All that
Jacob replied was, " Eat and may it do thee good! " But
the Lord said, " Thou despisest the birthright, therefore I
shall make thee despised in all generations." And by way
of punishment for denying God and the resurrection of the
dead, the descendants of Esau were cut off from the world."

As naught was holy to Esau, Jacob made him swear, concerning the birthright, by the life of their father, for he
knew Esau's love for Isaac, that it was strong." Nor did he
fail to have a document made out, duly signed by witnesses,
setting forth that Esau had sold him the birthright together
with his claim upon a place in the Cave of Machpelah."

Though no blame can attach to Jacob for all this, yet he
secured the birthright from him by cunning, and therefore
the descendants of Jacob had to serve the descendants of
Esau."

ISAAC WITH THE PHILISTINES

The life of Isaac was a faithful reflex of the life of his
father. Abraham had to leave his birthplace ; so also Isaac.
Abraham was exposed to the risk of losing his wife ; so also

Isaac. The Philistines were envious of Abraham; so also of
Isaac. Abraham long remained childless; so also Isaac.
Abraham begot one pious son and one wicked son; so also
Isaac. And, finally, as in the time of Abraham, so also in
the time of Isaac, a famine came upon the land.⁵²

At first Isaac intended to follow the example of his father
and remove to Egypt, but God appeared unto him, and
spake: "Thou art a perfect sacrifice, without a blemish,
and as a burnt offering is made unfit if it is taken outside of
the sanctuary, so thou wouldst be profaned if thou shouldst
happen outside of the Holy Land. Remain in the land, and
endeavor to cultivate it. In this land dwells the Shekinah,
and in days to come I will give unto thy children the realms
possessed by mighty rulers, first a part thereof, and the
whole in the Messianic time." ⁵³

Isaac obeyed the command of God, and he settled in
Gerar. When he noticed that the inhabitants of the place
began to have designs upon his wife, he followed the example of Abraham, and pretended she was his sister.⁵⁴ The
report of Rebekah's beauty reached the king himself, but he
was mindful of the great danger to which he had once exposed himself on a similar occasion, and he left Isaac and
his wife unmolested.⁵⁵ After they had been in Gerar for
three months, Abimelech noticed that the manner of Isaac,
who lived in the outer court of the royal palace, was that of
a husband toward Rebekah.⁵⁶ He called him to account,
saying, " It might have happened to the king himself to take
the woman thou didst call thy sister." ⁵⁷ Indeed, Isaac lay
under the suspicion of having illicit intercourse with Rebekah, for at first the people of the place would not believe

that she was his wife. When Isaac persisted in his statement,[58] Abimelech sent his grandees for them, ordered them to be arrayed in royal vestments, and had it proclaimed before them, as they rode through the city: " These two are man and wife. He that toucheth this man or his wife shall surely be put to death."

Thereafter the king invited Isaac to settle in his domains, and he assigned fields and vineyards to him for cultivation, the best the land afforded.[59] But Isaac was not self-interested. The tithe of all he possessed he gave to the poor of Gerar. Thus he was the first to introduce the law of tithing for the poor, as his father Abraham had been the first to separate the priests' portion from his fortune.[60] Isaac was rewarded by abundant harvests; the land yielded a hundred times more than was expected, though the soil was barren and the year unfruitful. He grew so rich that people wished to have " the dung from Isaac's she-mules rather than Abimelech's gold and silver."[61] But his wealth called forth the envy of the Philistines, for it is characteristic of the wicked that they begrudge their fellow-men the good, and rejoice when they see evil descend upon them, and envy brings hatred in its wake, and so the Philistines first envied Isaac, and then hated him. In their enmity toward him, they stopped the wells which Abraham had had his servants dig. Thus they broke their covenant with Abraham and were faithless, and they have only themselves to blame if they were exterminated later on by the Israelites.

Isaac departed from Gerar, and began to dig again the wells of water which they had digged in the days of Abraham his father, and which the Philistines had stopped. His

reverence for his father was so great that he even restored
the names by which Abraham had called the wells. To
reward him for his filial respect, the Lord left the name of
Isaac unchanged, while his father and his son had to submit
to new names."

After four attempts to secure water, Isaac was successful;
he found the well of water that followed the Patriarchs.
Abraham had obtained it after three diggings. Hence the
name of the well, Beer-sheba, " the well of seven diggings,"
the same well that will supply water to Jerusalem and its
environs in the Messianic time."

Isaac's success with his wells but served to increase the
envy of the Philistines, for he had come upon water in a
most unlikely spot and, besides, in a year of drouth. But
" the Lord fulfils the desire of them that fear Him." As
Isaac executed the will of his Creator, so God accomplished
his desire." And Abimelech, the king of Gerar, speedily
came to see that God was on the side of Isaac, for, to chastise
him for having instigated Isaac's removal from Gerar, his
house was ravaged by robbers in the night, and he himself
was stricken with leprosy." The wells of the Philistines
ran dry as soon as Isaac left Gerar, and also the trees failed
to yield their fruit. None could be in doubt but that these
things were the castigation for their unkindness.

Now Abimelech entreated his friends, especially the ad-
ministrator of his kingdom, to accompany him to Isaac and
help him win back his friendship." Abimelech and the Philistines spake thus to Isaac: " We have convinced ourselves
that the Shekinah is with thee, and therefore we desire thee
to renew the covenant which thy father made with us, that

thou wilt do us no hurt, as we also did not touch thee."
Isaac consented. It illustrates the character of the Philistines strikingly that they took credit unto themselves for
having done him no hurt. It shows that they would have
been glad to inflict harm upon him, for "the soul of the
wicked desireth evil."

The place in which the covenant was made between Isaac
and the Philistines was called Shib'ah, for two reasons, because an oath was "sworn" there, and as a memorial of the
fact that even the heathen are bound to observe the "seven"
Noachian laws.[67]

For all the wonders executed by God for Isaac, and all the
good he enjoyed throughout his life, he is indebted to the
merits of his father. For his own merits he will be rewarded in future.[68] On the great day of judgment it will
be Isaac who will redeem his descendants from Gehenna.
On that day the Lord will speak to Abraham, "Thy children
have sinned," and Abraham will make reply, "Then let
them be wiped out, that Thy Name be sanctified." The Lord
will turn to Jacob, thinking that he who had suffered so
much in bringing his sons to manhood's estate would display more love for his posterity. But Jacob will give the
same answer as Abraham. Then God will say: "The old
have no understanding, and the young no counsel. I will
now go to Isaac. Isaac," God will address him, "thy children have sinned," and Isaac will reply: "O Lord of the
world, sayest Thou *my* children, and not *Thine?* When
they stood at Mount Sinai and declared themselves ready to
execute all Thy bidding before even they heard it, Thou
didst call Israel 'My first-born,' and now they are *my* chil-

dren, and not *Thine!* Let us consider. The years of a man
are seventy. From these twenty are to be deducted, for
Thou inflictest no punishment upon those under twenty. Of
the fifty years that are left, one-half are to be deducted for
the nights passed in sleep. There remain only twenty-five
years, and these are to be diminished by twelve and a half,
the time spent in praying, eating, and attending to other
needs in life, during which men commit no sins. That leaves
only twelve years and a half. If Thou wilt take these upon
Thyself, well and good. If not, do Thou take one-half
thereof, and I will take the other half." The descendants of
Isaac will then say, "Verily, thou art our true father!"
But he will point to God, and admonish them, "Nay, give
not your praises to me, but to God alone," and Israel, with
eyes directed heavenward, will say, "Thou, O Lord, art our
Father; our Redeemer from everlasting is Thy name." [69]

It was Isaac, or, as he is sometimes called, Elihu the son of
Barachel, who revealed the wonderful mysteries of nature
in his arguments with Job. [70]

At the end of the years of famine, God appeared unto
Isaac, and bade him return to Canaan. Isaac did as he was
commanded, and he settled in Hebron. At this time he sent
his younger son Jacob to the Bet ha-Midrash of Shem and
Eber, to study the law of the Lord. Jacob remained there
thirty-two years. As for Esau, he refused to learn, and he
remained in the house of his father. The chase was his only
occupation, and as he pursued beasts, so he pursued men,
seeking to capture them with cunning and deceit.

On one of his hunting expeditions, Esau came to Mount
Seir, where he became acquainted with Judith, of the family

of Ham, and he took her unto himself as his wife, and brought her to his father at Hebron.

Ten years later, when Shem his teacher died, Jacob returned home, at the age of fifty. Another six years passed, and Rebekah received the joyful news that her sister-in-law 'Adinah, the wife of Laban, who, like all the women of his house, had been childless until then, had given birth to twin daughters, Leah and Rachel.[n] Rebekah, weary of her life on account of the woman chosen by her older son, exhorted Jacob not to marry one of the daughters of Canaan, but a maiden of the family of Abraham. He assured his mother that the words of Abraham, bidding him to marry no woman of the Canaanites, were graven upon his memory, and for this reason he was still unmarried, though he had attained the age of sixty-two, and Esau had been urging him for twenty-two years past to follow his example and wed a daughter of the people of the land in which they lived. He had heard that his uncle Laban had daughters, and he was resolved to choose one of them as his wife. Deeply moved by the words of her son, Rebekah thanked him and gave praise unto God with the words: "Blessed be the Lord God, and may His Holy Name be blessed for ever and ever, who hath given me Jacob as a pure son and a holy seed; for he is Thine, and Thine shall his seed be continually and throughout all the generations for evermore. Bless him, O Lord, and place in my mouth the blessing of righteousness, that I may bless him."

And when the spirit of the Lord came over her, she laid her hands upon the head of Jacob and gave him her maternal blessing. It ended with the words, " May the Lord of the

world love thee, as the heart of thy affectionate mother re-
joices in thee, and may He bless thee." "

Isaac Blesses Jacob

Esau's marriage with the daughters of the Canaanites
was an abomination not only in the eyes of his mother, but
also in the eyes of his father. He suffered even more than
Rebekah through the idolatrous practices of his daughters-
in-law. It is the nature of man to oppose less resistance
than woman to disagreeable circumstances. A bone is not
harmed by a collision that would shiver an earthen pot in
pieces. Man, who is created out of the dust of the ground,
has not the endurance of woman formed out of bone. Isaac
was made prematurely old by the conduct of his daughters-
in-law, and he lost the sight of his eyes. Rebekah had been
accustomed in the home of her childhood to the incense
burnt before idols, and she could therefore bear it under her
own roof-tree. Unlike her, Isaac had never had any such
experience while he abode with his parents, and he was stung
by the smoke arising from the sacrifices offered to their
idols by his daughters-in-law in his own house." Isaac's
eyes had suffered earlier in life, too. When he lay bound
upon the altar, about to be sacrificed by his father, the angels
wept, and their tears fell upon his eyes, and there they remained and weakened his sight.

At the same time he had brought the scourge of blindness
down upon himself by his love for Esau. He justified the
wicked for a bribe, the bribe of Esau's filial love, and loss of
vision is the punishment that follows the taking of bribes.
" A gift," it is said, " blinds the eyes of the wise."

Nevertheless his blindness proved a benefit for Isaac as well as Jacob. In consequence of his physical ailments, Isaac had to keep at home, and so he was spared the pain of being pointed out by the people as the father of the wicked Esau.[14] And, again, if his power of vision had been unimpaired, he would not have blessed Jacob. As it was, God treated him as a physician treats a sick man who is forbidden to drink wine, for which, however, he has a strong desire. To placate him, the physician orders that warm water be given him in the dark, and he be told that it is wine.[15]

When Isaac reached the age of one hundred and twenty-three, and was thus approaching the years attained by his mother, he began to meditate upon his end. It is proper that a man should prepare for death when he comes close to the age at which either of his parents passed out of life. Isaac reflected that he did not know whether the age allotted to him was his mother's or his father's, and he therefore resolved to bestow his blessing upon his older son, Esau, before death should overtake him.[16] He summoned Esau, and he said, " My son," and Esau replied, " Here am I," but the holy spirit interposed: " Though he disguises his voice and makes it sound sweet, put no confidence in him. There are seven abominations in his heart. He will destroy seven holy places—the Tabernacle, the sanctuaries at Gilgal, Shiloh, Nob, and Gibeon, and the first and the second Temple."

Gently though Esau continued to speak to his father, he yet longed for his end to come.[17] But Isaac was stricken with spiritual as well as physical blindness. The holy spirit deserted him, and he could not discern the wickedness of his older son. He bade him sharpen his slaughtering knives and beware of bringing him the flesh of an animal that had died of itself, or had been torn by a beast, and he was to guard also against putting an animal before Isaac that had been stolen from its rightful owner. " Then," continued Isaac, " will I bless him who is worthy of being blessed." ⁷⁸

This charge was laid upon Esau on the eve of the Passover, and Isaac said to him: " To-night the whole world will sing the Hallel unto God. It is the night when the storehouses of dew are unlocked. Therefore prepare dainties for me, that my soul may bless thee before I die." But the holy spirit interposed, " Eat not the bread of him that hath an evil eye." ⁷⁹ Isaac's longing for tidbits was due to his blindness. As the sightless cannot behold the food they eat, they do not enjoy it with full relish, and their appetite must be tempted with particularly palatable morsels.

Esau sallied forth to procure what his father desired, little recking the whence or how, whether by robbery or theft.⁸⁰ To hinder the quick execution of his father's order, God sent Satan on the chase with Esau. He was to delay him as long as possible. Esau would catch a deer and leave him lying bound, while he pursued other game. Immediately Satan would come and liberate the deer, and when Esau returned to the spot, his victim was not to be found. This was repeated several times. Again and again the quarry was run down, and bound, and liberated, so that Jacob was able meanwhile to carry out the plan of Rebekah whereby he would be blessed instead of Esau.

Though Rebekah had not heard the words that had passed between Isaac and Esau, they nevertheless were revealed to her through the holy spirit,⁸¹ and she resolved to restrain her husband from taking a false step. She was not actuated by love for Jacob, but by the wish of keeping Isaac from committing a detestable act.[*] Rebekah said to Jacob: "This night the storehouses of dew are unlocked; it is the night during which the celestial beings chant the Hallel unto God, the night set apart for the deliverance of thy children from Egypt, on which they, too, will sing the Hallel. Go now and prepare savory meat for thy father, that he may bless thee before his death.[*] Do as I bid thee, obey me as thou art wont, for thou art my son whose children, every one, will be good and God-fearing—not one shall be graceless."

In spite of his great respect for his mother,[*] Jacob refused at first to heed her command. He feared he might commit a sin,[*] especially as he might thus bring his father's curse down upon him. As it was, Isaac might still have a blessing for him, after giving Esau his. But Rebekah allayed his anxieties, with the words: "When Adam was cursed, the malediction fell upon his mother, the earth, and so shall I, thy mother, bear the imprecation, if thy father curses thee. Moreover, if the worst comes to the worst, I am prepared to step before thy father and tell him, 'Esau is a villain, and Jacob is a righteous man.'"

Thus constrained by his mother, Jacob, in tears and with body bowed, went off to execute the plan made by Rebekah.[*] As he was to provide a Passover meal, she bade him get two kids, one for the Passover sacrifice and one for the festival sacrifice.[*] To soothe Jacob's conscience, she added that her marriage contract entitled her to two kids daily. "And," she continued, "these two kids will bring good unto thee, the blessing of thy father, and they will bring good unto thy children, for two kids will be the atoning sacrifice offered on the Day of Atonement."

Jacob's hesitation was not yet removed. His father, he feared, would touch him and convince himself that he was not hairy, and therefore not his son Esau. Accordingly, Rebekah tore the skins of the two kids into strips and sewed them together, for Jacob was so tall a giant that otherwise they would not have sufficed to cover his hands.[⁸⁸] To make Jacob's disguise complete, Rebekah felt justified in putting Esau's wonderful garments on him. They were the high-priestly raiment in which God had clothed Adam, " the first-born of the world," for in the days before the erection of the Tabernacle all the first-born males officiated as priests. From Adam these garments descended to Noah, who trans-mitted them to Shem, and Shem bequeathed them to Abra-ham, and Abraham to his son Isaac, from whom they reached Esau as the older of his two sons. It was the opinion of Rebekah that as Jacob had bought the birthright from his brother, he had thereby come into possession of the gar-ments as well.[⁸⁹] There was no need for her to go and fetch them from the house of Esau. He knew his wives far too well to entrust so precious a treasure to them; they were in the safe-keeping of his mother. Besides, he used them most frequently in the house of his parents. As a rule, he did not lay much stress upon decent apparel. He was willing to appear on the street clad in rags, but he considered it his duty to wait upon his father arrayed in his best. " My father," Esau was in the habit of saying, " is a king in my sight, and it would ill become me to serve before him in any-

thing but royal apparel." To the great respect he manifested toward his father, the descendants of Esau owe all
their good fortune on earth. Thus doth God reward a good
deed.

Rebekah led Jacob equipped and arrayed in this way to
the door of Isaac's chamber. There she parted from him
with the words, "Henceforward may thy Creator assist
thee."[90] Jacob entered, addressing Isaac with "Father,"
and receiving the response, "Here am I! Who art thou,
my son?" he replied equivocally, "It is I, thy first-born
son is Esau." He sought to avoid a falsehood, and yet not
betray that he was Jacob.[91] Isaac then said: "Thou art
greatly in haste to secure thy blessing. Thy father Abraham was seventy-five years old when he was blessed, and
thou art but sixty-three." Jacob replied awkwardly, "Because the Lord thy God sent me good speed." Isaac concluded at once that this was not Esau, for he would not have
mentioned the name of God, and he made up his mind to
feel the son before him and make sure who he was. Terror
seized upon Jacob at the words of Isaac, "Come near, I
pray thee, that I may feel thee, my son." A cold sweat covered his body, and his heart melted like wax. Then God
caused the archangels Michael and Gabriel to descend. The
one seized his right hand, the other his left hand, while the
Lord God Himself supported him, that his courage might
not fail him. Isaac felt him, and, finding his hands hairy,
he said, "The voice is Jacob's voice, but the hands are the
hands of Esau," words in which he conveyed the prophecy
that so long as the voice of Jacob is heard in the houses of
prayer and of learning, the hands of Esau will not be able

to prevail against him. "Yes," he continued, "it is the
voice of Jacob, the voice that imposes silence upon those
on earth and in heaven," for even the angels may not raise
their voices in praise of God until Israel has finished his
prayers.

Isaac's scruples about blessing the son before him were
not yet removed, for with his prophetical eye he foresaw
that this one would have descendants who would vex the
Lord. At the same time, it was revealed to him that even
the sinners in Israel would turn penitents, and then he was
ready to bless Jacob. He bade him come near and kiss him,
to indicate that it would be Jacob who would imprint the
last kiss upon Isaac before he was consigned to the grave—
he and none other. When Jacob stood close to him, he
discerned the fragrance of Paradise clinging to him, and he
exclaimed, "See, the smell of my son is as the smell of the
field which the Lord hath blessed." [82]

The fragrance emanating from Jacob was not the only
thing about him derived from Paradise. The archangel
Michael had fetched thence the wine which Jacob gave his
father to drink, [83] that an exalted mood might descend upon
him, for only when a man is joyously excited the Shekinah
rests upon him. [84] The holy spirit filled Isaac, and he gave
Jacob his tenfold blessing: "God give thee of the dew of
heaven," the celestial dew wherewith God will awaken the
pious to new life in days to come; "and of the fatness of
the earth," the goods of this world; "and plenty of corn
and wine," the Torah and the commandments which bestow
the same joy upon man as abundant harvests; [85] "peoples
shall serve thee," the Japhethites and the Hamites; "nations

shall bow down to thee," the Shemite nations; "thou wilt be lord over thy brethren," the Ishmaelites and the descendants of Keturah; "thy mother's sons will bow down to thee," Esau and his princes; "cursed be every one that curseth thee," like Balaam; "and blessed be every one that blesseth thee," like Moses."

For each blessing invoked upon Jacob by his father Isaac, a similar blessing was bestowed upon him by God Himself in the same words. As Isaac blessed him with dew, so also God: ",And the remnant of Jacob shall be in the midst of many peoples as dew from the Lord." Isaac blessed him with the fatness of the earth, so also God: "And he shall give the rain of thy seed, that thou shalt sow the ground withal; and bread of the increase of the ground, and it shall be fat and plenteous." Isaac blessed him with plenty of corn and wine, so also God: "I will send you corn and wine." Isaac said, "Peoples shall serve thee," so also God: "Kings shall be thy nursing fathers, and their queens thy nursing mothers; they shall bow down to thee with their faces to the earth, and lick the dust of thy feet." Isaac said, "Nations shall bow down to thee," so also God: "And He will make thee high above all nations which He hath made, in praise, and in name, and in honor."

To this double blessing his mother Rebekah joined hers: "For He shall give His angels charge over thee, to keep thee in all thy ways. They shall bear thee up in their hands, lest thou dash thy feet against a stone. Thou shalt tread upon the lion and adder; the young lion and the serpent shalt thou trample under feet. Because he hath set his love upon me, therefore will I deliver him; I will set him on high, because he hath known my name."

The holy spirit added in turn: " He shall call upon me, and I will answer him; I will be with him in trouble; I will deliver him, and honor him. With long life will I satisfy him, and show him my salvation." [97]

Jacob left the presence of his father crowned like a bridegroom, adorned like a bride, and bathed in celestial dew, which filled his bones with marrow, and transformed him into a hero and a giant. [98]

Of a miracle done for him at that very moment Jacob himself was not aware. Had he tarried with his father an instant longer, Esau would have met him there, and would surely have slain him. It happened that exactly as Jacob was on the point of leaving the tent of his father, carrying in his hands the plates off which Isaac had eaten, he noticed Esau approaching, and he concealed himself behind the door. Fortunately, it was a revolving door, so that though he could see Esau, he could not be seen by him.

ESAU'S TRUE CHARACTER REVEALED

Esau arrived after a delay of four hours. [99] In spite of all the efforts he had put forth, he had not succeeded in catching any game, and he was compelled to kill a dog and prepare its flesh for his father's meal. [100] All this had made Esau ill-humored, and when he bade his father partake of the meal, the invitation sounded harsh. " Let my father arise," he said, " and eat of his son's venison." Jacob had spoken differently; he had said, " Arise, I pray thee, sit and eat of my venison." The words of Esau terrified Isaac greatly. His fright exceeded that which he had felt when his father was about to offer him as a sacrifice, and he cried

out, " Who then is he that hath been the mediator between
me and the Lord, to make the blessing reach Jacob?"—
words meant to imply that he suspected Rebekah of having
instigated Jacob's act.

Isaac's alarm was caused by his seeing hell at the feet of
Esau. Scarcely had he entered the house when the walls
thereof began to get hot on account of the nearness of hell,
which he brought along with him. Isaac could not but exclaim, " Who will be burnt down yonder, I or my son
Jacob? " and the Lord answered him, " Neither thou nor
Jacob, but the hunter."

Isaac told Esau that the meat set before him by Jacob had
had marvellous qualities. Any savor that one desired it
possessed, it was even endowed with the taste of the food
that God will grant the pious in the world to come. " I
know not," he said, " what the meat was. But I had only to
wish for bread, and it tasted like bread, or fish, or locusts, or
flesh of animals, in short, it had the taste of any dainty one
could wish for." When Esau heard the word " flesh," he
began to weep, and he said: " To me Jacob gave no more
than a dish of lentils, and in payment for it he took my
birthright. What must he have taken from thee for flesh
of animals? " Hitherto Isaac had been in great anguish on
account of the thought that he had committed a wrong in
giving his blessing to his younger son instead of the first-
born, to whom it belonged by law and custom. But when
he heard that Jacob had acquired the birthright from Esau,
he said, " I gave my blessing to the right one! "

In his dismay, Isaac had had the intention of cursing
Jacob for having wrested the blessing from him through

cunning. God prevented him from carrying out his plan.
He reminded him that he would but curse himself, seeing
that his blessing contained the words, " Cursed be every one
that curseth thee." But Isaac was not willing to acknowledge his blessing valid as applied to Jacob, until he was
informed that his second son was the possessor of the birthright. Only then did he say, " Yea, he shall be blessed,"
whereat Esau cried with an exceeding great and bitter cry.
By way of punishment for having been the cause of such
distress, a descendant of Jacob, Mordecai, was also made to
cry with a loud and bitter cry, and his grief was brought
forth by the Amalekite Haman, the descendant of Esau. At
the words of Isaac, " Thy brother came with wisdom, and
hath taken away thy blessing," Esau spat out in vexation,
and said, " He took away my birthright, and I kept silence,
and now that he takes away my blessing, should I also keep
silence?[101] Is not he rightly named Jacob? for he hath
supplanted me these two times."[102]

Isaac continued to speak to Esau: " Behold, I have made
him thy lord, he is thy king, and do what thou wilt, thy
blessings will still belong to him; all his brethren have I
given to him for slaves, and what slaves possess belongs to
their owner. There is nothing for it, thou must be content
that thou wilt receive thy bread baked from thy master."
The Lord took it ill of Isaac that he cheered him with such
kind words. " To Mine enemy," He reproached him, " thou
sayest, ' What shall I do for thee, my son? ' " Isaac replied,
" O that he might find grace with Thee! " God: " He is a
recreant." Isaac: " Doth he not act righteously when he
honors his parents? " God: " In the land of uprightness

will he deal wrongfully, he will stretch his hand forth in days to come against the Temple." **Isaac:** "Then let him enjoy much good in this world, that he may not behold the abiding-place of the Lord in the world to come." [102]

When it became plain to Esau that he could not induce his father to annul the blessing bestowed upon Jacob, he tried to force a blessing for himself by an underhand trick. He said: "Hast thou but one blessing, my father? bless me, even me also, O my father, else it will be said thou hast but one blessing to bestow. Suppose both Jacob and I had been righteous men, had not then thy God had two blessings, one for each?" The Lord Himself made reply: "Silence! Jacob will bless the twelve tribes, and each blessing will be different from every other." But Isaac felt great pity for his older son, and he wanted to bless him, but the Shekinah forsook him, and he could not carry out what he purposed. Thereupon Esau began to weep. He shed three tears—one ran from his right eye, the second from his left eye, and the third remained hanging from his eyelash. God said, "This villain cries for his very life, and should I let him depart empty-handed?" and then He bade Isaac bless his older son. [104]

The blessing of Isaac ran thus: "Behold, of the fat of the earth shall be thy dwelling," by which he meant Greater Greece, in Italy; "and of the dew of heaven from above," referring to Bet-Gubrin; "and by thy sword shalt thou live, and thou shalt serve thy brother," but when he casts off the yoke of the Lord, then shalt thou "shake his yoke from off thy neck," and thou wilt be his master. [105]

The blessing which Isaac gave to his older son was bound

to no condition whatsoever. Whether he deserved them or not, Esau was to enjoy the goods of this world. Jacob's blessing, however, depended upon his pious deeds; through them he would have a just claim upon earthly prosperity. Isaac thought: " Jacob is a righteous man, he will not murmur against God, though it should come to pass that suffering be inflicted upon him in spite of his upright life. But that reprobate Esau, if he should do a good deed, or pray to God and not be heard, he would say, ' As I pray to the idols for naught, so it is in vain to pray to God.' " For this reason did Isaac bestow an unconditional blessing upon Esau.[106]

Jacob Leaves His Father's House

Esau hated his brother Jacob on account of the blessing that his father had given him, and Jacob was very much afraid of his brother Esau, and he fled to the house of Eber, the son of Shem, and he concealed himself there fourteen years on account of his brother Esau, and he continued there to learn the ways of the Lord and His commandments. When Esau saw that Jacob had fled and escaped from him, and Jacob had cunningly obtained the blessing, then Esau grieved exceedingly, and he was also vexed at his father and mother. He also rose up and took his wife, and went away from his father and mother to the land of Seir. There he married his second wife, Basemath, the daughter of Elon the Hittite, and he called her name Adah, saying that the blessing had in that time passed from him. After dwelling in Seir for six months, Esau returned to the land of Canaan, and placed his two wives in his father's house in Hebron. And the wives of Esau vexed and provoked Isaac and Rebekah with their works, for they walked not in the ways of the Lord, but served their fathers' gods of wood and stone, as their fathers had taught them, and they were more wicked than their fathers. They sacrificed and burnt incense to the Baalim, and Isaac and Rebekah became weary of them. And at the end of fourteen years of Jacob's residing in the house of Eber, Jacob desired to see his father and his mother, and he returned home. Esau had forgotten in those days what Jacob had done to him, in having taken the blessing from him, but when Esau saw Jacob returning to his parents, he remembered what Jacob had done to him, and he was greatly incensed against him, and he sought to slay him.[107]

But Esau would not kill Jacob while his father was yet alive, lest Isaac beget another son. He wanted to be sure of being the only heir.[108] However, his hatred against Jacob was so great that he determined to hasten the death of his father and then dispatch Jacob. Such murderous plans Esau cherished in his heart, though he denied that he was harboring them. But God spoke, " Probably thou knowest not that I examine the hearts of men, for I am the Lord that searcheth the heart." And not God alone knew the secret desires of Esau. Rebekah, like all the Mothers, was a prophetess, and she delayed not to warn Jacob of the danger that hung over him. " Thy brother," she said to him, " is as sure of accomplishing his wicked purpose as though thou wert dead. Now therefore, my son, obey my voice, and arise, flee thou to Laban my brother, to Haran, and tarry with him for seven years, until thy brother's fury turn away." In the goodness of her heart, Rebekah could not but believe that the anger of Esau was only a fleeting passion, and would disappear in the course of time. But she was mistaken, his hate persisted until the end of his life.[109]

Courageous as he was, Jacob would not run away from danger. He said to his mother, " I am not afraid; if he wishes to kill me, I will kill him," to which she replied, " Let me not be bereaved of both my sons in one day." [110] By these words Rebekah again showed her prophetic gift. As she spoke, so it happened—when their time came, Esau was slain while the burial of Jacob was taking place.[111]

And Jacob said to Rebekah: " Behold, thou knowest that my father has become old and does not see, and if I leave him and go away, he will be angry and will curse me. I will not go; if he sends me, only then will I go." [112]

Accordingly, Rebekah went to Isaac, and amid tears she spoke to him thus: " If Jacob take a wife of the daughters of Heth, what good shall my life do me? " [113] And Isaac called Jacob, and charged him, and said unto him: " Thou shalt not take a wife of the daughters of Canaan, for thus did our father Abraham command us according to the word of the Lord, which He had commanded him, saying, ' Unto thy seed will I give the land; if thy children keep My covenant that I have made with thee, then will I also perform to thy children that which I have spoken unto thee, and I will not forsake them.' Now therefore, my son, hearken to my voice, to all that I shall command thee, and refrain from taking a wife from amongst the daughters of Canaan. Arise, go to Haran, to the house of Bethuel, thy mother's father, and take thee a wife from thence of the daughters of Laban, thy mother's brother. Take heed lest thou shouldst forget the Lord thy God and all His ways in the land to which thou goest, and shouldst join thyself to the people of the land, and pursue vanity, and forsake the Lord thy God. But when thou comest to the land, serve the Lord. Do not turn to the right or to the left from the way which I commanded thee, and which thou didst learn. And may the Almighty God grant thee favor before the people of the land, that thou mayest take a wife there according to thy choice, one who is good and upright in the way of the Lord. And may God give unto thee and thy seed the blessing of thy father Abraham and make thee fruitful and multiply thee, and mayest thou become a multitude of people in the land whither thou goest, and may God cause thee to return to thy land, the land of thy father's dwelling, with children and with great riches, with joy and with pleasure." [114]

As the value of a document is attested by its concluding words, the signature of the witnesses, so Isaac confirmed the blessing he had bestowed upon Jacob. [115] That none might say Jacob had secured it by intrigue and cunning, he blessed him again with three blessings, in these words, " In so far as I am endowed with the power of blessing, I bestow blessing upon thee. May God, with whom there is endless blessing, give thee His, and also the blessing wherewith Abraham desired to bless me, desisting only in order not to provoke the jealousy of Ishmael." [116]

Seeing with his prophetic eye that the seed of Jacob would once be compelled to go into exile, Isaac offered up one more petition, that God would bring the exiles back again. He said, " He shall deliver thee in six troubles, and in the seventh there shall no evil touch thee." And also Rebekah prayed to God in behalf of Jacob: " O Lord of the world, let not the purpose prosper which Esau harbors against Jacob. Put a bridle upon him, that he accomplish not all he wills to do." [117]

When Esau observed that even his father's love had passed from him to Jacob, he went away, to Ishmael, and he addressed him as follows: "Lo, as thy father gave all his possessions to thy brother Isaac, and dismissed thee with empty hands, so my father purposeth to do to me. Make thyself ready then, go forth and slay thy brother, and I will slay mine, and then we two shall divide the whole world between us." And Ishmael replied: "Why dost thou want me to slay thy father? thou canst do it thyself." Esau said: "It hath happened aforetime that a man killed his brother— Cain murdered Abel. But that a son should kill his father is unheard of."

Esau did not really shrink back from parricide, only it chanced not to fit the plan he had hatched. "If Ishmael slays my father," he said to himself, "I am the rightful redeemer, and I shall kill Ishmael to avenge my father, and if, then, I murder Jacob, too, everything will belong to me, as the heir of my father and my uncle." [118] This shows that Esau's marriage with Mahalath, the daughter of Ishmael and grandchild of Abraham, was not concluded out of regard for his parents, who were opposed to his two other wives, daughters of the Canaanites. All he desired was to enter into amicable relations with Ishmael in order to execute his devilish plan. [119]

But Esau reckoned without his host. The night before his wedding with Mahalath Ishmael died, and Nebaioth, the son of Ishmael, stepped into his father's place, and gave away his sister.[120] How little it had been in Esau's mind to make his parents happy by taking a granddaughter of Abraham to wife, appears from the fact that he kept his two other wives, the Canaanitish women. The daughter of Ishmael followed the example of her companions, and thus she but added to the grief caused the parents of Esau by their daughters-in-law.[121] And the opportunity might have been a most favorable one for Esau to turn aside from his godless ways and amend his conduct, for the bridegroom is pardoned on his wedding day for all his sins committed in years gone by.[122]

Scarcely had Jacob left his father's house, when Rebekah began to weep, for she was sorely distressed about him. Isaac comforted her, saying: "Weep not for Jacob! In peace doth he depart, and in peace will he return. The Lord, God Most High, will guard him against all evil and be with him. He will not forsake him all the days of his life. Have no fear for him, for he walketh on the right path, he is a perfect man, and he hath faith in God—he will not perish."[123]

Jacob Pursued by Eliphaz and Esau

When Jacob went away to go to Haran, Esau called his son Eliphaz, and secretly spoke unto him, saying: "Now hasten, take thy sword in thy hand and pursue Jacob, and pass before him in the road, and lurk for him and slay him with thy sword in one of the mountains, and take all belonging unto him, and come back." And Eliphaz was dexterous and expert with the bow, as his father had taught him, and he was a noted hunter in the field and a valiant man. And Eliphaz did as his father had commanded him. And Eliphaz was at that time thirteen years old, and he arose and went and took ten of his mother's brothers with him, and pursued Jacob. And he followed Jacob closely, and when he overtook him, he lay in ambush for him on the borders of the land of Canaan, opposite to the city of Shechem. And Jacob saw Eliphaz and his men pursuing after him, and Jacob stood in the place in which he was going in order to know what it was, for he did not understand their purpose. Eliphaz drew his sword and went on advancing, he and his men, toward Jacob, and Jacob said unto them, "Wherefore have you come hither, and why do you pursue with your swords?" Eliphaz came near to Jacob, and answered as follows, "Thus did my father command me, and now therefore I will not deviate from the orders which my father gave me." And when Jacob saw that Esau had impressed his command urgently upon Eliphaz, he approached and supplicated Eliphaz and his men, saying, "Behold, all that I have, and that which my father and mother gave unto me, that take unto thee and go from me, and do not slay me, and may this thing that thou wilt do with me be accounted unto thee as righteousness." And the Lord caused Jacob to find favor in the sight of Eliphaz and his men, and they hearkened to the voice of Jacob, and they did not put him to death, but took all his belongings, together with the silver and gold that he had brought with him from Beer-sheba. They left him nothing. When Eliphaz and his men returned to Esau, and told him all that had happened to them with Jacob, he was wroth with his son Eliphaz and with his men, because they had not put Jacob to

death. And they answered, and said unto Esau, " Because
Jacob supplicated us in this matter, not to slay him, our
pity was moved toward him, and we took all belonging to
him, and we came back." Esau then took all the silver and
gold which Eliphaz had taken from Jacob, and he put them
by in his house."

Nevertheless Esau did not give up the hope of intercept-
ing Jacob on his flight and slaying him. He pursued him,
and with his men occupied the road along which he had to
journey to Haran. There a great miracle happened to Jacob.
When he observed what Esau's intention was, he turned off
toward the Jordan river, and, with eyes directed to God, he
cleft the waters with his wanderer's staff, and succeeded in
crossing to the other side. But Esau was not to be deterred.
He kept up the pursuit, and reached the hot springs at
Baarus before his brother, who had to pass by there. Jacob,
not knowing that Esau was on the watch for him, decided
to bathe in the spring, saying, " I have neither bread nor
other things needful, so I will at least warm my body in the
waters of the well." While he was in the bath, Esau occupied every exit, and Jacob would surely have perished in
the hot water, if the Lord had not caused a miracle to come
to pass. A new opening formed of itself, and through it
Jacob escaped. Thus were fulfilled the words, " When
thou passest through the waters, I will be with thee; when
thou walkest through the fire, thou shalt not be burnt," for
Jacob was saved from the waters of the Jordan and from
the fire of the hot spring.

At the same time with Jacob, a rider, leaving his horse and
his clothes on the shore, had stepped into the river to cool

off, but he was overwhelmed by the waves, and he met his
death. Jacob put on the dead man's clothes, mounted his
horse, and went off. It was a lucky chance, for Eliphaz had
stripped him of everything, even his clothes, and the miracle
of the river had happened only that he might not be forced
to appear naked among men.[135]

Though Jacob was robbed of all his possessions, his
courage did not fail him. He said: " Should I lose hope in
my Creator? I set my eyes upon the merits of my fathers.
For the sake of them the Lord will give me His aid." And
God said: " Jacob, thou puttest thy trust in the merits of
thy fathers, therefore I will not suffer thy foot to be moved;
He that keepeth thee will not slumber. Yea, still more!
While a keeper watcheth only by day as a rule, and sleepeth
by night, I will guard thee day and night, for, behold, He
that keepeth Israel shall neither slumber nor sleep. The
Lord will keep thee from all evil, from Esau as well as
Laban; He will keep thy soul, that the Angel of Death do
thee no hurt; He will keep thy going out and thy coming in,
He will support thee now thou art leaving Canaan, and
when thou returnest to Canaan." [136]

Jacob was reluctant to leave the Holy Land before he received direct permission from God. " My parents," he reflected, " bade me go forth and sojourn outside of the land,
but who knows whether it be the will of God that I do as
they say, and beget children outside of the Holy Land?" [137]
Accordingly, he betook himself to Beer-sheba. There,
where the Lord had given permission to Isaac to depart from
Canaan and go to Philistia, he would learn the will of the
Lord concerning himself.

He did not follow the example of his father and grandfather and take refuge with Abimelech, because he feared
the king might force also him into a covenant, and make it
impossible for his descendants of many generations to take
possession of the Philistine land. Nor could he stay at home,
because of his fear that Esau might wrest the birthright
and the blessing from him, and to that he would not and
could not agree.[128] He was as little disposed to take up the
combat with Esau, for he knew the truth of the maxim, " He
who courts danger will be overcome by it; he who avoids
danger will overcome it." Both Abraham and Isaac had
lived according to this rule. His grandfather had fled from
Nimrod, and his father had gone away from the Philistines.[129]

THE DAY OF MIRACLES

Jacob's journey to Haran was a succession of miracles.
The first of the five that befell for his sake in the course of
it was that the sun sank while Jacob was passing Mount
Moriah, though it was high noon at the time. He was following the spring that appeared wherever the Patriarchs
went or settled. It accompanied Jacob from Beer-sheba to
Mount Moriah, a two days' journey. When he arrived at
the holy hill, the Lord said to him: " Jacob, thou hast bread
in thy wallet, and the spring of waters is near by to quench
thy thirst. Thus thou hast food and drink, and here thou
canst lodge for the night." But Jacob replied: " The sun
has barely passed the fifth of its twelve day stages, why
should I lie down to sleep at so unseemly an hour?" But
then Jacob perceived that the sun was about to sink, and he

prepared to make ready his bed.[129] It was the Divine purpose not to let Jacob pass the site of the future Temple without stopping; he was to tarry there at least one night. Also, God desired to appear unto Jacob, and He shows Himself unto His faithful ones only at night.[131] At the same time Jacob was saved from the pursuit of Esau, who had to desist on account of the premature darkness.[132]

Jacob took twelve stones from the altar on which his father Isaac had lain bound as a sacrifice, and he said: " It was the purpose of God to let twelve tribes arise, but they have not been begotten by Abraham or Isaac. If, now, these twelve stones will unite into a single one, then shall I know for a certainty that I am destined to become the father of the twelve tribes." At this time the second miracle came to pass, the twelve stones joined themselves together and made one, which he put under his head, and at once it became soft and downy like a pillow. It was well that he had a comfortable couch. He was in great need of rest, for it was the first night in fourteen years that he did not keep vigils. During all those years, passed in Eber's house of learning, he had devoted the nights to study. And for twenty years to come he was not to sleep, for while he was with his uncle Laban, he spent all the night and every night reciting the Psalms.[133]

On the whole it was a night of marvels. He dreamed a dream in which the course of the world's history was unfolded to him. On a ladder set up on the earth, with the top of it reaching to heaven, he beheld the two angels who had been sent to Sodom. For one hundred and thirty-eight years they had been banished from the celestial regions, because they had betrayed their secret mission to Lot. They had accompanied Jacob from his father's house thither, and now they were ascending heavenward. When they arrived there, he heard them call the other angels, and say, "Come ye and see the countenance of the pious Jacob, whose likeness appears on the Divine throne, ye who yearned long to see it," and then he beheld the angels descend from heaven to gaze upon him.¹³⁴ He also saw the angels of the four kingdoms ascending the ladder. The angel of Babylon mounted seventy rounds, the angel of Media, fifty-two, that of Greece, one hundred and eighty, and that of Edom mounted very high, saying, "I will ascend above the heights of the clouds, I will be like the Most High," and Jacob heard a voice remonstrating, "Yet thou shalt be brought down to hell, to the uttermost parts of the pit." God Himself reproved Edom, saying, "Though thou mount on high as the eagle, and though thy nest be set among the stars, I will bring thee down from thence." ¹³⁵

Furthermore, God showed unto Jacob the revelation at Mount Sinai, the translation of Elijah, the Temple in its glory and in its spoliation, Nebuchadnezzar's attempt to burn the three holy children in the fiery furnace, and Daniel's encounter with Bel.¹³⁶

In this, the first prophetic dream dreamed by Jacob,¹³⁷ God made him the promise that the land upon which he was lying would be given to him, but the land he lay upon was the whole of Palestine, which God had folded together and put under him. "And," the promise continued, "thy seed will be like unto the dust of the earth. As the earth survives all things, so thy children will survive all the nations of the earth. But as the earth is trodden upon by all, so thy children, when they commit trespasses, will be trodden upon by the nations of the earth." [138] And, furthermore, God promised that Jacob should spread out to the west and to the east, a greater promise than that given to his fathers Abraham and Isaac, to whom He had allotted a limited land. Jacob's was an unbounded possession. [139]

From this wondrous dream Jacob awoke with a start of fright, on account of the vision he had had of the destruction of the Temple. [140] He cried out, " How dreadful is this place! this is none other but the house of God, wherein is the gate of heaven through which prayer ascends to Him." He took the stone made out of the twelve, and set it up for a pillar, and poured oil upon the top of it, which had flowed down from heaven for him, and God sank this anointed stone unto the abyss, to serve as the centre of the earth, the same stone, the Eben Shetiyah, [141] that forms the centre of the sanctuary, whereon the Ineffable Name is graven, the knowledge of which makes a man master over nature, and over life and death. [142]

Jacob cast himself down before the Eben Shetiyah, and entreated God to fulfil the promise He had given him, and also he prayed that God grant him honorable sustenance. For God had not mentioned bread to eat and raiment to put on, that Jacob might learn to have faith in the Lord. Then he vowed to give the tenth of all he owned unto God, if He would but grant his petition. Thus Jacob was the first to take a vow upon himself, [143] and the first, too, to separate the tithe from his income. [144]

God had promised him almost all that is desirable, but

he feared he might forfeit the pledged blessings through his sinfulness,[145] and again he prayed earnestly that God bring him back to his father's house unimpaired in body, possessions, and knowledge,[146] and guard him, in the strange land whither he was going, against idolatry, an immoral life, and bloodshed.[147]

His prayer at an end, Jacob set out on his way to Haran, and the third wonder happened. In the twinkling of an eye he arrived at his destination. The earth jumped from Mount Moriah to Haran. A wonder like this God has executed only four times in the whole course of history.[148]

The first thing to meet his eye in Haran was the well whence the inhabitants drew their supply of water. Although it was a great city, Haran suffered from dearth of water, and therefore the well could not be used by the people free of charge. Jacob's sojourn in the city produced a change. By reason of his meritorious deeds the water springs were blessed, and the city had water enough for its needs.

Jacob saw a number of people by the well, and he questioned them, "My brethren, whence be ye?" He thus made himself a model for all to follow. A man should be companionable, and address others like brothers and friends, and not wait for them to greet him. Each one should strive to be the first to give the salutation of peace, that the angels of peace and compassion may come to meet him. When he was informed that the by-standers hailed from Haran, he made inquiry about the character and vocation of his uncle Laban, and whether they were on terms of friendly intercourse with him. They answered briefly: "There is peace between us, but if thou art desirous of inquiring further, here comes Rachel the daughter of Laban. From her thou canst learn all thou hast a mind to learn." They knew that women like to talk, wherefore they referred him to Rachel.[147]

Jacob found it strange that so many should be standing idle by the well, and he questioned further: "Are you day laborers? then it is too early for you to put by your work. But if you are pasturing your own sheep, why do you not water your flocks and let them feed?"[148] They told him they were waiting until all the shepherds brought their flocks thither, and together rolled the stone from the mouth of the well. While he was yet speaking with them, Rachel came with her father's sheep, for Laban had no sons, and a pest having broken out shortly before among his cattle, so few sheep were left that a maiden like Rachel could easily tend them. Now, when Jacob saw the daughter of his mother's brother approaching, he rolled the great stone from the mouth of the well as easily as a cork is drawn from a bottle—the fourth wonder of this extraordinary day. Jacob's strength was equal to the strength of all the shepherds; with his two arms alone he accomplished what usually requires the united forces of a large assemblage of men.[149] He had been divinely endowed with this supernatural strength on leaving the Holy Land. God had caused the dew of the resurrection to drop down upon him, and his physical strength was so great that even in a combat with the angels he was victorious.[150]

The fifth and last wonder of the day was that the water rose from the depths of the well to the very top, there was no need to draw it up, and there it remained all the twenty years that Jacob abode in Haran.[151]

JACOB WITH LABAN

Rachel's coming to the well at the moment when Jacob reached the territory belonging to Haran was an auspicious omen. To meet young maidens on first entering a city is a sure sign that fortune is favorable to one's undertakings. Experience proves this through Eliezer, Jacob, Moses, and Saul. They all encountered maidens when they approached a place new to them, and they all met with success.[154]

Jacob treated Rachel at once as his cousin, which caused significant whispering among the by-standers. They censured Jacob for his demeanor toward her, for since God had sent the deluge upon the world, on account of the immoral life led by men, great chastity had prevailed, especially among the people of the east. The talk of the men reduced Jacob to tears. Scarcely had he kissed Rachel when he began to weep, for he repented of having done it.

There was reason enough for tears. Jacob could not but remember sadly that Eliezer, his grandfather's slave, had brought ten camels laden with presents with him to Haran, when he came to sue for a bride for Isaac, while he had not even a ring to give to Rachel. Moreover, he foresaw that his favorite wife Rachel would not lie beside him in the grave, and this, too, made him weep.

As soon as Rachel heard that Jacob was her cousin, she ran home to tell her father about his coming. Her mother was no longer among the living, else she would naturally have gone to her. In great haste Laban ran to receive Jacob. He reflected, if Eliezer, the bondman, had come with ten camels, what would not the favorite son of the family bring with him, and when he saw that Jacob was unattended, he concluded that he carried great sums of money in his girdle, and he threw his arms about his waist to find out whether his supposition was true. Disappointed in this, he yet did not give up hope that his nephew Jacob was a man of substance. Perhaps he concealed precious stones in his mouth, and he kissed him in order to find out whether he had guessed aright. But Jacob said to him: "Thou thinkest I have money. Nay, thou art mistaken, I have but words." [155] Then he went on to tell him how it had come about that he stood before him empty-handed. He said that his father Isaac had sent him on his way provided with gold, silver, and money, but he had encountered Eliphaz, who had threatened to slay him. To this assailant Jacob had spoken thus: "Know that the descendants of Abraham have an obligation to meet, they will have to serve four hundred years in a land that is not theirs. If thou slayest me, then you, the seed of Esau, will have to pay the debt. It were better, therefore, to take all I have, and spare my life, so that what is owing may be paid by me. Hence," Jacob continued, "I stand before thee bare of all the substance carried off by Eliphaz." [156]

This tale of his nephew's poverty filled Laban with dismay. "What," he exclaimed, "shall I have to give food and drink for a month or, perhaps, even a year to this fellow, who has come to me empty-handed!" He betook himself to his teraphim, to ask them for counsel upon the matter, and they admonished him, saying: "Beware of sending him away from thy house. His star and his constellation are so lucky that good fortune will attend all his undertakings, and for his sake the blessing of the Lord will rest upon all thou doest, in thy house or in thy field."

Laban was satisfied with the advice of the teraphim, but he was embarrassed as to the way in which he was to attach Jacob to his house. He did not venture to offer him service, lest Jacob's conditions be impossible of fulfilment. Again he resorted to the teraphim, and asked them with what reward to tempt his nephew, and they replied: " A wife is his wage; he will ask nothing else of thee but a wife. It is his nature to be attracted by women, and whenever he threatens to leave thee, do but offer him another wife, and he will not depart." [157]

Laban went back to Jacob, and said, " Tell me, what shall thy wages be? " and he replied, " Thinkest thou I came hither to make money? I came only to get me a wife," [158] for Jacob had no sooner beheld Rachel than he fell in love with her and made her a proposal of marriage. Rachel consented, but added the warning: " My father is cunning, and thou art not his match." Jacob: " I am his brother in cunning." Rachel: " But is deception becoming unto the pious? " Jacob: " Yes, ' with the righteous righteousness is seemly, and with the deceiver deception.' But," continued Jacob, " tell me wherein he may deal cunningly with me." Rachel: " I have an older sister, whom he desires to see married before me, and he will try to palm her off on thee instead of me." To be prepared for Laban's trickery, Jacob and Rachel agreed upon a sign by which he would recognize her in the nuptial night. [159]

Thus warned to be on his guard against Laban, Jacob worded his agreement with him regarding his marriage to Rachel with such precision that no room was left for distortion or guile. Jacob said: " I know that the people of this

place are knaves, therefore I desire to put the matter very
clearly to thee. I will serve thee seven years for Rachel. hence
not Leah; for thy daughter, that thou bringest me not some
other woman likewise named Rachel; for the younger daughter, that thou exchangest not their names in the meantime."

Nothing of all this availed: "It profits not if a villain is
cast into a sawmill"—neither force nor gentle words can
circumvent a rascal. Laban deceived not only Jacob, but
also the guests whom he invited to the wedding.

THE MARRIAGE OF JACOB

After Jacob had served Laban seven years, he said to his
uncle: "The Lord destined me to be the father of twelve
tribes. I am now eighty-four years old, and if I do not take
thought of the matter now, when can I?"[160] Thereupon
Laban consented to let him have his daughter Rachel to
wife, and he was married forty-four years after his brother
Esau. The Lord often defers the happiness of the pious,
while He permits the wicked to enjoy the fulfilment of their
desires soon.[161] Esau, however, had purposely chosen his
fortieth year for his marriage; he had wanted to indicate
that he was walking in the footsteps of his father Isaac, who
had likewise married at forty years of age. Esau was like
a swine that stretches out its feet when it lies down, to show
that it is cloven-footed like the clean animals, though it is
none the less one of the unclean animals. Until his fortieth
year Esau made a practice of violating the wives of other
men, and then at his marriage he acted as though he were
following the example of his pious father. Accordingly,
the woman he married was of his own kind, Judith, a daugh-

ter of Heth, for God said: " This one, who is designed for
stubble, to be burnt by fire, shall take unto wife one of a
people also destined for utter destruction." They, Esau and
his wife, illustrated the saying, " Not for naught does the
raven consort with the crow; they are birds of a feather." [168]

Far different it was with Jacob. He married the two
pious and lovely sisters, Leah and Rachel, for Leah, like
her younger sister, was beautiful of countenance, form,
and stature. She had but one defect, her eyes were weak,
and this malady she had brought down upon herself, through
her own action. Laban, who had two daughters, and Rebekah, his sister, who had two sons, had agreed by letter,
while their children were still young, that the older son of the
one was to marry the older daughter of the other, and the
younger son the younger daughter. When Leah grew to
maidenhood, and inquired about her future husband, all her
tidings spoke of his villainous character, and she wept over
her fate until her eyelashes dropped from their lids. But
Rachel grew more and more beautiful day by day, for all
who spoke of Jacob praised and extolled him, and " good
tidings make the bones fat."

In view of the agreement between Laban and Rebekah,
Jacob refused to marry the older daughter Leah. As it was,
Esau was his mortal enemy, on account of what had happened regarding the birthright and the paternal blessing.
If, now, Jacob married the maiden appointed for him, Esau
would never forgive his younger brother. Therefore Jacob
resolved to take to wife Rachel, the younger daughter of
his uncle. [168]

Laban was of another mind. He purposed to marry off

his older daughter first, for he knew that Jacob would consent to serve him a second period of seven years for love of Rachel. On the day of the wedding he assembled the inhabitants of Haran, and addressed them as follows: " Ye know well that we used to suffer from lack of water, and as soon as this pious man Jacob came to dwell among us, we had water in abundance." " What hast thou in mind to do?" they asked Laban. He replied: " If ye have naught to say against it, I will deceive him and give him Leah to wife. He loves Rachel with an exceeding great love, and for her sake he will tarry with us yet seven other years." " Do as it pleaseth thee," his friends said. " Well, then," said Laban, " let each one of you give me a pledge that ye will not betray my purpose."

With the pledges they left with him, Laban bought wine, oil, and meat for the wedding feast, and he set a meal before them which they had themselves paid for. Because he deceived his fellow-citizens thus, Laban is called Arami, " the deceiver." They feasted all day long, until late at night, and when Jacob expressed his astonishment at the attention shown him, they said to him: " Through thy piety thou didst a great service of lovingkindness unto us, our supply of water was increased unto abundance, and we desire to show our gratitude therefor." And, indeed, they tried to give him a hint of Laban's purpose. In the marriage ode which they sang they used the refrain " Halia," in the hope that he would understand it as *Ha Leah*, " This is Leah." But Jacob was unsuspicious and noticed nothing.

When the bride was led into the nuptial chamber, the guests extinguished all the candles, much to Jacob's amazement. But their explanation satisfied him. "Thinkest thou," they said, "we have as little sense of decency as thy countrymen?" Jacob therefore did not discover the deception practiced upon him until morning. During the night Leah responded whenever he called Rachel, for which he reproached her bitterly when daylight came. "O thou deceiver, daughter of a deceiver, why didst thou answer me when I called Rachel's name?" "Is there a teacher without a pupil?" asked Leah, in return. "I but profited by thy instruction. When thy father called thee Esau, didst thou not say, Here am I?"[164]

Jacob was greatly enraged against Laban, and he said to him: "Why didst thou deal treacherously with me? Take back thy daughter, and let me depart, seeing thou didst act wickedly toward me."[165] Laban pacified him, however, saying, "It is not so done in our place, to give the younger before the first-born," and Jacob agreed to serve yet seven other years for Rachel, and after the seven days of the feast of Leah's wedding were fulfilled, he married Rachel.[166]

With Leah and Rachel, Jacob received the handmaids Zilpah and Bilhah, two other daughters of Laban, whom his concubines had borne unto him.[167]

The Birth of Jacob's Children

The ways of God are not like unto the ways of men. A man clings close to his friend while he has riches, and forsakes him when he falls into poverty. But when God sees a mortal unsteady and faltering, He reaches a hand out to him, and raises him up. Thus it happened with Leah. She was hated by Jacob, and God visited her in mercy. Jacob's aversion to Leah began the very morning after their wedding, when his wife taunted him with not being wholly free from cunning and craft himself. Then God said, " Help can come to Leah only if she gives birth to a child; then the love of her husband will return to her." [168] God remembered the tears she had shed when she prayed that her doom, chaining her to that recreant Esau, be averted from her, and so wondrous are the uses of prayer that Leah, besides turning aside the impending decree, was permitted to marry Jacob before her sister and be the first to bear him a child. There was another reason why the Lord was compassionately inclined toward Leah. She had gotten herself talked about. The sailors on the sea, the travellers along the highways, the women at their looms, they all gossiped about Leah, saying, " She is not within what her seeming is without. She appears to be pious, but if she were, she would not have deceived her sister." [169] To put an end to all this tattle, God granted her the distinction of bearing a son at the end of seven months after her marriage. He was one of a pair of twins, the other child being a daughter. So it was with eleven of the sons of Jacob, all of them except Joseph were born twins with a girl, and the twin sister and brother married later on. [170] Altogether it was an extraordinary childbirth, for Leah was barren, not formed by nature to bear children.

She called her first-born son Reuben, which means " See the normal man," for he was neither big nor little, neither dark nor fair, but exactly normal. [171] In calling her oldest child Reuben, " See the son," Leah indicated his future character. " Behold the difference," the name implied, " be-

tween my first-born son and the first-born son of my father-
in-law. Esau sold his birthright to Jacob of his own free
will, and yet he hated him. As for my first-born son, although his birthright was taken from him without his consent, and given to Joseph, it was nevertheless he who rescued
Joseph from the hands of his brethren." [112]

Leah called her second son Shime'on, " Yonder is sin," for
one of his descendants was that Zimri who was guilty of
vile trespasses with the daughters of Moab. [113]

The name of her third son, Levi, was given him by God
Himself, not by his mother. The Lord summoned him
through the angel Gabriel, and bestowed the name upon him
as one who is "crowned" with the twenty-four gifts that
are the tribute due to the priests. [114]

At the birth of her fourth son, Leah returned thanks to
God for a special reason. She knew that Jacob would beget
twelve sons, and if they were distributed equally among his
four wives, each would bear three. But now it appeared
that she had one more than her due share, and she called him
Jehudah, "thanks unto God." She was thus the first since
the creation of the world to give thanks to God, [115] and her
example was followed by David and Daniel, the descendants of her son Judah.

When Rachel saw that her sister had borne Jacob four
sons, she envied Leah. Not that she begrudged her the
good fortune she enjoyed, she only envied her for her piety,
saying to herself that it was to her righteous conduct that
she owed the blessing of many children. [116] Then she besought Jacob: "Pray unto God for me, that He grant me
children, else my life is no life. Verily, there are four that

may be regarded as though they were dead, the blind, the leper, the childless, and he who was once rich and has lost his fortune." Jacob's anger was kindled against Rachel, and he said: "It were better thou shouldst address thy petition to God, and not to me, for am I in God's stead, who hath withheld from thee the fruit of the womb?" ¹⁷⁷ God was displeased with this answer that Jacob made to his sad wife. He rebuked him with the words: "Is it thus thou wouldst comfort a grief-stricken heart? As thou livest, the day will come when thy children will stand before the son of Rachel, and he will use the same words thou hast but now used, saying, 'Am I in the place of the Lord?'"

Rachel also made reply to Jacob, saying: "Did not thy father, too, entreat God for thy mother with earnest words, beseeching Him to remove her barrenness?" Jacob: "It is true, but Isaac had no children, and I have several." Rachel: "Remember thy grandfather Abraham, thou canst not deny that he had children when he supplicated God in behalf of Sarah!" Jacob: "Wouldst thou do for me what Sarah did for my grandfather?" Rachel: "Pray, what did she?" Jacob: "She herself brought a rival into her house." Rachel: "If that is all that is necessary, I am ready to follow the example of Sarah, and I pray that as she was granted a child for having invited a rival, so may I be blessed, too." ¹⁷⁸ Thereupon Rachel gave Jacob Bilhah, her freed handmaid, to wife, and she bore him a son, whom Rachel called Dan, saying, "As the Lord was gracious unto me and gave me a son according to my petition, so He will permit Samson, the descendant of Dan, to judge his people, that it fall not into the hands of the Philistines." ¹⁷⁹ Bilhah's

second son Rachel named Naphtali, saying, " Mine is the
bond that binds Jacob to this place, for it was for my sake
that he came to Laban." At the same time she wanted to
convey by this name that the Torah, which is as sweet as
Nofet, " honeycomb," would be taught in the territory of
Naphtali.[180] And the name had still a third meaning: " As
God hath heard my fervent prayer for a son, so He will
hearken unto the fervent prayer of the Naphtalites when
they are beset by their enemies." [181]

Leah, seeing that she had left bearing, while Bilhah, her
sister's handmaid, bore Jacob two sons, concluded that it
was Jacob's destiny to have four wives, her sister and herself, and their half-sisters Bilhah and Zilpah. Therefore
she also gave him her handmaid to wife.[182] Zilpah was the
youngest of the four women. It was the custom of that time
to give the older daughter the older handmaid, and the
younger daughter the younger handmaid, as their dowry,
when they got married. Now, in order to make Jacob believe that his wife was the younger daughter he had served
for, Laban had given Leah the younger handmaid as her
marriage portion. This Zilpah was so young that her body
betrayed no outward signs of pregnancy, and nothing was
known of her condition until her son was born. Leah called
the boy Gad, which means " fortune," or it may mean " the
cutter," for from Gad was descended the prophet Elijah,
who brings good fortune to Israel, and he also cuts down
the heathen world.[183] Leah had other reasons, too, for choosing this name of double meaning. The tribe of Gad had the
good fortune of entering into possession of its allotment in
the Holy Land before any of the others,[184] and, also, Gad the
son of Jacob was born circumcised.[185]

To Zilpah's second son Leah gave the name of Asher, "praise," for, she said, "Unto me all manner of praise is due, for I brought my handmaid into the house of my husband as wife. Sarah did likewise, but only because she had no children, and so it was also with Rachel. But as for me, I had children, and nevertheless I subdued my passion, and without jealousy I gave my handmaid to my husband for wife. Verily, all will praise and extol me." [186] Furthermore she spoke: "As the women will praise me, so the sons of Asher will in time to come praise God for their fruitful possession in the Holy Land." [187]

The next son born unto Jacob was Issachar, "a reward," and once more it was Leah who was permitted to bring forth the child, as a reward from God for her pious desire to have the twelve tribes come into the world. To secure this result, she left no means untried. [188]

It happened once that her oldest son Reuben was tending his father's ass during the harvest, and he bound him to a root of dudaim, and went his way. On returning, he found the dudaim torn out of the ground, and the ass lying dead beside it. The beast had uprooted it in trying to get loose, and the plant has a peculiar quality, whoever tears it up must die. [189] As it was the time of the harvest, when it is permitted for any one to take a plant from a field, and as dudaim is, besides, a plant which the owner of a field esteems lightly, Reuben carried it home. Being a good son, he did not keep it for himself, but gave it to his mother. Rachel desired the dudaim, and she asked the plant of Leah, who parted with it to her sister, but on the condition that Jacob, when he returned from work in the evening, should

tarry with her for a while. It was altogether unbecoming
conduct in Rachel to dispose thus of her husband. She
gained the dudaim, but she lost two tribes. If she had
acted otherwise, she would have borne four sons instead of
two. And she suffered another punishment, her body was
not permitted to rest in the grave beside her husband's.

Jacob came home from the field after night had fallen, for
he observed the law obliging a day laborer to work until
darkness sets in, and Jacob's zeal in the affairs of Laban
was as great in the last seven years, after his marriage, as
in the first seven, while he was serving for the hand of
Rachel.[190] When Leah heard the braying of Jacob's ass,
she ran to meet her husband,[191] and without giving him
time to wash his feet, she insisted upon his turning aside
into her tent.[192] At first Jacob refused to go, but God
compelled him to enter, for unto God it was known that
Leah acted from pure, disinterested motives.[193] Her dudaim
secured two sons for her, Issachar, the father of the tribe
that devotes itself to the study of the Torah, whence his
name meaning "reward," and Zebulon, whose descendants
carried on commerce, using their profits to enable their
brethren of Issachar to keep at their studies.[194] Leah called
this last-born son of hers Zebulon, "dwelling-place," for
she said, "Now will my husband dwell with me, seeing that
I have borne him six sons, and, also, the sons of Zebulon
will have a goodly dwelling-place in the Holy Land."[195]

Leah bore once more, and this last time it was a daughter,
a man child turned into a woman by her prayer. When she
conceived for the seventh time, she spake as follows: "God
promised Jacob twelve sons. I bore him six, and each of the

two handmaids has borne him two. If, now, I were to bring forth another son, my sister Rachel would not be equal even unto the handmaids." Therefore she prayed to God to change the male embryo in her womb into a female, and God hearkened unto her prayer.[196]

Now all the wives of Jacob, Leah, Rachel, Zilpah, and Bilhah, united their prayers with the prayer of Jacob, and together they besought God to remove the curse of barrenness from Rachel. On New Year's Day, the day whereon God sits in judgment upon the inhabitants of the earth, He remembered Rachel, and granted her a son.[197] And Rachel spake, "God hath taken away my reproach," for all the people had said that she was not a pious woman, else had she borne children, and now that God had hearkened to her, and opened her womb, such idle talk no longer had any reason.[198]

By bearing a son, she had escaped another disgrace. She had said to herself: "Jacob hath a mind to return to the land of his birth, and my father will not be able to hinder his daughters who have borne him children from following their husband thither with their children. But he will not let me, the childless wife, go, too, and he will keep me here and marry me to one of the uncircumcised."[199] She said furthermore, "As my son hath removed my reproach, so Joshua, his descendant, will roll away a reproach from the Israelites, when he circumcises them beyond Jordan."[200]

Rachel called her son Joseph, "increase," saying, "God will give me an additional son." Prophetess as she was, she foresaw she would have a second son. But an increase added on by God is larger than the original capital itself.

Benjamin, the second son, whom Rachel regarded merely as a supplement, had ten sons, while Joseph begot only two. These twelve together may be considered the twelve tribes borne by Rachel.[201] Had Rachel not used the form of expression, " The Lord add to me another son," she herself would have begotten twelve tribes with Jacob.[202]

JACOB FLEES BEFORE LABAN

Jacob had only been waiting for Joseph to be born to begin preparations for his journey home. The holy spirit had revealed to him that the house of Joseph would work the destruction of the house of Esau, and, therefore, Jacob exclaimed at the birth of Joseph, " Now I need not fear Esau or his legions." [203]

About this time, Rebekah sent her nurse Deborah, the daughter of Uz, accompanied by two of Isaac's servants, to Jacob, to urge him to return to his father's house, now that his fourteen years of service had come to an end. Then Jacob approached Laban, and spoke, " Give me my wives and my children, that I may go unto mine own place, and to my country, for my mother has sent messengers unto me, bidding me to return to my father's house." [204] Laban answered, saying, " O that I might find favor in thine eyes! By a sign it was made known unto me that God blesseth me for thy sake." What Laban had in mind was the treasure he had found on the day Jacob came to him, and he considered that a token of his beneficent powers.[205] Indeed, God had wrought many a thing in the house of Laban that testified to the blessings spread abroad by the pious. Shortly before Jacob came, a pest had broken out among Laban's

cattle, and with his arrival it ceased.[206] And Laban had had
no son, but during Jacob's sojourn in Haran sons were born
unto him.[207]

All the hire he asked in return for his labor and for the
blessings he had brought Laban was the speckled and
spotted among the goats of his herd, and the black among
the sheep. Laban assented to his conditions, saying, " Behold, I would it might be according to thy word." The
arch-villain Laban, whose tongue wagged in all directions,
and who made all sorts of promises that were never kept,
judged others by himself, and therefore suspected Jacob of
wanting to deceive him.[208] And yet, in the end, it was Laban
himself who broke his word. No less than a hundred times
he changed the agreement between them. Nevertheless his
unrighteous conduct was of no avail. Though a three days'
journey had been set betwixt Laban's flocks and Jacob's, the
angels were wont to bring the sheep belonging to Laban
down to Jacob's sheep, and Jacob's droves grew constantly
larger and better.[209] Laban had given only the feeble
and sick to Jacob, yet the young of the flock, raised under
Jacob's tendance, were so excellent in quality that people
bought them at a heavy price.[210] And Jacob had no need to
resort to the peeled rods. He had but to speak, and the
flocks bare according to his desire.[211] What Laban deserved
was utter ruin, for having permitted the pious Jacob to work
for him without hire, and after his wages had been changed
ten times, and ten times Laban had tried to overreach him,
God rewarded him in this way.[212] But his good luck with
the flocks was only what Jacob deserved. Every faithful
laborer is rewarded by God in this world, quite regardless

of what awaits him in the world to come.[213] With empty
hands Jacob had come to Laban, and he left him with herds
numbering six hundred thousand. Their increase had been
marvellous, an increase that will be equalled only in the
Messianic time.[214]

The wealth and good fortune of Jacob called forth the
envy of Laban and his sons, and they could not hide their
vexation in their intercourse with him. And the Lord said
unto Jacob, " Thy father-in-law's countenance is not toward
thee as beforetime, and yet thou tarriest with him? Do
thou rather return unto the land of thy fathers, and there I
will let My Shekinah rest upon thee, for I cannot permit the
Shekinah to reside outside of the Holy Land." [215] Immediately Jacob sent the fleet messenger Naphtali [216] to Rachel
and Leah to summon them to a consultation, and he chose
as the place of meeting the open field, where none could
overhear what was said.[217]

His two wives approved the plan of returning to his home,
and Jacob resolved at once to go away with all his substance,
without as much as acquainting Laban with his intention
Laban was gone to shear his sheep, and so Jacob could execute his plan without delay.

That her father might not learn about their flight from his
teraphim, Rachel stole them, and she took them and concealed them upon the camel upon which she sat, and she
went on. And this is the manner they used to make the
images: They took a man who was the first-born, slew him
and took the hair off his head, then salted the head, and
anointed it with oil, then they wrote " the Name " upon a
small tablet of copper or gold, and placed it under his

tongue. The head with the tablet under the tongue was then put in a house where lights were lighted before it, and at the time when they bowed down to it, it spoke to them on all matters that they asked of it, and that was due to the power of the Name which was written upon it.[218]

THE COVENANT WITH LABAN

Jacob departed and crossed the Euphrates, and set his face toward Gilead, for the holy spirit revealed to him that God would bring help there to his children in the days of Jephthah. Meantime the shepherds of Haran observed that the well, which had been filled to overflowing since the arrival of Jacob in their place, ran dry suddenly. For three days they watched and waited, in the hope that the waters would return in the same abundance as before. Disappointed, they finally told Laban of the misfortune, and he divined at once that Jacob had departed thence, for he knew that the blessing had been conferred upon Haran only for the sake of his son-in-law's merits.[219]

On the morrow Laban rose early, assembled all the people of the city, and pursued Jacob with the intention of killing him when he overtook him. But the archangel Michael appeared unto him, and bade him take heed unto himself, that he do not the least unto Jacob, else would he suffer death himself.[220] This message from heaven came to Laban during the night, for when, in extraordinary cases, God finds it necessary to reveal Himself unto the heathen, He does it only in the dark, clandestinely as it were, while He shows Himself to the prophets of the Jews openly, during daylight.

Laban accomplished the journey in one day for which

Jacob had taken seven,[221] and he overtook him at the mountain of Gilead. When he came upon Jacob, he found him in the act of praying and giving praise unto God.[222] Immediately Laban fell to remonstrating with his son-in-law for having stolen away unawares to him. He showed his true character when he said, "It is in the power of my hand to do thee hurt, but the God of thy father spake unto me yesternight, saying, Take heed to thyself that thou speak not to Jacob either good or bad." That is the way of the wicked, they boast of the evil they can do. Laban wanted to let Jacob know that only the dream warning him against doing aught that was harmful to Jacob prevented him from carrying out the wicked design he had formed against him.[223]

Laban continued to take Jacob to task, and he concluded with the words, "And now, though thou wouldst needs be gone, because thou sore longedst after thy father's house, yet wherefore hast thou stolen my gods?" When he pronounced the last words, his grandchildren interrupted him, saying, "We are ashamed of thee, grandfather, that in thy old age thou shouldst use such words as 'my gods.'" Laban searched all the tents for his idols, going first to the tent of Jacob, which was Rachel's at the same time, for Jacob always dwelt with his favorite wife. Finding nothing, he went thence to Leah's tent, and to the tents of the two handmaids, and, noticing that Rachel was feeling about here and there, his suspicions were aroused, and he entered her tent a second time. He would now have found what he was looking for, if a miracle had not come to pass. The teraphim were transformed into drinking vessels, and Laban had to desist from his fruitless search.

Now Jacob, who did not know that Rachel had stolen her father's teraphim in order to turn him aside from his idolatrous ways, was wroth with Laban, and began to chide with him. In the quarrel between them, Jacob's noble character manifested itself. Notwithstanding his excitement, he did not suffer a single unbecoming word to escape him. He only reminded Laban of the loyalty and devotion with which he had served him, doing for him what none other would or could have done. He said: " I dealt wrongfully with the lion, for God had appointed of Laban's sheep for the lion's daily sustenance, and I deprived him thereof. Could another shepherd have done thus? Yes, the people abused me, calling me robber and sneak thief, for they thought that only by stealing by day and stealing by night could I replace the animals torn by wild beasts. And as to my honesty," he continued, " is it likely there is another son-in-law who, having lived with his father-in-law, hath not taken some little thing from the household of his father-in-law, a knife, or other trifle? But thou hast felt about all my stuff, what hast thou found of all thy household stuff? Not so much as a needle or a nail."

In his indignation, and conscious of his innocence, Jacob exclaimed, " With whomsoever thou findest thy gods, he shall not live," words which contained a curse—the thief was cursed with premature death, and therefore Rachel had to die in giving birth to Benjamin. Indeed, the curse would have taken effect at once, had it not been the wish of God that Rachel should bear Jacob his youngest son.²⁴

After the quarrel, the two men made a treaty, and with his gigantic strength Jacob set up a huge rock as a memo-

rial, and a heap of stones as a sign of their covenant. In
this matter Jacob followed the example of his fathers, who
likewise had covenanted with heathen nations, Abraham
with the Jebusites, and Isaac with the Philistines. Therefore Jacob did not hesitate to make a treaty with the Ara-
means.[125] Jacob summoned his sons, calling them brethren,
for they were his peers in piety and strength, and he bade
them cast up heaps of stones. Thereupon he swore unto
his father-in-law that he would take no wives beside his four
daughters, either while they were alive or after their death,
and Laban, on his part, swore that he would not pass over
the heaps or over the pillar unto Jacob with hostile
intent,[126] and he took the oath by the God of Abraham,
and the God of Nahor, while Jacob made mention of the
Fear of Isaac. He refrained from using the term "the
God of Isaac," because God never unites His name with that
of a living person, for the reason that so long as a man has
not ended his years, no trust may be put in him, lest he be
seduced by the evil inclination. It is true, when He appeared unto Jacob at Beth-el, God called Himself "the God
of Isaac." There was a reason for the unusual phrase.
Being blind, Isaac led a retired life, within his tent, and the
evil inclination had no power over him any more. But
though God had full confidence in Isaac, yet Jacob could not
venture to couple the name of God with the name of a living
man, wherefore he took his oath by "the Fear of Isaac."[127]

Early in the morning after the day of covenanting, Laban
rose up, and kissed his grandchildren and his daughters, and
blessed them. But these acts and words of his did not come
from the heart; in his innermost thoughts he regretted that

Jacob and his family and his substance had escaped him.
His true feelings he betrayed in the message which he sent to
Esau at once upon his return to Haran, by the hand of his
son Beor and ten companions of his son. The message read:
" Hast thou heard what Jacob thy brother has done unto me,
who first came to me naked and bare, and I went to meet him,
and took him to my house with honor, and brought him up,
and gave him my two daughters for wives, and also two of
my maids? And God blessed him on my account, and he increased abundantly, and had sons and daughters and maid-
servants, and also an uncommon stock of flocks and herds,
camels and asses, also silver and gold in abundance. But
when he saw that his wealth increased, he left me while I
went to shear my sheep, and he rose up and fled in secrecy.
And he put his wives and children upon camels, and he led
away all his cattle and substance which he acquired in my
land, and he resolved to go to his father Isaac, to the land of
Canaan. And he did not suffer me to kiss my sons and
daughters, and he carried away my daughters as captives
of the sword, and he also stole my gods, and he fled. And
now I have left him in the mountain of the brook of Jabbok,
he and all belonging to him, not a jot of his substance is lacking. If it be thy wish to go to him, go, and there wilt thou
find him, and thou canst do unto him as thy soul desireth."

Jacob had no need to fear either Laban or Esau, for on
his journey he was accompanied by two angel hosts, one
going with him from Haran to the borders of the Holy
Land, where he was received by the other host, the angels
of Palestine. Each of these hosts consisted of no less than
six hundred thousand angels, and when he beheld them,

Jacob said: " Ye belong neither to the host of Esau, who is preparing to go out to war against me, nor the host of Laban, who is about to pursue me again. Ye are the hosts of the holy angels sent by the Lord." And he gave the name Mahanaim, Double-Host, to the spot on which the second army relieved the first."

JACOB AND ESAU PREPARE TO MEET

The message of Laban awakened Esau's old hatred toward Jacob with increased fury, and he assembled his household, consisting of sixty men. With them and three hundred and forty inhabitants of Seir, he went forth to do battle with Jacob and kill him. He divided his warriors into seven cohorts, giving to his son Eliphaz his own division of sixty, and putting the other six divisions under as many of the Horites.

While Esau was hastening onward to meet Jacob, the messengers which Laban had sent to Esau came to Rebekah and told her that Esau and his four hundred men were about to make war upon Jacob, with the purpose of slaying him and taking possession of all he had. Anxious lest Esau should execute his plan while yet Jacob was on the journey, she hastily dispatched seventy-two of the retainers of Isaac's household, to give him help. Jacob, tarrying on the banks of the brook Jabbok, rejoiced at the sight of these men, and he greeted them with the words, " This is God's helping host," wherefore he called the place of their meeting Mahanaim, Host.

After the warriors sent by Rebekah had satisfied his questions regarding the welfare of his parents, they delivered hi◄

mother's message unto him, thus: " I have heard, my son, that thy brother Esau hath gone forth against thee on the road, with men of the children of Seir the Horite, and therefore, my son, hearken to my voice, and take counsel with thyself what thou wilt do, and when he cometh up to thee, supplicate him, and do not speak roughly to him, and give him a present from what thou possessest, and from what God has favored thee with. And when he asketh thee concerning thy affairs, conceal nothing from him, perhaps he may turn from his anger against thee, and thou wilt thereby save thy soul, thou and all belonging to thee, for it is thy duty to honor him, since he is thy elder brother."

And when Jacob heard the words of his mother which the messengers had spoken to him, he lifted up his voice and wept bitterly, and did as his mother commanded him.

He sent messengers to Esau to placate him, and they said unto him: " Thus speaketh thy servant Jacob: My lord, think not that the blessing which my father bestowed upon me profited me. Twenty years I served Laban, and he deceived me, and changed my hire ten times, as thou well knowest. Yet did I labor sorely in his house, and God saw my affliction, my labor, and the work of my hands, and afterward He caused me to find grace and favor in the sight of Laban. And through God's great mercy and kindness, I acquired oxen and asses and cattle and men-servants and maidservants. And now I am coming to my country and to my home, to my father and mother, who are in the land of Canaan. And I have sent to let my lord know all this in order to find favor in the eyes of my lord, so that he may not imagine that I have become a man of substance, or that the blessing with which my father blessed me has benefited me." [333]

Furthermore spake the messengers: "Why dost thou envy me in respect to the blessing wherewith my father blessed me? Is it that the sun shineth in my land, and not in thine? Or doth the dew and the rain fall only upon my land, and not upon thine? If my father blessed me with the dew of heaven, he blessed thee with the fatness of the earth, and if he spoke to me, Peoples will serve thee, he hath said unto thee, By thy sword shalt thou live. How long, then, wilt thou continue to envy me? Come, now, let us set up a covenant between us, that we will share equally all the vexations that may occur."

Esau would not agree to this proposal, his friends dissuaded him therefrom, saying, " Accept not these conditions, for God hath said to Abraham, Know of a surety that thy seed shall be a stranger in a land that is not theirs, and shall serve the people thereof, and the aliens shall afflict them four hundred years Wait, therefore, until Jacob and his family go down into Egypt to pay off this debt."

Jacob also sent word to Esau, saying: "Though I dwelt with that heathen of the heathen, Laban, yet have I not forgotten my God, but I fulfil the six hundred and thirteen commandments of the Torah. [334] If thy mind be set upon peace, thou wilt find me ready for peace. But if thy desire be war, thou wilt find me ready for war. I have with me men of valor and strength, they have but to utter a word, and God fulfils it. I tarried with Laban until Joseph should be born, he who is destined to subdue thee. [335] And though my descendants be held in bondage in this world, yet a day will come when they will rule over their rulers." [336]

In reply to all these gentle words, Esau spoke with arrogance: "Surely I have heard, and truly it has been told unto me what Jacob has been to Laban, who brought him up in his house, and gave him his daughters for wives, and he begot sons and daughters, and abundantly increased in wealth and riches in Laban's house and with his help. And when he saw that his wealth was abundant and his riches were great, he fled with all belonging to him from Laban's house, and he carried away Laban's daughters from their father as captives of the sword, without telling him of it. And not only to Laban hath Jacob done thus, but also unto me hath he done so, and he hath twice supplanted me, and shall I be silent? Now, I have this day come with my camp to meet him, and I will do unto him according to the desire of my heart."

The messengers dispatched by Jacob now returned to him, and reported these words of Esau unto him.[287] They also told him that his brother was advancing against him with an army consisting of four hundred crowned heads, each leading a host of four hundred men.[288] "It is true, thou art his brother, and thou treatest him as a brother should," they said to Jacob, "but he is an Esau, thou must be made aware of his villainy."[289]

Jacob bore in mind the promise of God, that He would bring him back to his father's house in peace, yet the report about his brother's purpose alarmed him greatly. A pious man may never depend upon promises of earthly good. God does not keep the promise if he is guilty of the smallest conceivable trespass, and Jacob feared that he might have forfeited happiness by reason of a sin committed by him.

Moreover, he was anxious lest Esau be the one favored by God, inasmuch as he had these twenty years been fulfilling two Divine commands that Jacob had had to disregard. Esau had been living in the Holy Land, Jacob outside of it; the former had been in attendance upon his parents, the latter dwelling at a distance from them. And much as he feared defeat, Jacob also feared the reverse, that he might be victorious over Esau, or might even slay his brother, which would be as bad as to be slain by him. And he was depressed by another apprehension, that his father had died, for he reasoned that Esau would not take such warlike steps against his own brother, were his father still alive.[240]

When his wives saw the anxiety that possessed Jacob, they began to quarrel with him, and reproach him for having taken them away from their father's house, though he knew that such danger threatened from Esau.[241] Then Jacob determined to apply the three means that might save him from the fate impending: he would cry to God for help, appease Esau's wrath with presents, and hold himself in readiness for war if the worst came to the worst.[242]

He prayed to God: " O Thou God of my father Abraham, and God of my father Isaac, God of all who walk in the ways of the pious and do like unto them! I am not worthy of the least of all the mercies, and of all the truth, which Thou hast showed unto Thy servant. O Lord of the world, as Thou didst not suffer Laban to execute his evil designs against me, so also bring to naught the purpose of Esau, who desireth to slay me. O Lord of the world, in Thy Torah which Thou wilt give us on Mount Sinai it is written, And whether it be cow or ewe, ye shall not kill it and her young both in one day. If this wretch should come and murder my children and their mothers at the same time, who would then desire to read Thy Torah which Thou wilt give us on Mount Sinai? And yet Thou didst speak, For the sake of thy merits and for the merits of thy fathers I will do good unto thee, and in the future world thy children shall be as numerous as the sand of the sea."

As Jacob prayed for his own deliverance, so also he prayed for the salvation of his descendants, that they might not be annihilated by the descendants of Esau.

Such was the prayer of Jacob when he saw Esau approaching from afar, and God heard his petition and looked upon his tears, and He gave him the assurance that for his sake his descendants, too, would be redeemed from all distress.[243]

Then the Lord sent three angels, and they went before Esau, and they appeared unto Esau and his people as hundreds and thousands of men riding upon horses. They were furnished with all sorts of weapons, and divided into four columns. And one division went on, and they found Esau coming with four hundred men, and the division ran toward them, and terrified them. Esau fell off his horse in alarm, and all his men separated from him in great fear, while the approaching column shouted after them, " Verily, we are the servants of Jacob, the servant of God, and who can stand against us?" Esau then said unto them, " O, then my lord and brother Jacob is your lord, whom I have not seen these twenty years, and now that I have this day come to see him, do you treat me in this manner?" The angels answered, " As the Lord liveth, were not Jacob thy brother, we had not left one remaining of thee and thy people, but on account of Jacob we will do nothing to thee." This division passed from Esau, and when he had gone from there about a league, the second division came toward him, and they also did unto Esau and his men as the first had done to them, and when they permitted him to go on, the third came and did like the first, and when the third had passed also, and Esau still continued with his men on the road to Jacob, the fourth division came and did to them as the others had done. And Esau was greatly afraid of his brother, because he thought that the four columns of the army which he had encountered were the servants of Jacob.

After Jacob had made an end of praying, he divided all that journeyed with him into two companies, and he set over them Damesek and Alinus, the two sons of Eliezer, the bondman of Abraham, and their sons.[344] Jacob's example teaches us not to conceal the whole of our fortune in one hiding-place, else we run the danger of losing everything at one stroke.

Of his cattle he sent a part to Esau as a present, first dividing it into three droves in order to impress his brother more. When Esau received the first drove, he would think he had the whole gift that had been sent to him, and suddenly he would be astonished by the appearance of the second portion, and again by the third. Jacob knew his brother's avarice only too well.[345]

The men who were the bearers of Jacob's present to Esau were charged with the following message, " This is an offering to my lord Esau from his slave Jacob." But God took these words of Jacob in ill part, saying, " Thou profanest

what is holy when thou callest Esau lord." Jacob excused himself; he was but flattering the wicked in order to
escape death at his hands.[346]

Jacob Wrestles with the Angel

The servants of Jacob went before him with the present
for Esau, and he followed with his wives and his children.
As he was about to pass over the ford of Jabbok, he observed
a shepherd, who likewise had sheep and camels. The
stranger approached Jacob and proposed that they should
ford the stream together, and help each other move their
cattle over, and Jacob assented, on the condition that his
possessions should be put across first. In the twinkling of
an eye Jacob's sheep were transferred to the other side of
the stream by the shepherd. Then the flocks of the shepherd were to be moved by Jacob, but no matter how many
he took over to the opposite bank, always there remained
some on the hither shore. There was no end to the cattle,
though Jacob labored all the night through. At last he lost
patience, and he fell upon the shepherd and caught him
by the throat, crying out, " O thou wizard, thou wizard, at
night no enchantment succeeds!" The angel thought,
" Very well, let him know once for all with whom he has
had dealings," and with his finger he touched the earth,
whence fire burst forth. But Jacob said, " What! thou
thinkest thus to affright me, who am made wholly of
fire?"[347]

The shepherd was no less a personage than the archangel
Michael, and in his combat with Jacob he was assisted by the
whole host of angels under his command. He was on the

point of inflicting a dangerous wound upon Jacob, when God appeared, and all the angels, even Michael himself, felt their strength ooze away. Seeing that he could not prevail against Jacob, the archangel touched the hollow of his thigh, and injured him, and God rebuked him, saying, " Dost thou act as is seemly, when thou causest a blemish in My priest Jacob? " Michael said in astonishment, " Why, it is I who am Thy priest! " But God said, " Thou art My priest in heaven, and he is My priest on earth." Thereupon Michael summoned the archangel Raphael, saying, " My comrade, I pray thee, help me out of my distress, for thou art charged with the healing of all disease," and Raphael cured Jacob of the injury Michael had inflicted.

The Lord continued to reproach Michael, saying, " Why didst thou do harm unto My first-born son? " and the archangel answered, " I did it only to glorify Thee," and then God appointed Michael as the guardian angel of Jacob and his seed unto the end of all generations, with these words: " Thou art a fire, and so is Jacob a fire ; thou art the head of the angels, and he is the head of the nations ; thou art supreme over all the angels, and he is supreme over all the peoples. Therefore he who is supreme over all the angels shall be appointed unto him who is supreme over all the peoples, that he may entreat mercy for him from the Supreme One over all."

Then Michael said unto Jacob, " How is it possible that thou who couldst prevail against me, the most distinguished of the angels, art afraid of Esau? "

When the day broke, Michael said to Jacob, " Let me go, for the day breaketh," but Jacob held him back, saying, " Art

thou a thief, or a gambler with dice, that thou fearest the
daylight?"   At that moment appeared many different hosts
of angels, and they called unto Michael: "Ascend, O Michael, the time of song hath come, and if thou art not in
heaven to lead the choir, none will sing."   And Michael
entreated Jacob with supplications to let him go, for he
feared the angels of 'Arabot would consume him with fire,
if he were not there to start the songs of praise at the proper
time.   Jacob said, "I will not let thee go, except thou bless
me," whereto Michael made reply: "Who is greater, the
servant or the son?   I am the servant, and thou art the son.
Why, then, cravest thou my blessing?"²⁴⁰   Jacob urged as
an argument, "The angels that visited Abraham did not
leave without blessing him," but Michael held, "They were
sent by God for that very purpose, and I was not."   Yet
Jacob insisted upon his demand, and Michael pleaded with
him, saying, "The angels that betrayed a heavenly secret
were banished from their place for one hundred and thirty-
eight years.   Dost thou desire that I should acquaint thee
with what would cause my banishment likewise?"   In the
end the angel nevertheless had to yield; Jacob could not be
moved, and Michael took counsel with himself thus: "I will
reveal a secret to him, and if God demands to know why I
revealed it, I will make answer, Thy children stand upon
their wishes with Thee, and Thou dost yield to them.   How,
then, could I have left Jacob's wish unfulfilled?"

Then Michael spoke to Jacob, saying: "A day will come
when God will reveal Himself unto thee, and He will change
thy name, and I shall be present when He changeth it.²⁴¹
Thy name shall be called no more Jacob, but Israel, for

happy thou, of woman born, who didst enter the heavenly palace, and didst escape thence with thy life." And Michael blessed Jacob with the words, " May it be the will of God that thy descendants be as pious as thou art." [350]

At the same time the archangel reminded Jacob that he had promised to give a tithe of his possessions unto God, and at once Jacob separated five hundred and fifty head of cattle from his herds, which counted fifty-five hundred. Then Michael went on, " But thou hast sons, and of them thou hast not set apart the tenth." Jacob proceeded to pass his sons in review: Reuben, Joseph, Dan, and Gad being the first-born, each of his mother, were exempt, and there remained but eight sons, and when he had named them, down to Benjamin, he had to go back and begin over again with Simon, the ninth, and finish with Levi as the tenth.

Michael took Levi with him into heaven, and presented him before God, saying, " O Lord of the world, this one is Thy lot, and the tenth belonging unto Thee," and God stretched forth His hand and blessed Levi with the blessing that his children should be the servants of God on earth as the angels were His servants on high. Michael spoke again, " Doth not a king provide for the sustenance of his servants?" whereupon God appointed for the Levites all that was holy unto the Lord. [351]

Then Jacob spoke to the angel: " My father conferred the blessing upon me that was intended for Esau, and now I desire to know whether thou wilt acknowledge the blessing as mine, or wilt bring charges against me on account of it." And the angel said: " I acknowledge the blessing to be thine by right. Thou didst not gain it by craft and cunning, and I and all the heavenly powers recognize it to be valid, for thou hast shown thyself master over the mighty powers of the heavens as over Esau and his legions."[253]

And even then Jacob would not let the angel depart, he had to reveal his name to him first, and the angel made known to him that it was Israel, the same name that Jacob would once bear.[253]

At last the angel departed, after Jacob had blessed him, and Jacob called the place of wrestling Penuel, the same place to which before he had given the name Mahanaim, for both words have but one meaning, the place of encounter with angels.[254]

THE MEETING BETWEEN ESAU AND JACOB

At the break of day the angel left off from wrestling with Jacob. The dawn on that day was of particularly short duration. The sun rose two hours before his time, by way of compensation for having set early, on the day on which Jacob passed Mount Moriah on his journey to Haran, to induce him to turn aside and lodge for a night on the future Temple place.[255] Indeed, the power of the sun on this same day was altogether remarkable. He shone with the brilliance and ardor with which he was invested during the six days of the creation, and as he will shine at the end of days, to make whole the halt and the blind among the Jews and to consume the heathen. This same healing and devastating property he had on that day, too, for Jacob was cured, while Esau and his princes were all but burnt up by his terrible heat.[256]

Jacob was in dire need of healing lotions for the injury

he had sustained in the encounter with the angel. The combat between them had been grim, the dust whirled up by the scuffle rose to the very throne of God.[267] Though Jacob prevailed against his huge opponent, as big as one-third of the whole world, throwing him to the ground and keeping him pinned down, yet the angel had injured him by clutching at the sinew of the hip which is upon the hollow of the thigh, so that it was dislocated, and Jacob halted upon his thigh.[258] The healing power of the sun restored him, nevertheless his children took it upon themselves not to eat the sinew of the hip which is upon the hollow of the thigh, for they reproached themselves with having been the cause of his mishap, they should not have left him alone in that night.[269]

Now, although Jacob had prepared for the worst, for open hostilities even, yet when he saw Esau and his men, he thought it discreet to make separate divisions of the households of Leah, Rachel, and the handmaids, and divide the children unto each of them. And he put the handmaids and their children foremost, and Leah and her children after, and Rachel and Joseph hindermost. It was the stratagem which the fox used with the lion. Once upon a time the king of beasts was wroth with his subjects, and they looked hither and thither for a spokesman who mastered the art of appeasing their ruler. The fox offered himself for the undertaking, saying, "I know three hundred fables which will allay his fury." His offer was accepted with joy. On the way to the lion, the fox suddenly stood still, and in reply to the questions put to him, he said, "I have forgotten one hundred of the three hundred fables." "Never mind," said those accompanying him, "two hundred will serve the purpose." A little way further on the fox again stopped suddenly, and, questioned again, he confessed that he had forgotten half of the two hundred remaining fables. The animals with him still consoled him that the hundred he knew would suffice. But the fox halted a third time, and then he admitted that his memory had failed him entirely, and he had forgotten all the fables he knew, and he advised that every animal approach the king on his own account and endeavor to appease his anger. At first Jacob had had courage enough to enter the lists with Esau in behalf of all with him. Now he came to the conclusion to let each one try to do what he could for himself.

However, Jacob was too fond a father to expose his family to the first brunt of the danger. He himself passed over before all the rest, saying, "It is better that they attack me than my children." [260] After him came the handmaids and their children. His reason for placing them there was that, if Esau should be overcome by passion for the women, and try to violate them, he would thus meet the handmaids first, and in the meantime Jacob would have the chance of preparing for more determined resistance in the defense of the honor of his wives. [261] Joseph and Rachel came last, and Joseph walked in front of his mother, though Jacob had ordered the reverse. But the son knew both the beauty of his mother and the lustfulness of his uncle, and therefore he tried to hide Rachel from the sight of Esau. [262]

In the vehemence of his rage against Jacob, Esau vowed that he would not slay him with bow and arrow, but would bite him dead with his mouth, and suck his blood. But he was doomed to bitter disappointment, for Jacob's neck turned as hard as ivory, and in his helpless fury Esau could but gnash his teeth.[268] The two brothers were like the ram and the wolf. A wolf wanted to tear a ram in pieces, and the ram defended himself with his horns, striking them deep into the flesh of the wolf. Both began to howl, the wolf because he could not secure his prey, and the ram from fear that the wolf renew his attacks. Esau bawled because his teeth were hurt by the ivory-like flesh of Jacob's neck, and Jacob feared that his brother would make a second attempt to bite him.[264]

Esau addressed a question to his brother. "Tell me," he said, "what was the army I met?" for on his march against Jacob he had had a most peculiar experience with a great host of forty thousand warriors. It consisted of various kinds of troops, armor-clad soldiers walking on foot, mounted on horses, and seated in chariots, and they all threw themselves upon Esau when they met. He demanded to know whence they came, and the strange soldiers hardly interrupted their savage onslaught to reply that they belonged to Jacob. Only when Esau told them that Jacob was his brother did they leave off, saying, "Woe to us if our master hears that we did thee harm." This was the army and the encounter Esau inquired about as soon as he met his brother. But the army was a host of angels, who had the appearance of warriors to Esau and his men.[265] Also the messengers sent by Jacob to Esau had been angels, for no mere human being could be induced to go forth and face the recreant.[266]

Jacob now gave Esau the presents intended for him, a tenth of all his cattle,[267] and also pearls and precious stones,[268] and, besides, a falcon for the chase.[369] But even the animals refused to give up their gentle master Jacob and become the property of the villain Esau. They all ran away when Jacob wanted to hand them over to his brother, and the result was that the only ones that reached Esau were the feeble and the lame, all that could not make good their escape.[370]

At first Esau declined the presents offered to him. Naturally, that was a mere pretense. While refusing the gifts with words, he held his hand outstretched ready to receive them.[371] Jacob took the hint, and insisted that he accept them, saying: " Nay, I pray thee, if now I have found grace in thy sight, then receive my present at my hand, forasmuch as I have seen thy face, as I have seen the face of angels, and thou art pleased with me." The closing words were chosen with well-calculated purpose. Jacob wanted Esau to derive the meaning that he had intercourse with angels, and to be inspired with awe. Jacob was like the man invited to a banquet by his mortal enemy who has been seeking an opportunity to slay him. When the guest divines the purpose for which he has been brought thither, he says to the host: " What a magnificent and delicious meal this is! But once before in my life did I partake of one like it, and that was when I was bidden by the king to his table "—enough to drive terror to the heart of the would-be slayer. He takes good care not to harm a man on such intimate terms with the king as to be invited to his table ![372]

Jacob had valid reason for recalling his encounter with the angel, for it was the angel of Esau who had measured his strength with Jacob's, and had been overcome.[373]

As Esau accepted the presents of Jacob willingly on **this**

first occasion, so he continued to accept them for a whole
year; daily Jacob gave him presents as on the day of their
meeting, for, he said, "'A gift doth blind the eyes of the
wise,' and how much more doth it blind the wicked! Therefore will I give him presents upon presents, perhaps he will
let me alone." Besides, he did not attach much value to
the possessions he had acquired outside of the Holy Land.
Such possessions are not a blessing, and he did not hesitate
to part with them.

Beside the presents which Jacob gave Esau, he also paid
out a large sum of money to him for the Cave of Machpelah.
Immediately upon his arrival in the Holy Land he sold
all he had brought with him from Haran, and a pile of gold
was the proceeds of the sale. He spoke to Esau, saying:
"Like me thou hast a share in the Cave of Machpelah, wilt
thou take this pile of gold for thy portion therein?" "What
care I for the Cave?" returned Esau. "Gold is what I
want," and for his share in Machpelah he took the gold
realized from the sale of the possessions Jacob had accumu-
lated outside of the Holy Land. But God "filled the vacuum
without delay," and Jacob was as rich as before.[314]

Wealth was not an object of desire to Jacob. He would
have been well content, in his own behalf and in behalf
of his family, to resign all earthly treasures in favor of
Esau and his family. He said to Esau: "I foresee that
in future days suffering will be inflicted by thy children
upon mine. But I do not demur, thou mayest exercise thy
dominion and wear thy crown until the time when the Messiah springs from my loins, and receives the rule from
thee." These words spoken by Jacob will be realized in days

to come, when all the nations will rise up against the kingdom of Edom, and take away one city after another from
him, one realm after another, until they reach Bet-Gubrin,
and then the Messiah will appear and assume his kingship.
The angel of Edom will flee for refuge to Bozrah, but God
will appear there, and slay him, for though Bozrah is one of
the cities of refuge, yet will the Lord exercise the right of
the avenger therein. He will seize the angel by his hair,
and Elijah will slaughter him, letting the blood spatter the
garments of God.[375] All this Jacob had in mind when he said
to Esau, " Let my lord, I pray thee, pass over before his
servant, until I come unto my lord unto Seir." Jacob himself never went to Seir. What he meant was the Messianic
time when Israel shall go to Seir, and take possession
thereof.[376]

Jacob tarried in Succoth a whole year, and he opened a
house of learning there.[377] Then he journeyed on to
Shechem, while Esau betook himself to Seir, saying to
himself, " How long shall I be a burden to my brother ? " for
it was during Jacob's sojourn at Succoth that Esau received
daily presents from Jacob.[378]

And Jacob, after abiding these many years in a strange
land, came to Shechem in peace, unimpaired in mind and
body. He had forgotten none of the knowledge he had acquired before; the gifts he gave to Esau did not encroach
upon his wealth; the injury inflicted by the angel that
wrestled with him had been healed, and likewise his children
were sound and healthy.[379]

Jacob entered Shechem on a Friday, late in the afternoon,
and his first concern was to lay out the boundaries of the

city, that the laws of the Sabbath might not be transgressed. As soon as he was settled in the place, he sent presents to the notables. A man must be grateful to a city from which he derives benefits. No less did the common people enjoy his bounty. For them he opened a market where he sold all wares at low prices.[280]

Also he lost no time in buying a parcel of ground, for it is the duty of every man of substance who comes to the Holy Land from outside to make himself the possessor of land there.[281] He gave a hundred lambs for his estate, a hundred yearling sheep, and a hundred pieces of money, and received in return a bill of sale, to which he attached his signature, using the letters Yod-He for it. And then he erected an altar to God upon his land, and he said, " Thou art the Lord of all celestial things, and I am the lord of all earthly things." But God said, " Not even the overseer of the synagogue arrogates privileges in the synagogue, and thou assumest lordship with a high hand? Forsooth, on the morrow thy daughter will go abroad, and she shall be humbled." [282]

THE OUTRAGE AT SHECHEM

While Jacob and his sons were sitting in the house of learning, occupied with the study of the Torah,[283] Dinah went abroad to see the dancing and singing women, whom Shechem had hired to dance and play in the streets in order to entice her forth.[284] Had she remained at home, nothing would have happened to her. But she was a woman, and all women like to show themselves in the street.[285] When Shechem caught sight of her, he seized her by main force, young though she was,[286] and violated her in beastly fashion.[287]

This misfortune befell Jacob as a punishment for his excessive self-confidence. In his negotiations with Laban, he had used the expression, " My righteousness shall answer for me hereafter." Besides, on his return to Palestine, when he was preparing to meet his brother, he concealed his daughter Dinah in a chest, lest Esau desire to have her for wife, and he be obliged to give her to him. God spoke to him, saying: " Herein hast thou acted unkindly toward thy brother, and therefore Dinah will have to marry Job, one that is neither circumcised nor a proselyte. Thou didst refuse to give her to one that is circumcised, and one that is uncircumcised will take her. Thou didst refuse to give her to Esau in lawful wedlock, and now she will fall a victim to the ravisher's illicit passion." [388]

When Jacob heard that Shechem had defiled his daughter, he sent twelve servants to fetch Dinah from Shechem's house, but Shechem went out to them with his men, and drove them from his house, and he would not suffer them to come unto Dinah, and he kissed and embraced her before their eyes. Jacob then sent two maidens of his servants' daughters to remain with Dinah in the house of Shechem. Shechem bade three of his friends go to his father Hamor, the son of Haddakum, the son of Pered, and say, " Get me this damsel to wife." Hamor tried at first to persuade his son not to take a Hebrew woman to wife, but when Shechem persisted in his request, he did according to the word of his son, and went forth to communicate with Jacob concerning the matter. In the meanwhile the sons of Jacob returned from the field, and, kindled with wrath, they spoke unto their father, saying, " Surely death is due to this man and his household, because the Lord God of the whole earth commanded Noah and his children that man shall never rob nor commit adultery. Now, behold, Shechem has ravaged and committed fornication with our sister, and not one of all the people of the city spake a word to him." And whilst they were speaking, Hamor came to speak to Jacob the words of his son concerning Dinah, and after he ceased to speak, Shechem himself came to Jacob and repeated the request made by his father. Simon and Levi answered Hamor and Shechem deceitfully, saying: "All you have spoken unto us we will do. And, behold, our sister is in your house, but keep away from her until we send to our father Isaac concerning this matter, for we can do nothing without his counsel. He knows the ways of our father Abraham, and whatever he saith unto us we will tell you, we will conceal nothing from you."

Shechem and his father went home thereafter, satisfied with the result achieved, and when they had gone, the sons of Jacob asked him to seek counsel and pretext in order to kill all the inhabitants of the city, who had deserved this punishment on account of their wickedness. Then Simon said to them: "I have good counsel to give you. Bid them be circumcised. If they consent not, we shall take our daughter from them, and go away. And if they consent to do this, then, when they are in pain, we shall attack them and slay them." The next morning Shechem and his father came again to Jacob, to speak concerning Dinah, and the sons of Jacob spoke deceitfully to them, saying: "We told our father Isaac all your words, and your words pleased him, but he said, that thus did Abraham his father command him from God, that any man that is not of his descendants, who desireth to take one of his daughters to wife, shall cause every male belonging to him to be circumcised."

Shechem and his father hastened to do the wishes of the sons of Jacob, and they persuaded also the men of the city to do likewise, for they were greatly esteemed by them, being the princes of the land.

On the next day, Shechem and his father rose up early in the morning, and they assembled all the men of the city, and they called for the sons of Jacob, and they circumcised Shechem, his father, his five brothers, and all the males in the city, six hundred and forty-five men and two hundred and seventy-six lads. Haddakum, the grandfather of Shechem, and his six brothers would not be circumcised, and they were greatly incensed against the people of the city for submitting to the wishes of the sons of Jacob.

In the evening of the second day, Shechem and his father sent to have eight little children whom their mothers had concealed brought to them to be circumcised. Haddakum and his six brothers sprang at the messengers, and sought to slay them, and sought to slay also Shechem, Hamor, and Dinah. They chided Shechem and his father for doing a thing that their fathers had never done, which would raise the ire of the inhabitants of the land of Canaan against them, as well as the ire of all the children of Ham, and that on account of a Hebrew woman. Haddakum and his brothers finished by saying: "Behold, to-morrow we will go and assemble our Canaanitish brethren, and we will come and smite you and all in whom you trust, that there shall not be a remnant left of you or them."

When Hamor and his son Shechem and all the people of
the city heard this, they were sore afraid, and they repented
what they had done, and Shechem and his father answered
Haddakum and his brothers: "Because we saw that the
Hebrews would not accede to our wishes concerning their
daughter, we did this thing, but when we shall have obtained
our request from them, we will then do unto them that which
is in your hearts and in ours, as soon as we shall become
strong."

Dinah, who heard their words, hastened and dispatched
one of her maidens whom her father had sent to take care of
her in Shechem's house, and informed Jacob and his sons of
the conspiracy plotted against them. When the sons of
Jacob heard this, they were filled with wrath, and Simon and
Levi swore, and said, " As the Lord liveth, by to-morrow
there shall not be a remnant left in the whole city."

They began the extermination by killing eighteen of the
twenty young men who had concealed themselves and were
not circumcised, and two of them fled and escaped to some
lime pits that were in the city. Then Simon and Levi slew
all the city, not leaving a male over, and while they were
looking for spoils outside of the city, three hundred women
rose against them and threw stones and dust upon them, but
Simon single-handed slew them all, and returned to the city,
where he joined Levi. Then they took away from the people
outside of the city their sheep, their oxen, their cattle, and
also the women and the little children, and they led all these
away, and took them to the city to their father Jacob. The
number of women whom they did not slay, but only took captive, was eighty-five virgins, among them a young damsel of

great beauty by the name of Bunah, whom Simon took to wife. The number of the males which they took captive and did not slay was forty-seven, and all these men and women were servants to the sons of Jacob, and to their children after them, until the day they left Egypt.

A War Frustrated

When Simon and Levi had gone from the city, the two young men who had concealed themselves in the lime pits, and were not slain amongst the people of the city, rose up, and they found the city desolate, without a man, only weeping women, and they cried out, saying, " Behold, this is the evil which the sons of Jacob did who destroyed one of the Canaanite cities, and were not afraid of all the land of Canaan."

They left the city and went to Tappuah, and told the inhabitants all that the sons of Jacob had done to the city of Shechem. Jashub, the king of Tappuah, sent to Shechem to see whether these young men told the truth, for he did not believe them, saying, " How could two men destroy a large city like Shechem? " The messengers of Jashub returned, and they reported, " The city is destroyed, not a man is left there, only weeping women, neither are there flocks and cattle there, for all that was in the city was taken away by the sons of Jacob."

Jashub wondered thereat, for the like had not been heard from the days of Nimrod, and not even from the remotest times, that two men should be able to destroy so large a city, and he decided to go to war against the Hebrews, and avenge the cause of the people of Shechem. His counsellors said to him: "If two of them laid waste a whole city, surely if thou goest against them, they all will rise up against us, and destroy us. Therefore, send to the kings round about, that we all together fight against the sons of Jacob, and prevail against them."

The seven kings of the Amorites, when they heard the evil that the sons of Jacob had done to the city of Shechem, assembled together, with all their armies, ten thousand men, with drawn swords, and they came to fight against the sons of Jacob. And Jacob was greatly afraid, and he said to Simon and Levi, "Why have you brought such evil upon me? I was at rest, and you provoked the inhabitants of the land against me by your acts."

Then Judah spoke to his father: "Was it for naught that Simon and Levi killed the inhabitants of Shechem? Verily, it was because Shechem dishonored our sister, and transgressed the command of our God to Noah and his children, and not one of the inhabitants of the city interfered in the matter. Now, why art thou afraid, and why art thou displeased at my brethren? Surely, our God, who delivered the city of Shechem and its people into their hand, He will also deliver into our hands all the Canaanitish kings who are coming against us. Now cast away thy fears, and pray to God to assist us and deliver us."

Judah then addressed his brethren, saying: "The Lord our God is with us! Fear naught, then! Stand ye forth, each man girt with his weapons of war, his bow and his sword, and we will go and fight against the uncircumcised. The Lord is our God, He will save us."

Jacob, his eleven sons, and one hundred servants belonging to Isaac, who had come to their assistance, marched forward to meet the Amorites, a people exceedingly numerous, like unto the sand upon the sea-shore. The sons of Jacob sent unto their grandfather Isaac, at Hebron, requesting him to pray unto the Lord to protect them from the hand of the Canaanites, and he prayed as follows: " O Lord God, Thou didst promise my father, saying, I will multiply thy seed as the stars of heaven, and also me Thou didst promise that Thou wouldst establish Thy word to my father. Now, O Lord, God of the whole world, pervert, I pray Thee, the counsel of these kings, that they may not fight against my sons, and impress the hearts of their kings and their people with the terror of my sons, and bring down their pride that they turn away from my sons. Deliver my sons and their servants from them with Thy strong hand and outstretched arm, for power and might are in Thy hands to do all this."

Jacob also prayed unto God, and said: " O Lord God, powerful and exalted God, who hast reigned from days of old, from then until now and forever! Thou art He who stirreth up wars and causeth them to cease. In Thy hand are power and might to exalt and to bring low. O may my prayer be acceptable unto Thee, that Thou mayest turn to me with Thy mercies, to impress the hearts of these kings and their people with the terror of my sons, and terrify them and their camps, and with Thy great kindness deliver all those that trust in Thee, for Thou art He who subdues the peoples under us, and the nations under our feet."

God heard the prayers of Isaac and Jacob, and He filled the hearts of all the advisers of the Canaanite kings with great fear and terror, and when the kings, who were unde-

cided whether to undertake a campaign against the sons of
Jacob, consulted them, they said: " Are you silly, or is there
no understanding in you, that you propose to fight with the
Hebrews? Why do you take delight in your own destruction this day? Behold, two of them came to the city of
Shechem without fear or terror, and they put all the inhabitants of the city to the sword, no man stood up against them,
and how will you be able to fight with them all? "

The royal counsellors then proceeded to enumerate all the
mighty things God had done for Abraham, Jacob, and the
sons of Jacob, such as had not been done from days of old
and by any of the gods of the nations. When the kings
heard all the words of their advisers, they were afraid of
the sons of Jacob, and they would not fight against them.
They turned back with their armies on that day, each to his
own city. But the sons of Jacob kept their station that day
till evening, and seeing that the kings did not advance to do
battle with them in order to avenge the inhabitants of Shechem whom they had killed, they returned home.[289]

The wrath of the Lord descended upon the inhabitants of
Shechem to the uttermost on account of their wickedness.
For they had sought to do unto Sarah and Rebekah as they
did unto Dinah, but the Lord had prevented them. Also they
had persecuted Abraham when he was a stranger, and they
had vexed his flocks when they were big with young, and
Eblaen, one born in his house, they had handled most shame-
fully. And thus they did to all strangers, taking away their
wives by force.[290]

THE WAR WITH THE NINEVITES

The destruction of Shechem by Simon and Levi terrified the heathen all around. If two sons of Jacob had succeeded in ruining a great city like Shechem, they argued, what would Jacob and all his sons accomplish acting together? Jacob meanwhile left Shechem, hindered by none, and with all his possessions he set out, to betake himself to his father Isaac. But after an eight days' march he encountered a powerful army, which had been dispatched from Nineveh to levy tribute upon the whole world and subjugate it. On coming in the vicinity of Shechem, this army heard to what the city had been exposed at the hands of the sons of Jacob, and fury seized the men, and they resolved to make war upon Jacob.

But Jacob said to his sons: " Fear not, God will be your helper, and He will fight for you against your enemies. Only you must put away from you the strange gods in your possession, and you must purify yourselves, and wash your garments clean."

Girt with his sword, Jacob advanced against the enemy, and in the first onslaught he slew twelve thousand of the weak in the army. Then Judah spake to him, and said, " Father, thou art tired and exhausted, let me fight the enemy alone." And Jacob replied, saying, " Judah, my son, I know thy strength and thy bravery, that they are exceeding great, so that none in the world is like unto thee therein." His countenance like a lion's and inflamed with wrath, Judah attacked the army, and slew twelve myriads of tried and famous warriors. The battle raged hot in front and in the rear, and Levi his brother hastened to his aid, and together they won a victory over the Ninevites. Judah alone slew five thousand more soldiers, and Levi dealt blows right and left with such vigor that the men of the enemy's army fell like grain under the scythe of the reaper.

Alarmed about their fate, the people of Nineveh said: "How long shall we fight with these devils? Let us return to our land, lest they exterminate us root and branch, without leaving a remnant." But their king desired to restrain them, and he said: "O ye heroes, ye men of might and valor, have you lost your senses that you ask to return to your land? Is this your bravery? After you have subdued many kingdoms and countries, ye are not able to hold out against twelve men? If the nations and the kings whom we have made tributary to ourselves hear of this, they will rise up against us as a man, and make a laughing-stock of us, and do with us according to their desire. Take courage, ye men of the great city of Nineveh, that your honor and your name be exalted, and you become not a mockery in the mouth of your enemies."

These words of their king inspired the warriors to continue the campaign. They sent messengers to all the lands to ask for help, and, reinforced by their allies, the Ninevites assaulted Jacob a second time. He spoke to his sons, saying, "Take courage and be men, fight against your enemies." His twelve sons then took up their stand in twelve different places, leaving considerable intervals between one and another, and Jacob, a sword in his right hand and a bow in his left, advanced to the combat. It was a desperate encounter for him. He had to ward off the enemy to the right and the left. Nevertheless he inflicted a severe blow, and when a band of two thousand men beset him, he leapt up in the air and over them and vanished from their sight. Twenty-two myriads he slew on this day, and when evening came he planned to flee under cover of darkness. But suddenly ninety thousand men appeared, and he was compelled to continue the fight. He rushed at them with his sword, but it broke, and he had to defend himself by grinding huge rocks into lime powder, and this he threw at the enemy and blinded them so that they could see nothing. Luckily, darkness was about to fall, and he could permit himself to take rest for the night.

In the morning, Judah said to Jacob, " Father, thou didst fight the whole of yesterday, and thou art weary and exhausted. Let me fight this day." When the warriors caught sight of Judah's lion face and his lion teeth, and heard his lion voice, they were greatly afraid. Judah hopped and jumped over the army like a flea, from one warrior to the next, raining blows down upon them incessantly, and by evening he had slain eighty thousand and ninety-six men, armed with swords and bows. But fatigue overcame him, and Zebulon took up his station at his brother's left hand, and mowed down eighty thousand of the enemy. Meantime Judah regained some of his strength, and, rising up in wrath and fury, and gnashing his teeth with a noise like unto thunder claps in midsummer, he put the army to flight. It ran a distance of eighteen miles, and Judah could enjoy a respite that night.

But the army reappeared on the morrow, ready for battle again, to take revenge on Jacob and his children. They blew their trumpets, whereupon Jacob spake to his sons,

"Go forth and fight with your enemies." Issachar and Gad
said that this day they would take the combat upon themselves, and their father bade them do it while their brothers
kept guard and held themselves in readiness to aid and relieve the two combatants when they showed signs of weari-
ness and exhaustion.

The leaders of the day slew forty-eight thousand warriors, and put to flight twelve myriads more, who concealed
themselves in a cave. Issachar and Gad fetched trees from
the woods, piled the trunks up in front of the opening of
the cave, and set fire to them. When the fire blazed with a
fierce flame, the warriors spoke, saying: "Why should we
stay in this cave and perish with the smoke and the heat?
Rather will we go forth and fight with our enemies, then
we may have a chance of saving ourselves." They left the
cave, going through openings at the side, and they attacked
Issachar and Gad in front and behind. Dan and Naphtali
saw the plight of their brothers and ran to their assistance.
They laid about with their swords, hewing a way for themselves to Issachar and Gad, and, united with them, they, too,
opposed the foe.

It was the third day of the conflict, and the Ninevites
were reinforced by an army as numerous as the sand on the
sea-shore. All the sons of Jacob united to oppose it, and they
routed the host. But when they pursued after the enemy,
the fugitives faced about and resumed the battle, saying:
"Why should we run away? Let us rather fight them, perhaps we may be victorious, now they are weary." A stub-
born combat ensued, and when Jacob saw the vehement
attack upon his children, he himself sprang into the thick of

the battle and dealt blows right and left. Nevertheless the heathen were victorious, and succeeded in separating Judah from his brethren. As soon as Jacob was aware of the peril of his son, he whistled, and Judah responded, and his brethren hastened to his aid. Judah was fatigued and parched with thirst, and there was no water for him to drink, but he dug his finger into the ground with such force that water gushed out in the sight of the whole army. Then said one warrior to another, " I will flee before these devils, for God fights on their side," and he and all the army fled precipitately, pursued by the sons of Jacob. Soldiers without number they slew, and then they went back to their tents. On their return they noticed that Joseph was missing, and they feared he had been killed or taken captive. Naphtali ran after the retreating enemy, to make search for Joseph, and he found him still fighting against the Ninevite army. He joined Joseph, and killed countless soldiers, and of the fugitives many drowned, and the men that were besetting Joseph ran off and left him in safety.

At the end of the war Jacob continued his journey, unhindered, to his father Isaac.²¹¹

THE WAR WITH THE AMORITES

At first the people that lived round about Shechem made no attempt to molest Jacob, who had returned thither after a while, together with his household, to take up his abode there and establish himself. But at the end of seven years the heathen began to harass him. The kings of the Amorites assembled together against the sons of Jacob to slay them in the Valley of Shechem. " Is it not enough," they said,

" that they have slain all the men of Shechem? Should they be permitted now to take possession of their land, too? " and they advanced to render battle.

Judah leapt into the midst of the ranks of the foot soldiers of the allied kings, and slew first of all Jashub, the king of Tappuah, who was clad in iron and brass from top to toe. The king was mounted, and from his horse he cast his spears downward with both hands, in front of him and in back, without ever missing his aim, for he was a mighty warrior, and he could throw javelins with one hand or the other. Nevertheless Judah feared neither him nor his prowess. He ran toward him, snatching a stone of sixty sela'im from the ground and hurling it at him. Jashub was at a distance of one hundred and seventy-seven ells and one-third of an ell, and, protected with iron armor and throwing spears, he moved forward upon Judah. But Judah struck him on his shield with the stone, and unhorsed him. When the king attempted to rise, Judah hastened to his side to slay him before he could get on his feet. But Jashub was nimble, he stood ready to attack Judah, shield to shield, and he drew his sword to cut off Judah's head. Quickly Judah raised his shield to catch the blow upon it, but it broke in pieces. What did Judah now? He wrested the shield of his opponent away from him, and swung his sword against Jashub's feet, cutting them off above the ankles. The king fell prostrate, his sword slipped from his grasp, and Judah hastened to him and severed his head from his body.

While Judah was removing the armor of his slain adversary, nine of Jashub's followers appeared. Judah slung a stone against the head of the first of them that approached him, with such force that he dropped his shield, which Judah snatched from the ground and used to defend himself against his eight assailants. His brother Levi came and stood next to him, and shot off an arrow that killed Elon, king of Gaash, and then Judah killed the eight men. And his father Jacob came and killed Zerori king of Shiloh. None of the heathen could prevail against these sons of Jacob, they had not the courage to stand up before them, but took to flight, and the sons of Jacob pursued after them, and each slew a thousand men of the Amorites on that day, before the going down of the sun. And the other sons of Jacob set forth from the Hill of Shechem, where they had taken up their stand, and they also pursued after them as far as Hazor. Before this city they had another severe encounter with the enemy, more severe than that in the Valley of Shechem. Jacob let his arrows fly, and slew Pirathon king of Hazor, and then Pasusi king of Sartan, Laban king of Aram, and Shebir king of Mahanaim.

Judah was the first to mount the walls of Hazor. As he approached the top, four warriors attacked him, but he slew them without stopping in his ascent, and before his brother Naphtali could bring him succor. Naphtali followed him, and the two stood upon the wall, Judah to the right and Naphtali to the left, and thence they dealt out death to the warriors. The other sons of Jacob followed their two brothers in turn, and made an end of exterminating the heathen host on that day. They subjugated Hazor, slew the warriors thereof, let no man escape with his life, and despoiled the city of all therein.

On the day following they went to Sartan, and again a

bloody battle took place. Sartan was situated upon high
land, and the hill before the city was likewise very high, so
that none could come near unto it, and also none could come
near unto the citadel, because the wall thereof was high.
Nevertheless they made themselves masters of the city. They
scaled the walls of the citadel, Judah on the east side being
the first to ascend, then Gad on the west side, Simon and
Levi on the north, and Reuben and Dan on the south, and
Naphtali and Issachar set fire to the hinges upon which the
gates of the city were hung.

In the same way the sons of Jacob subdued five other
cities, Tappuah, Arbel, Shiloh, Mahanaim, and Gaash, making an end of all of them in five days. On the sixth day all
the Amorites assembled, and they came to Jacob and his sons
unarmed, bowed down before them, and sued for peace.
And the sons of Jacob made peace with the heathen, who
ceded Timna to them, and all the land of Ḥarariah. In that
day also Jacob concluded peace with them, and they made
restitution to the sons of Jacob for all the cattle they had
taken, two head for one, and they restored all the spoil they
had carried off. And Jacob turned to go to Timna, and
Judah went to Arbel, and thenceforth the Amorites troubled
them no more.²⁰²

Isaac Blesses Levi and Judah

If a man voweth a vow, and he does not fulfil it in good
time, he will stumble through three grave sins, idolatry,
unchastity, and bloodshed. Jacob had been guilty of not
accomplishing promptly the vow he had taken upon himself
at Beth-el, and therefore punishment overtook him—his

daughter was dishonored, his sons slew men, and they kept
the idols found among the spoils of Shechem.²⁹³ Therefore,
when Jacob prostrated himself before God after the bloody
outrage at Shechem, He bade him arise, and go to Beth-el
and accomplish the vow he had vowed there.²⁹⁴ Before
Jacob set out for the holy place to do the bidding of God,
he took the idols which were in the possession of his sons,
and the teraphim which Rachel had stolen from her father,
and he shivered them in pieces, and buried ²⁹⁵ the bits under
an oak upon Mount Gerizim,²⁹⁶ uprooting the tree with one
hand, concealing the remains of the idols in the hollow left
in the earth, and planting the oak again with one hand.²⁹⁷

Among the destroyed idols was one in the form of a dove,
and this the Samaritans dug up later and worshipped.

On reaching Beth-el he erected an altar to the Lord, and
on a pillar he set up the stone whereon he had rested his
head during the night which he had passed there on his
journey to Haran.²⁹⁸ Then he bade his parents come to
Beth-el and take part in his sacrifice. But Isaac sent him a
message, saying, "O my son Jacob, that I might see thee
before I die," whereupon Jacob hastened to his parents,
taking Levi and Judah with him. When his grandchildren
stepped before Isaac, the darkness that shrouded his eyes
dropped away, and he said, "My son, are these thy children,
for they resemble thee?" And the spirit of prophecy entered his mouth, and he grasped Levi with his right hand
and Judah with his left in order to bless them, and he spoke
these words to Levi: "May the Lord bring thee and thy
seed nigh unto Him before all flesh, that ye serve in His
sanctuary like the Angel of the Face and the Holy Angels.

Princes, judges, and rulers shall they be unto all the seed of
the children of Jacob. The word of God they will proclaim
in righteousness, and all His judgments they will execute in
justice, and they will make manifest His ways unto the children of Jacob, and unto Israel His paths." And unto Judah
he spake, saying: " Be ye princes, thou and one of thy sons,
over the sons of Jacob. In thee shall be the help of Jacob,
and the salvation of Israel shall be found in thee. And when
thou sittest upon the throne of the glory of thy justice, perfect peace shall reign over all the seed of the children of my
beloved Abraham."

On the morrow, Isaac told his son that he would not accompany him to Beth-el on account of his great age, but he
bade him not delay longer to fulfil his vow, and gave him
permission to take his mother Rebekah with him to the holy
place. And Rebekah and her nurse Deborah went to Beth-el
with Jacob.²⁹⁹

Joy and Sorrow in the House of Jacob

Deborah, the nurse of Rebekah, and some of the servants
of Isaac had been sent to Jacob by his mother, while he still
abode with Laban, to summon him home at the end of his
fourteen years' term of service. As Jacob did not at once
obey his mother's behest, the two servants of Isaac returned
to their master, but Deborah remained with Jacob then and
always. Therefore, when Deborah died in Beth-el, Jacob
mourned for her, and he buried her below Beth-el under the
palm-tree,³⁰⁰ the same under which the prophetess Deborah
sat later, when the children of Israel came to her for
judgment.³⁰¹

But a short time elapsed after the death of the nurse Deborah, and Rebekah died, too. Her passing away was not made the occasion for public mourning. The reason was that, as Abraham was dead, Isaac blind, and Jacob away from home, there remained Esau as the only mourner to appear in public and represent her family, and beholding that villain, it was feared, might tempt a looker-on to cry out, "Accursed be the breasts that gave thee suck." To avoid this, the burial of Rebekah took place at night.

God appeared unto Jacob to comfort him in his grief,[402] and with Him appeared the heavenly family. It was a sign of grace, for all the while the sons of Jacob had been carrying idols with them the Lord had not revealed Himself to Jacob.[403] At this time God announced to Jacob the birth of Benjamin soon to occur, and the birth of Manasseh and Ephraim, who also were to be founders of tribes, and furthermore He told him that these three would count kings among their descendants, Saul and Ish-bosheth, of the seed of Benjamin, Jeroboam the Ephraimite, and Jehu of the tribe of Manasseh. In this vision, God confirmed the change of his name from Jacob to Israel, promised him by the angel with whom he had wrestled on entering the Holy Land, and finally God revealed to him that he would be the last of the three with whose names the Name of God would appear united, for God is called only the God of Abraham, the God of Isaac, and the God of Jacob, and never the God of any one else.[404]

In token of this revelation from God, Jacob set up a pillar of stone, and he poured out a drink offering thereon, as in a later day the priests were to offer libations in the Temple on the Feast of Tabernacles,[306] and the libation brought by Jacob at Beth-el was as much as all the waters in the Sea of Tiberias.[306]

At the time when Deborah and Rebekah died, occurred also the death of Rachel, at the age of thirty-six,[307] but not before her prayer was heard, that she bear Jacob a second son, for she died in giving birth to Benjamin. Twelve years she had borne no child, then she fasted twelve days, and her petition was granted her. She brought forth the youngest son of Jacob, whom he called Benjamin, the son of days, because he was born in his father's old age,[308] and with him a twin sister was born.[309]

Rachel was buried in the way to Ephrath, because Jacob, gifted with prophetic spirit, foresaw that the exiles would pass this place on their march to Babylon, and as they passed, Rachel would entreat God's mercy for the poor outcasts.[310]

Jacob journeyed on to Jerusalem.[311]

During Rachel's lifetime, her couch had always stood in the tent of Jacob. After her death, he ordered the couch of her handmaid Bilhah to be carried thither. Reuben was sorely vexed thereat, and he said, "Not enough that Rachel alive curtailed the rights of my mother, she must needs give her annoyance also after death!" He went and took the couch of his mother Leah and placed it in Jacob's tent instead of Bilhah's couch.[312] Reuben's brothers learned of his disrespectful act from Asher. He had found it out in one way or another, and had told it to his brethren, who ruptured their relations with him, for they would have nothing to do with an informer, and they did not become reconciled with Asher until Reuben himself confessed his transgression.[234] For it was not long before Reuben recognized that he had acted reprehensibly toward his father, and he fasted and put on sackcloth, and repented of his misdeed. He was the first among men to do penance, and therefore God said to him: "Since the beginning of the world it hath not happened that a man hath sinned and then repented thereof. Thou art the first to do penance, and as thou livest, a prophet of thy seed, Hosea, shall be the first to proclaim, 'O Israel, return.'"[234]

Esau's Campaign against Jacob

When Isaac felt his end approaching, he called his two sons to him, and charged them with his last wish and will, and gave them his blessing. He said: "I adjure you by the exalted Name, the praised, honored, glorious, immutable, and mighty One, who hath made heaven and earth and all things together, that ye fear Him, and serve Him, and each shall love his brother in mercy and justice, and none wish evil unto the other, now and henceforth unto all eternity, all the days of your life, that ye may enjoy good fortune in all your undertakings, and that ye perish not."

Furthermore he commanded them to bury him in the Cave of Machpelah, by the side of his father Abraham, in the grave which he had dug for himself with his own hands. Then he divided his possessions between his two sons, giving Esau the larger portion, and Jacob the smaller. But Esau said, "I sold my birthright to Jacob, and I ceded it to him, and it belongs unto him." Isaac rejoiced greatly that Esau acknowledged the rights of Jacob of his own accord, and he closed his eyes in peace.[235]

The funeral of Isaac was not disturbed by any unseemly act, for Esau was sure of his heritage in accordance with the last wishes expressed by his father. But when the time came to divide Isaac's possessions between the two brothers, Esau said to Jacob, "Divide the property of our father into two portions, but I as the elder claim the right of choosing the portion I desire." What did Jacob do? He knew well that "the eye of the wicked never beholds treasures enough to satisfy it," so he divided their common heritage in the following way: all the material possessions of his father formed one portion, and the other consisted of Isaac's claim upon the Holy Land, together with the Cave of Machpelah, the tomb of Abraham and Isaac. Esau chose the money and the other things belonging to Isaac for his inheritance, and to Jacob were left the Cave and the title to the Holy Land. An agreement to this effect was drawn up in writing in due form, and on the strength of the document Jacob insisted upon Esau's leaving Palestine. Esau acquiesced, and he and his wives and his sons and daughters journeyed to Mount Seir, where they took up their abode.[216]

Though Esau gave way before Jacob for the nonce, he returned to the land to make war upon his brother. Leah had just died, and Jacob and the sons borne by Leah were mourning for her, and the rest of his sons, borne unto him by his other wives, were trying to comfort them, when Esau came upon them with a powerful host of four thousand men, well equipped for war, clad in armor of iron and brass, all furnished with bucklers, bows, and swords. They surrounded the citadel wherein Jacob and his sons dwelt at that time with their servants and children and households, for

they had all assembled to console Jacob for the death of
Leah, and they sat there unconcerned, none entertained a
suspicion that an assault upon them was meditated by any
man. And the great army had already encircled their castle,
and still none within suspected any harm, neither Jacob
and his children nor the two hundred servants. Now when
Jacob saw that Esau presumed to make war upon them,
and sought to slay them in the citadel, and was shooting
darts at them, he ascended the wall of the citadel and spake
words of peace and friendship and brotherly love to Esau.
He said: "Is this the consolation which thou hast come to
bring me, to comfort me for my wife, who hath been taken
by death? Is this in accordance with the oath thou didst
swear twice unto thy father and thy mother before they died?
Thou hast violated thy oath, and in the hour when thou
didst swear unto thy father, thou wast judged." But Esau
made reply: "Neither the children of men nor the beasts
of the field swear an oath to keep it unto all eternity, but on
every day they devise evil against one another, when it is
directed against an enemy, or when they seek to slay an
adversary. If the boar will change his skin and make his
bristles as soft as wool, or if he can cause horns to sprout
forth on his head like the horns of a stag or a ram, then
shall I observe the tie of brotherhood with thee."

Then spoke Judah to his father Jacob, saying: "How long
wilt thou stand yet wasting words of peace and friendship
upon him? And he attacks us unawares, like an enemy, with
his mail-clad warriors, seeking to slay us." Hearing these
words, Jacob grasped his bow and killed Adoram the Edomite, and a second time he bent his bow, and the arrow struck

Esau upon the right thigh. The wound was mortal, and his sons lifted Esau up and put him upon his ass, and he came to Adora, and there he died.

Judah made a sally to the south of the citadel, and with him were Naphtali and Gad, aided by fifty of Jacob's servants; to the east Levi and Dan went forth with fifty servants; Reuben, Issachar, and Zebulon with fifty servants, to the north; and Simon, Benjamin, and Enoch, the last the son of Reuben, with fifty servants, to the west. Judah was exceedingly brave in battle. Together with Naphtali and Gad he pressed forward into the ranks of the enemy, and captured one of their iron towers. On their bucklers they caught the sharp missiles hurled against them in such numbers that the light of the sun was darkened by reason of the rocks and darts and stones. Judah was the first to break the ranks of the enemy, of whom he killed six valiant men, and he was accompanied on the right by Naphtali and by Gad on the left. They also hewed down two soldiers each, while their troop of servants killed one man each. Nevertheless they did not succeed in forcing the army away from the south of the citadel, not even when all together, Judah and his brethren, made an united attack upon the enemy, each of them picking out a victim and slaying him. And they were still unsuccessful in a third combined attack, though this time each killed two men.

When Judah saw now that the enemy remained in possession of the field, and it was impossible to dislodge them, he girded himself with strength, and an heroic spirit animated him. Judah, Naphtali, and Gad united, and together they pierced the ranks of the enemy, Judah slaying ten of them, and his brothers each eight. Seeing this, the servants took courage, and they joined their leaders and fought at their side. Judah laid about him to right and to left, always aided by Naphtali and Gad, and so they succeeded in forcing the enemy one ris further to the south, away from the citadel. But the hostile army recovered itself, and maintained a brave stand against all the sons of Jacob, who were faint from the hardships of the combat, and could not continue to fight. Thereupon Judah turned to God in prayer, and God hearkened unto his petition, and He helped them. He set loose a storm from one of His treasure chambers, and it blew into the faces of the enemy, and filled their eyes with darkness, and they could not see how to fight. But Judah and his brothers could see clearly, for the wind blew upon their backs. Now Judah and his two brothers wrought havoc among them, they hewed the enemy down as the reaper mows down the stalks of grain and heaps them up for sheaves.

After they had routed the division of the army assigned to them on the south, they hastened to the aid of their brothers, who were defending the east, north, and west of the citadel with three companies. On each side the wind blew into the faces of the enemy, and so the sons of Jacob succeeded in annihilating their army. Four hundred were slain in battle, and six hundred fled, among the latter Esau's four sons, Reuel, Jeush, Lotan, and Korah. The oldest of his sons, Eliphaz, took no part in the war, because he was a disciple of Jacob, and therefore would not bear arms against him.

The sons of Jacob pursued after the fleeing remnant of

the army as far as Adora. There the sons of Esau abandoned the body of their father, and continued their flight to
Mount Seir. But the sons of Jacob remained in Adora over
night, and out of respect for their father they buried the
remains of his brother Esau. In the morning they went on
in pursuit of the enemy, and besieged them on Mount Seir.
Now the sons of Esau and all the other fugitives came and
fell down before them, bowed down, and entreated them
without cease, until they concluded peace with them. But
the sons of Jacob exacted tribute from them.[117]

The Descendants of Esau

The worthiest among the sons of Esau was his first-born
Eliphaz. He had been raised under the eyes of his grandfather Isaac, from whom he had learnt the pious way of
life.[118] The Lord had even found him worthy of being endowed with the spirit of prophecy, for Eliphaz the son of
Esau is none other than the prophet Eliphaz, the friend of
Job. It was from the life of the Patriarchs that he drew the
admonitions which he gave unto Job in his disputes with him.
Eliphaz spake: "Thou didst ween thyself the equal of
Abraham, and thou didst marvel, therefore, that God should
deal with thee as with the generation of the confusion of
tongues. But Abraham stood the test of ten temptations,
and thou faintest when but one toucheth thee. When any
that was not whole came to thee, thou wouldst console him.
To the blind thou wouldst say, If thou didst build thyself a
house, thou wouldst surely put windows in it, and if God
hath denied thee light, it is but that He may be glorified
through thee in the day when ' the eyes of the blind shall be

opened.' To the deaf thou wouldst say, If thou didst fashion
a water pitcher, thou wouldst surely not forget to make ears
for it, and if God created thee without hearing, it is but
that He may be glorified through thee in the day when ' the
ears of the deaf shall be unstopped.' In such wise thou
didst endeavor to console the feeble and the maimed. But
now it is come unto thee, and thou art troubled. Thou
sayest, I am an upright man, why doth He chastise me? But
who, I pray thee, ever perished, being innocent? Noah was
saved from the flood, Abraham from the fiery furnace, Isaac
from the slaughtering knife, Jacob from angels, Moses from
the sword of Pharaoh, and Israel from the Egyptians that
were drowned in the Sea. Thus shall all the wicked fare."

Job answered Eliphaz, and said, "Look at thy father
Esau!"

But Eliphaz returned: "I have nothing to do with him,
the son should not bear the iniquity of the father. Esau will
be destroyed, because he executed no good deeds, and likewise his dukes will perish. But as for me, I am a prophet,
and my message is not unto Esau, but unto thee, to make
thee render account of thyself." But God rebuked Eliphaz,
and said: "Thou didst speak harsh words unto My servant
Job. Therefore shall Obadiah, one of thy descendants,
utter a prophecy of denunciation against thy father's house,
the Edomites." [119]

The concubine of Eliphaz was Timna, a princess of royal
blood, who had asked to be received into the faith of Abraham and his family, but they all, Abraham, Isaac, and Jacob,
had rejected her, and she said, "Rather will I be a maid-
servant unto the dregs of this nation, than mistress of an-

other nation," and so she was willing to be concubine to Eliphaz. To punish the Patriarchs for the affront they had offered her, she was made the mother of Amalek, who inflicted great injury upon Israel.[120]

Another one of Esau's descendants, Anah, had a most unusual experience. Once when he was pasturing his father's asses in the wilderness, he led them to one of the deserts on the shores of the Red Sea, opposite the wilderness of the nations, and while he was feeding the beasts, a very heavy storm came from the other side of the sea, and the asses could not move. Then about one hundred and twenty great and terrible animals came out from the wilderness at the other side of the sea, and they all came to the place where the asses were, and they placed themselves there. From the middle down, these animals were in the shape of a man, and from the middle up some had the likeness of bears, some of apes, and they all had tails behind them like the tail of the dukipat, from between their shoulders reaching down to the earth. The animals mounted the asses, and they rode away with them, and unto this day no eye hath seen them. One of them approached Anah, and smote him with its tail, and then ran off.

When Anah saw all this, he was exceedingly afraid on account of his life, and he fled to the city, where he related all that had happened to him. Many sallied forth to seek the asses, but none could find them. Anah and his brothers went no more to the same place from that day forth, for they were greatly afraid on account of their lives.[121]

This Anah was the offspring of an incestuous marriage; his mother was at the same time the mother of his father

Zibeon. And as he was born of an unnatural union, so he tried to bring about unnatural unions among animals. He was the first to mix the breed of the horse and the ass and produce the mule. As a punishment, God crossed the snake and the lizard, and they brought forth the ḥabarbar, whose bite is certain death, like the bite of the white she-mule.[322]

The descendants of Esau had eight kings before there reigned any king over the descendants of Jacob. But a time came when the Jews had eight kings during whose reign the Edomites had none and were subject to the Jewish kings. This was the time that intervened between Saul, the first Israelitish king, who ruled over Edom, and Jehoshaphat, for Edom did not make itself independent of Jewish rule until the time of Joram, the son of Jehoshaphat. There was a difference between the kings of Esau's seed and the kings of Jacob's seed. The Jewish people always produced their kings from their own midst, while the Edomites had to go to alien peoples to secure theirs.[323] The first Edomite king was the Aramean Balaam,[324] called Bela in his capacity as ruler of Edom. His successor Job, called Jobab also, came from Bozrah, and for furnishing Edom with a king this city will be chastised in time to come. When God sits in judgment on Edom, Bozrah will be the first to suffer punishment.[325]

The rule of Edom was of short duration, while the rule of Israel will be unto all times, for the standard of the Messiah shall wave forever and ever.[326]